US BMD and Deterrence Postures: The New Cold War Era
Perspective on the Wartime Use of Active Missile Defenses

US BALLISTIC MISSILE DEFENSE AND DETERRENCE POSTURES

The New Cold War Era Perspective on the Wartime Use of Active Missile Defenses

GRZEGORZ NYCZ

Westphalia Press

An Imprint of the Policy Studies Organization

Washington, DC

2020

Contents

Introduction ix

**Chapter I. Evolution of US Deterrence Policies Since the Cold
War to the "New Cold War": Political, Strategic, and
Technological Perspectives** 1

    1. Introduction. Deterrence Concepts of the United States
    Since the Dawn of the Era of 'The Absolute Weapon' and
    Missile Defense 1

    2. Hydrogen Bomb-Era Deterrence Developments 4

    3. Post-Cold War Deterrence Shifts 6

    4. BMD and Deterrence Since the 1990s to the "The New
    Cold War" 8

    Summary of the Chapter 11

    Statistical Overview. Missile Defense Effectiveness
    Probability Analysis: The Case of the US BMD Systems in
    the Twenty-First Century 13

**Chapter II. BMD History. Missile Defense Pre-Trump
Presidency** 39

    1. Historical Introduction 39

    2. The North Korean Danger 45

    3. BMD in Post-ABM Perspective 46

    4. "New Cold War"? Stages of Conflict, INF Treaty Problem 48

    5. Back to SDI? Long-Range BMD Perspectives in the
    Twenty-First Century 53

    6. The 2000s' BMD Developments and Polish Missile
    Defense Base 56

    7. BMDS Components: Midcourse, Terminal and Boost-
    Phase Interception. BMD Costs 59

        a) An Overview 59

        b) BMDS/Aegis 60

c) GBI 61

d) Terminal High Altitude Area Defense (THAAD) and
Patriot Advanced Capability (PAC) 63

8. New Strategic Arms Reduction Treaty (START) 65

9. BMD Effectiveness: Probability Analysis 69

Summary of the Chapter 79

**Chapter III. Trump's Global Advocacy: Opportunities,
Chances, Qualified Perspectives on the Defense and Foreign
Policy Choices** 81

1. Threat to INF Treaty 81

2. Sanctions Against North Korean WMD Program 88

a) The US' Sanctions Against North Korean Nuclear
Program 88

b) The EU's sanctions against North Korea 92

c) Attempts to Stop North Korean WMD Program and
the Rise of 2018 Détente 94

**Chapter IV. Regional Extended Deterrence and Missile Defense
in the Twenty-First Century: Theory and Probability Analysis** 97

1. Extended Deterrence. Theory and Practice 97

2. Analyses of Extended Deterrence Based on Empirical
Evidence 101

3. Deterrence Theory and Extended Deterrence After the
Cold War 107

4. US Extended Deterrence in the Far East 109

5. Eastern Europe: US Forward Deployments 114

6. BMD Probability Analysis in the Extended Deterrence
Context 119

7. Finite Deterrence, Minimum Deterrence, Basic Deterrence 130

**Chapter V. Since the Gulf War to Layered BMD: An Overview
of US PAC Intercept Performance** 137

1. The Controversy of PAC Performance in the year 1991 137

2. PAC Improved Performance During the 2003 Iraq War 144

3. The Stages of PAC Improvements 147

4. Israeli BMD Improvements Supported by the US Since the
1991 PAC-2 Introduction 152

5. Layered US-Led BMD Systems in the Twenty-First Century:
The Cases of Eastern Europe and East Asia 162

6. Probability Analysis in the Context of PAC Improvements 167

Chapter Summary 170

**Chapter VI. Case Study. Yemen Missile War and Patriot
Interceptors: A New Perspective on Tactical BMD?** 179

1. Introduction. PAC and the Middle Eastern Challenge:
The Case of Yemen 179

2. The Background of PAC Engagement Against Yemen Missile
Threat 180

3. The Role of PAC Missile Defense in Saudi-Led Intervention
in Yemen 182

4. The Controversy of Iranian Arms Deliveries for Houthis 183

5. Houthi Missile Attacks and PAC Defense 185

6. Summary and Analysis: The Improvement of Patriot
Engagements Since 1990-1991 (US-Iraq Wars and After) 189

    a) Summary: PAC Performance During Desert Storm 189

    b) Summary: PAC Performance During the 2003 Iraq War 190

    c) Summary: Israeli Patriot-Related BMD Improvements 191

7. Probability Analysis in Scenarios of Hypothetical PAC-Level
Effective BMD Engagements 193

Conclusion 195

Final Conclusions 203

Addendum. BMD costs after the Cold War: Tables 205

References 213

Introduction

This book aims to investigate the most significant shifts in US deterrence postures since the end of the Cold War until "the New Cold War", i.e. in the 1987-2019 timeframe, with a special focus on the role of ballistic missile defense (BMD), largely improved in operational capacities since the early introduction of the Patriot in the 1980s. Among the key components of modern 2010s deterrence capacities of Western US allies are new missile defense technologies, including the Terminal High Altitude Area Defense (THAAD), Aegis Ashore, and PAC-3. By the early twenty-first century, the long-range Ground-based Midcourse Defense (GMD) layer of the US BMD still fell behind the ambitions of Reagan's Strategic Defense Initiative (SDI), but the maturing technologies of intercontinental ballistic missiles (ICBMs) encouraged rivals of the West to invest in controversial missile deployments, which gradually led to Intermediate-Range Nuclear Forces (INF) withdrawal. Among the key cases in the BMD-deterrence circle stood the defense of South Korea (THAAD) against potential North Korean's ballistic-nuclear threat, East European Aegis and Patriot investments in the context of Iranian ballistic program (which worsened relations with Russia), Israeli Iron Dome deployments, and PAC engagements on the Arabian Peninsula during the Yemen war.

CHAPTER I

Evolution of US Deterrence Policies Since the Cold War During the "New Cold War": Political, Strategic, and Technological Perspectives

1. Introduction. US Deterrence Concepts Since the Dawn of the Era of 'The Absolute Weapon' and Missile Defense

N otably, the significance of missile defense in US security policies grew in the post-Cold War second nuclear age of increased weapons of mass destruction (WMD) proliferation threats, including challenges posed by authoritarian lesser powers (rogue states), regional conflicts, and terrorist dangers.[1] Such regional (including WMD) and terrorist threats, examined by the fourth wave of deterrence theories, developed since the 1990s[2] after waves centered on bipolar rivalry and its flaws,[3] led after the September 11, 2001 (9/11) terrorist attacks to a revised US deterrence posture. The US deterrence policy was 'tailored' in the 2000s to respond to an increasingly varied range of potential adversaries, from major powers to loosely organized militants with a possibility of low-level conflicts engaging missile and WMD hazards.[4] Among the

---

1   Colin Gray, *The Second Nuclear Age* (Boulder: Lynne Rienner, 1999): 5–9, 12–14; Keith Payne, *Deterrence in the Second Nuclear Age* (Lexington: The University Press of Kentucky, 1996), 167; Lawrence Freedman, *The Evolution of Nuclear Strategy* (London, UK: Palgrave Macmillan UK, 2003), 443–447, 451, https://doi.org/10.1057/9780230379435; Paul Bracken, *The Second Nuclear Age. Strategy, Danger, and the New Power Politics* (New York: St. Martin's Griffin, 2013), 271–272; Robert Jervis, *How Statesmen Think. The Psychology of International Politics* (Princeton: Princeton University Press, 2017), 24–25.

2   Amir Lupovici, "The Emerging Fourth Wave of Deterrence Theory—Toward a New Research Agenda," *International Studies Quarterly* 54, no. 3 (2010): 710; Reuben Steff, *Strategic Thinking, Deterrence and the US Ballistic Missile Defense Project From Truman to Obama* (Farnham: Ashgate, 2013), 7, 23–26, 68.

3   Robert Jervis, "Deterrence Theory Revisited, Review Article, Reviewed Work: Deterrence in American Foreign Policy: Theory and Practice, by Alexander George and Richard Smoke," *World Politics* 31, no. 2 (1979): 291–314; Conf. Alexander L. George and Richard Smoke, *Deterrence in American Foreign Policy: Theory and Practice* (New York: Columbia University Press, 1974).

4   Elinor Sloan, *Modern Military Strategy. An Introduction* (New York: Routledge, 2017), 59–64; US Department of Defense (QDR) Donald H. Rumsfeld, *Quadrennial Defense Review Report (QDR), February 6, 2006* (Washington DC, 2006), vi, http://

earlier BMD research that was important for the assessment of US missile defense capacities, it is important to note (apart from others mentioned in the text) the works of Stephen Cimbala, Andrew Futter, Donald Baucom, Ernest Yanarella, Scott McMahon, Peter Mantle, Michael Mayer, and Reuben Steff.[5]

The first deployment of nuclear weapons by the United States (since the atomic bombing of Japanese cities of Hiroshima and Nagasaki in August, 1945) was not consecutive with the new standing of the general role of those developments in terms of its political and military role in defense posture.

To begin with, a most often recalled voice on the matter, Bernard Brodie (a leading theorist of deterrence), pointed out as early as 1946 that for the general public, the introduction of an atomic bomb meant either total destruction scenarios or the vision of fully mature mankind, willing to choose compromise over conflict, which this nuclear policy pioneer found unlikely in terms of empirical facts related to human behavior over ages.[6] In order to analyze the main outcomes of atomic weapons' revolutionary engagement, Brodie presented eight theses, summarized in the following lines:

    1.   any city in the world could be destroyed by 1-10 atomic bombs,

---

        archive.defense.gov/pubs/pdfs/QDR20060203.pdf; US Strategic Command (DO JOC) James E. Cartwright, *Deterrence Operations Joint Operating Concept (DO JOC)* (Washington DC, 2006), 7, 11, http://www.jcs.mil/Portals/36/Documents/Doctrine/concepts/joc_deterrence.pdf?ver=2017-12-28-162015-337.

5   Stephen Cimbala, *Shield of Dreams. Missile Defenses in US and Russian Nuclear Strategy* (Annapolis: Naval Institute Press, 2008); Andrew Futter, *Ballistic Missile Defense and US National Security Policy. Normalisation and Acceptance after the Cold War* (London, UK: Routledge, 2013); Steff, *Strategic Thinking*; Donald Baucom, *US Missile Defense Program, 1944-1994: A Protracted Revolution* (1995), www.dtic.mil/dtic/tr/fulltext/u2/a338560.pdf; Ernest Yanarella, *The Missile Defense Controversy. Technology in Search of a Mission* (Lexington: University of Kentucky Press, 2002); Scott McMahon, *Pursuit of the Shield. The US Quest for Limited Ballistic Missile Defense* (Lanham, MD: University Press of America, 1997); Peter J. Mantle, *The Missile Defense Equation: Factors for Decision Making* (Reston, MD: American Institute of Aeronautics and Astronautics, 2004); Michael Mayer, *US Missile Defense Strategy. Engaging the Debate* (Boulder: First Forum Press, 2015).

6   Bernard Brodie, "War in the Atomic Age," in *The Absolute Weapon: Atomic Power and World Order*, ed. by Bernard Brodie (New York: Harcourt, Brace and Company, 1946), 21.

2. there was no effective defense against such bombs and no per-spectives for one in the future,

3. atomic weapons lead to an increased emphasis on the deploy-ment of new weapon carriers and the modernization of existing weapon carriers,

4. superiority of air forces no longer guaranteed security,

5. a higher number of any bombs could not provide by itself strate-gic superiority,

6. one should not think of a use of atomic weapons mainly as a tool of sabotage, whereas a surprise attack could be largely strength-ened on the nuclear level,

7. due to atomic weapons' power, the significance of related re-sources (uranium ore) significantly grew,

8. it was supposed to be understood that other powers (beyond the US-Britain-Canada triangle) would possess nuclear weapons within 5-10 years regardless of any US government decisions.[7]

Such framework of analyses could help one keep in mind that since the early looks on atomic age dogmas, many of the first conclusions remained up-to-date even in the time of twenty-first-century technological oppor-tunities.

Basil Liddell Hart's interesting comment on the atomic bomb's perceived unmatched powers lead to an optimistic vision of a possible "antidote," an equally capable defense tool, which could ultimately end the era of the advantage of aggressive means of warfare over defensive ones provided by nuclear forces in a scenario of a new Pearl Harbor-like surprise attack, degrading non-nuclear players to non-regular warfare.[8] Similarly, "the fa-ther of the atomic bomb," J. Robert Oppenheimer, declared in Novem-ber 1945 that this dangerous new weapon gave advantage to aggression (shaking a balance between offensive and defensive arms) leading to a state of common danger.[9] On the other hand, in 1946, Jacob Viner (and

---

7   Brodie, "War in the Atomic Age," 24–69.

8   Basil H. Liddell Hart, *The Revolution in Warfare* (London: Faber and Faber, 1946), 84–85.

9   J. Robert Oppenheimer, "Speech to the Association of Los Alamos Scientists, Los

Brodie) persuaded others that the retaliatory capacities of nuclear powers could effectively deter opponents from using such a weapon in advance, leading to a state balance of chances for both atomic bomb-equipped sides of a conflict.[10] Similarly, Brodie claimed that nuclear weapons would not become primarily a tool of surprise attacks, knowing the atomic retaliatory powers of the power defending itself.[11]

2. Hydrogen Bomb-Era Deterrence Developments

The introduction of hydrogen bomb by the US in 1952 and its development in 1953 by the USSR (who had possessed atomic capacities since 1949) forced the US administration to reorganize its deterrence policies, which was based, until the early 1960s, on the posture of massive retaliation employed to deter the Soviet Union from a large scale conventional attack against the weak West European allies of the North Atlantic Treaty Organization (NATO). Dwight Eisenhower's administration (with John Foster Dulles as Secretary of State) combined massive retaliation with brinksmanship, used to increase pressure on the Soviet Union in the East-West Cold War conflict, serving US containment strategy in Europe and the Far East. Still, Soviet hydrogen capacities led to a shift in US deterrence policies, signaled by Gen. Maxwell Taylor's concept of flexible response: engaging tactical nuclear and conventional deterrence in place of overreliance on massive retaliation, which was less credible in the time of near-equivalent Soviet thermonuclear powers.[12]

Herman Kahn, known for his "doomsday machine" vision (based on automatic nuclear war design systems), distinguished between three types of deterrence:

1.   retaliation as a reliable imminent consequence of a direct attack,

Alamos, November 2, 1945," in *Robert Oppenheimer, Letters and Recollections*, ed. by Alice Kimball Smith and Charles Weiner (Stanford: Stanford University Press, 1995), 318–319.

10   Jacob Viner, "The Implications of the Atomic Bomb for International Relations," *Proceedings of the American Philosophical Society* 90, no. 1 (1946): 53–54, http://www.jstor.org/stable/3301039.

11   Bernard Brodie, "Implications for Military Policy," in *The Absolute Weapon: Atomic Power and World Order*, ed. by Bernard Brodie (New York: Harcourt, Brace and Company, 1946), 73, 85.

12   Maxwell D. Taylor, *The Uncertain Trumpet* (New York: Harper & Brothers, 1960).

2. deterring an enemy from taking dangerous steps (not directly targeted against the US) by the threat of strategic attack,

3. pressure on the enemy side leading to its potential actions, deterred by limited deterrence (and nonmilitary) warnings.[13]

Robert McNamara recognized the Mutual Assured Destruction (MAD) paradigm, but judged it not fully effective in terms of deterring all forms of Soviet aggression, which under the flexible response doctrine meant conventional build-up to deter lower than strategic levels of conflict.[14] MAD paradigm's vitality in the Multiple Independently Target Reentry Vehicles (MIRV) era was strengthened (as a peace-conditioning mutual vulnerability balance) by the Anti-Ballistic Missile (ABM) treaty limitation agreed to during the US-Soviet SALT negotiations, from 1972 Moscow and 1974 Vladivostok agreements to the limit of 2400 deployed strategic nuclear launchers on both sides. Notably, the 1972 ABM treaty limited missile defense up to two areas, with only 100 interceptors (limited in 1974 to one area).[15]

During the Ronald Reagan-era Strategic Defense Initiative (SDI) and Strategic Defense Initiative Organization (SDIO), space-based kinetic Kill Vehicles (KVs) were rooted, as Donald Baucom noted, in 1960s Project Defender.[16] George Bush Sr.-era Global Protection Against Limited Strikes (GPALS) changed the perspective from all-out US-Soviet conflicts to threats of unauthorized or low-number missile attacks.[17] In 1991, the US' focus was shifting towards regional threats, countered by Theatre Missile Defense (TMD).[18]

---

13 Herman Kahn, *On Thermonuclear War* (Princeton: Princeton University Press, 1960), 126, 145.

14 Robert S. McNamara, *The Essence of Security. Reflections in Office* (New York: Harper & Row, 1968), 59.

15 The US Anti-Ballistic Missile (ABM) programs, Sentinel (Lyndon Johnson's era defense of cities) and Safeguard (the Richard Nixon-era defense of Grand Forks' ICBM base), were based on nuclear tipped Nike-Zeus interceptors turned Spartan, supported by shorter-range Sprint missiles. Baucom, *US Missile Defense Program*, 2–3.

16 Homing Overlay Experiment (HOE) 1984 intercept outside the atmosphere contributed to further orbital concept: Space-based interceptors: Smart Rocks, then BP. Donald Baucom, "The Rise and Fall of Brilliant Pebbles," *The Journal of Social, Political and Economic Studies* 29, no. 2 (2004): 143–146, http://highfrontier.org/oldarchive/Archive/hf/The Rise and Fall of Brilliant Pebbles-Baucom.pdf.

17 Baucom, *US Missile Defense Program*, 164–165.

18 Daniel Fink, Fred Hoffman and William Delaney, *Final Report of the Defense Sci-*

This security dilemma (increased arms race expenditures of one side lead-ing to its increased sense of security and decreased perception of security of the other) remained a foundation of the analyses of the Cold War arms competition.[19] Next to that framework, among the important and still accurate problems of deterrence discovered in the Cold War empirical analyses stood the paradox of stability-instability, which meant a policy of acceptance of scenarios of low-level conflicts, seen as not very risky in the conditions of mutual strategic deterrence and as such, perceived as a possible outcome without clear consciousness of its possible escalation scenario to the level posing a risk of all-out nuclear war.[20]

As Robert Jervis noted in the "second wave of deterrence theories" found-ed by Albert Wohlstetter, Thomas Schelling, and Glenn Snyder (follow-ing Brodie), the significance of game theory became evident, including the threat of stubbornness of both superpowers in their massive confron-tation postures ("playing chicken"), which led to a paradox of deterrence based on a heavy losses scenario in non-defense postures as a contribu-tion to peace, not achievable by purely defensive measures.[21]

The third wave of deterrence theories (appearing with Alexander George and Richard Smoke's "Deterrence in American Foreign Policy"), as Law-rence Freedman pointed out, questioned the previous rationality of deci-sion-makers and rational actor theory (in light of the failures of the Viet-nam war, among others) and remained valid until the end of the Cold War.[22] The environment of the Cold War (and the later war on terror) led to the fourth wave of deterrence theories, which were centered on region-al and asymmetrical threats.

3. Post-Cold War Deterrence Shifts

The "second nuclear age" after the Cold War included a threat of hori-zontal proliferation on a regional scale (an increased number of nuclear

ence Board/Defense Policy Board Task Force on Ballistic Missile Defense (BMD), 1991, 1, https://www.dod.mil/pubs/foi/Reading_Room/Homeland_Defense/06-F-041 9_FINAL_RESPONSE-ocrd.pdf.

19   Robert Jervis, *Perception and Misperception in International Politics* (Princeton: Princeton University Press, 2017), 65–66.

20   Steff, 14–15.

21   Jervis, "Deterrence Theory Revisited," 291–292.

22   Lawrence Freedman, *Deterrence* (Cambridge, UK: Polity Press, 2004), 23–25.

powers) in place of vertical proliferation on global scale led mainly by two rival superpowers.[23]

As Keith Payne noted, in the time of the "second nuclear age," the abandoned rigorous control of the two competing blocs areas of influence left regional powers unchecked and free to take part in any local hostilities in their neighborhood, posing a challenge to the United States, while the post-Cold War proliferation of WMD and missile technologies opened paths for secondary military state actors to quickly boost their capabilities.[24]

Notably, in the post-Cold War environment, Stephen Quackenbush (after Frank Zagare and Marc Kilgour) proposed perfect deterrence (stressing the reliability of threats) in place of Robert Powell's 1990 model of traditional deterrence, adapted to the stability expected in the balance that includes the possible first strike option of nuclear super-powers, expected after the inevitability of nuclear conflict surpassed its threshold of probability at the level of $(N-1)/N$ for N nuclear power, beyond which, due to anticipated conflict, a first strike the safer option.[25]

The fourth wave of deterrence theories observed after the Cold War (and with a new focus after the 9/11 attacks) led to a growing significance of "rogue country" threats in US foreign policy, involving "tailored deterrence" that recognized a much more varied environment of potential enemies (state and non-state actors) than in the time of the Cold War, when deterrence doctrines were centered on the Soviet rival.[26] As Elinor Sloan noted, the September 11th attacks led to the US administration's loss of confidence in deterrence tools (visible in National Security Strategy [NSS] of the year 2002). These deterrence tools were seen as incompat-

---

23   Dale C. Walton, "Weapons of Mass Destruction," in *Understanding Modern Warfare* (Cambridge: Cambridge University Press, 2016), 22–24.

24   Payne, *Deterrence in the Second Nuclear Age,* 168.

25   Stephen Quackenbush *Understanding General Deterrence. Theory and Application* (New York: Palgrave Macmillan, 2011), 742–743, 750; Robert Powell, *Nuclear Deterrence Theory. The Search for Credibility* (Cambridge: Cambridge University Press, 1990), 113–130. Conf. Stephen L. Quackenbush, "General Deterrence and International Conflict: Testing Perfect Deterrence Theory," *International Interactions* 36, no. 1 (2010): 60–85, https://doi.org/10.1080/03050620903554069; Frank Zagare and Marc Kilgour, *Perfect Deterrence* (Cambridge: Cambridge University Press, 2000), 287–289.

26   Steff, 23–26.

ible with the characteristics of terrorist threats. Enemy groups not connected with any particular territory or any specific nation (population) therefore could hardly be deterred using strategic-level US strike capabilities.[27] As the US NSS of 2002 stated, traditional views of deterrence, effective during the Cold War, were not suitable to counter terrorist organizations (stateless, suicide-attack oriented), whereas "rogue states" (and sponsors of terrorism) appeared to be able to easily employ WMD to limit the conventional advantage of the United States.[28] Notably, the claims of the George W. Bush administration related to the threat of Iraqi WMD as a cause of the 2003 intervention were not supported by any evidence (as shown by post-intervention official US and British investigations).[29]

4. BMD and Deterrence Since the 1990s to the "The New Cold War"

Most of the Ronald Reagan's SDI-era BMD projects (implemented in 1983) were cancelled just after the Cold War and labeled as too futuristic.[30] The Bill Clinton administration-era budget limitations reduced SBI (a cornerstone of SDI), including small satellites designed to reduce the ICBMs called Brilliant Pebbles (BP) to zero, and turned BP into a technological base.[31]

The Clinton administration's National Missile Defense's (NMD) advanced stages included radar system developments in a gradually en-

---

27   Sloan, *Modern Military Strategy*, 70. Conf. The White House (NSS 2002), *National Security Strategy (NSS) of the United States of America* (Washington DC, 2002), https://www.state.gov/documents/organization/63562.pdf.

28   The White House (NSS 2002), 15.

29   Charles Duelfer, *Comprehensive Report of the Special Advisor to the DCI on Iraq's WMD. Volume I* (Washington, DC, 2004), https://www.cia.gov/library/readingroom/docs/DOC_0001156395.pdf; John Chilcot, *The Report of the Iraq Inquiry. Executive Summary* (London, 2016), http://www.iraqinquiry.org.uk/media/247921/the-report-of-the-iraq-inquiry_executive-summary.pdf.

30   Sharon Weinberger, "The Most Outlandish Ideas for Missile Defence Systems," *BBC Future* (2013), http://www.bbc.com/future/story/20130805-rise-and-fall-of-missile-defences; Ronald Reagan, *Address to the Nation on Defense and National Security*, 23 March 1983 (1983), https://www.reaganlibrary.archivep.gov/archives/speeches/1983/32383d.htm. Conf. Brilliant Pebbles (BP)-based Astrid. John Whitehead, Lee Pittenger, and Nicholas Colella, "Astrid Rocket Flight Test," *Energy and Technology Review* (1994), 11–17, https://str.llnl.gov/etr/pdfs/07_94.2.pdf.

31   Malcolm O'Neill, *Memorandum for Secretary of Defense* (1993), http://www.dod.mil/pubs/foi/Reading_Room/Selected_Acquisition_Reports/485.pdf.

larged NMD system, as Thomas Karako and Ian Williams noted, from twenty through 100 to 250 Ground-Based Interceptors (GBIs) (in place of previously planned 1000 GBI and SBI of SDI phase 1 and 750 GBI ad 1000 SBI of GPALS).[32]

The George W. Bush-era Ground-based Midcourse Defense (GMD) and Aegis investments meant a reinvigoration of missile defense efforts in post-ABM environment with a special focus on regional-level limited missile threats, including "axis of evil" powers (Iran, Iraq, and North Korea).[33]

Donald Rumsfeld 2002 secretary of defense annual report introduced a new strategic triad, linking nuclear and conventional tools to increase the global outreach of executable deterrence and tactical technological edges of the US (unipolar period) preponderance.[34]

Prompt Global Strike of the G. W. Bush administration was using conventional technologies to increase range of US air attacks, to provide for the fully global dimension of "war against terrorism" unilateral preemptive attacks.[35]

Keir Lieber and Daryl Press argued that the post-ABM treaty US strategic capabilities, surmounted by a possible BMD hedge against retaliatory strike allowed the DC planners to provide for successful first strike force in a possible attempt to disarm Russia and degrade its strategic force to non-equal level.[36]

32　New X-band radars were replacing Cold War early warning facilities. Thomas Karako and Ian Williams, *Missile Defense 2020. Next Steps for Defending the Homeland* (2017), 16–17, 33, http://espap.eu/orbis/sites/default/files/generated/document/en/170406_Karako_MissileDefense2020_Web.pdf.

　　Conf. James M. Lindsay and Michael O'Hanlon, *Defending America. The Case for Limited National Missile Defense* (Washington, DC: Brookings, 2001).

33　George W. Bush, *The President's State of the Union Address* (2002), http://georgewbush-whitehouse.archivep.gov/news/releases/2002/01/20020129-11.html.

34　Donald H. Rumsfeld, *Annual Report to the President and the Congress* (2002), 84–85, http://history.defense.gov/Portals/70/Documents/annual_reports/2002_DoD_AR.pdf.

35　US Strategic Command (DO JOC) Cartwright, *Deterrence Operations Joint Operating Concept*, 40.

36　Keir Lieber and Daryl Press, "The Rise of US Nuclear Primacy," *Foreign Affairs* 85, no. 2 (2006): 51.

New "tailored" deterrence introduced in US Deterrence Operations Joint Operating Concept (DO JOC) of 2006 pressed for next stages in adapting selected deterrent policies and tools on regional and local scale, to diversify the range of responses design to counter more and more diverse range of possible enemies, from state actors armed with heavy military equipment to loosely formed local non-state militant groups or terrorist organizations.[37]

The Barack Obama-era European Phased Adaptive Approach (EPAA) reduced the proposed number of missile defense sites for GMD interceptors in Poland (and Czech radar) for intermediate level Aegis bases. Obama's vision of a world free of nuclear weapons brought him a Nobel Peace Prize, but the true progress appeared to be achievable only in terms of the nuclear arms reduction agreement signed by the US and Russian presidents in Prague in 2010, which led to a further arsenal limitation to 1550 deployed warheads on each side.[38]

The 2014 Russian aggression against Ukraine, the illegal annexation of Crimea, violated the 1994 Budapest memorandum, signed by Russia, which guaranteed Ukrainian territorial integrity in return for its accession to the Non-Proliferation Treaty (NPT). Russia's support for separatist military units in Eastern Ukraine led to a serious clash with the EU and US, which decided to impose sanctions to force Moscow to withdraw from the Crimean Peninsula.[39] Despite Western efforts, Vladimir

---

37   US Strategic Command (DO JOC) Cartwright; US Department of Defense (QDR) Rumsfeld, vi; Conf. Steff, 23–26; Sloan, 59, 63–64; Payne, 33-53, 199; Gray, *The Second Nuclear Age*, 7–8.

38   US Department of State, *New START* (2019), https://www.state.gov/t/avc/newstart/; Nobel Media AB, "The Nobel Peace Prize for 2009 to President Barack Obama—Press Release" (2017), https://www.nobelprize.org/nobel_prizes/peace/laureates/2009/press.html.

39   European Union External Action Service, *EU Restrictive Measures in Force* (2017), https://eeas.europa.eu/sites/eeas/files/restrictive_measures-2017-08-04.pdf; European Commission Service for Foreign Policy Instruments, *European Union Consolidated Financial Sanctions List* (2019), https://webgate.ec.europa.eu/europeaid/fsd/fsf/public/files/pdfFullSanctionsList/content?token=dG9rZW4tMjAx Nw; Estonian Presidency of the Council of the EU, *EU Sanctions Map* (2019), https://www.sanctionsmap.eu/#/main; European Council, *EU Restrictive Measures in Response to the Crisis in Ukraine* (2019), http://www.consilium.europa.eu/en/policies/sanctions/ukraine-crisis/; US Department of Treasury Office of Foreign Assets Control, *Ukraine-/Russia-Related Sanctions* (2019), https://www.treasury.gov/resource-center/sanctions/Programs/Pages/ukraine.aspx; US Department of Trea-

Putin's authoritarian Russia seemed more than secure with its new territorial gains, reached through military expansion (after seizing portions of Georgia). The New Cold War[40] between Russia and the West could sound unnatural in light of the post-World War II mass scale fierce military competition between the capitalist and socialist worlds, but the scope of Russian influence in Europe, as measured by higher rates of trust for Putin than for Donald Trump in West-European countries and French, German, and Italian reluctance to support military aid in NATO's eastern flank countries under Russian attack scenario, could prove that Moscow has regained much of its pre-1991 Soviet partition influence.[41]

Summary of the Chapter

Since the Cold War, the main body of deterrence theory related to a possible outcome of a nuclear-based threat on both sides attempting to perform certain military actions that are seen by the deterring state actor as hostile and the likelihood of a successful outcome of such efforts.

sury Office of Foreign Assets Control, *Ukraine/Russia-Related Sanctions Program* (2016) , https://www.treasury.gov/resource-center/sanctions/Programs/Documents/ukraine.pdf.

40 For broader views on the New Cold War, see Marvin Kalb, *Imperial Gamble: Putin, Ukraine, and the New Cold War* (Washington DC: Brookings, 2015); Walter Laqueur, *Putinism. Russia and Its Future in the West*, Kindle (New York: Thomas Dunne Books, 2015); Robert Legvold, *Return to Cold War* (Cambridge: Polity Press, 2016); Edward Lucas, *The New Cold War. Putin's Threat to Russia and the World* (London: Bloomsbury, 2014); Mark MacKinnon, *He New Cold War. Revolutions, Rigged Elections and Pipeline Politics in the Former Soviet Union* (Toronto: Vintage Canada, 2008); Menon Rajan and Eugene Rumer, *Conflict in Ukraine. The Unwindling of the Post-Cold War Order* (Cambridge, MA: The Massachusetts Institute of Technology Press, 2015); Nikolas Gvosdev and Christopher Marsh, *Russian Foreign Policy. Interests, Vectors, and Sectors* (Thousand Oaks: CQ Press, 2014); Fiona Hill and Clifford Gaddy, *New and Expanded Mr Putin. Operative in the Kremlin* (Washington, DC: Brookings, 2015); Stephen Pifer, *The Eagle and the Trident. US-Ukraine Relations in Turbulent Times* (Washington, DC: Brookings, 2017); Steven Rosefielde, *The Kremlin Strikes Back. Russia and the West after Crimea's Annexation* (New York: Cambridge University Press, 2017); Richard Sakwa, *Frontline Ukraine. Crisis in the Borderlands* (London, UK: I. B. Tauris, 2016).

41 Pew Research Center, *Topline Questionnaire, Pew Research Center Spring 2015 Global Attitudes Survey* (2015), 27, http://www.pewglobal.org/category/datasets/2015/; Katie Simmons, Bruce Stokes, and Jacob Poushter, *NATO Publics Blame Russia for Ukrainian Crisis but Reluctant to Provide Military Aid. In Russia, Anti-Western Views and Support for Putin Surge* (2015), 5, http://assets.pewresearch.org/wp-content/uploads/sites/2/2015/06/Pew-Research-Center-Russia-Ukraine-Report-FINAL-June-10-2015.pdf.

In the hydrogen age, the gradual development of comparably devastating nuclear arsenals and delivery means of two superpowers (in a state of a relative equilibrium since the early 1970s), deadlocked in the MAD stalemate, opened a path to an age of strategic arms limitations, interrupted by a Reagan era return to the East-West confrontation. After the end of the Cold War, the second nuclear age brought a threat of a horizontal (in place of a limited two superpowers' vertical) proliferation and new nuclear-capable state challengers, aspiring to the role of regional powers. The US deterrence doctrine has evolved since the time of the Cold War from radical massive retaliation (during the time of American nuclear advantage and conventional weakness of Western Europe) through flexible response and MAD-era mutual vulnerability, supplemented by the 1970s' modernized counterforce concept, and the 1980s' SDI-era futuristic vision of BMD-based mutual survival, to the post-bipolar regionally-focused deterrence, tailored after 9/11 to engage conventional capabilities of state and non-state challengers. In the post-ABM era, US investments in BMD systems appeared to be one of the main new technological edges of the Pentagon's global outreach and modified strategic triad, enhanced by new conventional tools of long-distance warfare. New deployments of US Ballistic Missile Defense System (BMDs), justified by such threats as Iranian and North Korean nuclear/ballistic programs, were among the important factors of tensions between the US and Russia (next to the enlargement of Western area of alliances after the Cold War and the pressure of the West leading to the support of democratization in the former Soviet Union). Due to the Ukrainian crisis of 2014, some scholars questioned the predominant historical narrative of the final cessation of Cold War hostilities between the Western powers and Moscow in the time of geopolitical change 1989 to 1991. Notably, the conflict between Putin's Russian authoritarian regime and Western powers overshadowed the potential rise of tensions between the new Chinese emerging superpower and the US system of alliances, forcing the West to review its deterrence capabilities in the scenario of a possible military clash with the expanding modernized Russian (Soviet-based) US-equivalent strategic power, aided by newly adapted-to-information-warfare conventional forces.

Statistical Overview. Missile Defense Effectiveness Probability Analysis: The Case of the US BMD Systems in the Twenty-First Century

Table 1. Probability of defeating BMD with 0 to 5 attacking warheads (out of 5) when:

Single Shot Kill Probability (SSKP) of interceptor attacking single warhead equals 81%:

Warheads	0	1	2	3	4	5
probability	0.349	0.409	0.192	0.045	0.005	0.000

SSKP of interceptor attacking single warhead equals 84%:

Warheads	0	1	2	3	4	5
probability	0.418	0.398	0.152	0.029	0.003	0.000

Source: own counting (using Microsoft Excel) according to the equation (bullet operator represents here multiplication symbol)

$$P(x) = \{W!/[x! \cdot (W - x)!]\} \cdot (1 - K_w)^x \cdot K_w^{W-x}$$

based on Dean Wilkening's model (Bernoulli distribution), where $P(x)$ is the probability of defeating the missile defense by x number of incoming warheads, K_w is the probability of interception of an incoming warhead by a single interceptor missile, W is the number of incoming warheads.

In a scenario of a leak-proof defense (intercepting all incoming warheads), i.e., x = 0 and $P(0) = (K_w)^W$ and

$$P(0) = 1 - (1 - p)^n$$

based on George N. Lewis's model, for p counted for a leak-proof defense in the cases of attacks of 5, 6, 7, ... 30 incoming warheads (in Bernoulli distribution).

Dean Wilkening, "A Simple Model for Calculating Ballistic Missile Defense Effectiveness," *Science & Global Security* 8, no. 2 (1999): 191, https://cisac.fsi.stanford.edu/sites/default/files/Simple_Model_for_BMD.pdf. George N. Lewis, "Technical Controversy. Can Missile Defense Work?" *Regional Missile Defense from a Global Perspective*, ed. Catherine McArdle Kelleher, Peter Dombrowski, op. cit., ibidem. See also Missile Defense Agency (MDA), *Ballistic Missile Defense Intercept Flight Test Record (as of May 30, 2017)*, https://www.mda.mil/global/documents/pdf/testrecord.pdf. See also Laura Grego, George N. Lewis, and David Wright, *Shielded from Oversight. The Disastrous US Approach to Strategic Missile Defense*, Union of Concerned Scientists (July 2016), http://www.ucsusa.org/sites/default/files/attach/2016/07/Shielded-from-Oversight-appendix-8.pdf. Conf. *Parentheses, Braces & Brackets in Math*, Saxon Algebra ½ Homeschool: Online Textbook Help, https://study.com/academy/lesson/parentheses-braces-brackets-in-math.html

Chart 1. Probability of defeating the BMD by from 0 to 5 attacking warheads (out of 5) when SSKP of interceptor attacking a single warhead equals 81%.

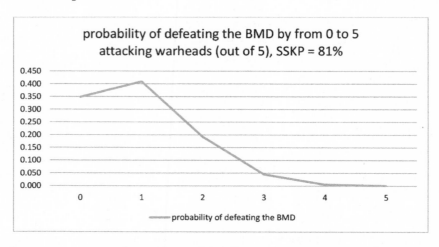

Source: own counting (using Microsoft Excel) according to the equation (where bullet operator represents multiplication symbol)

$$P(x) = \{W!/[x! \cdot (W-x)!]\} \cdot (1-K_w)^x \cdot K_w^{W-x}$$

based on Wilkening's model (Bernoulli distribution), and

$$P(0) = 1 - (1-p)^n$$

based on G. Lewis's model, for p counted for a leak-proof defense in the cases of attacks of 5, 6, 7, ... 30 incoming warheads (in Bernoulli distribution).

Wilkening, "A Simple Model for Calculating Ballistic Missile Defense Effectiveness," 191. G. Lewis, "Technical Controversy." See also MDA, *Ballistic Missile Defense Intercept Flight Test Record (as of May 30, 2017),* https://www.mda.mil/global/documents/pdf/testrecord.pdf.

Table 2. Probability of leak-proof interception using additional (up to 15 interceptors against single attacking warhead, in a salvos up to 30 attacking consecutively), with SSKP 81%.

Warheads	Interceptors														
	1	2	3	4	5	6	7	8	9	10	11	12	13	14	15
1	0.81	0.96	0.99	1.00	1.00	1.00	1.00	1.00	1.00	1.00	1.00	1.00	1.00	1.00	1.00
2	0.66	0.88	0.96	0.99	1.00	1.00	1.00	1.00	1.00	1.00	1.00	1.00	1.00	1.00	1.00
3	0.53	0.78	0.90	0.95	0.98	0.99	1.00	1.00	1.00	1.00	1.00	1.00	1.00	1.00	1.00
4	0.43	0.68	0.82	0.89	0.94	0.97	0.98	0.99	0.99	1.00	1.00	1.00	1.00	1.00	1.00
5	0.35	0.58	0.72	0.82	0.88	0.92	0.95	0.97	0.98	0.99	0.99	0.99	1.00	1.00	1.00
6	0.28	0.49	0.63	0.73	0.81	0.86	0.90	0.93	0.95	0.96	0.97	0.98	0.99	0.99	0.99
7	0.23	0.41	0.54	0.65	0.73	0.79	0.84	0.87	0.90	0.93	0.94	0.96	0.97	0.97	0.98
8	0.19	0.34	0.46	0.56	0.64	0.71	0.76	0.81	0.84	0.87	0.90	0.91	0.93	0.94	0.95
9	0.15	0.28	0.39	0.48	0.56	0.62	0.68	0.73	0.77	0.80	0.83	0.86	0.88	0.90	0.91
10	0.12	0.23	0.32	0.40	0.48	0.54	0.60	0.65	0.69	0.73	0.76	0.79	0.81	0.84	0.86
11	0.10	0.19	0.27	0.34	0.40	0.46	0.52	0.56	0.61	0.65	0.68	0.71	0.74	0.77	0.79
12	0.08	0.15	0.22	0.28	0.34	0.39	0.44	0.49	0.53	0.56	0.60	0.63	0.66	0.69	0.71
13	0.06	0.13	0.18	0.23	0.28	0.33	0.37	0.41	0.45	0.49	0.52	0.55	0.58	0.61	0.63
14	0.05	0.10	0.15	0.19	0.24	0.28	0.31	0.35	0.38	0.42	0.45	0.48	0.50	0.53	0.55
15	0.04	0.08	0.12	0.16	0.19	0.23	0.26	0.29	0.32	0.35	0.38	0.41	0.43	0.45	0.48
16	0.03	0.07	0.10	0.13	0.16	0.19	0.22	0.24	0.27	0.29	0.32	0.34	0.37	0.39	0.41

	0.03	0.05	0.08	0.11	0.13	0.16	0.18	0.20	0.22	0.25	0.27	0.29	0.31	0.33	0.34
17	0.03	0.05	0.08	0.11	0.13	0.16	0.18	0.20	0.22	0.25	0.27	0.29	0.31	0.33	0.34
18	0.02	0.04	0.07	0.09	0.11	0.13	0.15	0.17	0.19	0.20	0.22	0.24	0.26	0.27	0.29
19	0.02	0.04	0.05	0.07	0.09	0.10	0.12	0.14	0.15	0.17	0.18	0.20	0.21	0.23	0.24
20	0.01	0.03	0.04	0.06	0.07	0.09	0.10	0.11	0.13	0.14	0.15	0.16	0.18	0.19	0.20
21	0.01	0.02	0.04	0.05	0.06	0.07	0.08	0.09	0.10	0.11	0.12	0.13	0.14	0.16	0.17
22	0.01	0.02	0.03	0.04	0.05	0.06	0.07	0.07	0.08	0.09	0.10	0.11	0.12	0.13	0.14
23	0.01	0.02	0.02	0.03	0.04	0.05	0.05	0.06	0.07	0.08	0.08	0.09	0.10	0.10	0.11
24	0.01	0.01	0.02	0.03	0.03	0.04	0.04	0.05	0.06	0.06	0.07	0.07	0.08	0.09	0.09
25	0.01	0.01	0.02	0.02	0.03	0.03	0.04	0.04	0.05	0.05	0.06	0.06	0.06	0.07	0.07
26	0.00	0.01	0.01	0.02	0.02	0.02	0.03	0.03	0.04	0.04	0.04	0.05	0.05	0.06	0.06
27	0.00	0.01	0.01	0.02	0.02	0.02	0.02	0.03	0.03	0.03	0.04	0.04	0.04	0.05	0.05
28	0.00	0.01	0.01	0.01	0.01	0.02	0.02	0.02	0.02	0.03	0.03	0.03	0.04	0.04	0.04
29	0.00	0.00	0.01	0.01	0.01	0.01	0.02	0.02	0.02	0.02	0.02	0.03	0.03	0.03	0.03
30	0.00	0.00	0.01	0.01	0.01	0.01	0.01	0.01	0.02	0.02	0.02	0.02	0.02	0.02	0.03

Source: own counting (using Microsoft Excel) according to the equation (bullet operator represents multiplication)

$$P(x) = \{W!/[x! \cdot (W-x)!]\} \cdot (1 - K_w)^x \cdot K_w^{W-x}$$

based on Wilkening's model (Bernoulli distribution), and

$$P(0) = 1 - (1-p)^n$$

based on G. Lewis's model, for p counted for a leak-proof defense in the cases of attacks of 5, 6, 7, … 30 incoming warheads (in Bernoulli distribution).

Wilkening, 191. G. Lewis. See also MDA, *Ballistic Missile Defense Intercept Flight Test Record.*

Chart 2. Probability of leak-proof interception using additional (up to 15 interceptors against single one out of attacking warheads, in a salvos up to 30 attacking consecutively), with SSKP 81%.

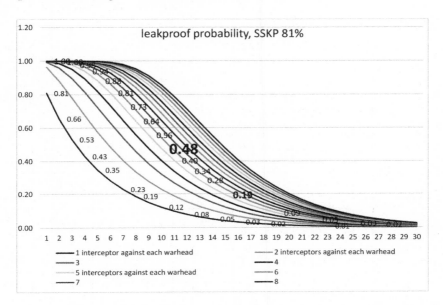

Source: own counting (using Microsoft Excel) according to the equation (bullet operator represents multiplication)

$$P(x) = \{W!/[x! \cdot (W - x)!]\} \cdot (1 - K_W)^x \cdot K_W^{W-x}$$

based on Wilkening's model (Bernoulli distribution), and

$$P(0) = 1 - (1 - p)^n$$

based on Lewis's model, for p counted for a leak-proof defense in the cases of attacks of 5, 6, 7, ... 30 incoming warheads (in Bernoulli distribution).

Wilkening, 191. G. Lewis. See also MDA, *Ballistic Missile Defense Intercept Flight Test Record.*

Table 3. Probability of leak-proof interception using additional (up to 15 interceptors against single attacking warhead, in a salvo of up to 30 attacking consecutively), with SSKP 84%.

Warheads	Interceptors														
	1	2	3	4	5	6	7	8	9	10	11	12	13	14	15
1	0.84	0.97	1.00	1.00	1.00	1.00	1.00	1.00	1.00	1.00	1.00	1.00	1.00	1.00	1.00
2	0.71	0.91	0.97	0.99	1.00	1.00	1.00	1.00	1.00	1.00	1.00	1.00	1.00	1.00	1.00
3	0.59	0.83	0.93	0.97	0.99	1.00	1.00	1.00	1.00	1.00	1.00	1.00	1.00	1.00	1.00
4	0.50	0.75	0.87	0.94	0.97	0.98	0.99	1.00	1.00	1.00	1.00	1.00	1.00	1.00	1.00
5	0.42	0.66	0.80	0.89	0.93	0.96	0.98	0.99	0.99	1.00	1.00	1.00	1.00	1.00	1.00
6	0.35	0.58	0.73	0.82	0.89	0.93	0.95	0.97	0.98	0.99	0.99	0.99	1.00	1.00	1.00
7	0.30	0.50	0.65	0.75	0.83	0.88	0.91	0.94	0.96	0.97	0.98	0.98	0.99	0.99	0.99
8	0.25	0.43	0.57	0.68	0.76	0.82	0.86	0.90	0.92	0.94	0.96	0.97	0.98	0.98	0.99
9	0.21	0.37	0.50	0.61	0.69	0.75	0.80	0.85	0.88	0.90	0.92	0.94	0.95	0.96	0.97
10	0.17	0.32	0.44	0.54	0.62	0.68	0.74	0.79	0.82	0.85	0.88	0.90	0.92	0.93	0.94
11	0.15	0.27	0.38	0.47	0.55	0.61	0.67	0.72	0.76	0.80	0.83	0.85	0.87	0.89	0.91
12	0.12	0.23	0.33	0.41	0.48	0.55	0.60	0.65	0.69	0.73	0.77	0.79	0.82	0.84	0.86
13	0.10	0.20	0.28	0.35	0.42	0.48	0.54	0.58	0.63	0.67	0.70	0.73	0.76	0.78	0.81
14	0.09	0.17	0.24	0.31	0.37	0.42	0.47	0.52	0.56	0.60	0.63	0.66	0.69	0.72	0.75
15	0.07	0.14	0.20	0.26	0.32	0.37	0.41	0.46	0.50	0.53	0.57	0.60	0.63	0.65	0.68
16	0.06	0.12	0.17	0.22	0.27	0.32	0.36	0.40	0.43	0.47	0.50	0.53	0.56	0.59	0.61

	0.05	0.10	0.15	0.19	0.23	0.27	0.31	0.35	0.38	0.41	0.44	0.47	0.50	0.52	0.55
17	0.05	0.08	0.12	0.16	0.20	0.23	0.27	0.30	0.33	0.36	0.39	0.41	0.44	0.46	0.49
18	0.04	0.07	0.11	0.14	0.17	0.20	0.23	0.26	0.28	0.31	0.34	0.36	0.38	0.41	0.43
19	0.04	0.06	0.09	0.12	0.14	0.17	0.20	0.22	0.24	0.27	0.29	0.31	0.33	0.35	0.37
20	0.03	0.05	0.08	0.10	0.12	0.14	0.17	0.19	0.21	0.23	0.25	0.27	0.29	0.31	0.32
21	0.03	0.05	0.06	0.08	0.10	0.12	0.14	0.16	0.18	0.20	0.21	0.23	0.25	0.26	0.28
22	0.02	0.04	0.05	0.07	0.09	0.10	0.12	0.14	0.15	0.17	0.18	0.20	0.21	0.23	0.24
23	0.02	0.04	0.04	0.06	0.07	0.09	0.10	0.12	0.13	0.14	0.16	0.17	0.18	0.19	0.21
24	0.02	0.03	0.04	0.05	0.06	0.07	0.09	0.10	0.11	0.12	0.13	0.14	0.15	0.16	0.18
25	0.01	0.03	0.04	0.04	0.05	0.06	0.07	0.08	0.09	0.10	0.11	0.12	0.13	0.14	0.15
26	0.01	0.03	0.03	0.04	0.04	0.05	0.06	0.07	0.08	0.09	0.09	0.10	0.11	0.12	0.13
27	0.01	0.02	0.03	0.03	0.04	0.04	0.05	0.06	0.07	0.07	0.08	0.09	0.09	0.10	0.11
28	0.01	0.02	0.02	0.03	0.04	0.04	0.04	0.05	0.06	0.06	0.07	0.07	0.08	0.09	0.09
29	0.01	0.01	0.02	0.03	0.03	0.04	0.04	0.05	0.06	0.06	0.07	0.07	0.08	0.09	0.09
30	0.01	0.01	0.02	0.02	0.03	0.03	0.04	0.04	0.05	0.05	0.06	0.06	0.07	0.07	0.08

Source: own counting (using Microsoft Excel) according to the equation (bullet operator represents multiplication)

$$P(x) = \{W!/[x! \cdot (W - x)!]\} \cdot (1 - K_w)^x \cdot K_w^{W-x}$$

based on Wilkening's model (Bernoulli distribution), and

$$P(0) = 1 - (1 - p)^n$$

based on G. Lewis's model, for p counted for a leak-proof defense in the cases of attacks of 5, 6, 7, … 30 incoming warheads (in Bernoulli distribution).

Wilkening, 191. G. Lewis. See also MDA, Ballistic Missile Defense Intercept Flight Test Record.

Chart 3. Probability of leak-proof interception using additional (up to 15 interceptors against single attacking warhead, in a salvo of up to 30 attacking consecutively), with SSKP 84%.

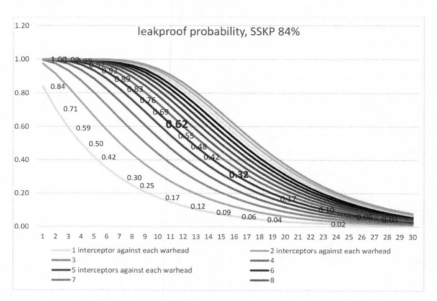

Source: own counting (using Microsoft Excel) according to the equation (bullet operator represents multiplication)

$$P(x) = \{W!/[x! \cdot (W-x)!]\} \cdot (1 - K_w)^x \cdot K_w^{W-x}$$

based on Wilkening's model (Bernoulli distribution), and

$$P(0) = 1 - (1 - p)^n$$

based on G. Lewis's model, for p counted for a leak-proof defense in the cases of attacks of 5, 6, 7, ... 30 incoming warheads (in Bernoulli distribution).

Wilkening, 191. G. Lewis. See also MDA, *Ballistic Missile Defense Intercept Flight Test Record*.

Table 4. Probability of leak-proof interception using additional (up to 15 interceptors against single attacking warhead, in a salvo of up to 30 attacking consecutively), with SSKP 89%.

Warheads	Interceptors														
	1	2	3	4	5	6	7	8	9	10	11	12	13	14	15
1	0.89	0.99	1.00	1.00	1.00	1.00	1.00	1.00	1.00	1.00	1.00	1.00	1.00	1.00	1.00
2	0.79	0.96	0.99	1.00	1.00	1.00	1.00	1.00	1.00	1.00	1.00	1.00	1.00	1.00	1.00
3	0.70	0.91	0.97	0.99	1.00	1.00	1.00	1.00	1.00	1.00	1.00	1.00	1.00	1.00	1.00
4	0.63	0.86	0.95	0.98	0.99	1.00	1.00	1.00	1.00	1.00	1.00	1.00	1.00	1.00	1.00
5	0.56	0.80	0.91	0.96	0.98	0.99	1.00	1.00	1.00	1.00	1.00	1.00	1.00	1.00	1.00
6	0.50	0.75	0.87	0.94	0.97	0.98	0.99	1.00	1.00	1.00	1.00	1.00	1.00	1.00	1.00
7	0.44	0.69	0.83	0.90	0.95	0.97	0.98	0.99	0.99	1.00	1.00	1.00	1.00	1.00	1.00
8	0.39	0.63	0.78	0.86	0.92	0.95	0.97	0.98	0.99	0.99	1.00	1.00	1.00	1.00	1.00
9	0.35	0.58	0.73	0.82	0.88	0.92	0.95	0.97	0.98	0.99	0.99	0.99	1.00	1.00	1.00
10	0.31	0.53	0.67	0.78	0.85	0.89	0.93	0.95	0.97	0.98	0.98	0.99	0.99	0.99	0.99
11	0.28	0.48	0.62	0.73	0.80	0.86	0.90	0.93	0.95	0.96	0.97	0.98	0.99	0.99	0.99
12	0.25	0.43	0.57	0.68	0.76	0.82	0.86	0.90	0.92	0.94	0.96	0.97	0.97	0.98	0.99
13	0.22	0.39	0.53	0.63	0.71	0.77	0.82	0.86	0.89	0.92	0.93	0.95	0.96	0.97	0.98
14	0.20	0.35	0.48	0.58	0.66	0.73	0.78	0.82	0.86	0.89	0.91	0.93	0.94	0.95	0.96
15	0.17	0.32	0.44	0.53	0.62	0.68	0.74	0.78	0.82	0.85	0.88	0.90	0.92	0.93	0.94
16	0.15	0.29	0.40	0.49	0.57	0.64	0.69	0.74	0.78	0.81	0.84	0.87	0.89	0.91	0.92

	0.14	0.26	0.36	0.45	0.52	0.59	0.65	0.69	0.74	0.77	0.80	0.83	0.85	0.87	0.89
17	0.14	0.26	0.36	0.45	0.52	0.59	0.65	0.69	0.74	0.77	0.80	0.83	0.85	0.87	0.89
18	0.12	0.23	0.32	0.41	0.48	0.54	0.60	0.65	0.69	0.73	0.76	0.79	0.82	0.84	0.86
19	0.11	0.21	0.29	0.37	0.44	0.50	0.56	0.60	0.65	0.69	0.72	0.75	0.78	0.80	0.82
20	0.10	0.19	0.26	0.34	0.40	0.46	0.51	0.56	0.60	0.64	0.68	0.71	0.74	0.76	0.78
21	0.09	0.17	0.24	0.30	0.36	0.42	0.47	0.52	0.56	0.60	0.63	0.66	0.69	0.72	0.74
22	0.08	0.15	0.21	0.27	0.33	0.38	0.43	0.47	0.51	0.55	0.59	0.62	0.65	0.67	0.70
23	0.07	0.13	0.19	0.25	0.30	0.35	0.39	0.43	0.47	0.51	0.54	0.57	0.60	0.63	0.66
24	0.06	0.12	0.17	0.22	0.27	0.31	0.36	0.40	0.43	0.47	0.50	0.53	0.56	0.59	0.61
25	0.05	0.11	0.15	0.20	0.24	0.28	0.32	0.36	0.39	0.43	0.46	0.49	0.52	0.54	0.57
26	0.05	0.09	0.14	0.18	0.22	0.26	0.29	0.33	0.36	0.39	0.42	0.45	0.47	0.50	0.52
27	0.04	0.08	0.12	0.16	0.20	0.23	0.26	0.30	0.33	0.36	0.38	0.41	0.44	0.46	0.48
28	0.04	0.08	0.11	0.14	0.18	0.21	0.24	0.27	0.30	0.32	0.35	0.37	0.40	0.42	0.44
29	0.03	0.07	0.10	0.13	0.16	0.19	0.22	0.24	0.27	0.29	0.32	0.34	0.36	0.38	0.41
30	0.03	0.06	0.09	0.12	0.14	0.17	0.19	0.22	0.24	0.26	0.29	0.31	0.33	0.35	0.37

Source: own counting (using Microsoft Excel) according to the equation (bullet operator represents multiplication)

$$P(x) = \{W! / [x! \cdot (W-x)!]\} \cdot (1 - K_W)^x \cdot K_W^{W-x}$$

based on Wilkening's model (Bernoulli distribution), and

$$P(0) = 1 - (1-p)^n$$

based on G. Lewis's model, for p counted for a leak-proof defense in the cases of attacks of 5, 6, 7, … 30 incoming warheads (in Bernoulli distribution).

Wilkening, 191. G. Lewis. See also MDA, *Ballistic Missile Defense Intercept Flight Test Record.*

Chart 4. Probability of leak-proof interception using additional (up to 15 interceptors against single attacking warhead, in a salvo of up to 30 attacking consecutively), with SSKP 89%.

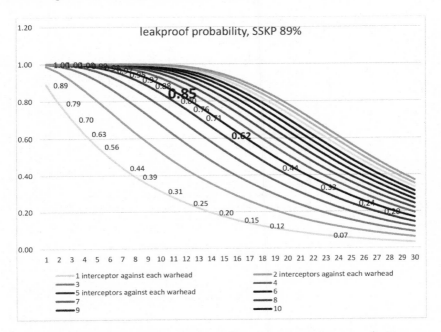

Source: own counting (using Microsoft Excel) according to the equation (bullet operator represents multiplication)

$$P(x) = \{W!/[x! \cdot (W-x)!]\} \cdot (1-K_W)^x \cdot K_W^{W-x}$$

based on Wilkening's model (Bernoulli distribution), and

$$P(0) = 1 - (1-p)^n$$

based on G. Lewis's model, for p counted for a leak-proof defense in the cases of attacks of 5, 6, 7, ... 30 incoming warheads (in Bernoulli distribution).

Wilkening, 191. G. Lewis. See also MDA, *Ballistic Missile Defense Intercept Flight Test Record*.

Table 5. Probability of leak-proof interception using additional (up to 15 interceptors against single attacking warhead, in a salvo of up to 30 attacking consecutively)), with SSKP 93%.

Warheads	Interceptors														
	1	2	3	4	5	6	7	8	9	10	11	12	13	14	15
1	0.93	1.00	1.00	1.00	1.00	1.00	1.00	1.00	1.00	1.00	1.00	1.00	1.00	1.00	1.00
2	0.86	0.98	1.00	1.00	1.00	1.00	1.00	1.00	1.00	1.00	1.00	1.00	1.00	1.00	1.00
3	0.80	0.96	0.99	1.00	1.00	1.00	1.00	1.00	1.00	1.00	1.00	1.00	1.00	1.00	1.00
4	0.75	0.94	0.98	1.00	1.00	1.00	1.00	1.00	1.00	1.00	1.00	1.00	1.00	1.00	1.00
5	0.70	0.91	0.97	0.99	1.00	1.00	1.00	1.00	1.00	1.00	1.00	1.00	1.00	1.00	1.00
6	0.65	0.88	0.96	0.98	0.99	1.00	1.00	1.00	1.00	1.00	1.00	1.00	1.00	1.00	1.00
7	0.60	0.84	0.94	0.97	0.99	1.00	1.00	1.00	1.00	1.00	1.00	1.00	1.00	1.00	1.00
8	0.56	0.81	0.91	0.96	0.98	0.99	1.00	1.00	1.00	1.00	1.00	1.00	1.00	1.00	1.00
9	0.52	0.77	0.89	0.95	0.97	0.99	0.99	1.00	1.00	1.00	1.00	1.00	1.00	1.00	1.00
10	0.48	0.73	0.86	0.93	0.96	0.98	0.99	0.99	1.00	1.00	1.00	1.00	1.00	1.00	1.00
11	0.45	0.70	0.83	0.91	0.95	0.97	0.98	0.99	1.00	1.00	1.00	1.00	1.00	1.00	1.00
12	0.42	0.66	0.80	0.89	0.93	0.96	0.98	0.99	0.99	1.00	1.00	1.00	1.00	1.00	1.00
13	0.39	0.63	0.77	0.86	0.92	0.95	0.97	0.98	0.99	0.99	1.00	1.00	1.00	1.00	1.00
14	0.36	0.59	0.74	0.83	0.89	0.93	0.96	0.97	0.98	0.99	0.99	1.00	1.00	1.00	1.00
15	0.34	0.56	0.71	0.81	0.87	0.91	0.94	0.96	0.98	0.98	0.99	0.99	1.00	1.00	1.00
16	0.31	0.53	0.68	0.78	0.85	0.89	0.93	0.95	0.97	0.98	0.98	0.99	0.99	0.99	1.00

	0.99	0.99	0.99	0.98	0.98	0.97	0.95	0.94	0.91	0.87	0.82	0.75	0.64	0.50	0.29
17	0.99	0.99	0.99	0.98	0.98	0.97	0.95	0.94	0.91	0.87	0.82	0.75	0.64	0.50	0.29
18	0.99	0.99	0.98	0.98	0.97	0.96	0.94	0.92	0.89	0.85	0.79	0.72	0.61	0.47	0.27
19	0.99	0.98	0.98	0.97	0.96	0.95	0.93	0.90	0.87	0.82	0.77	0.69	0.58	0.44	0.25
20	0.98	0.98	0.97	0.96	0.95	0.93	0.91	0.88	0.85	0.80	0.74	0.66	0.55	0.41	0.23
21	0.97	0.97	0.96	0.95	0.93	0.91	0.89	0.86	0.82	0.77	0.71	0.63	0.52	0.39	0.22
22	0.97	0.96	0.95	0.93	0.92	0.90	0.87	0.84	0.79	0.74	0.68	0.60	0.49	0.36	0.20
23	0.96	0.95	0.93	0.92	0.90	0.88	0.85	0.81	0.77	0.71	0.65	0.57	0.47	0.34	0.19
24	0.94	0.93	0.92	0.90	0.88	0.85	0.82	0.79	0.74	0.69	0.62	0.54	0.44	0.32	0.18
25	0.93	0.92	0.90	0.88	0.86	0.83	0.80	0.76	0.71	0.66	0.59	0.51	0.41	0.30	0.16
26	0.92	0.90	0.88	0.86	0.84	0.81	0.77	0.73	0.68	0.63	0.56	0.48	0.39	0.28	0.15
27	0.90	0.88	0.86	0.84	0.81	0.78	0.75	0.70	0.65	0.60	0.53	0.46	0.37	0.26	0.14
28	0.88	0.86	0.84	0.81	0.79	0.75	0.72	0.68	0.63	0.57	0.50	0.43	0.34	0.24	0.13
29	0.86	0.84	0.82	0.79	0.76	0.73	0.69	0.65	0.60	0.54	0.48	0.41	0.32	0.23	0.12
30	0.84	0.81	0.79	0.76	0.73	0.70	0.66	0.62	0.57	0.51	0.45	0.38	0.30	0.21	0.11

Source: own counting (using Microsoft Excel) according to the equation (bullet operator represents multiplication)

$$P(x) = \{W! / [x! \cdot (W - x)!]\} \cdot (1 - K_w)^x \cdot K_w^{W-x}$$

based on Wilkening's model (Bernoulli distribution), and

$$P(0) = 1 - (1 - p)^n$$

based on G. Lewis's model, for p counted for a leak-proof defense in the cases of attacks of 5, 6, 7, … 30 incoming warheads (in Bernoulli distribution).

Wilkening, 191. G. Lewis. See also MDA, *Ballistic Missile Defense Intercept Flight Test Record.*

Chart 5. Probability of leak-proof interception using additional (up to 15 interceptors against single attacking warhead, in a salvo of up to 30 attacking consecutively), with SSKP 93%.

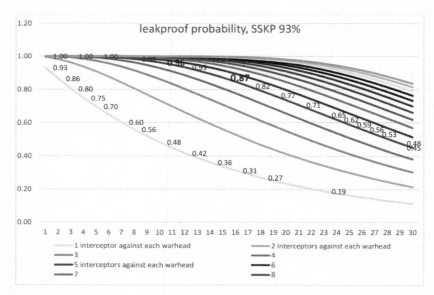

Source: own counting (using Microsoft Excel) according to the equation (bullet operator represents multiplication)

$$P(x) = \{W!/[x! \cdot (W-x)!]\} \cdot (1 - K_w)^x \cdot K_w^{W-x}$$

based on Wilkening's model (Bernoulli distribution), and

$$P(0) = 1 - (1-p)^n$$

based on G. Lewis's model, for p counted for a leak-proof defense in the cases of attacks of 5, 6, 7, ... 30 incoming warheads (in Bernoulli distribution).

Wilkening, 191. G. Lewis. See also MDA, *Ballistic Missile Defense Intercept Flight Test Record.*

Table 6. Probability of leak-proof interception using additional (up to 15 interceptors against single attacking warhead, in a salvo of up to 30 attacking consecutively), with SSKP 96%.

Warheads	Interceptors														
	1	2	3	4	5	6	7	8	9	10	11	12	13	14	15
1	0.96	1.00	1.00	1.00	1.00	1.00	1.00	1.00	1.00	1.00	1.00	1.00	1.00	1.00	1.00
2	0.92	0.99	1.00	1.00	1.00	1.00	1.00	1.00	1.00	1.00	1.00	1.00	1.00	1.00	1.00
3	0.88	0.99	1.00	1.00	1.00	1.00	1.00	1.00	1.00	1.00	1.00	1.00	1.00	1.00	1.00
4	0.85	0.98	1.00	1.00	1.00	1.00	1.00	1.00	1.00	1.00	1.00	1.00	1.00	1.00	1.00
5	0.82	0.97	0.99	1.00	1.00	1.00	1.00	1.00	1.00	1.00	1.00	1.00	1.00	1.00	1.00
6	0.78	0.95	0.99	1.00	1.00	1.00	1.00	1.00	1.00	1.00	1.00	1.00	1.00	1.00	1.00
7	0.75	0.94	0.98	1.00	1.00	1.00	1.00	1.00	1.00	1.00	1.00	1.00	1.00	1.00	1.00
8	0.72	0.92	0.98	0.99	1.00	1.00	1.00	1.00	1.00	1.00	1.00	1.00	1.00	1.00	1.00
9	0.69	0.91	0.97	0.99	1.00	1.00	1.00	1.00	1.00	1.00	1.00	1.00	1.00	1.00	1.00
10	0.66	0.89	0.96	0.99	1.00	1.00	1.00	1.00	1.00	1.00	1.00	1.00	1.00	1.00	1.00
11	0.64	0.87	0.95	0.98	0.99	1.00	1.00	1.00	1.00	1.00	1.00	1.00	1.00	1.00	1.00
12	0.61	0.85	0.94	0.98	0.99	1.00	1.00	1.00	1.00	1.00	1.00	1.00	1.00	1.00	1.00
13	0.59	0.83	0.93	0.97	0.99	1.00	1.00	1.00	1.00	1.00	1.00	1.00	1.00	1.00	1.00
14	0.56	0.81	0.92	0.96	0.98	0.99	1.00	1.00	1.00	1.00	1.00	1.00	1.00	1.00	1.00
15	0.54	0.79	0.90	0.96	0.98	0.99	1.00	1.00	1.00	1.00	1.00	1.00	1.00	1.00	1.00
16	0.52	0.77	0.89	0.95	0.97	0.99	0.99	1.00	1.00	1.00	1.00	1.00	1.00	1.00	1.00

17	0.50	0.75	0.87	0.94	0.97	0.98	0.99	1.00	1.00	1.00	1.00	1.00	1.00	1.00	1.00
18	0.48	0.73	0.86	0.93	0.96	0.98	0.99	0.99	1.00	1.00	1.00	1.00	1.00	1.00	1.00
19	0.46	0.71	0.84	0.92	0.95	0.98	0.99	0.99	1.00	1.00	1.00	1.00	1.00	1.00	1.00
20	0.44	0.69	0.83	0.90	0.95	0.97	0.98	0.99	0.99	1.00	1.00	1.00	1.00	1.00	1.00
21	0.42	0.67	0.81	0.89	0.94	0.96	0.98	0.99	0.99	1.00	1.00	1.00	1.00	1.00	1.00
22	0.41	0.65	0.79	0.88	0.93	0.96	0.97	0.98	0.99	0.99	1.00	1.00	1.00	1.00	1.00
23	0.39	0.63	0.77	0.86	0.92	0.95	0.97	0.98	0.99	0.99	1.00	1.00	1.00	1.00	1.00
24	0.38	0.61	0.76	0.85	0.90	0.94	0.96	0.98	0.99	0.99	0.99	1.00	1.00	1.00	1.00
25	0.36	0.59	0.74	0.83	0.89	0.93	0.96	0.97	0.98	0.99	0.99	1.00	1.00	1.00	1.00
26	0.35	0.57	0.72	0.82	0.88	0.92	0.95	0.97	0.98	0.99	0.99	0.99	1.00	1.00	1.00
27	0.33	0.55	0.70	0.80	0.87	0.91	0.94	0.96	0.97	0.98	0.99	0.99	0.99	1.00	1.00
28	0.32	0.54	0.68	0.78	0.85	0.90	0.93	0.95	0.97	0.98	0.98	0.99	0.99	1.00	1.00
29	0.31	0.52	0.67	0.77	0.84	0.89	0.92	0.95	0.96	0.97	0.98	0.99	0.99	0.99	1.00
30	0.29	0.50	0.65	0.75	0.82	0.88	0.91	0.94	0.96	0.97	0.98	0.98	0.99	0.99	0.99

Source: own counting (using Microsoft Excel) according to the equation (bullet operator represents multiplication)

$$P(x) = \{W! / [x! \cdot (W - x)!]\} \cdot (1 - K_W)^x \cdot K_W^{W-x}$$

based on Wilkening's model (Bernoulli distribution), and

$$P(0) = 1 - (1 - p)^n$$

based on G. Lewis's model, for p counted for a leak-proof defense in the cases of attacks of 5, 6, 7, … 30 incoming warheads (in Bernoulli distribution).

Wilkening, 191. G. Lewis. See also MDA, *Ballistic Missile Defense Intercept Flight Test Record.*

Chart 6. Probability of leak-proof interception using additional (up to 15 interceptors against single attacking warhead, in a salvo of up to 30 attacking consecutively), with SSKP 96%.

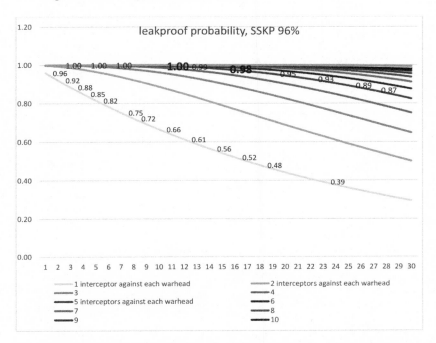

Source: own counting (using Microsoft Excel) according to the equation (bullet operator represents multiplication)

$$P(x) = \{W!/[x! \cdot (W - x)!]\} \cdot (1 - K_W)^x \cdot K_W^{W-x}$$

based on Wilkening's model (Bernoulli distribution), and

$$P(0) = 1 - (1 - p)^n$$

based on G. Lewis's model, for p counted for a leak-proof defense in the cases of attacks of 5, 6, 7, … 30 incoming warheads (in Bernoulli distribution).

Wilkening, 191. G. Lewis. See also MDA, *Ballistic Missile Defense Intercept Flight Test Record.*

Table 7. Leak-proof intercept probability at 81% SSKP for 1-30 attacking warheads.

Attacking (salvo)	Leak-proof intercept probability (81% SSKP)
1	0.81
2	0.65
3	0.53
4	0.43
5	0.35
6	0.28
7	0.23
8	0.18
9	0.15
10	0.12
11	0.10
12	0.08
13	0.06
14	0.05
15	0.04
16	0.03
17	0.03
18	0.02
19	0.02
20	0.01
21	0.01
22	0.01
23	0.01
24	0.01
25	0.00
26	0.00
27	0.00
28	0.00
29	0.00
30	0.00

Source: own counting (using Microsoft Excel) according to the equation (bullet operator represents multiplication)

$$P(x) = \{W!/[x! \cdot (W-x)!]\} \cdot (1 - K_w)^x \cdot K_w^{W-x}$$

based on Wilkening's model (Bernoulli distribution), and

$$P(0) = 1 - (1 - p)^n$$

based on G. Lewis's model, for p counted for a leak-proof defense in the cases of attacks of 5, 6, 7, ... 30 incoming warheads (in Bernoulli distribution).

Wilkening, 191. G. Lewis. See also MDA, *Ballistic Missile Defense Intercept Flight Test Record.*

Table 8. Likely effects of an engagement of two interceptors against each of 1-30 incoming warheads, chances (probability) of 0-12 warheads to pass through BMD (with interceptors' 81% SSKP).

Attacking warheads	Chances of n 1-30 warheads defeating BMD												
	0	1	2	3	4	5	6	7	8	9	10	11	12
1	**0.96**	0.34	0.00	0.00	0.00	0.00	0.00	0.00	0.00	0.00	0.00	0.00	0.00
2	**0.88**	0.52	0.07	0.00	0.00	0.00	0.00	0.00	0.00	0.00	0.00	0.00	0.00
3	**0.78**	0.61	0.17	0.01	0.00	0.00	0.00	0.00	0.00	0.00	0.00	0.00	0.00
4	**0.68**	0.64	0.26	0.04	0.00	0.00	0.00	0.00	0.00	0.00	0.00	0.00	0.00
5	0.58	**0.65**	0.35	0.09	0.01	0.00	0.00	0.00	0.00	0.00	0.00	0.00	0.00
6	0.49	**0.64**	0.41	0.14	0.03	0.00	0.00	0.00	0.00	0.00	0.00	0.00	0.00
7	0.41	**0.61**	0.46	0.20	0.05	0.01	0.00	0.00	0.00	0.00	0.00	0.00	0.00
8	0.34	**0.57**	0.49	0.25	0.08	0.01	0.00	0.00	0.00	0.00	0.00	0.00	0.00
9	0.28	**0.53**	0.51	0.30	0.11	0.03	0.00	0.00	0.00	0.00	0.00	0.00	0.00
10	0.23	0.49	**0.51**	0.34	0.15	0.04	0.01	0.00	0.00	0.00	0.00	0.00	0.00
11	0.19	0.44	**0.51**	0.38	0.19	0.06	0.02	0.00	0.00	0.00	0.00	0.00	0.00
12	0.15	0.40	**0.50**	0.40	0.22	0.09	0.02	0.00	0.00	0.00	0.00	0.00	0.00
13	0.13	0.36	**0.48**	0.42	0.26	0.11	0.04	0.01	0.00	0.00	0.00	0.00	0.00
14	0.10	0.31	**0.46**	0.43	0.29	0.14	0.05	0.01	0.00	0.00	0.00	0.00	0.00
15	0.08	0.28	0.43	**0.44**	0.32	0.17	0.07	0.02	0.00	0.00	0.00	0.00	0.00
16	0.07	0.24	0.40	**0.43**	0.34	0.20	0.09	0.03	0.01	0.00	0.00	0.00	0.00
17	0.05	0.21	0.37	**0.43**	0.36	0.23	0.11	0.04	0.01	0.00	0.00	0.00	0.00
18	0.04	0.18	0.34	**0.42**	0.37	0.26	0.13	0.06	0.02	0.00	0.00	0.00	0.00

19	0.04	0.16	0.31	**0.40**	0.38	0.28	0.16	0.07	0.03	0.01	0.00	0.00	0.00
20	0.03	0.13	0.29	**0.39**	0.39	0.30	0.18	0.09	0.03	0.01	0.00	0.00	0.00
21	0.02	0.11	0.26	0.37	<u>0.39</u>	0.32	0.20	0.11	0.04	0.02	0.00	0.00	0.00
22	0.02	0.10	0.23	0.35	**0.38**	0.33	0.23	0.13	0.06	0.02	0.01	0.00	0.00
23	0.02	0.08	0.21	0.33	**0.38**	0.34	0.25	0.14	0.07	0.03	0.01	0.00	0.00
24	0.01	0.07	0.18	0.30	**0.37**	0.35	0.26	0.16	0.08	0.04	0.01	0.00	0.00
25	0.01	0.06	0.16	0.28	**0.36**	0.35	0.28	0.18	0.10	0.04	0.02	0.01	0.00
26	0.01	0.05	0.14	0.26	0.34	<u>0.35</u>	0.29	0.20	0.12	0.06	0.02	0.01	0.00
27	0.01	0.04	0.13	0.24	0.33	**0.35**	0.31	0.22	0.13	0.07	0.03	0.01	0.00
28	0.01	0.04	0.11	0.22	0.31	**0.35**	0.31	0.24	0.15	0.08	0.04	0.01	0.00
29	0.00	0.03	0.10	0.20	0.29	**0.34**	0.32	0.25	0.17	0.09	0.04	0.02	0.01
30	0.00	0.03	0.08	0.18	0.28	**0.33**	<u>0.32</u>	<u>0.27</u>	<u>0.18</u>	<u>0.11</u>	<u>0.05</u>	<u>0.02</u>	<u>0.01</u>

*underlined - here, if 10 warheads attack and there are 2 interceptors with SSKP 81% then the highest ranked is 2 warheads passing through the BMD, that could mean that it takes at least 10 warhead to get the slight majority of chances to move 2 warheads through the defense of 81-% SSKP.

**in bold here - the highest ranked probability of moving 0-12 warheads through the BMD of 81% SSKP, e.g. for 30 warheads attacking its relatively most likely to move 5 through the defense (at 33%) against moving 6 (at 32% likelihood).

Source: own counting (using Microsoft Excel) according to the equation (bullet operator represents multiplication symbol)

$$P(x) = \{W!/[x! \cdot (W - x)!]\} \cdot (1 - K_w)^x \cdot K_w^{W-x}$$

based on Wilkening's model (Bernoulli distribution), and

$$P(0) = 1 - (1 - p)^n$$

based on G. Lewis's model, for p counted for a leak-proof defense in the cases of attacks of 5, 6, 7, ... 30 incoming warheads (in Bernoulli distribution).

Wilkening, 191. G. Lewis. See also MDA, *Ballistic Missile Defense Intercept Flight Test Record.*

Chart 7. Likely effects of an engagement of two interceptors against each of 1-30 incoming warheads, chances (probability) of 0-12 warheads passing through BMD (with interceptors' 81% SSKP).

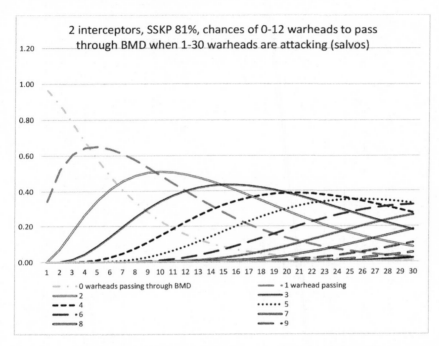

Source: own counting (using Microsoft Excel) according to the equation (bullet operator represents multiplication)

$$P(x) = \{W!/[x! \cdot (W-x)!]\} \cdot (1 - K_w)^x \cdot K_w^{W-x}$$

based on Wilkening's model (Bernoulli distribution), and

$$P(0) = 1 - (1-p)^n$$

based on G. Lewis's model, for p counted for a leak-proof defense in the cases of attacks of 5, 6, 7, ... 30 incoming warheads (in Bernoulli distribution).

Wilkening, 191. G. Lewis. See also MDA, *Ballistic Missile Defense Intercept Flight Test Record*.

Table 9. World's nuclear powers' arsenals and military spending since 2015 to 2018.

Country			Year	2015	2016	2017	2018
USA	Military budget	As % of GDP (The White House)		3.3	3.2	3.1	3.1
		in $ bn	Current $ (The White House)	589.7	593.4	598.7	631.2
			constant 2017 $ (SIPRI)	616.5	612.9	605.8	633.6
	Nuclear warheads (SIPRI)	deployed		2080	1930	1800	1750
		other		5180	5070	5000	4700
Russia	Military budget	As % of GDP (SIPRI)		4.9	5.5	4.2	3.9
		in $ bn	Average market exchange (IISS)	65.6	58.9	61.2	63.1
			constant 2017 $ (SIPRI)	77.0	82.6	66.5	64.2
	Nuclear warheads (SIPRI)	deployed		1780	1790	1950	1600
		other		5720	5500	5050	5250
China	Military budget	As % of GDP (SIPRI)		1.9	1.9	1.9	1.9
		in $ bn	Average market (IISS)	145.8	145.0	150.5	168.2
			constant 2017 $ exchange (SIPRI)	204.2	215.7	227.8	239.2
	Nuclear warheads (SIPRI)	deployed		n.d.	n.d.	n.d.	n.d.
		other		260	260	270	280

UK	Military budget	As % of GDP (SIPRI)	1.9	1.8	1.8	1.8
		in $ bn — Average market (IISS)	56.2	52.5	50.7	56.1
		in $ bn — constant 2017 $ exchange (SIPRI)	46.8	46.9	46.4	46.9
	Nuclear warheads (SIPRI)	deployed	150	120	120	120
		other	65	95	95	95
France	Military budget	As % of GDP (SIPRI)	2.3	2.3	2.3	2.3
		in $ bn — Average market exchange (IISS)	46.8	47.2	48.6	53.4
		in $ bn — constant 2017 $ (SIPRI)	56.7	58.8	60.4	59.5
	Nuclear warheads (SIPRI)	deployed	290	280	280	280
		other	10	20	20	20
India	Military budget	As % of GDP (SIPRI)	2.4	2.5	2.5	2.4
		in $ bn — Average market exchange (IISS)	48.0	51.1	52.5	57.9
		in $ bn — constant 2017 $ (SIPRI)	54.7	60.3	64.5	66.6
	Nuclear warheads (SIPRI)	deployed	n.d.	n.d.	n.d.	n.d.
		other	90-110	100-120	120-130	130-140
Pakistan	Military budget	As % of GDP (SIPRI)	3.6	3.6	3.8	4.0
		in $ bn — Current $ (SIPRI)	9.5	10.0	11.5	11.4
		in $ bn — constant 2017 $ (SIPRI)	10.0	10.4	11.5	12.7
	Nuclear warheads (SIPRI)	deployed	n.d.	n.d.	n.d.	n.d.
		other	100-120	110-130	130-140	140-150

Israel	Military budget	As % of GDP (SIPRI)	5.6	4.6	4.4	4.3
		in $ bn — Average market exchange (IISS)	18.6	19.0	21.6	21.6
		constant 2017 $ (SIPRI)	18.2	15.7	15.6	15.7
	Nuclear warheads (SIPRI)	deployed	n.d.	n.d.	n.d.	n.d.
		other	80	80	80	80
North Korea	Military budget	As % of GDP (SIPRI)	n.d.	n.d.	n.d.	n.d.
		in $ bn — Average market exchange (IISS)	n.d.	n.d.	n.d.	n.d.
		constant 2017 $ (SIPRI)	n.d.	n.d.	n.d.	n.d.
	Nuclear warheads (SIPRI)	deployed	n.d.	n.d.	n.d.	n.d.
		other	6-8	10	10-20	10-20

Sources: SIPRI, Annual Yearbook 2015-2018; SIPRI Military Expenditure Database 1949-2018; IISS ("The Military Balance"), *Comparative Defense Statistics*, 2016-2019; The White House Office of Management and Budget, Historical Tables, 2019.[42]

Chart 8. Hypothetical growth of Chinese defense expenditures (by 5% annually), based on SIPRI and IISS estimates for 2015-2018.

42   John Chipman, "Chapter Two: Comparative Defence Statistics," *The Military Balance* 116, no. 1 (2016): 19–26, https://doi.org/10.1080/04597222. 2016.1127562; John Chipman, "Chapter One: Defence and Military Analysis," *The Military Balance* 117, no. 1 (2017): 7–18, 21-27, https://doi.org/10.1080/04597222.2017.1271206; Shannon N. Kile and Hans M. Kristensen, "World Nuclear Forces," *SIPRI Annual Yearbook 2016* (Oxford: Oxford University Press, 2016), 610, https://www.sipri.org/sites/default/files/SIPRIYB16c16s0.pdf; Shannon N. Kile and Hans M. Kristensen, "World Nuclear Forces," in *SIPRI Annual Yearbook 2017* (Oxford University Press, 2017), https://www.sipri.org/yearbook/2017/11; Shannon N. Kile and Hans M. Kristensen, "World Nuclear Forces," in *SIPRI Yearbook 2018* (Oxford: Oxford University Press, 2018), 236, https://www.sipri.org/sites/default/files/SIPRIYB18c06.pdf; SIPRI, *SIPRI Military Expenditure Database 1949-2018* (2019), https://www.sipri.

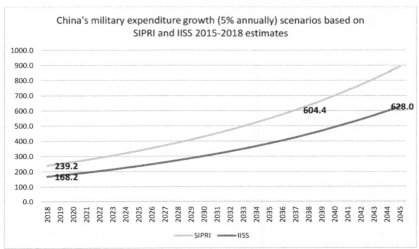

in relation to the previous year, used to calculate percentage change (absolute change of production divided by the amount of production in the previous year, multiplied by 100). Here in this exemplary equation % change of annual production is labeled as ΔP, Pcy stands for production in the current year and Ppy is production in the previous year (bullet operator represents multiplication)

$$\Delta P = \left[(P_{cy} - P_{py}) / P_{py} \right] \cdot 100$$

Begg, Fischer, and Dornbusch. *Economics*. London, UK: McGraw-Hill Higher Education, 2008, 24.

Defense expenditures data from SIPRI, Annual Yearbook 2015-2018; SIPRI Military Expenditure Database 1949-2018; IISS ("The Military Balance"), *Comparative Defense Statistics*, 2016-2019.

The chart related to China's defense expenditure growth scenario relied on SIPRI and IISS estimates for 2015-2018, which stated that the People's Republic of China (PRC) increased its defense budget by 5% a year on average.[43] If such a growth rate was sustained in the following decades,

---

org/sites/default/files/SIPRI-Milex-data-1949-2018_0.xlsx; The White House Office of Managament and Budget, *Historical Tables* (2019), 58, https://www.whitehouse.gov/wp-content/uploads/2019/03/hist-fy2020.pdf; Shannon N. Kile and Hans M. Kristensen, "World Nuclear Forces," *SIPRI Yearbook 2015* (Oxford: Oxford University Press, 2015), 460, https://www.sipri.org/sites/default/files/SIPRIYB15c11s0.pdf.

43   Data based on SIPRI, Annual Yearbook 2015-2018; SIPRI Military Expenditure

the overall amount of PRC defense spending would match US spending by 2037 (in SIPRI's estimate of 2015-2018 PRC spending) or by 2045 (in accordance with the average market exchange estimate of PRC defense spending for 2015-2018 IISS's).[44]

Table 10. Percentage growth of China's defense expenses (compared to the preceding year) in SIPRI and IISS estimates for 2015-2018.

Year	2016	2017	2018	Annual average (2016-2018)
SIPRI	5.632	5.610	5.004	5.415
IISS	-0.55	3.79	11.76	5.002

Sources: own counting based on annual growth of production % rate, as explained by Begg, Fischer, and Dornbusch, *Economics*. London, UK: McGraw-Hill Higher Education, 2008, 24. Defense data based on SIPRI, Annual Yearbook 2015-2018; SIPRI Military Expenditure Database 1949-2018; IISS ("The Military Balance"), *Comparative Defense Statistics*, 2016-2019.

Database 1949-2018; IISS ("The Military Balance"), *Comparative Defense Statistics*, 2016-2019.

44 Ibidem. As Begg, Fischer and Dornbusch clarified, a percentage change in economic growth is measured by an equation where the absolute change of production (i.e., previous year minus current year) is divided by previous year and multiplied by 100: David Begg, Stanley Fischer, and Rudiger Dornbusch, *Economics* (London, UK: McGraw-Hill Higher Education, 2008), 24.

CHAPTER II
BMD History: Missile Defense
Pre-Trump Presidency

1. Historical Introduction

After the dawn of the missile age, which came with pioneering Robert Goddard's developments and the corresponding achievements of Hermann Oberth, Konstantin Ciolkowsky, and Werner von Braun, the first stages towards BMD were made after the Autumn 1944 V-2 attacks against London and Brussels.[45]

As Gen. Clare Armstrong et al.'s report noted, on September 8, 1944, the first V-2 rocket fell on Paris, which was a target of lower importance, in the next few hours a V-2 attacked London, and then the missile campaign was enhanced to engage Low Countries targets: on September 13 and 14, V-2s fell in the area of Brussels; from September 14 to October 12, more than four V-2s daily attacked Liege. Afterwards until the end of the war, Antwerp became the main target of V-2 bombings (reaching its height on November 2, 1944 of 24 missiles).[46] As Martin Gilbert

---

45   Robert H. Goddard, *A Method of Reaching Extreme Altitudes* (1919), http://www2.clarku.edu/research/archives/pdf/ext_altitudep.pdf; Rob Garner and Brian Dunbar, "Dr. Robert H. Goddard, American Rocketry Pioneer," *Goddard Space Flight Center National Aeronautics and Space Administration* (2016), https://www.nasa.gov/centers/goddard/about/history/dr_goddard.html; Robert H. Goddard, *US Patents, Rocket Apparatus* (1914), https://patents.google.com/patent/US1102653; Clark University, *Robert H. Goddard Papers* (2019), https://www2.clarku.edu/research/archives/goddard/articles.cfm; Mike Wright, *Notes on Hermann Oberth. Space Pioneer Hermann Oberth Was von Braun Mentor* (2019), https://history.msfc.nasa.gov/earlyra/hoberth_notes.html; Rick Smith, *100 Years of Possibility: Celebrating the Centennial Birthday of Dr. Wernher von Braun* (2012), https://www.nasa.gov/topics/history/features/vonbraun.html; Gerard K. O'Neill, "The Colonization of Space," *Physics Today* 27, no. 9 (1974): 32–40, http://www.nsp.org/settlement/physicstoday.htm. V stood for *Vergeltungswaffe* (vengeance weapon), while in Nazi Germany, the missile program series was labeled A (*Aggregat*); A-4 was named V-2 for propaganda reasons. Smithsonian National Air and Space Museum, *V-2 Missile* (2019), https://airandspace.si.edu/collection-objects/missile-surface-surface-v-2-4.

46   Clare Armstrong, *V-2 Rocket Attacks and Defense* 1, no. 945, 11–12, http://usacac.army.mil/cac2/cgsc/carl/eto/eto-042.pdf.

stressed, seizing the launch sites of the V-2s attacking the critically important port of Antwerp, indispensable for allied offensive in Germany, was a top priority of the failed Market Garden paratroopers operation.[47]

The first British missile defense involved anti-aircraft artillery (in the prototype system of Gen. Frederick Pile).[48]

US post-World War II developments included the Wasserfall-modeled air defense guided missiles Hermes for Army Ordnance Project.[49] Importantly, Wernher von Braun's contribution to the US ballistic programs allowed American space military enterprises to keep their technological edge in the Cold War superpower rivalry.[50]

Bomarc missiles, developed post-1946 and forming a base of long-range antiaircraft interception, have been deployed since 1959, with a range of 440 miles.[51]

Among the early 1960s, BMD developments were the first partly successful tests of nuclear warheads of interceptors engaging incoming missiles without hitting the target, which as Edward Teller noted, became difficult with the 1963 Limited Test Ban Treaty.[52]

---

47   Martin Gilbert, "Attacking Antwerp," *Forbes* (May 6, 2008), https://www.forbes.com/2008/06/05/antwerp-port-wwII-tech-logistics08-cx_mg_0605antwerp.html.

48   John Dabrowski, *Missile Defense. The First 70 Years* (2013), 2–3, https://www.mda.mil/global/documents/pdf/first70.pdf.

49   *Wasserfall* was an experimental German prototype of air-defense surface guided missile. M. Leroy Spearman, *Historical Development of Worldwide Guided Missiles* (1983), 10, 14, https://ntrp.nasa.gov/archive/nasa/casi.ntrp.nasa.gov/19830027720.pdf; Conf. Smithsonian National Air and Space Museum, *Missile, Surface-To-Surface, Liquid Propellant, Hermes A-1* (2019), https://airandspace.si.edu/collection-objects/missile-surface-surface-liquid-propellant-hermes-1; Frank Schubert and Theresa Kraus, *The Whirlwind War. The United States Army in Operations Desert Shield and Desert Storm*, 236, http://www.history.army.mil/books/www/WWINDX.HTM; US Army Center of Military History, *History of Strategic Air and Ballistic Missile Defense, Vol. I, 1945-1955* (1975), 3, http://www.history.army.mil/html/books/bmd/BMDV1.pdf.

50   Michael J. Neufeld, *Von Braun. Dreamer of Space, Engineer of War* (New York: Vintage Books, 2007).

51   John Lonnquest and David Winkler, *To Defend and to Deter: The Legacy of the United States Cold War Missile Program* (1996), 3, http://www.dtic.mil/cgi-bin/GetTRDoc?Location=U2&doc=GetTRDoc.pdf&AD=ADA337549.

52   Edward Teller and Judith Schoolery, *Memoirs. A Twentieth-Century Journey in Science*

In the context of guided missile construction, George Siouris mentioned maximization of SSKP through minimization of missed distance (conf. CEP), sources of which were:

- heading mistake at initial level,

- biased accelerating mode,

- gyroscopic drifting causing destabilization of a seeker,

- noise coming from sparkling (glinting),

- noise of the receiver,

- noise fading,

- noise connected with diverse frequency (angle).[53]

Those efforts were heading towards Prompt Global Strike, precise munitions after the Cold War.

The 1950s Nike program led to first SAM Nike Ajax and its successor, a tactical nuclear tipped Nike-Hercules interceptor.[54]

Importantly, McNamara saw the MAD paradigm as insufficient against all forms of Soviet aggression, correspondingly with flexible response doctrine, bringing a need of conventional build-up to deter on lower levels than the strategic one.[55]

Sentinel BMD of the Lyndon Johnson era (defense of cities) and Safe-

---

and Politics (Cambridge, Massachusetts: Perseus Publishers, 2001), 466.

53   George Siouris, *Missile Guidance and Control Systems* (New York: Springer, 2004), 101; Conf. Horace Jacobs and Eunice Engelke Whitney, *Missile and Space Projects Guide 1962* (New York: Springer, 1962); Xu Zheng, Suochang Yang and Dan Fang, "Research on Simulation Identification Technology of Loitering Missile" (2019), 1459–1465, https://doi.org/10.1007/978-981-10-6571-2_176; Ajey Lele, "Missile and Nuclear Conundrums," in *Asian Space Race: Rhetoric or Reality?* (India: Springer India, 2013), 125–141, https://doi.org/10.1007/978-81-322-0733-7_10; Shiquan Zhu and others, "Investigations on the Influence of Control Devices to the Separation Characteristics of a Missile from the Internal Weapons Bay," *Journal of Mechanical Science and Technology* 32, no. 5 (2018): 2047–2057, https://doi.org/10.1007/s12206-018-0414-3.

54   Kenneth P. Werrell, *Archie to SAM. A Short Operational History of Ground-Based Air Defense* (Maxwell Air Force Base, 2005), 84–85, http://www.dtic.mil/dtic/tr/fulltext/u2/a439255.pdf; Lonnquest and Winkler, *To Defend and to Deter*.

55   McNamara, *The Essence of Security*, 59.

guard (the Richard Nixon era, defense of Grand Forks ICBM base) programs interceptors were based on nuclear tipped Nike-Zeus (tested in 1962), turned Spartan, supplemented by shorter-range Sprint missiles.[56]

Notably, 1972-1974 ABM treaty limited missile defense up to two, then one, area, with only 100 interceptors.

The Reagan-era SDI (and SDIO) space-based kinetic KVs were rooted, as Donald Baucom noted, in 1960s Project Defender.[57] The Homing Overlay Experiment (HOE) 1984 intercept outside the atmosphere contributed to a further orbital concept: space-based interceptors (Smart Rocks, and then Brilliant Pebbles, BP).[58]

BP, a smaller (40 inches long and weighing only 100 pounds), more cost-effective solution of a SBI-capable vehicle was supposed (according to a 1989 estimation) to be supported by $25 billion in the SDIO budget, which was used to develop the orbital system, while the cost of the 1987-introduced SBI Phase I (placing interceptors on fewer than 200 orbital platforms) accounted for $69 billion.[59]

Teller noted that the concepts of Smart Rocks (a few thousand small, inexpensive satellites able to use projectiles against incoming ICBMs), discussed in November 1986 by SDI experts Lowell Wood and Gregory Canavan, were redesigned in Lawrence Livermore Laboratory towards BP, adopted by the Pentagon in March 1992, but cancelled after Clinton's victory in the presidential election.[60] Wood and Scott estimated in

---

56 Baucom, *US Missile Defense Program*, 2–3.

57 Baucom, "The Rise and Fall of Brilliant Pebbles," 143–146.

58 Baucom, "The Rise and Fall of Brilliant Pebbles," 143–146; Lockheed Martin, *Missile Defense* (2019), http://www.lockheedmartin.com/us/what-we-do/aerospace-defense/missile-defense.html; SMDC/ARSTRAT Historical Office, "An Old Concept for a New Era in Missile Defense," *The Eagle* (2007), 10, http://www.smdc.army.mil/2008/Historical/Eagle/HittoKill-AnOldConceptforaNewErainMissile-Defense.pdf; Reagan, *Address to the Nation*; Baucom, *US Missile Defense Program*; Lockheed Martin, *Missile vs. Missile* (2019), https://www.lockheedmartin.com/en-us/news/features/history/missile-defense.html.

59 Baker Spring and James Gattuso, *"Brilliant Pebbles": The Revolutionary Idea for Strategic Defense* (The Backgrounder, 1990), 3–5, http://s3.amazonaws.com/thf_media/1990/pdf/bg748.pdf.

60 Edward Teller, "The Ultimate Defense, 2002," in *Memoirs: A Twentieth-Century Journey in Science and Politics*, ed. by Hoover Institution (Perseus Publishers), http://www.hoover.org/research/ultimate-defense.

June 1989 that BP (reduced Smart Rocks) hardware ($500,000 per unit) would account for $5 billion (for 10000 interceptors placed in space) to serve for a decade (made cheaper due to propulsion developments and lower weight).[61]

In 1984, Wood was afraid of the high costs of launching SBI-architecture into orbit and proposed laser propulsion for space equipment delivery to orbit, following Arthur Kantrowitz's model.[62]

What is interesting is the SDI-era BMD cooperation between the US and its allies, notably Israel, Germany, and Japan, brought significant results, such as Arrow and the Iron Dome's David's Sling in Israel's US-supported missile defense programs, German's Patriot development co-produced with Italy MEADS,[63] Japan's BMD-GMD components, radar, and Aegis SM3-IIA development.

Importantly, twenty-first century European mergers and acquisitions in the defense sector also supported short-range BMD efforts (according to Military Balance 2017).[64]

Notably, Robert Everett's panel in 1989 recommended the further development of BP as an interesting cost-effective concept related to SBI (not ready to replace the latter), concluding that both BP and SBI research, exploration, and construction efforts should be further continued.[65]

Simultaneously, the Missile Technology Control Regime (MTCR) of the late 1980s (1987) was developed by Western partners to counter du-

---

61 Lowell Wood and Walter Scott, *Brilliant Pebbles* (1989), 8, https://e-reports-ext.llnl.gov/pdf/212611.pdf.

62 Lowell Wood and Roderick Hyde, *Science and Technology in Space during the Coming Decade*, 1984, 2, https://e-reports-ext.llnl.gov/ pdf/203612.pdf; Arthur Kantrowitz, "Laser Propulsion to Earth Orbit – Has Its Time Come?" in *Second Beamed Space-Power Workshop* (1989), 41–56, http://ntrp.nasa.gov/archive/nasa/casi.ntrp.nasa.gov/19900000827.pdf; Arthur Kantrowitz, *Laser Propulsion to Earth Orbit* (1975), 67, http://arc.aiaa.org/doi/abs/10.2514/6.1975-2009.

63 The hit-to-kill concept in Patriot (replacing blast warheads in the first PAC) was developed in the 1980s, including the Flexible Lightweight Agile Experiment (FLAGE) of 1983 and upgraded in 1987 to Extended Range Intercept Technology (ERINT), which was used in PAC-3. Werrell, *Archie to SAM*, 239–243.

64 Chipman, "Chapter One," 7–9.

65 Robert Everett, *Report of Defense Science Board on SDIO Brilliant Pebbles Space Based Interceptor Concept* (Washington, DC, 1989), 1–7, http://www.dod.mil/pubs/foi/Reading_Room/Homeland_Defense/06-F-0419_FINAL_RESPONSE-ocrd.pdf.

al-use technology transfer during the final East-West arms race rivalry.[66]

The 1990 RAND report led toward using nation-wide BMD to build protection against limited strikes (lower quantity, unauthorized, or accidental ballistic launches during third party attacks) in a manner non-threatening to the stability of the first-strike capabilities of both superpowers.[67] RAND experts recommended the introduction of limited BMD (of potential within a range of 500-1000 vehicles) through bilateral US-Soviet negotiations on ABM treaty modification.[68]

The Bush Sr.-era GPALS stressed the changed perspective from all-out US-Soviet conflicts to threats of unauthorized or low-number missile attacks.[69] In 1991, the US focus shifted toward regional threats, countered by TMD.[70]

Most SDI-era BMD projects were cancelled just after the Cold War and labeled as too futuristic.[71] The Clinton-era limitations reduced SBI to zero and turned BP into technological bases.[72]

NMD's advanced stages included radar system developments in a gradually enlarged NMD system, as Karako and Williams noted, from 20 through 100 to 250 GBIs (in place of previously planned 1000 GBI and SBI of SDI phase 1 and 750 GBI ad 1000 SBI of GPALS).[73]

---

66   J. Molas-Gallart, "Conversion and Control of Technological Capabilities in the Missile Field: The 'Dual-Use Paradox,'" in *Defense Conversion Strategies* (Dordrecht: Springer Netherlands, 1997), 196, https://doi.org/10.1007/978-94-017-1213-2_11; MTCR, "Missile Technology Control Regime" (2019), http://mtcr.info/partners/; Kelsey Davenport, *Missile Technology Control Regime (MTCR)* (2019), https://www.armscontrol.org/factsheets/mtcr.

67   Glenn A. Kent and David E. Thaler, *First-Strike Stability and Strategic Defenses. Part II of a Methodology for Evaluating Strategic Forces*, 1990, vi, 33–34, 36, http://www.dtic.mil/get-tr-doc/pdf?AD=ADA231524.

68   Kent and Thaler, *First-Strike Stability and Strategic Defenses*, vi, 33–34, 36.

69   Henry F. Cooper, *Brilliant Pebbles* (2016), http://highfrontier.org/category/brilliant-pebbles/; Baucom, "The Rise and Fall of Brilliant Pebbles," 164–165, 168; Spring and Gattuso, "*Brilliant Pebbles*," 7.

70   Fink, Hoffman and Delaney, *Final Report of the Defense Science Board*, 1.

71   Weinberger, "The Most Outlandish Ideas"; Whitehead, Pittenger and Colella, "Astrid Rocket Flight Test."

72   M. O'Neill, *Memorandum for Secretary of Defense*.

73   New X-band radars replaced Cold War early warning facilities. Karako and Williams, *Missile Defense 2020*, 16–17, 33; Conf. Lindsay and O'Hanlon, *Defending America*.

2. The North Korean Danger

A new North Korean threat grew in 2017 to the size of a new potentially ultra-radical dangerous thermonuclear-tipped communist force, equipped with possible maneuvering reentry vehicle (MaRV) even if not yet MIRV missiles.[74] Dave Majumdar wrote that, according to Nikolai Sokov, Russia would be able to test in September 2017 a MaRV warhead on a Topol 12M ICBM; Pavel Podvig claimed otherwise, stating that it could be only a set of decoys.[75] By December 2017, the North Korea MIRV capability remained unclear, but intelligence information in July 2017 (between South Korea and the US) revealed that Pyongyang was developing a MIRV-ready ICBM.[76] Majumdar noted that the North Korean development of a road-mobile Hwasong-15 (HS-15) missile with a possible range of 13000 km could lead to its MIRV capability.[77] There remained no proof of already possessed MIRV North Korean capacities in Spring 2017.[78] On August 28, 2017, the media reported that a possible (not confirmed) North Korean ICBM with MIRV capacity flew close to Japan, when the missile broke into parts and then fell into the water 700 miles east of Hokkaido. It was examined whether it was a technical failure or a rather (uncertain) MIRV flight test.[79]

---

74   CSIS, *Missile Threat, KN-18 (MaRV Scud Variant)*, https://missilethreat.csip.org/missile/kn-18-marv-scud-variant/.

75   Dave Majumdar, "Here Is Everything We Know (And Don't) About Russia's Mysterious ICBM Tests," *The National Interest* (September 2017), http://national interest.org/blog/the-buzz/here-everything-we-know-dont-about-russias-mysterious-icbm-22502.

76   Lee Chul-Jae, "North May Have Multiple-ICBM Technology," *Korea JoongAng Daily* (July 5, 2017), http://koreajoongangdaily.joins.com/news/article/article.aspx?aid=3035462.

77   Dave Majumdar, "Does North Korea's New Hwasong-15 ICBM Have Soviet and Chinese 'DNA?'" *The National Interest* (November 2017), http://nationalinterest.org/blog/the-buzz/does-north-koreas-new-hwasong-15-icbm-have-soviet-or-chinese-23434.

78   Keith Rogers, "North Korean Missiles Could Reach Las Vegas, Experts Say," *Las Vegas Review-Journal* (April 2017), https://www.reviewjournal.com/news/military/north-korean-missiles-could-reach-las-vegas-experts-say/; Conf. BBC News, "What We Know about North Korea's Missile Programme," *BBC* (August 10, 2017), http://www.bbc.com/news/world-asia-17399847; Andrew Buncombe, "Pentagon Says North Korea's ICBM Was a Missile They've Never Seen before," *The Independent* (July 5, 2017), http://www.independent.co.uk/news/world/asia/north-korea-missile-icbm-pentagon-trump-not-seen-before-a7825541.html.

79   Tyler Rogoway, "North Korea Sends Missile Flying Over Japan (Updating Live)," *The Drive* (August 28, 2017), http://www.thedrive.com/the-war-zone/13898/

The 2018 Panmunjeom Declaration of the leaders of Koreas confirmed progress in the denuclearization goal, allowing the prospect of ending the dangerous North Korean ballistic and nuclear program due to Moon Jae-in's diplomatic skill and US pressure on Kim Jong-un.[80] The Panmunjeom commitment of North Korea to denuclearize was sustained due to the Trump-Kim Singapore summit, ending in a successful declaration (June 2018).[81] Nevertheless, the February 2019 Hanoi Trump-Kim summit brought no progress.[82] As Andrei Lankov's earlier November 2018 analysis correctly predicted, North Korea was in fact unready to give up on nuclear weapons as a key factor of its totalitarian regime's survival.[83]

3. BMD in Post-ABM Perspective

Importantly, the 2019 US Intermediate-Range Nuclear Forces (INF) treaty withdrawal (NATO-supported), due to Russia's ground-launched cruise missile testing (SSC-8), led to the greater significance of BMD in Europe and beyond. INF, a 1987 treaty between the US and USSR, was the cornerstone of the post-Cold War order. INF eliminated both medium-range (1000-5500 km) and shorter-range (500-1000 km) missiles (land-based and ground-launched cruise), including Pershing II (US) countering Soviet SS-20 Intermediate Range Ballistic Missile (IRBM), which threatened European capitals.[84] The gradual decline of INF treaty

---

north-korea-sends-missile-flying-over-japan-updating-live.

80   Moon Jae-in and Kim Jong-un, *Panmunjeom Declaration for Peace, Prosperity and Unification of the Korean Peninsula* (2018), http://www.korea.net/Government/ Current-Affairs/National-Affairs/view?affairId=656&subId=641&articleId=3354.

81   The White House, *Joint Statement of President Donald J. Trump of the United States of America and Chairman Kim Jong Un of the Democratic People's Republic of Korea at the Singapore Summit, June 12, 2018* (2018), https://www.whitehouse.gov/briefings-statements/joint-statement-president-donald-j-trump-united-states-america-chairman-kim-jong-un-democratic-peoples-republic-korea-singapore-summit/.

82   The White House, *Remarks by President Trump and Chairman Kim Jong Un of the Democratic People's Republic of Korea in a 1:1 Conversation, Hanoi, Vietnam, February 27, 2019* (2019), https://www.whitehouse.gov/briefings-statements/remarks-president-trump-chairman-kim-jong-un-democratic-peoples-republic-korea-11-conversation-hanoi-vietnam/.

83   Andrei Lankov, *Strategic Stability in the Twenty-First Century: The North Korean Nuclear Threat* (2018), https://carnegie.ru/commentary/77735.

84   Article VII of the INF treaty (Treaty between the United States of America and the Union of Soviet Socialist Republics on the Elimination of Their Intermediate-Range and Shorter-Range Missiles). Office of the Under Secretary of Defense for Acqui-

proved that the long-questioned overview of the post-2014 Russian invasion of Crimea and its illegal annexation labelling the newly-heightened Russia rivalry with the West 'a new Cold War' was fully justified.

Similarly, Iran's hostile steps in 2019 bringing the nuclear weapon option closer against the remnant Lausanne ordeal proved the valid priority of supplementing sanctions policies aimed at rogue countries with BMD improvements. In 2018, Trump gave up on the Iran deal, seeing it as ineffective, while the EU chose to comply.[85] In May 2019, Iran President Hassan Rouhani suspended part of its Lausanne deal commitment to limit uranium enrichment.[86]

The December 13, 2001 US ABM treaty withdrawal, justified by terrorist and rogue states' WMD threat, did not stop the prepared SORT treaty agreement, concluded in Moscow on May 24, 2002.[87] ABM was presented by the George W. Bush administration as obsolete after the Cold War.[88] Russian leader Putin stated in June 2001 that the ABM 1972 agreement remained a centerpiece of international security, but did not strongly oppose the US withdrawal from the ABM treaty in the July 2001 meeting.[89]

---

sition, *Treaty between the United States of America and the Union of Soviet Socialist Republics on the Elimination of Their Intermediate-Range and Shorter-Range Missiles* (1987), https://www.acq.osd.mil/tc/inf/INFtext.htm; CSIS Missile Threat, *SSC-8 (Novator 9M729)* (2019), https://missilethreat.csis.org/missile/ssc-8-novator-9m729/.

85 The White House, *President Trump Says the Iran Deal Is Defective at Its Core. A New One Will Require Real Commitments, May 11, 2018* (2018), https://www.white house.gov/articles/president-trump-says-iran-deal-defective-core-new-one-will-require-real-commitments/.

86 BBC News, "Iran Nuclear Deal: Tehran May Increase Uranium Enrichment" (May 8, 2019), https://www.bbc.com/news/world-middle-east-48197628.

87 The White House, *ABM Treaty Fact Sheet* (2001), https://georgewbush-white-house.archives.gov/news/releases/2001/12/20011213-2.html.

88 The White House, *Press Briefing by National Security Advisor Condoleezza Rice, June 15, 2001* (2001), https://georgewbush-whitehouse.archives.gov/news/releases/2001/06/20010615-2.html; The White House, *Press Briefing by National Security Advisor Condoleezza Rice on President's Travel to Europe, June 6, 2001* (2001), https://georgewbush-whitehouse.archives.gov/news/releases/2001/06/20010606-6.html; The White House, *Dr. Rice Discusses Bilateral Meeting of President Bush and Russian President Putin, July 22, 2001* (2001), https://georgewbush-whitehouse.archives.gov/news/releases/2001/07/20010722-7.html; The White House, *President Holds Prime Time News Conference, October 11, 2001* (2001), https://georgewbush-whitehouse.archives.gov/news/releases/2001/10/20011011-7.html.

89 The White House, *Press Conference by President Bush and Russian Federation President Putin (Brdo Pri Kranju, Slovenia), June 16, 2001* (2001), https://georgewbush-

On December 24, 2001, Putin said that the withdrawal of the US from ABM treaty posed no threat to Russian national security or US-Russia relations, although he called it a mistake.[90]

4. "New Cold War"? Stages of Conflict, INF Treaty Problem

The point of major difference in US-Russia relations was connected to the democratization of parts of the former Soviet Union. As Peter Conradi noted, the Rose Revolution of 2003 in Georgia and the Ukrainian Orange Revolution of 2004 seemed to prove the success of George W. Bush's "freedom agenda," raising hopes for democratic change in Russia as well; for Putin's regime, the Color Revolutions (including the Tulip Revolution in Kyrgystan in 2005) meant a loss of influence in the nearest neighborhood and the possible removal of former junior partners from the orbit of authoritarian Russia.[91] Conradi stressed that the prime sign of the New Cold War came with the February 2007 Munich Security Conference, when Putin criticized the unipolar US-dominated world order.[92] Other 2007 signs of the New Cold War, as Edward Lucas pointed out, included the Russian return to bipolar-era aircraft maneuvers inside Western airspace (i.e., Tupolev-95 bombers) and increased military investments, to deliver challenging air defense S-400 system, surpassing the range of Patriot missiles, new Topol-M ICBMs, Bulava SLBM, and 8 Borei SSBNs (with the first, Yuri Dolgoruky, built in 2007).[93]

Putin suspended Russian participation in the Conventional Forces in Eu-

---

whitehouse.archives.gov/news/releases/2001/06/20010618.html; The White House, *Press Conference by President Bush and President Putin (Genoa, Italy), July 22, 2001* (2001), https://georgewbush-whitehouse.archives.gov/news/releases /2001/07/20010722-3.html.

90   President of Russia, *Live with President Vladimir Putin - Hot Line (Excerpts), December 24, 2001* (2001), http://en.kremlin.ru/events/president/transcripts/21457; BBC News, "America Withdraws from ABM Treaty" (December 13, 2001), http:// news.bbc.co.uk/2/hi/americas/1707812.stm; The White House, *Response to Russian Statement on US ABM Treaty Withdrawal, December 13, 2001* (2001), https:// georgewbush-whitehouse.archives.gov/news/releases/2001/12/20011213-8.html.

91   Peter Conradi, *Who Lost Russia? How the World Entered a New Cold War*, Kindle (London: A Oneworld Book, 2017), 3171-3184, 3290-3302.

92   Conradi, *Who Lost Russia?* 3351; see also the Washington Post, *Putin's Prepared Remarks at 43rd Munich Conference on Security Policy, February 12, 2007 (Transcript)* (2007), http://www.washingtonpost.com/wp-dyn/content/article/2007/02/12/ AR2007021200555.html.

93   Lucas, *The New Cold War*, 3919-3931.

rope (CFE) Treaty in 2007 and withdrew completely in 2015.[94] Among the reasons for Russia's CFE Treaty withdrawal were US plans of deployment of GMD elements in Poland and the Czech Republic.[95] Kremlin's CFE suspension in 2007 caused concern in the Caucasus that increased arms race and Russian military engagement might occur (and did shortly after, in Georgia).[96]

Among the key factors in Russia's conflict with the West are the war in Ukraine, the illegal annexation of Crimea by Russia, military support for pro-Russian separatists in eastern Ukraine, and problems with the Minsk 2015 agreement implementation. The February 12, 2015 Minsk agreements (signed by Russia, Ukraine, Germany, France, and the leaders of pro-Russian militants), replacing the failed Minsk Protocol of September 5, 2014, which was violated by Russian-oriented separatists, led to the withdrawal of heavy weapons from the area of conflict and a cease-fire.[97]

The threat of Russian-Western conflict had been growing since the April 2008 Bucharest NATO summit, when the West failed to support US plans to provide for Membership Action Plan (MAP) for Georgia and

---

94   OSCE, *Russia's Withdrawal from CFE Treaty Work a "Dangerous Move," Says OSCE PA Security Chair* (2015), http://www.osce.org/pa/144946; Peter Finn, "Putin Withdraws Russia From Major Arms Treaty," *The Washington Post* (December 1, 2007), http://www.washingtonpost.com/wp-dyn/content/article/2007/11/30/AR2007113000221.html.

95   Andrew E. Kramer and Thom Shanker, "Russia Suspends Arms Agreement Over US Shield," *The New York Times* (July 15, 2007), http://www.nytimes.com/2007/07/15/world/europe/15russia.html.

96   Sergei Minasyan, "Moratorium on the CFE Treaty and South Caucasian Security," *Russia in Global Affairs* 3 (2008), http://eng.globalaffairs.ru/number/n_11279; Duncan Hollis, "Russia Suspends CFE Treaty Participation," *American Society of International Law Insights* 111, no. 19 (2007), https://www.asil.org/insights/volume/11/issue/19/russia-suspends-cfe-treaty-participation.

97   Naja Bentzen and Evarts Anosovs, *Minsk Peace Agreement: Still to Be Consolidated on the Ground* (2015), http://www.europarl.europa.eu/EPRS/EPRS-Briefing-548991-Minsk-peace-summit-FINAL.pdf; the Economist, "The Economist Explains. What Are the Minsk Agreements? The Plan to Bring Lasting Peace to Ukraine Is Riddled with Loose Language" (September 2016), http://www.economist.com/blogs/economist-explains/2016/09/economist-explains-7; United Nations, *Package of Measures for the Implementation of the Minsk Agreements* (2015), http://peacemaker.un.org/sites/peacemaker.un.org/files/UA_150212_MinskAgreement_en.pdf; Voice of America News, "Agreement to Send Armed European Police Force to Eastern Ukraine" (October 16, 2016), https://www.voanews.com/a/germany-hosts-meeting-to-review-minsk-agreements-on-ukraine/3557662.html.

Ukraine.[98] The NATO declaration stated that MAP was the next step for Georgia and Ukraine on their path to NATO membership ("We agreed today that these countries will become members of NATO").[99] Russia used the next opportunity to attack Georgia due to its attempt to restore control over the separatist region of South Ossetia. The Russian authoritarian regime increased its pressure on Ukraine to stop the association agreement negotiations with the EU. The corrupt, pro-Russian Yanukovych regime decided not to sign the association agreement with the EU in October 2013.[100] The Maidan protests proved that democratic pro-Western forces in Ukraine were large enough to challenge the regime, which used most brutal methods of suppression, including snipers shooting at the protestors.[101] Some of the protestors in response also used firearms against the Yanukovych regime forces.[102] On February 20, 2014, the Yanukovych regime apparatus on the most violent day of repressions killed (shot down) more than fifty protestors in the Kiev Maidan area, while on February 22, another twenty protestors were killed by the Yanukovych-governed special riot police: Berkut.[103] Yanukovych was ousted by the Ukrainian parliament in February 2014; Russia then attacked Crimea and supported armed pro-Russian units to start a domestic war in

98   Paul Gallis, *The NATO Summit at Bucharest, 2008* (2008), 1, 5, https://fas.org/sgp/crs/row/RS22847.pdf.

99   NATO, *Bucharest Summit Declaration. Issued by the Heads of State and Government Participating in the Meeting of the North Atlantic Council in Bucharest on 3 April 2008* (2008), http://www.nato.int/cps/in/natohq/official_texts_8443.htm point 23.

100 Naja Bentzen, *Ukraine and the Minsk II Agreement. On a Frozen Path to Peace?* (2016), 2, http://www.europarl.europa.eu/RegData/etudes/BRIE/2016/573951/EPRS_BRI(2016)573951_EN.pdf.

101 Ian Traynor, "Ukraine's Bloodiest Day: Dozens Dead as Kiev Protesters Regain Territory from Police," *The Guardian* (February 21, 2014), https://www.theguardian.com/world/2014/feb/20/ukraine-dead-protesters-police.

102 Gabriel Gatehouse, "The Untold Story of the Maidan Massacre," *BBC News Magazine* (February 12, 2015), http://www.bbc.com/news/magazine-31359021.

103 Daniel Sandford, "Ukraine Crisis: What We Know about the Kiev Snipers," *BBC News* (April 3, 2014), http://www.bbc.com/news/world-europe-26866069; Natalya Golitsina and Ron Synovitz, "Photos Link Yanukovych's Troops To Maidan Massacre," *Radio Free Europe, Radio Liberty* (April 2, 2014), https://www.rferl.org/a/ukraine-snipers-sbu-photos-video/25318776.html; Conf. Damien Sharkov, "Ukraine Has Found the Weapon Used in the 'Maidan Massacre,'" *Newsweek* (July 14, 2016), http://www.newsweek.com/ukraine-claims-find-sniper-maidan-massacre-480406.

the eastern regions of Doneck and Lugansk in Ukraine.[104] The EU and the US decided to introduce broad sanctions against Russia to exert pressure that was intended to lead to the withdrawal of Moscow from Crimea.[105] Vladimir Popov noted that Western sanctions led to a further reorientation of the Russian economy toward Asia, helping to increase China's position in international trade.[106]

Marvin Kalb observed that in Putin's eyes, the Maidan leaders were Western agents, which led to his military actions against Ukraine.[107]

Notably, the illegality of Russia's annexation of the Crimean Peninsula on the basis of a non-recognized independence referendum was clear in light of the UN General Assembly resolution of March 27, 2014.[108] The UN Crimean resolution of March 2014 mentioned the Budapest memorandum of 1994, signed by Ukraine, Russia, the US, and the UK, which guaranteed the sovereignty and territorial integrity of Ukraine in return for the transfer of Ukrainian nuclear weapons and Russia's and Ukraine's accession to the NPT.[109]

Robert Legvold viewed the Ukraine crises as a part of the growing tendency among Western powers and Russia's military postures to return to the Cold War standoff in a divided Europe.[110]

The main challenges to the twenty-first-century US-Russian equation in-

---

104 The Economist, "The Economist Explains."

105 US Department of Treasury Office of Foreign Assets Control, *Ukraine/Russia-Related Sanctions Program*; European Union External Action Service, *EU Restrictive Measures in Force.*

106 Vladimir Popov, "Western Economic Sanctions and East-West Economic Orientation of Russia," in *The Return of the Cold War. Ukraine, the West and Russia*, ed. by J. L. Black, Michael Johns, and Alanda D. Theriault, Kindle (London: Routledge, 2016), 3988.

107 Kalb, *Imperial Gamble*, 4752.

108 UN General Assembly, *Resolution Adopted by the General Assembly on 27 March 2014, 68/262, Territorial Integrity of Ukraine* (2014), http://www.un.org/en/ga/search/view_doc.asp?symbol=A/RES/68/262.

109 UN General Assembly; Leonid D. Kuchma and others, *Letter Dated 7 December 1994 from the Permanent Representatives of the Russian Federation, Ukraine, the United Kingdom of Great Britain and Northern Ireland and the United States of America to the United Nations Addressed to the Secretary General. Annex I* (1994), https://www.un.org/en/ga/search/view_doc.asp?symbol=S/1994/1399.

110 Legvold, *Return to Cold War*, 947.

cluded the abandonment of the CFE treaty and the threat of the violation of the INF treaty by new deployments of intermediate range cruise missiles by Russia. The violations of the 1987 INF Treaty by Russian cruise developments were reported by the US administration for the first time in 2014.[111]

On October 20, 2018, Trump declared withdrawal from the INF possible.[112] In January 2019, Trump's Missile Defense Review (MDR) added to the BMD capacity, countering Russia and China's missiles, in place of an earlier focus on smaller rogue states, such as Iran or North Korea.[113] MDR 2019 explained that the Aegis Ashore base in Poland will be completed and armed with SM-3 Blk IIA missiles, as the operating Romanian Aegis Ashore base.[114] The latter missile was to be tested against an ICBM-range target in 2020.[115] A newly developed low-power laser demonstrator on Unmanned Aerial Vehicles (UAVs) was supposed to increase boost-phase intercept capacities, strengthened by F-35 skills, while 64 (by 2023) GBI-strong GMD force potential was supplemented by the Multi-Object Kill Vehicle (MOKV).[116] The Russian deployment of SSC-8 intermediate cruise missile was described by MDR as an INF treaty violation.[117] Among the main BMD challenges are hypersonic glide vehicles (HGV) and Russian and Chinese MIRV and MaRV.[118]

---

111 Oliver Meier and Steven Pifer, *Russia's Missile Treaty Violations Directly Threaten Europe—So Europe Should Speak Up* (2017), https://www.brookings.edu/blog/order-from-chaos/2017/05/05/russias-missile-treaty-violations-directly-threaten-europe-so-europe-should-speak-up/; Ryan Browne, Jim Sciutto and Barbara Starr, "Russia Deploys Missile in Apparent Treaty Violation," *CNN* (February 14, 2017), http://edition.cnn.com/2017/02/14/politics/russia-cruise-missile-spy-ship/index.html.

112 The White House, *Remarks by President Trump Before Air Force One Departure, October 20, 2018* (2018), https://www.whitehouse.gov/briefings-statements/remarks-president-trump-air-force-one-departure-4/.

113 Lara Seligman, "Trump's Muscular New Plan to Fend Off Russian and Chinese Missiles," *Foreign Policy* (January 2019), https://foreignpolicy.com/2019/01/17/trumps-muscular-new-plan-to-fend-off-russian-and-chinese-missiles-missile-defense-space/.

114 US Department of Defense (MDR), *Missile Defense Review* (2019), xii–xiv, https://media.defense.gov/2019/Jan/17/2002080666/-1/-1/1/2019-MISSILE-DEFENSE-REVIEW.PDF.

115 US Department of Defense (MDR), *Missile Defense Review*, xii–xiv.

116 US Department of Defense (MDR), xi, xiii–xiv.

117 US Department of Defense (MDR), iv.

118 US Department of Defense (MDR), iv.

New arms control questions of the late 2010s of more than bilateral importance also include the fate of the New START treaty after it ends in 2021.[119]

The US-China rivalry, first economic, and gradually international, reached military levels with technologically upgraded Chinese missile capacities becoming a threat to the US fleet and bases from the "Guam Express" (DF-26 missile).[120] The threat became more visible after the US's INF abandonment in 2018, due to Russian (and possible Chinese) missile development.

The growing missile threat to Europe in the turbulent post-Cold War environment led to NATO BMD investments. In Europe, George W. Bush's view on the missile threat of rogue countries was largely rejected, as Vincent Garrido Rebolledo and Belén Lara Fernandez explained, due to a suspicion that the US was exaggerating the missile danger to gain more leverage to possess unilateral hegemony worldwide.[121]

5. Back to SDI? Long-Range BMD Perspectives in the Twenty-First Century

The George W. Bush-era investments in GMD and Aegis meant a reinvigoration of missile defense efforts in the post-ABM environment, with a special focus on regional-level limited missile threats, including the "axis of evil" powers (Iran, Iraq, and North Korea).[122]

The Obama-era EPAA reduced the proposed missile defense sites for GMD interceptors in Poland (and Czech radar) to intermediate level Aegis Ashore bases.[123]

---

119 NTI, *New START* (2019), http://www.nti.org/learn/treaties-and-regimes/treaty-between-the-united-states-of-america-and-the-russian-federation-on-measures-for-the-further-reduction-and-limitation-of-strategic-offensive-arms/.

120 James Johnson, *The US-China Military and Defense Relationship during the Obama Presidency* (Cham: Springer International Publishing, 2018), 95–109, 194, https://doi.org/10.1007/978-3-319-75838-1_5.

121 Vicente Garrido Rebolledo and Belén Lara Fernández, "Is There a Missile Threat for Europe? Justifications for a European Missile Defence in Europe and in the Mediterranean" (2003), 419, https://doi.org/10.1007/978-3-642-558542_25.

122 Bush, *The President's State of the Union Address.*

123 The White House, *Fact Sheet: Implementing Missile Defense in Europe, September 15, 2011* (2011), https://obamawhitehouse.achives.gov/the-press-office/2011/09/15

THAAD deployment in South Korea and future South Korean Aegis participation showed the increased significance of regional defense against a nuclear North Korea, increasing the range of its missile forces under Kim Jong Un's dictatorial leadership.[124]

Henry Cooper, O'Neill, et al. noted that, due to Adm. Bill Gortney's (NORAD commander) assessment of the North Korean threat, despite the capability of shooting down its missiles, the US needed to develop boost-phase interception options. This led, according to those scholars, to BP reengagement in the twenty-first-century environment (as the most cost-effective of known systems).[125] Similarly, Karako judged that the current (Obama-era) US BMD constructions' lack of boost-phase capability meant that MDA was not fulfilling its mission of seeking all-phase interception: in this context, UAV lasers were recommended.[126]

The National Academies (NAP) 2012 report stressed that MKV, terminated by the Obama administration, was very valuable (as a "hedge"); the MDA 2002 KEI ground-based boost-phase interceptor program was also cancelled in 2009, as was the Space Test Bed program, important for possible Space-Based Interceptors and valuable in terms of geographic accessibility of all locations of enemy missiles—not easily reachable from neighboring countries for political reasons.[127] Notably, the 2012 NAP report recommended quitting boost-phase development in favor of improved GMD capabilities with the new interceptor GMD-E and improved Exo-atmospheric Kill Vehicle (EKV), based on recommendations of the 2004 American Physical Society (APS) report.[128] The APS 2004

/fact-sheet-implementing-missile-defense-europe.

124 John Chipman, "Chapter Six: Asia," *The Military Balance* 117, no. 1 (2017): 244, https://doi.org/10.1080/04597222.2017.1271212.

125 Henry F. Cooper and others, *Missile Defense. Challenges and Opportunities for the Trump Administration* (2016), http://www.ifpa.org/pdf/IWGWhitePaper16.pdf; Bill Gortney, *Department of Defense Press Briefing by Admiral Gortney in the Pentagon Briefing Room, April 7, 2015* (2015), https://www.defense.gov/News/Transcripts/Transcript-View/Article/607034/departmentof-defense-press-briefing-by-admiral-gortney-in-the-pentagon-briefin/.

126 Karako and Williams, xxix.

127 L. David Montague and Walter B. Slocombe, *Making Sense of Ballistic Missile Defense: An Assessment of Concepts and Systems for US Boost-Phase Missile Defense in Comparison to Other Alternatives* (2012), 11, 32–33, 38–39, https://download.nap.edu/cart/download.cgi?record_id=13189.

128 Montague and Slocombe, *Making Sense of Ballistic Missile Defense,* 128, 131, 149–50;

report stressed that a boost-phase defense against liquid-propellant ballistic missiles was feasible, while such attempts against solid-propellant long range missiles attacking US territory would be hardly imaginable, including the use of space-based interceptors, which were ineffective (requiring 1000 intercepting vehicles against a single ICBM) and very costly due to the high rate of required orbital flights.[129] The APS report stated that the SBI designed for boost-phase interception would have to carry massive KVs as GBIs and a very large number of interceptors, due to short orbiting time of a low-orbit satellite-launcher over a selected target.[130] According to the APS study, a system resembling BP placed in orbit would require 1600 satellites to intercept a North Korean ICBM (by keeping at least one satellite at the position of interception).[131] APS experts estimated that an interceptor's (orbiting at an altitude of 300km) mass would reach 820 kg, a kill vehicle could weigh 136 kg, and an entire 1600-satellite system's mass would be as high as 2000 tons, which would lead to extensive costs of deployment. (With a cost of low orbit delivery at $10,000 per pound, the SBI transportation to orbit could require $44.4 billion).[132]

Critics of space-based boost-phase interception, such as Laura Grego, George N. Lewis, and David Wright of the Union of Concerned Scientists (UCS), stressed its high costs and a lack of meaningful assessments in the matter (in the context of 2016 Congressional funding feasibility study).[133] As the UCS report noted, GBI (composed of ATK Orion 50 XLG first stage motor, Orion 50 XL second stage rocket, and Orion 38

Conf. Daniel Kleppner and Frederick K. Lamb, "Report of the American Physical Society Study Group on Boost-Phase Intercept Systems for National Missile Defense: Scientific and Technical Issues," *Review of Modern Physics* 76, no. S1 (2004): 243–244, 250–251, https://journals.aps.org/rmp/pdf/10.1103/RevModPhys.76.S1.

129   Kleppner and Lamb, "Report of the American Physical Society Study Group," xxi–xxii, xxv.

130   Kleppner and Lamb, xxi–xxii, xxv.

131   Kleppner and Lamb, S103-104.

132   Kleppner and Lamb, S103-104; Conf. National Institute of Standards and Technology, *Approximate Conversions from US Customary Measures to Metric* (2010), https://www.nist.gov/pml/weights-and-measures/approximate-conversions-us-customary-measures-metric.

133   Laura Grego, George N. Lewis and David Wright, *Shielded from Oversight. The Disastrous US Approach to Strategic Missile Defense* (2016), 17, http://www.ucsusa.org/sites/default/files/attach/2016/07/Shielded-from-Oversight-full-report.pdf.

third stage motor) reaches a design speed (in vertical boost) of 7.2 kilometers per second (maximum), while the burnout speed (in non-vertical flight) could reach 8.3 km/p.[134]

Notably, the Trump-era missile defense was supposed to be more robust than in the 1999 NMD act, due to a December 2016 Congressional amendment.[135] The FY2020 MDA budget plan included an investment in a potentially deployable space-based layer of BMD, including the technological maturation of a Neutral Particle Beam, which was to be considered within Space-Based Directed Energy interceptors.[136]

6. The 2000s' BMD Developments and Polish Missile Defense Base

Notably, the NATO Active Layered Theater Ballistic Missile Defence (ALTBMD) was approved in 2005.[137] The August 2008 agreement between the George W. Bush administration and Polish authorities, including the construction of silos for 10 GBI of GMD systems protecting the United States from long-range ICBM missile attack, was amended for the purpose of EPAA.[138]

Due to Obama's controversial shift in the concept of BMD in September 17, 2009, after a simulated Russian nuclear attack against Poland,[139] the

---

134 Laura Grego, George N. Lewis and David Wright, *Shielded from Oversight. The Disastrous US Approach to Strategic Missile Defense. Appendix 6. The Ground Based Interceptor and Kill Vehicle*, 2016, 1, http://www.ucsusa.org/sites/default/files/attach/2016/07/Shielded-from-Oversight-appendix-6.pdf.

135 US Congress (sponsor John McCain), *National Defense Authorization Act for Fiscal Year 2017, Public Law 114-328, January 4, 2016* (Washington, DC: US Congress, 2016), 2000–2968, https://www.congress.gov/bill/114th-congress/senate-bill/2943/text; US Congress, *National Missile Defense Act of 1999, Public Law 106-38, 106th Congress, July 22, 1999* (1999), https://www.congress.gov/106/plaws/publ38/PLAW-106publ38.pdf.

136 MDA, *Fiscal Year (FY) 2020 Budget Estimates, March 7, 2019* (2019), 11, https://www.mda.mil/global/documents/pdf/budgetfy20.pdf.

137 NATO, *NATO, BMD, Where We Are* (2017), https://www.ncia.nato.int/BMD/Pages/Where-we-are.aspx; NATO, *NATO, Ballistic Missile Defence Programme* (2017), https://www.ncia.nato.int/BMD/pages/ballistic-missile-defence.aspx.

138 George W. Bush and Radosław Sikorski, *Agreement between the Government of the United States of America and the Government of the Republic of Poland Concerning the Deployment of Ground-Based Ballistic Missile Defense Interceptors in the Territory of the Republic of Poland, Warsaw, August 20, 2008* (2008), https://www.state.gov/documents/organization/180542.pdf.

139 Stratfor, *In Zapad Exercises, Russia Flexes Its Military Strength* (2009), https://www.

BMD agreement between the US and Poland was changed in a manner suited to Russia's reluctance to any ICBM-capable missile defense.

Obama's administration replaced the GMD base in Poland with an Aegis Ashore base, to deliver intermediate-range missile defense (with a plan to increase the interception range in the future). Aegis-based EPAA systems had been deployed since March 2011.[140] In March 2013, the US Department of Defense abandoned the ICBM-level of interception through Aegis SM-3 Block IIB's[141] previous phase four of EPAA (2020).[142] The Romanian Deveselu base reached its operational capabilities in 2015. The Aegis Ashore Redzikowo base construction started on May 13, 2016, as European Phase Adaptive Approach phase 3.[143] The Aegis Ashore Missile Defense System (AAMDS) with Polish Force Protection Battalion will

stratfor.com/article/zapad-exercises-russia-flexes-its-military-strength; Matthew Day, "Russia 'Simulates' Nuclear Attack on Poland," *The Telegraph* (November 1, 2009), http://www.telegraph.co.uk/news/worldnews/europe/poland/6480227/Russia-simulates-nuclear-attack-on-Poland.html; John Noonan, "Russia 'Simulates' Nuclear Attack on Poland," *The Weekly Standard* (November 3, 2009), http://www.weeklystandard.com/russia-simulates-nuclear-attack-on-poland/article/271383.

140   MDA, *Aegis Ballistic Missile Defense* (2019), https://www.mda.mil/system/aegis_bmd.html.

141   Cristina Chaplain, *Missile Defense. Mixed Progress in Achieving Acquisition Goals and Improving Accountability* (2014), 11, http://www.gao.gov/assets/670/662194.pdf; James D. Syring, *Department of Defense Briefing by Vice Adm. Syring on the Fiscal Year 2016 Missile Defense Agency Budget Request in the Pentagon Briefing Room, February 2, 2015* (2015), https://www.defense.gov/News/Transcripts/Transcript-View/Article/607005/department-of-defense-briefing-by-vice-adm-syring-on-the-fiscal-year-2016-missi/; James D. Winnefeld, *Adm. Winnefeld's Remarks at the Center for Strategic and International Studies* (2015), http://www.jcs.mil/Media/Speeches/Article/589289/adm-winnefelds-remarks-at-the-center-for-strategic-and-international-studies/; CSIS, *Missile Defense Project, Standard Missile-3 (SM-3), Missile Threat, Center for Strategic and International Studies, June 14, 2016, Last Modified September 28, 2018* (2016), https://missilethreat.csis.org/defsys/sm-3/; Jacek Durkalec, "The Role of Missile Defence in NATO Deterrence," in *Regional Approached to the Role of Missile Defence in Reducing Nuclear Threats,* ed. by Marcin Andrzej Piotrowski (Warsaw: The Polish Institute of International Affairs, 2013), 20, https://www.pism.pl/files/?id_plik=14446.

142   US Embassy in Romania, *A "Phased, Adaptive Approach" for Missile Defense in Europe* (2016), https://ro.usembassy.gov/a-phased-adaptive-approach-for-missile-defense-in-europe/.

143   US Embassy Warsaw, *United States and Poland Start Construction of Redzikowo Missile Defense Facility, May 18, 2016* (2016), https://pl.usembassy.gov/facility/; US Embassy Warsaw, *US Congressional Delegation Visits Redzikowo, April 19, 2017* (2017), https://pl.usembassy.gov/u-s-congressional-delegation-visits-redzikowo/.

host SM-3 Block IIA missiles.[144] The Polish Aegis base, according to the US Department of Defense, was not aimed at Russia and remained unable to threaten Russian strategic forces.[145] Polish Minister for Foreign Affairs, Witold Waszczykowski, confirmed the non-significance of the base in the context of Russian ICBM capabilities.[146]

The Romanian Aegis base underwent an update in 2019, secured by THAAD battery deployed in April from Fort Hood for three months.[147] Among other THAAD deployments (next to South Korea) was the March 2019 introduction of a battery in South Israel, connected to the Iranian threat.[148]

Aside from Redzikowo, Poland attempted to persuade Trump to build a second permanent US base (Fort Trump) and were willing to pay $2 billion, according to the Duda-Trump White House September 2018 meeting.[149] Although Trump gave no clear final opinion on the matter in

---

144 Commander Navy Installations Command (CNIC), *Naval Support Facility Redzikowo* (2019), https://www.cnic.navy.mil/regions/cnreurafswa/installations/nsf_redzikowo.html; EUCOM, *US, Poland Break Ground on Aegis Ashore Site in Poland* (2016), https://www.eucom.mil/media-library/pressrelease/35358/u-s-poland-break-ground-on-aegis-ashore-site-in-poland; Alex Perrien, *NSF Redzikowo Signs Premiere Training Agreement with Polish Forces* (2017), https://pl.usembassy.gov/agreement/.

145 Lisa Ferdinando, *Work Joins Groundbreaking for Ballistic Missile Defense Site in Poland* (2016), https://www.defense.gov/News/Article/Article/759662/work-joins-groundbreaking-for-ballistic-missile-defense-site-in-poland/.

146 Ministry of Foreign Affairs Republic of Poland, *Minister Witold Waszczykowski: Redzikowo Base Will Significantly Strengthen Poland's Security* (2016), http://www.msz.gov.pl/en/news/minister_witold_waszczykowski__redzikowo_base_will_significantly_strengthen_poland_s_security.

147 Jason Epperson, *US Deploys THAAD Anti-Missile System in First Deployment to Romania* https://www.cnic.navy.mil/regions/cnreurafswa/installations/nsf_deveselu/news/US-deploys-THAAD-anti-missile-system-to-Romania.html; NATO Public Affairs, *Aegis Ashore Missile Defence System in Romania Undergoes Scheduled Update* (2019), https://www.cnic.navy.mil/regions/cnreurafswa/installations/nsf_deveselu/news/Aegis-Ashore-missile-defence-system-in-Romania-undergoes-scheduled-update.html.

148 Jen Judson, "US Army Terminal Missile Defense System Is Headed to Eastern Europe," *DefenseNews* (April 11, 2019), https://www.defensenews.com/land/2019/04/11/us-army-terminal-missile-defense-system-is-headed-to-eastern-europe/; Isabel Debre, "In First, US Deploys THAAD Anti-Missile System in Israel," *DefenseNews* (March 4, 2019), https://www.defensenews.com/land/2019/03/04/in-first-us-deploys-thaad-anti-missile-system-in-israel/.

149 Tara Copp, "'Fort Trump' Would Be the Second US Site in Poland," *Military Times*

the first place, he stressed that he valued a declared financial contribution (also in the context of unsatisfactory commitments of wealthy NATO members in Europe to common defense and aggressive military actions of Russia) and promised to conduct an in-depth review of the matter of the new permanent US base.[150]

7. BMDS Components: Midcourse, Terminal and Boost-Phase Interception. BMD Costs

a) Overview

The midcourse stage of a flight of incoming missile interception devices includes ICBM-level capable GMD, composed of 36 GBI. As of April 2017 and located at Fort Greely (Alaska) and Vandenberg (California), each GBI is aimed to intercept an incoming missile in the Earth's orbit using EKV, a separate vehicle lifted by multi-stage boosters.[151]

The midcourse stage of the intermediate level missile-interception ready system, Aegis, consisted in 2016 of 33 ships, five cruisers, and 28 destroyers, divided into Pacific (17) and Atlantic (16) Fleets, while the system was operationally deployed for the first time in 2004. There are an additional four Aegis-capable ships, which are Japanese Kongo-class destroyers.[152]

Aegis Ashore bases consist of a Deveselu complex armed with SM-3 Block IB missiles and the Polish Redzikowo facility, to be equipped with SM-3 Block IB and IIA missiles.[153]

The terminal stage interception (apart from Aegis) is provided by THAAD (higher level) and PAC-3 (lower level) interceptors.

(September 19, 2018), https://www.militarytimes.com/news/your-military/2018/09/19/fort-trump-would-be-the-second-us-site-in-poland/.

150   The White House, *Remarks by President Trump and President Duda of the Republic of Poland in Joint Press Conference, September 18, 2018* (2018), https://www.whitehouse.gov/briefings-statements/remarks-president-trump-president-duda-republic-poland-joint-press-conference/.

151   MDA, *Ground-Based Midcourse Defense Fact Sheet* (2017), https://www.mda.mil/global/documents/pdf/gmdfacts.pdf.

152   MDA, *Aegis Ballistic Missile Defense Fact Sheet* (2016), https://www.mda.mil/global/documents/pdf/aegis.pdf.

153   MDA, *Aegis Ashore* (2019), https://www.mda.mil/system/aegis_ashore.html.

Six THAAD batteries were deployed from 2008 to 2016, including three launchers (eight interceptors per launcher) in a battery.[154]

The boost-phase interception is to be developed by the US through new technologies including UAVs and possible SM-3 Aegis improvements.[155]

According to US Government Accountability Office (GAO), from 2002 to 2014 the Department of Defense spent $98 billion to develop BMD.[156] According to the GAO April 28, 2016 report, the Missile Defense Agency (MDA) has received $123 billion since 2002, with an additional $38 billion to be granted through fiscal year (FY) 2020.[157] The December 2012 estimation of THAAD operating costs, including the support of six batteries accounted for $6.5 billion in a twenty-year perspective.[158]

b) BMDS/Aegis

According to GAO, MDA received $123 billion from 2002 to April 2016 to develop BMDS (the GAO-assessed BMDS elements apart from additional in the MDA) including:

- Aegis BMD:
    - SM-3 Block IB,
    - SM-3 Block IIA,
    - Aegis Ashore,
- Command, Control, Battle Management and Communications (C2BMC),

---

154 MDA, *Terminal High Altitude Area Defense Fact Sheet* (2016), https://www.mda. mil/global/documents/pdf/thaad.pdf.

155 MDA, *A System of Elements* (2019), https://www.mda.mil/system/elements.html; MDA, *Elements. Potential New Technologies* (2019), https://www.mda.mil/system/ potential_new_technologies.html.

156 Annual costs on average amounted to $7.5 billion. John H. Pendleton, *Ballistic Missile Defense. Actions Needed to Address Implementation Issues and Estimate Long-Term Costs for European Capabilities* (2014), 1, http://www.gao.gov/assets/670/662492. pdf.

157 Annual costs (yearly on average, 2002-2016) reached 8.2 billion, and in the time framework 2002-2020: $7.9 billion. Cristina Chaplain, *Ballistic Missile Defense System Testing Delays Affect Delivery of Capabilities* (2016), 1, http://www.gao.gov/assets /680/676855.pdf.

158 Pendleton, *Ballistic Missile Defense*, 19.

- GMD – Capability Enhancement-I (CE-I), CE-II,

- Targets and Countermeasures,

- THAAD.[159]

On May 13, 2016, construction in Redzikowo officially started, a day after the Romanian official opening of a base in Deveselu.[160] The deployment of Aegis Ashore operational site in Poland was planned on December, 2018. (The Deveselu base was deployed in December 2015, completed 2016, with vulnerabilities before 2018.)

c) GBI

CE-II Block I had been planned to be produced since 2014, while the GAO recommended MDA delay it until the demonstration flights results. The Department of Defense maintained that it would endanger a goal of fielded 44 interceptors before 2018.[161]

On June 22, 2014, GMD Contractor Boeing, leader of an industry team, achieved a successful test intercept of an enhanced EKV.[162] Boeing has been a leader since 1998, while other contractors were Northrop Grumman, Raytheon, and Orbital Sciences.[163] Orbital ATK was the successor to Orbital Sciences following the 2015 merger.[164]

---

159 Ranges: short-range 621 miles, medium range 621-1864 miles, intermediate-range 1864-3418 miles, and intercontinental range 3418 miles. Chaplain, *Ballistic Missile Defense System Testing Delays*, 1.

160 EUCOM.

161 Cristina Chaplain, *Missile Defense: Assessment of DOD's Reports on Status of Efforts and Options for Improving Homeland Missile Defense* (2016), 7–8, http://www.gao.gov/assets/680/675263.pdf.

162 Terence Williams, *Boeing-Led Missile Defense Team Achieves Intercept in Flight Test, June 22, 2014*, http://boeing.mediaroom.com/Boeing-led-Missile-Defense-Team-Achieves-Intercept-in-Flight-Test.

163 Boeing, *Ground-Based Midcourse Defense* (2019), http://www.boeing.com/defense/missile-defense/ground-based-midcourse/index.page#.

164 Anthony J. Valento, *Report of Organizational Actions Affecting Basis of Securities, Orbital ATK, Inc.* (2015), http://investor.northropgrumman.com/static-files/4ed20b33-b405-4ac1-95a8-91ec553367bd; Orbital ATK, *About Leadership* (2017), http://www.orbitalatk.com/about/leadership/default.aspx; Orbital ATK, *David A. Thompson* (2017), http://www.orbitalatk.com/about/leadership/files/Thompson_David_OA.pdf; Northrop Grumman, *Orbital ATK Merged with Northrop Grumman in 2018. Orbital ATK Merger* (2019), http://investor.northropgrumman.com/orbital-

CE-II Block I was planned for 2017 (upgraded CE-II and RKV for 30 interceptors were to be placed in the field by that time, while 14 remaining were to be fielded before 2018): 24 CE-I and 22 CE-II were successfully delivered and 10 CE-II Block I have been expected to be delivered since 2017 (according to a GAO April 2016 report).[165]

The Obama administration delayed the development of key technology (MOKV) by cancelling the program in 2009, finally admitting its critical value (MOKV development contract was granted in 2015 to Raytheon).[166]

In 2014, 36 GBI were operational in Fort Greely, Alaska and Vandenberg, California.[167]

As MDA Chief Adm. Syring claimed in 2014, there were 30 GBI to protect the US from North Korea and Iran-based BMD threats.[168]

As Karako, Williams, and Wes Rumbaugh stated, the chances for GBI improvements in terms of shooting capabilities are connected to MKV,

---

atk-merger; Northrop Grumman Corporation (Tim Paynter & Steve Movius) & Globe Newswire, *Northrop Grumman Completes Orbital ATK Acquisition, Blake Larson Elected to Lead New Innovation Systems Sector* (2018), https://northropgrumman.gcs-web.com/news-releases/news-release-details/northrop-grumman-completes-orbital-atk-acquisition-blake-larson; https://www.globenewswire.com/news-release/2018/06/06/1518052/0/en/Northrop-Grumman-Completes-Orbital-ATK-Acquisition-B; PRNews Wire & Northrop Grumman (Tim Paynter & Steve Movius) & Orbital ATK (Barron Beneski), *Northrop Grumman to Acquire Orbital ATK for $9.2 Billion* (2017), https://www.prnewswire.com/news-releases/northrop-grumman-to-acquire-orbital-atk-for-92-billion-300521034.html.

165 Chaplain, *Ballistic Missile Defense System Testing Delays*, 1–3, 47–48, 51–52, 55.

166 Raytheon, *Kill Vehicle* (2019), http://www.raytheon.com/capabilities/products/ekv/; Raytheon, *Raytheon Completes $9.2 Million Space Factory Expansion* (2018), http://www.raytheon.com/news/feature/factory_expansion.html; Michaela Dodge, *President Obama's Missile Defense Policy: A Misguided Legacy*, http://www.heritage.org/defense/report/president-obamas-missile-defense-policy-misguided-legacy; Dov Zakheim, "Evaluating the Opportunity and Financial Costs of Ballistic Missile Defense," in *Regional Missile Defense from a Global Perspective*, ed. by Catherine McArdle Kelleher and Peter Dombrowski, Kindle (Stanford: Stanford University Press, 2015), 5629.

167 MDA, *Ground-Based Midcourse Defense Fact Sheet*; MDA, *Elements. Ground-Based Midcourse Defense (GMD)* (2019), https://www.mda.mil/system/gmd.html.

168 James D. Syring, *Unclassified Statement of Vice Admiral James D. Syring, Director, Missile Defense Agency, Before the House Armed Service Committee Subcommittee on Strategic Forces, March 25, 2014* (2014), 7, https://www.mda.mil/global/documents/pdf/ps_syring_032514_HASC.pdf.

which was delayed by the Obama administration.[169]

Rocket motors of MX-Peacekeeper missiles after their withdrawal from service were used as components of the interceptor Minotaur (IV, V, VI), produced by Orbital ATK, which delivers GBI boosters for Boeing as a contractor, hired for MDA GMD program development.[170] Earlier, MX missiles were used as targets, and the selection of launch vehicles included Taurus, Athena, and Conestoga.[171]

Orbital interceptors' development included Pegasus, Taurus, and Minotaur boosters for three-stage GMD rocket improvements (EKV was developed by Raytheon).[172]

Interestingly, Orbital ATK used Russian cooperation as well to build Antares space launch engines (NPO Energomash company); Orbital used American-repaired Soviet propulsion (a design from the 1960s) for Antares, replaced after the 2014 accident by new Russian delivery.[173]

d) THAAD and Patriot Advanced Capability (PAC)

THAAD, an endo and low-exo-atmospheric[174] terminal phase BMDS

---

169 Karako and Williams, 82; Conf. Grego, Lewis and Wright, *Shielded from Oversight. The Disastrous US Approach to Strategic Missile Defense.*

170 Orbital ATK, *Flight Systems* (2016), https://www.orbitalatk.com/flight-systems/ overview/; Orbital ATK, *Interceptors* (2016), https://www.orbitalatk.com/flight-systems/missile-defense-systems/interceptors/default.aspx; Boeing.

171 US Army Space and Missile Defense Command & MDA, *Ground-Based Midcourse Defense (GMD) Extended Test Range (ETR), Final Environmental Impact Statement, Volume 1 of 3: Chapters 1-4* (2003), 2–7, https://www.mda.mil/global/documents/ pdf/env_gmd_etr_covch2.pdf.

172 Orbital ATK, *Interceptors*; Orbital ATK, *Missile Defense Systems* (2016), https://www. orbitalatk.com/flight-systems/missile-defense-systems/overview/default.aspx; Orbital ATK, *GMD Boost Vehicle, Fact Sheet* (2015), https://www.orbitalatk.com/ flight-systems/missile-defense-systems/interceptors/docs/BR06009_3862GMD_ R2.pdf; Bob Granath, *Pegasus XL Mated to L-1011 Stargazer Carrier Aircraft* (2016), https://www.nasa.gov/image-feature/pegasus-xl-mated-to-l-1011-stargazer-carrier-aircraft.

173 Loren Grush, "Orbital ATK to Launch Antares Rocket This Weekend—Two Years after 2014 Explosion," *The Verge* (2016), https://www.theverge.com/2016/10/ 14/13225592/orbital-atk-antares-rocket-launch-2014-explosion; William Graham, *Antares 230 Successfully Returns with Launch of OA-5 Cygnus* (2016), https://www. nasaspaceflight.com/2016/10/antares-230-launch-oa-5-cygnus/.

174 Lockheed Martin, *Terminal High Altitude Area Defense THAAD* (2019), https:// www.lockheedmartin.com/en-us/products/thaad.html.

has been in full procurement since 2012 (first two batteries included six launchers and 48 interceptors).[175]

The first THAAD battery was deployed in 2008, waiting for full capabilities through 2012 (a missile was aimed to counter short and medium ballistic threats at a range of 124 miles).[176]

According to the GAO, in 1996 the total THAAD costs were estimated at $16.7 billion, 10 interceptors per launcher were used in the THAAD prototype - User Operational Evaluation System (UOES); a total of 40 were completed before testing.[177] Later eight interceptors per launcher were used.

Due to delays, the total cost of THAAD grew to $17.9 billion from $16.8 billion. All four first intercept tests failed, including the March 1997 test, while the Department of Defense expected three intercept successes to admit THAAD to production phase (as the GAO report stated in 1997).[178]

THAAD acquisition costs were extended to $15.5 billion; $3.3 billion was spent by the Department of Defense on this program through April 1999 (according to a GAO 1999 report).[179]

---

175 MDA, *Terminal High Altitude Area Defense* (2014), http://www.mda.mil/global/documents/pdf/thaad.pdf; Ballistic Missile Defense Organization (US Department of Defense), *User Operational Evaluation System (UOES) THAAD Missile Configuration* (2000), http://fas.org/spp/starwars/program/38112.pdf; Federation of American Scientists (FAS), *THAAD TMD* (2016), http://fas.org/spp/starwars/program/thaad.htm.

176 Robert Wisher, "Patriot Air and Missile Defense System," in *Nalysis of System Training Impact for Major Defense Acquisition Programs (MDAPs): Training Systems Acquisition*, ed. by Frederick Hartman (2012), 6, 8–9, 18, http://www.dtic.mil/cgi-bin/GetTRDoc?AD=ADA570775; MDA, *Terminal High Altitude Area Defense*; Federation of American Scientists (FAS), *THAAD TMD*.

177 Henry L. Hinton and others, *Ballistic Missile Defense. Issues Concerning Acquisition of THAAD Prototype System* (1996), 1–3, http://www.gao.gov/assets/230/222810.pdf; Conf. Thomas Schulz, *Letter to William J. Perry, The Secretary of Defense* (1997), http://www.gao.gov/assets/90/86108.pdf.

178 Allen Li, Tom Schulz, and others, *Ballistic Missile Defense. Improvements Needed in THAAD Acquisition Planning* (1997), 2–4, http://www.gao.gov/assets/230/224624.pdf.

179 Allen Li, Lee Edwards, and others, *Missile Defense. THAAD Restructure Addresses Problems But Limits Early Capability* (1999), 3–4, http://www.gao.gov/assets/230/227724.pdf.

Lockheed delivered the 100th THAAD missile in July 2015.[180]

As Robert A. Wisher explained, short-range missile defense units SAM/D (renamed Patriot in 1975) were deployed in 1984 after being developed in full scale since 1976 with MIM-104 and MIM-104A of 70 km range.[181] Patriot Advanced Capability (PAC)-1 was first fielded in 1988, with MIM-104B protected against electronic countermeasures and a 70-km range.[182] PAC-2 MIM-104C was deployed in 1990, with a 160-km range (four versions of Guidance Enhanced Missiles [GEM] to PAC-2 were introduced in 1990s-2000s, while PAC-3 has been full scale-produced since 2002.[183] PAC-3 units were armed with 16 interceptors per launcher (four in PAC-2).[184] Those interceptors were used in Operation Iraqi Freedom with GEM and C-5 airplanes as transportation.[185]

8. New Strategic Arms Reduction Treaty (START)

New START 2010 limits include within seven years after the introduction of the treaty by law, i.e., February 2018, aggregate numbers of up to 700 deployed ICBMs, SLBMs, and heavy bombers, altogether, 1550 deployed warheads on three legs of the triad, 800 deployed and non-deployed ICBMs, and SLBMs launchers and heavy bombers, altogether.[186]

---

180   Lockheed Martin, *Lockheed Martin Completes 100th THAAD Interceptor* (2015), http://www.lockheedmartin.com/us/news/press-releases/2015/july/mfc-lockheed-martin-completes-100th-thaad-interceptor.html; Lockheed Martin, *Lockheed Martin Receives $528 Million THAAD Missile Defense Contract* (2016), http://www.lockheedmartin.com/us/news/press-releases/2016/january/mfc-010416-lockheed-martin-receives-528-million-THAAD-contract.html.

181   Wisher, "Patriot Air and Missile Defense System," 6, 8–9, 18.

182   Wisher, 6, 8–9, 18.

183   Wisher, 6, 8–9, 18.

184   Lockheed Martin, *Patriot Advanced Capability-3 (PAC-3®)* (2010), https://www.lockheedmartin.com/content/dam/lockheed-martin/mfc/pc/pac-3/mfc-pac-3-pc.pdf.

185   MDA, *Patriot Advanced Capability-3* (2016), https://www.mda.mil/global/documents/pdf/pac3.pdf; Federation of American Scientists (FAS), *Patriot TMD* (2000), http://fas.org/spp/starwars/program/patriot.htm.

186   US Department of State, *Report on the Reasons That Continued Implementation of the New Start Treaty Is in the National Security Interests of the United States* (2018), https://www.state.gov/wp-content/uploads/2019/05/AVC-New-START-December-2018.pdf; US Department of State, *Annual Report on the Implementation of the New Start Treaty, January 2016* (2016), https://www.state.gov/t/avc/rls/rpt/2016/255558.htm.

The data on the New START treaty implementation since 2011 to 2016 show a decrease in the deployed strategic warheads arsenal on the US side and a slight growth of deployed warheads on Russian side.[187] By 2019, there were deployed strategic warhead reductions on both sides, to levels below 1500, fulfilling the treaty obligations.[188]

Table 1. New START Treaty implementation (Aggregate numbers of strategic arms as of September 1, 2011)

category	USA	Russia
deployed ICBMs, SLBMs and heavy bombers	822	516
warheads on deployed ICBMs, SLBMs and heavy bombers	1790	1566
deployed and non-deployed ICBMs and SLBMs launchers and heavy bombers	1043	871

Source: US Department of State, *Annual Report on the Implementation of the New Start Treaty,* January 31, 2012, https://www.state.gov/t/avc/rls/rpt/197087.htm.

Table 2. New START Treaty implementation (as of September 1, 2015)

category	USA	Russia
deployed ICBMs, SLBMs and heavy bombers	762	526
warheads on deployed ICBMs, SLBMs and heavy bombers	1538	1648
deployed and non-deployed ICBMs and SLBMs launchers and heavy bombers	898	877

Source: US Department of State, *Annual Report on the Implementation of the New Start Treaty,* January 2016, https://www.state.gov/t/avc/rls/rpt/2016/255558.htm.

---

187   Hans M. Kristensen, *New START Data Shows Russian Warhead Increase Before Expected Decrease* (2016), https://fas.org/blogs/security/2016/10/new-start-data-2016/; Hans M. Kristensen, *Assembled Documents: New START Treaty Aggregate Numbers of Strategic Offensive Arms As of September 1, 2011* (2011), https://fas.org/programs/ssp/nukes/armscontrol/NewSTART-USnumbers090111.pdf; US Department of State, *Annual Report on the Implementation of the New Start Treaty, January 31, 2012* (2012), https://www.state.gov/t/avc/rls/rpt/197087.htm; US Department of State, *Annual Report on the Implementation of the New Start Treaty, January 2016*; US Department of State, *Annual Report on the Implementation of the New Start Treaty, January 2017* (2017), https://www.state.gov/annual-report-on-implementation-of-the-new-start-treaty-2017/.

188   US Department of State, *New START Treaty Aggregate Numbers of Strategic Offensive Arms Fact Sheet, March 1, 2019* (2019), https://www.state.gov/wp-content/uploads/2019/05/AVC-03012019.pdf.

Table 3. New START Treaty implementation (as of September 1, 2016)

category	USA	Russia
deployed ICBMs, SLBMs and heavy bombers	681	508
warheads on deployed ICBMs, SLBMs and heavy bombers	1367	1796
deployed and non-deployed ICBMs and SLBMs launchers and heavy bombers	848	847

Source: US Department of State, *Annual Report on the Implementation of the New Start Treaty,* January 2017, 3, https://www.state.gov/wp-content/uploads/2019/05/AVC-New-START-January-2017.pdf.

Table 4. New START Treaty implementation (September 1, 2017)

category	USA	Russia
deployed ICBMs, SLBMs and heavy bombers	660	501
warheads on deployed ICBMs, SLBMs and heavy bombers	1393	1561
deployed and non-deployed ICBMs and SLBMs launchers and heavy bombers	800	790

Source: US Department of State, *Annual Report on Implementation of the New Start Treaty,* January 2018, 3, https://www.state.gov/wp-content/uploads/2019/05/AVC-New-START-January-2018.pdf.

According to the US Department of State's assessment, by 2018 both parts of the New START treaty had managed to implement its goals: since February 5, 2011, when the treaty became effective, and within 7 years, the US and Russia had managed to reach the designed strategic arms reduction objectives.[189] At the same time, the US Department of State noted that in March 2018, Putin announced plans for new Russian nuclear (and nuclear-powered) strategic weapons deployment (nuclear-powered and armed cruise missile, nuclear-powered underwater intercontinental-range UAV, air-launched missile, a gliding vehicle, and a new heavy ICBM), scheduled before the expiration of the New Start treaty in February 2021.[190] Among the challenges to the New START extension were the US withdrawal from the INF treaty and the dispute over Russia's Comprehensive Test Ban Treaty (CTBT) violations in 2019. (Russia ratified

---

189   US Department of State, *Report on the Reasons.*

190   US Department of State, *Report on the Reasons.*

CTBT, but the US has not and the treaty is not in force until all 44 signatories join, which are required for ratification. Those that did not ratify include China, North Korea, Egypt, Iran, Israel, and Pakistan).[191]

Table 5. New START Treaty implementation (September 1, 2018)

category	USA	Russia
deployed ICBMs, SLBMs and heavy bombers	659	517
warheads on deployed ICBMs, SLBMs and heavy bombers	1398	1420
deployed and non-deployed ICBMs and SLBMs launchers and heavy bombers	800	775

Source: *Report on the Reasons that Continued Implementation of the New Start Treaty is in the National Security Interests of the United States,* US DoS, December 2018, https://www.state.gov/wp-content/uploads/2019/05/AVC-New-START-December-2018.pdf.

Table 6. New START Treaty implementation (March, 1 2019)

category	USA	Russia
deployed ICBMs, SLBMs and heavy bombers	656	524
warheads on deployed ICBMs, SLBMs and heavy bombers	1365	1461
deployed and non-deployed ICBMs and SLBMs launchers and heavy bombers	800	760

Source: US Department of State, DoS, *New START Treaty Aggregate Numbers of Strategic Offensive Arms Fact Sheet,* March 1, 2019, https://www.state.gov/wp-content/uploads/2019/05/AVC-03012019.pdf.

---

191 Stratfor, *Russia, US: What To Make of an Accusation of a Test Ban Treaty Violation* (2019), https://worldview.stratfor.com/article/russia-us-what-make-accusation-test-ban-treaty-violation-nuclear-arms-race; United Nations Office for Disarmament Affairs, *Comprehensive Nuclear-Test-Ban Treaty (CTBT)* (2019), https://www.un.org/disarmament/wmd/nuclear/ctbt/; Comprehensive Test Ban Treaty Organization (CTBTO) Preparatory Commission, *Status of Signature and Ratification* (2019), https://www.ctbto.org/the-treaty/status-of-signature-and-ratification/; Nuclear Threat Initiative (NTI), *Comprehensive Test Ban Treaty (CTBT)* (2019), https://www.nti.org/learn/treaties-and-regimes/comprehensive-nuclear-test-ban-treaty-ctbt/.

Chart 1. US and Russia's reductions of deployed strategic warheads due to New START treaty (2011-2019)

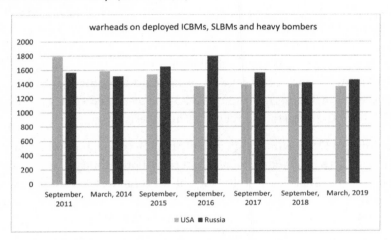

Sources: US Department of State New START Treaty implementation reports.[192]

9. BMD Effectiveness: Probability Analysis

The first successful ICBM intercept by GBI took place on May 30, 2017.[193] The interception was achieved by CE-II Block 1 EKV in a Configuration 2 (C2) three-stage launch vehicle.[194]

---

192   US Department of State, *Annual Report on Implementation of the New Start Treaty, January 2018* (2018), https://www.state.gov/wp-content/uploads/2019/05/AVC-New-START-January-2018.pdf; US Department of State, *New START Treaty Aggregate Numbers of Strategic Offensive Arms Fact Sheet, March 1, 2019*; US Department of State, *Annual Report on the Implementation of the New Start Treaty, January 2017*; US Department of State, *Annual Report on the Implementation of the New Start Treaty, January 2016*; US Department of State, *Annual Report on the Implementation of the New Start Treaty, January 31, 2012*; US Department of State, *New START Treaty Aggregate Number of Strategic Offensive Arms, April 1, 2014* (2014), http://www.state.gov/documents/organization/224449.pdf; US Department of State, *Report on the Reasons*; Conf. Kristensen, *New START Data Shows Russian Warhead Increase Before Expected Decrease*; Kristensen, *Assembled Documents: New START Treaty Aggregate Numbers of Strategic Offensive Arms As of September 1, 2011.*

193   MDA, *Homeland Missile Defense System Successfully Intercepts ICBM Target, May 30, 2017* (2017), https://www.mda.mil/news/17news0003.html.

194   James D. Syring, *Statement before the House Armed Service Committee Subcommittee on Strategic Forces, June 7, 2017* (2017), 7, https://www.mda.mil/global/documents/pdf/FY18_WrittenStatement_HASC_SFP.PDF; MDA, *Ground-Based Midcourse Defense (GMD) Program Overview, May 24, 2016* (2016), https://mda.mil/global/documents/pdf/osbp_16conf_GMD_Next_Follow_On_Barrow.pdf.

GMD's efficiency accounted for 10 successes and eight failures from 1999 to 2017.[195] Aegis interceptors hit the targets in 35 out of 42 tests from 2002 to 2017 (effectively in 83.3%), including 29 out of 36 successful intercepts of SM-3, four out of four SM-2 Block IV interceptions and two out of two SM-6 Dual I tests. The THAAD system was successful in all 13 tests from 2006 to 2015.[196] In all elements of BMDS (including PAC-3, THAAD, Aegis, and GMD), the hit-to-kill ratio accounted for 81.5% (i.e., 75 successes in 92 tests); without PAC-3, the overall efficiency is lower, at ca. 79.4% (50 successful interceptions in 63 tests).[197]

According to Dean Wilkening's model of the Bernoulli binomial distribution to analyze BMD effectiveness in terms of probability of interception of incoming warheads, the following equation can be used: (binomial coefficient "n choose k, n over k", i.e. ${}_nC_k$, is written here as ${}_wC_x$ i.e. "W over x", bullet operator represents multiplication symbol[198])

$$P(x) = {}_wC_x \cdot q^x \cdot (1-q)^{W-x} = {}_wC_x \cdot (1-K_W)^x \cdot (K_W)^{W-x} = \{W!/[x! \cdot (W-x)!]\} \cdot (1-K_W)^x \cdot K_W^{W-x}$$

where $P(x)$ is the probability of defeating the missile defense by x number of incoming warheads, q is a probability that a warhead would defeat BMD, K_W is the probability of interception of an incoming warhead by a single interceptor missile ($K_W = 1 - q$), W is the number of incoming warheads. In a scenario of a leak-proof defense (intercepting all incoming warheads), $x = 0$ and $P(0) = (K_W)^W$.[199]

195   MDA, *Ballistic Missile Defense Intercept Flight Test Record (as of May 30, 2017)* (2017), https://www.mda.mil/global/documents/pdf/testrecord.pdf.

196   MDA, *Ballistic Missile Defense Intercept Flight Test Record (as of May 30, 2017)*; MDA, *Aegis Ballistic Missile Defense Testing* (2017) https://www.mda.mil/global/documents/pdf/aegis_tests.pdf.

197   PAC-3 was 86% effective in 25 out of 29 tests. MDA, *Ballistic Missile Defense Intercept Flight Test Record (as of May 30, 2017)*.

198   On writing binomial combinations see MathBits, Binomial Theorem https://mathbits.com/MathBits/TISection/Algebra2/binomialtheorem.htm

      Marco Taboga, Binomial coefficient, StatLect, https://www.statlect.com/glossary/binomial-coefficient

199   Dean Wilkening, "A Simple Model for Calculating Ballistic Missile Defense Effectiveness," *Science & Global Security* 8, no. 2 (1999): 187–188, http://scienceandglobalsecurity.org/archive/sgs08wilkening.pdf.

Table 7. Probability of defeating the BMD by a given number (from 0 to 5) of incoming warheads when single interception probability equals 88% and 5 warheads are attacking (Bernoulli trial)

x	0	1	2	3	4	5
P(x)	0.528	0.360	0.098	0.013	0.0009	0.00002

Source: own counting (using Microsoft Excel) according to the equation (bullet operator represents multiplication symbol)

$$P(x) = \{W!/[x! \cdot (W-x)!]\} \cdot (1 - K_w)^x \cdot K_w^{W-x}$$

based on Dean Wilkening's model (Bernoulli distribution).

Wilkening, 187-188. See also MDA, *Ballistic Missile Defense Intercept Flight Test Record.*

Chart 2. Probability of defeating the BMD by a given number (from 0 to 5) of incoming warheads when single interception probability equals 88% and 5 warheads are attacking (Bernoulli trial)

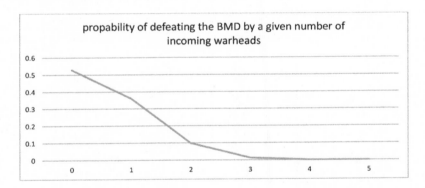

Source: own counting (using Microsoft Excel) according to the equation (bullet operator represents multiplication symbol)

$$P(x) = \{W!/[x! \cdot (W-x)!]\} \cdot (1 - K_w)^x \cdot K_w^{W-x}$$

based on Dean Wilkening's model (Bernoulli distribution)

Wilkening, 187-188. See also MDA, *Ballistic Missile Defense Intercept Flight Test Record.*

A Union of Concerned Scientists model concerning the probability of defeating the BMD by 1 or more missiles equaled

$$1 - P(0) = 1 - p^n$$

where n is the number of incoming warheads and p is the probability of a single inceptor missile intercepting an incoming warhead.[200]

Following Lewis, the effectiveness of a layered BMD (in terms of the introduction of more than one interceptor against an incoming warhead) can be measured by an equation

$$P(0) = 1 - (1 - p)^n$$

where p is the probability of a single interception and n is the amount of interceptors used against an incoming warhead.[201]

Table 8. Leak-proof interception probabilities for x (from 5 to 30) attacking warheads and n additional interceptors (from 2 to 10) against every single incoming warhead when Single Interception Kill Probability (SSKP) = 88%.

x\n	2	3	4	5	6	7	8	9	10
5	0.777	0.895	0.950	0.977	0.989	0.995	0.998	0.999	0.999
6	0.713	0.846	0.918	0.956	0.976	0.987	0.993	0.996	0.998
7	0.650	0.793	0.878	0.928	0.957	0.975	0.985	0.991	0.995
8	0.590	0.737	0.832	0.892	0.931	0.956	0.972	0.982	0.988
9	0.533	0.681	0.782	0.851	0.898	0.930	0.952	0.967	0.978
10	0.479	0.624	0.729	0.804	0.859	0.898	0.927	0.947	0.962
11	0.430	0.570	0.675	0.755	0.815	0.860	0.895	0.920	0.940
12	0.385	0.518	0.622	0.703	0.767	0.817	0.857	0.888	0.912
13	0.344	0.468	0.569	0.651	0.717	0.771	0.814	0.850	0.878
14	0.306	0.422	0.519	0.599	0.666	0.722	0.768	0.807	0.839
15	0.272	0.379	0.471	0.548	0.615	0.671	0.720	0.761	0.796
16	0.242	0.340	0.425	0.500	0.564	0.621	0.670	0.712	0.750
17	0.215	0.304	0.383	0.453	0.516	0.571	0.620	0.663	0.701
18	0.190	0.271	0.344	0.410	0.469	0.522	0.570	0.613	0.652

---

200 Laura Grego, George N. Lewis, and David Wright, *Shielded from Oversight. The Disastrous US Approach to Strategic Missile Defense. Appendix 8* (Cambridge, Massachusetts, 2016), 1, 5, http://www.ucsusa.org/sites/default/files/attach/2016/07/Shielded-from-Oversight-appendix-8.pdf; Wilkening, A Simple Model for Calculating Ballistic Missile Defense Effectiveness," 187–188.

201 George N. Lewis, "Technical Controversy. Can Missile Defense Work?" in *Regional Missile Defense from a Global Perspective*, ed. by Catherine McArdle Kelleher and Peter Dombrowski, Kindle (Stanford: Stanford University Press, 2015), 1418-1438.

19	0.169	0.242	0.309	0.370	0.425	0.476	0.522	0.564	0.603
20	0.149	0.215	0.276	0.332	0.384	0.432	0.476	0.516	0.554
21	0.132	0.191	0.246	0.298	0.346	0.390	0.432	0.471	0.507
22	0.117	0.170	0.219	0.266	0.310	0.352	0.391	0.427	0.462
23	0.103	0.150	0.195	0.238	0.278	0.316	0.352	0.387	0.419
24	0.091	0.133	0.173	0.212	0.249	0.284	0.317	0.349	0.379
25	0.080	0.118	0.154	0.189	0.222	0.254	0.284	0.313	0.342
26	0.071	0.104	0.136	0.168	0.198	0.226	0.254	0.281	0.307
27	0.062	0.092	0.121	0.149	0.176	0.202	0.227	0.252	0.275
28	0.055	0.081	0.107	0.132	0.156	0.180	0.203	0.225	0.246
29	0.048	0.072	0.095	0.117	0.139	0.160	0.180	0.200	0.220
30	0.043	0.063	0.084	<u>0.103</u>	0.123	0.142	0.160	0.178	0.196

Source: own counting (using Microsoft Excel) according to the equation (bullet operator represents multiplication symbol)

$$P(x) = \{W!/[x! \cdot (W - x)!]\} \cdot (1 - K_w)^x \cdot K_w^{W-x}$$

based on Wilkening's model (Bernoulli distribution), and

$$P(0) = 1 - (1 - p)^n$$

based on G. Lewis's model, for p counted for a leak-proof defense in the cases of attacks of 5, 6, 7, ... 30 incoming warheads (in Bernoulli distribution).

Wilkening, 187-188. G. Lewis. See also MDA, *Ballistic Missile Defense Intercept Flight Test Record.*

Chart 3. Leak-proof interception probabilities for x (from 5 to 30) attacking warheads and n additional interceptors (from 2 to 10) against every single incoming warhead when SSKP = 88%.

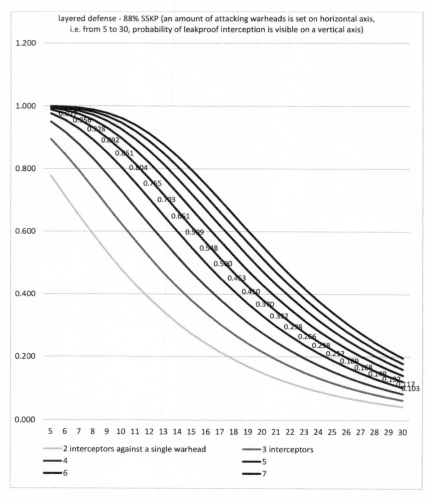

Source: own counting (using Microsoft Excel) according to the equation (bullet operator represents multiplication symbol)

$$P(x) = \{W!/[x! \cdot (W-x)!]\} \cdot (1 - K_w)^x \cdot K_w^{W-x}$$

based on Wilkening's model (Bernoulli distribution), and

$$P(0) = 1 - (1 - p)^n$$

based on G. Lewis's model, for p counted for a leak-proof defense in the cases of attacks of 5, 6, 7, ... 30 incoming warheads (in Bernoulli distribution). Wilkening, 187-188. G. Lewis. See also MDA, *Ballistic Missile Defense Intercept Flight Test Record.*

Table 9. Probability of defeating the BMD by a given number (from 0 to 5) of incoming warheads when single interception probability equals 94% and 5 warheads are attacking (Bernoulli trial).

x	0	1	2	3	4	5
P(x)	0.734	0.234	0.030	0.002	0.000	0.000

Source: own counting (using Microsoft Excel) according to the equation (bullet operator represents multiplication symbol)

$$P(x) = \{W! / [x! \cdot (W - x)!]\} \cdot (1 - K_w)^x \cdot K_w^{W-x}$$

based on Wilkening's model (Bernoulli distribution). Wilkening, 187-188. See also MDA, *Ballistic Missile Defense Intercept Flight Test Record*.

Chart 4. Probability of defeating the BMD by a given number (from 0 to 5) of incoming warheads when single interception probability equals 94% and 5 warheads are attacking (Bernoulli trial).

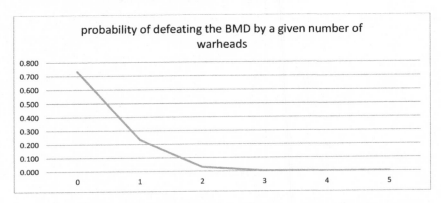

Source: own counting (using Microsoft Excel) according to the equation (bullet operator represents multiplication symbol)

$$P(x) = \{W! / [x! \cdot (W - x)!]\} \cdot (1 - K_w)^x \cdot K_w^{W-x}$$

based on Wilkening's model (Bernoulli distribution). Wilkening, 187-188. See also MDA, *Ballistic Missile Defense Intercept Flight Test Record*.

Table 10. Leak-proof interception probabilities for x (from 5 to 30) attacking warheads and n additional interceptors (from 2 to 10) against every single incoming warhead (single interception probability = 94%).

x\n	2	3	4	5	6	7	8	9	10
5	0.929	0.981	0.995	0.999	1.000	1.000	1.000	1.000	1.000
6	0.904	0.970	0.991	0.997	0.999	1.000	1.000	1.000	1.000
7	0.876	0.957	0.985	0.995	0.998	0.999	1.000	1.000	1.000
8	0.848	0.940	0.977	0.991	0.996	0.999	0.999	1.000	1.000
9	0.818	0.922	0.967	0.986	0.994	0.997	0.999	1.000	1.000
10	0.787	0.902	0.955	0.979	0.990	0.996	0.998	0.999	1.000
11	0.756	0.880	0.941	0.971	0.986	0.993	0.996	0.998	0.999
12	0.725	0.856	0.925	0.960	0.979	0.989	0.994	0.997	0.998
13	0.695	0.831	0.907	0.948	0.972	0.984	0.991	0.995	0.997
14	0.664	0.805	0.887	0.935	0.962	0.978	0.987	0.993	0.996
15	0.634	0.779	0.866	0.919	0.951	0.970	0.982	0.989	0.993
16	0.605	0.752	0.844	0.902	0.938	0.961	0.976	0.985	0.990
17	0.577	0.724	0.821	0.883	0.924	0.951	0.968	0.979	0.986
18	0.549	0.697	0.796	0.863	0.908	0.938	0.959	0.972	0.981
19	0.522	0.670	0.772	0.842	0.891	0.924	0.948	0.964	0.975
20	0.496	0.642	0.746	0.820	0.872	0.909	0.936	0.954	0.967
21	0.471	0.615	0.720	0.796	0.852	0.892	0.922	0.943	0.959
22	0.447	0.589	0.694	0.773	0.831	0.874	0.906	0.930	0.948
23	0.424	0.563	0.668	0.748	0.809	0.855	0.890	0.916	0.937
24	0.402	0.537	0.642	0.723	0.786	0.834	0.872	0.901	0.923
25	0.380	0.512	0.616	0.698	0.762	0.813	0.853	0.884	0.909
26	0.360	0.488	0.591	0.673	0.738	0.791	0.832	0.866	0.893
27	0.341	0.465	0.566	0.647	0.714	0.768	0.811	0.847	0.876
28	0.322	0.442	0.541	0.622	0.689	0.744	0.789	0.826	0.857
29	0.305	0.420	0.517	0.597	0.664	0.720	0.766	0.805	0.838
30	0.288	0.399	0.493	<u>0.572</u>	0.639	0.696	0.743	0.783	0.817

Source: own counting (using Microsoft Excel) according to the equation (bullet operator represents multiplication symbol)

$$P(x) = \{W!/[x! \cdot (W - x)!]\} \cdot (1 - K_W)^x \cdot K_W^{W-x}$$

based on Wilkening's model (Bernoulli distribution), and

$$P(0) = 1 - (1 - p)^n$$

based on G. Lewis's model, for p counted for a leak-proof defense in the cases of attacks of 5, 6, 7, ... 30 incoming warheads (in Bernoulli distribution). Wilkening, 187-188. G. Lewis. See also MDA, *Ballistic Missile Defense Intercept Flight Test Record*.

Chart 5. Leak-proof interception probabilities for x (from 5 to 30) attacking warheads and n additional interceptors (from 2 to 10) against every single incoming warhead when SSKP = 94%.

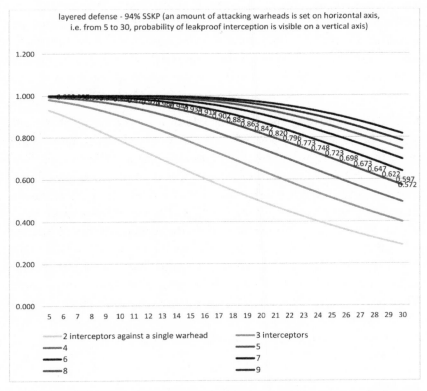

Source: own counting (using Microsoft Excel) according to the equation (bullet operator represents multiplication symbol)

$$P(x) = \{W!/[x! \cdot (W-x)!]\} \cdot (1 - K_W)^x \cdot K_W^{W-x}$$

based on Wilkening's model (Bernoulli distribution), and

$$P(0) = 1 - (1 - p)^n$$

based on G. Lewis's model, for p counted for a leak-proof defense in the cases of attacks of 5, 6, 7, ... 30 incoming warheads (in Bernoulli distribution). Wilkening, 187-188. G. Lewis. See also MDA, *Ballistic Missile Defense Intercept Flight Test Record*.

The tables above explain the perspectives of using additional interceptors against incoming warheads in the case of a salvo interception scenario. US forces used similar measures (to increase PAC batteries' effectiveness) during the 1990-1991 Gulf War, when Saddam Hussein's regime used ballistic missiles against Saudi Arabia and Israel. As Victoria Samson noted, on February 25, 1991, three or more Patriot missiles launched in Tel Aviv fell on the ground (and exploded) rather than reaching their targets, causing one death and forty-four injuries. That record, among many others, proved that the PAC-2 of the time was truly unready for high performance combat.[202] The results of the US engagement at the time (when PAC-2 performance had yet to be improved) were mixed; using even three interceptors against a single attacking warhead could not secure a successful interception.[203]

Both SSKP improvements and using additional interceptors changes the odds of BMD against a salvo of incoming warheads much more significantly than the plain arithmetical comparison of a single shot probability would show. The analysis of the example presented above (Table 10, Chart 5) proved that the SSKP increased from 88% to 94% (while constituting a plain increase of 6 percentage points could give more than 5 times increased interception efficiency in the scenario of using 5 interceptors against each of the 30 attacking warheads). In the 88% reliable single shot interception, using 5 interceptors against each of the 30 attacking warheads gave only ca. a 10% probability of a leak-proof interception. When SSKP grows to 94%, the leak-proof interception chances in the 30 incoming warheads scenario account for more than 57% when using 5 interceptors against each of the attacking warheads.

---

202   Victoria Samson, *American Missile Defense. Guide to the Issues* (Santa Barbara: Praeger, 2010), 101.

203   Steven Hildreth, *Evaluation of US Army Assessment of Patriot Antitactical Missile Effectiveness in the War Against Iraq* (Washington, DC, 1992), 2, http://www.dtic.mil/gettr-doc/pdf?AD=ADA344634; Robert Shuey, *Theater Missile Defense: Issues for Congress* (Washington, DC, 2001), 1–2, http://www.au.af.mil/au/awc/awcgate/crs/ib98028.pdf; Jeremiah Sullivan and others, "Technical Debate over Patriot Performance in the Gulf War," *Science & Global Security*, 8 (1999): 42, 55; Theodore Postol and George N. Lewis, "Video Evidence on the Effectiveness of Patriot during the 1991 Gulf War," *Science & Global Security* 4 (1993): 34; Theodore Postol, *Optical Evidence Indicating Patriot High Miss Rates during the Gulf War* (2004), http://ee162.caltech.edu/notes/postol.pdf.

Summary of the Chapter

The New Cold War environment (an increased likelihood of armed conflict between NATO and Russia, which is capable of attacking Poland with Iskander nuclear short-range missiles), as well as the severe North Korean ballistic-thermonuclear crisis (and the deployments of THAAD BMD next to Patriot in South Korea), drew attention to the present-day efficiency of US-developed missile defense systems. A careful analysis of the PAC-3 effectiveness (86%) shows that it needs additional backing and investments to provide for a leak-proof scenario in the case of a possible attack of more than twenty ballistic missiles, even using a few interceptors against the attacking warheads (as in the 1990-1991 Gulf War).

It is therefore more advisable in the time of PAC-3 purchase negotiated by the Polish government to take a deeper look at the performance of particular missile configurations (including Missile Segment Enhancement) for the needs of the Polish armed forces who are preparing for the worst-case scenario of an attack of nuclear-tipped short range Russian Iskander missiles against Polish soft targets (cities) from the Kaliningrad circle.

CHAPTER III

Trump's Global Advocacy: Opportunities, Chances, Qualified Perspectives on the Defense and Foreign Policy Choices

1. Threat to INF treaty

Since 2014, the US has claimed that Russia is violating the treaty by flight tests of GLCM SSC-8 missile system (designated by Russia as 9M729), developed by Novator Design Bureau and Titan Central Design Bureau; accordingly, the US sought resolution through INF Special Verification Commission (SVC).[204] Russian claims on US INF noncompliance referred to Aegis Ashore, ballistic target missiles, and UAVs.[205]

On October 20, 2018, Trump declared INF withdrawal possible.[206] Among the supporters of such decision was Polish president Andrzej Duda.[207]

---

204 US Department of State, *INF Treaty: At a Glance, Fact Sheet*, 2017, https://www. state.gov/inf-treaty-at-a-glance/; US Department of State, *US Response to the Russian Federation's INF Treaty Violation: Integrated Strategy*, 2017, https://www.state.gov /u-s-response-to-the-russian-federations-inf-treaty-violation-integrated-strategy/; Michael R. Pompeo, *US Intent To Withdraw from the INF Treaty*, 2019, https:// www.state.gov/u-s-intent-to-withdraw-from-the-inf-treaty-february-2-2019/; US Department of State, *Adherence to and Compliance with Arms Control, Nonproliferation, and Disarmament Agreements and Commitments* (2018), 12, https://www.state. gov/documents/organization/280774.pdf; US Department of State, *Diplomacy in Action, Intermediate-Range Nuclear Forces (INF) Treaty* (2018), https://www.state. gov/t/avc/inf/index.htm.

205 US Department of State, *Refuting Russian Allegations of US Noncompliance with the INF Treaty, Fact Sheet* https://www.state.gov/refuting-russian-allegations-of-u-s-noncompliance-with-the-inf-treaty/.

206 US Department of State, *Diplomacy in Action, Intermediate-Range Nuclear Forces (INF) Treaty*; The White House, *Remarks by President Trump Before Air Force One Departure, October 20, 2018.*

207 Stratfor, *Poland: President Supports US Departure From Nuclear Proliferation Treaty, October 26, 2018* (2018), https://worldview.stratfor.com/situation-report/po-land-president-supports-us-departure-nuclear-proliferation-treaty; Monika Sierad-ka, "Poland Supports US Withdrawal from INF," *Deutsche Welle* (October 25, 2018), https://www.dw.com/en/poland-supports-us-withdrawal-from-inf/a-46049028; Conf. Stratfor, *Russia: European Countries Will Be Targeted If They Host US Nuclear Missiles, Putin Says*, 2018, https://worldview.stratfor.com/situation-report/russia-european-countries-will-be-targeted-if-they-host-us-nuclear-missiles-putin; Stratfor, *Russia: UN Draft Resolution to Preserve INF Treaty*, 2018, https://world

Apart from 9M729, the controversy of INF withdrawal referred to ICBM RS-26 Rubezh of ranges of Intermediate Range Ballistic Missiles (IRBM s).[208]

As *The Economist* assessed Poland and Baltic states, who were afraid of Russian invasion and occupation (reaching beyond "new cold war" scenarios that had been escalating since the Russian invasion of Ukraine in 2014); they could be interested in possible deployments of new US IRBMs developed after the abolishment of the INF treaty, but such developments are not likely to occur soon due to technological delays causes by the INF regime.[209] SSC-8, a ground-launched derivative of 3M14 naval cruise missile, was used in late 2017 by two battalions and included 36 missiles altogether with a 2500 km range (naval 3M14 was used in Syria in 2015).[210]

The Nuclear Posture Review (NPR) of 2018 stated that Russia's decision to retain numerous non-strategic nuclear weapons despite the US reductions under the START framework, Russian investments in nuclear forces (strategic and nonstrategic) combined with its military strategies based on nuclear escalation as a condition of success and, importantly, the annexation of Crimea accompanied by nuclear threats against US allies proved that Russia had turned toward a competitive path in relations with the US in terms of power politics on international stage (a "return to Great Power competition").[211] Deterrence policy would remain tailored

---

view.stratfor.com/situation-report/russia-un-draft-resolution-preserve-inf-treaty; Michelle Nichols, "Russia, US Clash over INF Arms Treaty at United Nations," *Reuters* (October 26, 2018), https://www.reuters.com/article/us-usa-nuclear-russia-un/russia-us-clash-over-inf-arms-treaty-at-united-nations-idUSKCN1N02FI; Radio Free Europe/ Radio Liberty (RFERL), "Russia Fails In Bid To Schedule UN Vote On Nuclear Treaty Spurned By Trump," *RFERL* (October 27, 2018), https://www.rferl.org/a/russia-fails-bid-schedule-un-vote-nuclear-treaty-inf-spurned-by-trump/29566690.html.

208   The Economist, "What is the INF treaty?" (October 26, 2018), https://www.economist.com/the-economist-explains/2018/10/26/what-is-the-inf-treaty.

209   The Economist, "America Tears up an Arms Treaty and Harms Itself" (October 2018), https://www.economist.com/united-states/2018/10/25/america-tears-up-an-arms-treaty-and-harms-itself.

210   The Economist, "Russia Is Undermining a Symbol of Cold War Diplomacy" (December 2017), https://www.economist.com/europe/2017/12/09/russia-is-undermining-a-symbol-of-cold-war-diplomacy.

211   Jim Mattis, *Nuclear Posture Review. Preface* (2018), 1, https://www.defense.gov/News/Special-Reports/0218_npr/, https://media.defense.gov/2018/Feb/02/2001872

to respond flexibly to a broad range of potential adversaries by moderniz-ing nuclear options and integrating nuclear and non-nuclear forces.[212] The 2018 US strategic triad was composed of:

- 14 Ohio-class SSBN (to be replaced by Columbia-class for the next decades),

- 400 single-warhead Minuteman III ICBM in underground silos (in service until 2029, when Ground-Based Strategic Deterrent would replace those),

- 46 B-52H bombers (with Air-Launched Cruise Missile, which is outdated and to be replaced by the Long-Range Stand-Off cruise missile) and 20 B-2A nuclear capable bombers (to be sup-plemented and replaced by the new B-21 Raider since the mid-2020s).[213]

US forces also included nuclear non-strategic gravity bombs B61 deliv-ered by F-15E and US allies' aircraft, preparing for the introduction of the F-35 to replace the currently used dual-capable aircrafts.[214] Among the important challenges mentioned by the NPR are the Russian violation of the INF treaty and other arms control obligations and its unwillingness to negotiate reductions in non-strategic arms, noting that the New START was in force through 2021 and could be prolonged to 2026.[215]

NPR 2018 stressed that Russia and China followed the opposite path to the US reduction of nuclear forces, instead expanding such arsenals, while at the same time North Korea's nuclear armaments violated UN Security Council resolutions.[216] Among the Russian nuclear delivery im-

---

886/-1/-1/1/2018-NUCLEAR-POSTURE-REVIEW-FINAL-REPORT.PDF; Conf. Donald J. Trump, *Statement by President Donald J. Trump on the Nuclear Posture Review, February 2, 2018* (2018), https://www.whitehouse.gov/briefings-statements/statement-president-donald-j-trump-nuclear-posture-review/.

212 US Department of Defense (NPR), *Nuclear Posture Review. Executive Summary* (2018), vii–viii, https://media.defense.gov/2018/Feb/02/2001872886/-1/-1/1/2018-NUCLEAR-POSTURE-REVIEW-FINAL-REPORT.PDF.

213 US Department of Defense (NPR), *Nuclear Posture Review. Executive Summary*, x.

214 US Department of Defense (NPR), *Nuclear Posture Review. Executive Summary*, x.

215 US Department of Defense (NPR), *Nuclear Posture Review. Executive Summary*, xvii.

216 US Department of Defense (NPR), *Nuclear Posture Review* (2018), 2–3, https://media.defense.gov/2018/Feb/02/2001872886/-1/-1/1/2018-NUCLEAR-

provements since 2010, NPR 2018 emphasized the fielding of:

- SS-27 Mod 2 ICBM,
- SSC-08 GLCM,
- Borei SSBN,
- SS-N-32 SLBM,
- SS-n-30 SLCM,
- Yason SSGN,
- Kh-102 ALCM,

and the development of:

- SS-X-28 ICBM,
- SS-X-29 ICBM,
- SS-19 Mod-X-4 ICBM,
- Status-6 AUV,
- Kh-32 ALCM,
- PAK-DA bomber
- PAK-FA DCA.[217]

Chinese improvements to their nuclear force since 2010 included the deployments of:

- CSS-4 Mod 2/3 ICBM,
- CSS-10 Mod ½ ICBM,
- CSS-5 Mod 6 MRBM,

POSTURE-REVIEW-FINAL-REPORT.PDF.

217   US Department of Defense (NPR), *Nuclear Posture Review*, 8; Dave Majumdar, "Russia's New PAK-DA Stealth Bomber Just Took a Big Step Forward," *The National Interest* (March 2017), http://nationalinterest.org/blog/the-buzz/russias-new-pak-da-stealth-bomber-just-took-big-step-forward-19656; Dave Majumdar, "The Big Problem Russia's New PAK-FA Stealth Fighter and America's F-22 Share," *The National Interest* (July 2017), http://nationalinterest.org/blog/the-buzz/the-big-problem-russias-new-pak-fa-stealth-fighter-americas-21654; Dave Majumdar, "Just How Much of a Threat Is Russia's Status-6 Nuclear Torpedo?" *The National Interest* (January 2018), http://nationalinterest.org/blog/the-buzz/just-how-much-threat-russias-status-6-nuclear-torpedo-24094; US Navy, *Fact File. Guided Missile Submarines - SSGN* (2019), https://www.navy.mil/navydata/fact_display.asp?cid=4100&ct=4&tid=300.

- Type 094 SSBN
- JL-2 SLBM,

and the development of:

- DF-26 IRBM,
- CSS-X-20 ICBM,
- Type 096 SSBN,
- JL-3 SLBM.[218]

North Korean investments since 2010 included, according to NPR 2018, the deployment of:

- Scud C SRBM,
- ER Scud MRBM,
- Nodong MRBM,
- Musudan IRBM,

and research and development (R&D) on:

- Hwasong-12 IRBM,
- Hwasong-14 ICBM,
- Pukguksong-2 MRBM,
- Hwaong-13 ICBM,
- Hwasong-15 ICBM,
- Gorae SSB,
- Pukguksong-1 SLBM.[219]

NPR 2018 stressed that Russia retained ca. 2000 non-strategic nuclear weapons and various delivery vehicles (while the US possessed only B61 gravity bombs).[220] According to SIPRI, the US stored 150 B61 bombs on its territory in 2017, while 150 more were kept by NATO allies.[221]

---

218 US Department of Defense (NPR), *Nuclear Posture Review*, 8.

219 US Department of Defense (NPR), *Nuclear Posture Review*, 8.

220 A couple hundred. US Department of Defense (NPR), *Nuclear Posture Review*, 53.

221 Shannon N. Kile and Hans M. Kristensen, *Trends in World Nuclear Forces* (2017), 2, https://www.sipri.org/sites/default/files/2017-06/fs_1707_wnf.pdf.

According to SIPRI, the US deployed 1800 warheads (and stored 2200, and retired 2800), while Russia deployed 1950 and stored 2350 warheads (and retired 2700).[222]

In Trump's 2018 State of the Union Address, Russia and China were named US rivals, challenging US interests, economy, and values.[223] Trump declared as key issues the modernization of the nuclear arsenal, countering the North Korean threat, sanctions against socialist regimes of Cuba and Venezuela, support for Iranians struggling against their corrupt regime, and combating ISIS and Al-Qaeda.[224] In the area of internal affairs, Trump set as priorities infrastructure investments, tax cuts, combating organized crime and drugs trading, immigration control to protect from criminal gangs moving in through the border, grace for 1.8 million illegal immigrants who came to the US at a young age, and a path to citizenship.[225]

The NSS of December 2017 selected North Korea's rogue regime and ISIS as the main threats.[226] NSS 2017 was based on four pillars:

1. protecting Americans, their homeland and their way of life (by defending them from WMD threats, jihadists, and international crime, a.o.),

2. promoting the prosperity of Americans by strengthening the domestic economic environment, justified trade relations, R&D, innovations, and "energy dominance,"

3. fighting to keep international peace by means of the Reaganite "peace through strength" motto,

4. advancing American influence worldwide.[227]

---

222 Kile and Kristensen, *Trends in World Nuclear Forces*, 2.

223 Donald J. Trump, *State of the Union Address* (2018), https://www.whitehouse.gov/briefings-statements/remarks-president-trump-state-union-address/.

224 Trump, *State of the Union Address*.

225 Trump, *State of the Union Address*.

226 The White House, *National Security Strategy (NSS) of the United States of America. Introduction of Donald J. Trump* (2017), 1, https://www.whitehouse.gov/wp-content/uploads/2017/12/NSS-Final-12-18-2017-0905.pdf.

227 The White House (NSS 2017), *National Security Strategy (NSS) of the United States*

The foremost threats depicted in the December 2017 US NSS were related to the North Korean attempts to threaten Americans by using nuclear WMD against the US, Iranian Muslim terrorist connections, and ISIS or Al-Qaeda jihadists.[228] The Trump administration's strategy of December 2017 clearly stated that Russia was trying to undermine US global influence, seeing NATO and the EU as dangers and increasing its military outreach, while maintaining its nuclear force, posing an "existential threat" to the US, and creating a new area of instability in Eurasia.[229]

A certain innovation (in the context of previous US national security strategies[230] is the regional focus of the tailored US engagements, adapting to the changing regional balance of power, centered on three key regions:

- Indo-Pacific, where the Trump administration saw important geopolitical rivalry between "the free world" and oppressive political regimes, North Korea's rapidly growing threat, and increased Chinese military capacities,

- Europe, threatened by Russian military aggression (particularly after Russia's wars against Georgia and Ukraine) and under growing Chinese "strategic" influence, while facing a severe danger from jihadist campaigns,

- the Middle East, seen as a region where neither democracy promotion nor disengagement could bring closer the US vision of non-dominance of any hostile power and stabilization of energy markets and still affected by jihadists.[231]

---

of America (2017), v–vi, https://www.whithouse.gov/wp-content/uploads/2017/12/NSS-Final-12-18-2017-0905.pdf.

228 In this context, the strategy stressed the importance of disrupting the terrorist networks' WMD powers internationally. The White House (NSS 2017), 7–8, 10.

229 The White House (NSS 2017), 25–26.

230 On NSS 1987-2006, see the Historical Office (Office of the Secretary of Defense), "National Security Strategy" (2019), https://history.defense.gov/Historical-Sources/National-Security-Strategy/; The White House (NSS 2010), *National Security Strategy (NSS), May 2010* (2010), https://obamawhitehouse.archives.gov/sites/default/files/rss_viewer/national_security_strategy.pdf; the White House (NSS 2015), *National Security Strategy (NSS), February 2015* (2015), https://obamawhitehouse.archives.gov/sites/default/files/docs/2015_national_security_strategy_2.pdf.

231 The White House (NSS 2017), 45–49.

Trump as a Reagan follower used for campaign purposes Reagan's 1980 "peace through strength" motto, leading to his key objective to "Make America Strong Again," resembling Reagan's inaugural goal (1981) of reaching "greater strength around the world."[232]

The US and Polish presidents discussed the US base in Poland ("Fort Trump") during their meeting in the White House on September 18, 2018 (in the context of a US-Polish strategic partnership).[233] Among the priority issues for Trump remained a new US deal with Iran.[234] In Poland July 2017, Trump declared that Three Seas Summit Initiative was supported by the US.[235]

2. Sanctions Against North Korean WMD Program

a) The US sanctions against North Korean nuclear program

Until the 2018 détente, the North Korean nuclear weapons program remained an example of failed international non-proliferation regime and sanctions policies. Since the introduction of UN sanctions against the Democratic People's Republic of Korea (DPRK) due to its 1950 invasion against its Southern neighbor,[236] the US government maintained restric-

---

232 Ronald Reagan, *A Strategy for Peace in the 80s, October 10, 1980* (1980), https://www. reaganlibrary.gov/major-speeches-index/10-archives/reference/12-10-19-80; Ronald Reagan, *Inaugural Address, January 20, 1981* (1981), https://www.reaganlibrary. archives.gov/archives/speeches/1981/12081a.htm; Donald J. Trump, "Donald J. Trump," https://www.donaldjtrump.com/.

233 The White House, *Remarks by President Trump and President Duda of the Republic of Poland in Joint Press Conference, September 18, 2018*; The White House, *Joint Statement of President Donald J. Trump of the United States of America and Chairman Kim Jong Un of the Democratic People's Republic of Korea at the Singapore Summit, June 12, 2018*; Stratfor, *Stuck Between the US and the EU, Poland Explores Its Options, July 10, 2018* (2018), https://worldview.stratfor.com/article/stuck-between-us-and-eu-poland-explores-its-options; Stratfor, *Poland: Warsaw's Push for a US Base Faces and Uphill Climb, September 19, 2018* (2018), https://worldview.stratfor.com/article/poland-warsaw-tries-win-washington-approval-us-base-polish-soil.

234 Stratfor, *US Diplomat Floats the Idea of a Treaty With Iran, September 19, 2018* (2018), https://worldview.stratfor.com/article/us-diplomat-floats-idea-treaty-iran-nuclear-deal.

235 Donald J. Trump, *Remarks by President Trump to the People of Poland, July 6, 2017* (2017),https://www.whitehouse.gov/briefings-statements/remarks-president-trump-people-poland/; The White House, *President Trump in Poland, July 6, 2017* (2017), https://www.whitehouse.gov/articles/president-trump-poland/.

236 Albert Esgain, "The Spectrum of Responses to Treaty Violations," *Ohio State Law Jour-*

88

tions aimed at the Pyongyang dictatorship, while the post-Cold War attempts to negotiate the revocation of punitive measures were hampered by the North Korean nuclear weapons and ballistic missiles programs.[237]

The ballistic missile threat posed by North Korea became clear after the surprising non-notified launch of a missile-propelled object near the coast of Japan on August 31, 1998.[238] The North Korean consent to a cessation of missile tests opened a path to Clinton's decision to lift the majority of US exports sanctions against Pyongyang, while the restrictions related to DPRK's engagement in international terrorism (due to the possible involvement of North Korea in a bombing of South Korean airplane on November 29, 1987) were formally kept until 2008.[239] As Rennack explained, North Korea was removed by the US from the list of countries supporting terrorism in 2008 and later reintroduced to the list (as a state sponsor of terrorism) in 2017.[240]

The six-party talks, conducted since 2003 with North Korean participation by the US, China, Japan, Russia, and South Korea, attempted without success to bring an end to the proliferation threats posed by Pyongyang through the preliminary agreement of September 2005.[241] In the Joint Statement of 2005, North Korea agreed to support non-proliferation (denuclearization) agreements in return for energy assistance.[242] In 2006, however, North Korea decided to perform multiple ballistic missile

---

nal 26, no. 1 (1965): 1–42, https://kb.osu.edu/dspace/bitstream/handle/1811/68754/OSLJ_V26N1_0001.pdf.

237   Diane Rennack, *North Korea: Legislative Basis for US Economic Sanctions* (2019), Summary, https://fas.org/sgp/crs/row/R41438.pdf; Conf. US Department of Treasury Office of Foreign Assets Control, *North Korea Sanctions Program* (2016), https://www.treasury.gov/resource-center/sanctions/Programs/Documents/nkorea.pdf.

238   UNSC, *UNSC Resolution 1695 (2006), July 15* (United Nations Security Council, 2006), http://www.un.org/en/ga/search/view_doc.asp?symbol=S/RES/1695(2006); Thomas Melito, *North Korea Sanctions* (2015), 6, http://www.gao.gov/assets/680/670170.pdf.

239   Diane Rennack, *North Korea: Economic Sanctions* (2006), 10–11, https://fas.org/sgp/crs/row/RL31696.pdf.

240   Rennack, *North Korea: Legislative Basis for US Economic Sanctions,* 6.

241   Rennack, *North Korea: Economic Sanctions,* Summary.

242   US Department of State, *Joint Statement of the Fourth Round of the Six-Party Talks, Beijing, September 19, 2005* (2005), https://www.state.gov/p/eap/regionalc15455.htm.

launches (on July 5), followed by the first nuclear weapon test on October 6, condemned by the UN Security Council.[243] In response to the North Korean test, the US Congress amended the Iran and Syria Non-proliferation Act to include the Pyongyang regime.[244] The Iran, Syria, and North Korea Nonproliferation Act (INKSNA) included a ban on trade restricted by the Nuclear Suppliers Group, the Missile Technology Control Regime, the Australia Group (biological or chemical weapons), and the Chemical Weapons Convention, as well as the Wassenaar Arrangement (dual-use goods and technologies) control measures, while prohibiting any supplies contributing to the construction of WMD and missiles (cruise or ballistic).[245]

Ruediger Frank noted that sanctions (until the year 2006) had the opposite than intended effect on the North Korean missile and nuclear program, which has not been stopped, but rather sped up.[246]

The six-party talks of 2007 provided for an agreement on the abandonment of the North Korean nuclear program conducted in Yongbyon facility, which became effective in June 2008. The US then lifted the Trading with the Enemy Act (TWEA) restrictions against North Korea in return for its willingness to cooperate on limitations of plutonium-based activities, but the cooperation ended in April 2009, with an expulsion of the international inspection team, which was followed by a second nuclear weapon test.[247] The June 26, 2008 US restrictions, i.e.,

243   UNSC, *UNSC Resolution 1695 (2006), July 15*; UNSC, *UNSC Resolution 1718 (2006), October 14* (United Nations Security Council), http://www.un.org/en/ga/search/view_doc.asp?symbol=S/RES/1718(2006); Melito, *North Korea Sanctions*, 6.

244   Melito, 6; US Congress, *North Korea Nonproliferation Act, October 13, 2006* (2006), http://uscode.house.gov/statutes/pl/109/353.pdf; US Department of State, *Iran and Syria Nonproliferation Act Sanctions* (2017), https://www.state.gov/iran-north-korea-and-syria-nonproliferation-act-sanctions/.

245   US Department of State, *Iran, Syria and North Korea Nonproliferation Act (INKSNA)* (2019), https://www.state.gov/t/isn/inksna/; Benjamin A. Gilman, *Iran Nonproliferation Act of 2000, Public Law 106-178, March 14* (US Congress, 2000), https://www.congress.gov/106/plaws/publ178/PLAW-106publ178.pdf.

246   Ruediger Frank, "The Political Economy of Sanctions against North Korea," *Asian Affairs* 30, no. 3 (2006): 34, http://www.jstor.org/stable/42704552.

247   Emma Chanlett-Avery, Ian Rinehart and Mary Nikitin, *North Korea: US Relations, Nuclear Diplomacy, and Internal Situation* (2016), 5–6, https://fas.org/sgp/crs/nuke/R41259.pdf.

the blocking of North Korean property under TWEA (and limitations of vessel registration), were explained in the context of further progress of North Korean WMD program, which was seen as truly threatening US national security.[248]

As Sang-young Rhyu and Jong-Yun Bae stressed, a firm US decision to erase North Korea from the list of terrorist-supporting countries in 2008 was sustained despite the continued North Korean nuclear weapons program.[249] In 2009, a second North Korean nuclear test proved that sanctions could not play a decisive role in stopping the proliferation program.[250]

In August 30, 2010, the US introduced extended property blocking (against restricted individuals) after North Korea's March 2010 attack against the South Korean navy ship Cheonan, which led to the death of 46 sailors.[251] US import restrictions imposed in 2011 were aimed at possible violations of the previous US and UN embargoes.[252]

Despite those efforts, in 2013, the third North Korean nuclear test confirmed the stubborn stance of the Pyongyang regime in ignoring international non-proliferations efforts.[253] In January 2015, US sanctions were broadened by an executive order related to cyber actions of North Korea and human rights abuses.[254] Unfortunately, in 2016 and 2017, the North Korean regime surprised the world again with new WMD capabilities, including hydrogen-level explosion and intercontinental missile tests.

---

248   George W. Bush, *Executive Order 13466, June 26, 2008* (2008), https://www.treasury. gov/resource-center/sanctions/Documents/nkeo.pdf.

249   Sang-young Rhyu and Jong-Yun Bae, "The Politics of Economic Sanctions against North Korea: The Bush Administration's Strategy toward a Multilateral Governance," *Pacific Focus*, 25, no.1 (2010): 113, https://doi.org/10.1111/j.1976-5118.2010. 01037.x.

250   Melito, 6.

251   Barack Obama, *Executive Order 13551, August 30, 2010* (2010), https://www. treasury.gov/resource-center/sanctions/Programs/Documents/Executive Order 13551.pdf.

252   Barack Obama, *Executive Order 13570, April 18, 2011* (2011), https://www.treasury. gov/resource-center/sanctions/Programs/Documents/04182011_nk_eo.pdf.

253   Melito, 6.

254   Barack Obama, *Executive Order 13687, January 2, 2015* (2015), https://www.treas ury.gov/resource-center/sanctions/Programs/Documents/13687.pdf.

b) The EU Sanctions Against North Korea

The sanctions against North Korea introduced by the EU implemented the provisions of the UN Security Council resolutions introduced to limit the North Korean nuclear weapon program (since 2006).[255] The common position of November 2006 implemented UNSCR 1718, responding to the North Korean nuclear test on October 9, 2006 and calling for the North Korean regime to suspend its ballistic missile program and withdraw from nuclear weapons development.[256] The UNSCR 1718 sanctions included a trade ban (including importation and exportation) on selected conventional military equipment, goods and technology supporting DPRK nuclear and ballistic missile program, and luxurious products, as well as an assets freeze and entry ban against individuals and entities engaged in North Korean ballistic and WMD programs.[257] The council regulation of 2007 defined and specified the measures set forth in the common position of 2006 due to UNSCR 1718 provisions, by introducing a list of luxurious goods, a.o.[258]

In a 2009 decision, the EU listed thirteen individuals (including heads of party-controlled defense industry bodies, as well as military, civilian, and scientific institutions engaged in prohibited activities) and four entities (Yongbyon Nuclear Research Centre and others involved) that contributed to the UN-forbidden ballistic and nuclear weapon programs.[259]

---

255 EEAS, "EU-Democratic People's Republic of Korea (DPRK) Relations" (2016), https://eeas.europa.eu/headquarters/headquarters-homepage/4003/eu-demo cratic-peoples-republic-korea-dprk-relations_en; Conf. EEAS, *Statement on the Nuclear Test in the DPRK, September 9, 2016* (2016), https://eeas.europa.eu/headquarters/headquarters-homepage/9582/statement-nuclear-test-dprk_en.

256 European Council, *Council Common Position 2006/795/CFSP, November 20, 2006* (2006), http://eur-lex.europa.eu/legal-content/EN/TXT/PDF/?uri=CELEX:32 006E0795&from=EN; UNSC, *UNSC Resolution 1718 (2006), October 14.*

257 UNSC, *UNSC Resolution 1718 (2006), October 14*; Conf. Jean-Marc de La Sablière, *Letter Dated 13 October 2006 from the Permanent Representative of France to the United Nations Addressed to the President of the Security Council, S/2006/814* (2006), https://undocs.org/S/2006/814.

258 European Council, *Council Regulation No 329/2007, March 27, 2007* (2007), http://eur-lex.europa.eu/LexUriServ/LexUriServ.do?uri=OJ:L:2007:088: 0001:0011:EN:PDF; European Council, *Council Regulation 1334/2000, June 22, 2000* (2000), http://eur-lex.europa.eu/legal-content/EN/TXT/PDF/?uri=CEL-EX:32000R1334&from=EN.

259 European Council, *Council Decision 2009/1002/CFSP, December 22, 2009* (2009),

The common position of July 2009 and the regulation of December 2009 introduced measures prescribed by UNSCR 1874, enhancing the restrictions against North Korea due to its nuclear test May 25, 2009 and the violation of UNSCR 1718 provisions by broadening military trade sanctions to include all arms deliveries and preventing member states from adding financial assistance to DPRK, apart from humanitarian purposes and development assistance connected with civilian necessities.[260]

The council's decision of 2010 provided for additional control measures against restricted financial transactions with North Korea, including monitoring DPRK's banks and enhancing the lists of individuals and entities engaged in illegal WMD and ballistic programs, by mining and defense companies, banks, and trading firms under the DPRK's regime supervision, as well as research centers.[261] In 2011, Council's decision amendment revealed new data on restricted activities of Office 39 (the Korean Workers Party fundraising entity), including the production and distribution of narcotics (methamphetamine, opium, and heroin).[262]

In a response to North Korean nuclear test on February 12, 2013, UNSCR resolution 2087 (related to DPRK's ballistic launch on December 12, 2012), and UNSCR 2094 (including reviewed restrictions related to UN-forbidden nuclear weapon program, i.e., broadened financial and travel limitations), the Council's Spring 2013 regulation and decision broadened sanctions by bonds trade prohibition, gold and precious metals embargo, further travel control, entry restrictions, and monitoring of

---

http://eur-lex.europa.eu/LexUriServ/LexUriServ.do?uri=OJ:L:2009:346:0047:0050:EN:PDF.

260 European Council, *Council Common Position 2009/573/CFSP, July 27, 2009* (2009), http://eur-lex.europa.eu/LexUriServ/LexUriServ.do?uri=OJ:L:2009:197:0111:0116:EN:PDF; UN Security Council, *Resolution 1874 (2009), June 12, 2009* (2009), http://www.un.org/en/ga/search/view_doc.asp?symbol=S/RES/1874 (2009); European Council, *Council Regulation 1283/2009, December 22, 2009* (2009), http://eur-lex.europa.eu/LexUriServ/LexUriServ.do?uri=OJ:L:2009:346:0001:0025:EN:PDF.

261 European Council, *Council Decision 2010/800/CFSP, December 22, 2010* (2010), http://eur-lex.europa.eu/LexUriServ/LexUriServ.do?uri=OJ:L:2010:341:0032:0044:EN:PDF.

262 European Council, *Council Decision 2011/860CFSP, December 19, 2011* (2011), http://eur-lex.europa.eu/legal-content/EN/TXT/PDF/?uri=CELEX:32011D0860&-from=EN.

teaching of North Korea's citizens contributing to banned development of WMD or its systems of delivery.[263]

c) Attempts to Stop North Korean WMD Program and the Rise of the 2018 Détente

The failure of international efforts to stop the North Korean nuclear weapons program was clearly visible in early 2016, when the Kim Jong Un regime ignored UN pressure and WMD restrictions by conducting another nuclear test (January 6) and ballistic launch (February 7).[264] The international community was shocked both by the fourth North Korean nuclear test and the possible thermonuclear weapon capabilities of Pyongyang.[265] In a response to those threats, UNSC 2270 broadened the 2006 arms embargo and provided measures against DPRK representatives acting to omit international sanctions.[266] Similar enhanced measures were introduced by the EU's Council's May 2016 decision.[267] The February 2016 US North Korea Sanctions and Policy Enhancement Act was justified by the ongoing threat of the North Korean nuclear weapons program and its violations of UN resolutions.[268] In March 2016, the US administration blocked the property of North Korea's government and the ruling Workers Party.[269] The sanctions were clarified by the Secretary of

---

263 European Council, *Council Decision 2013/183/CFSP, April 22, 2013* (2013), http://eur-lex.europa.eu/legal-content/EN/TXT/PDF/?uri=CELEX:32013D0183&-from=EN; UN Security Council, *Resolution 2094 (2013), March 7, 2013* (2013), http://www.un.org/en/ga/search/view_doc.asp?symbol=S/RES/2094(2013); UN Security Council, *Resolution 2087 (2013), January 22, 2013*, 2013, http://www.un.org/en/ga/search/view_doc.asp?symbol=S/RES/2087(2013); European Council, *Council Regulation 296/2013, March 26, 2013* (2013), http://eur-lex.europa.eu/LexUriServ/LexUriServ.do?uri=OJ:L:2013:090:0004:0009:EN:PDF.

264 European Council, *Council Decision 2016/849, May 27, 2016, Repealing Decision 2013/183/CFSP* (2016), http://eur-lex.europa.eu/legal-content/EN/TXT/PDF/?uri=CELEX:32016D0849&from=EN.

265 Chanlett-Avery, Rinehart and Nikitin, *North Korea*, Summary.

266 UNSC, *UNSC Resolution 2270 (2016), March 2* (2016), http://www.un.org/en/ga/search/view_doc.asp?symbol=S/RES/2270(2016).

267 European Council, *Council Decision 2016/849*.

268 Sponsor: Edward R. Royce, *Public Law 114-122, North Korea Sanctions and Policy Enhancement Act of 2016* (US Congress, 2016), https://www.congress.gov/114/plaws/publ122/PLAW-114publ122.pdf.

269 Barack Obama, *Executive Order 13722, March 15, 2016* (2016), https://www.treasury.gov/resource-center/sanctions/Programs/Documents/nk_eo_20160316.pdf.

Trade determination of March 16, 2016, involving a US property freeze of persons and entities engaged in DPRK's transport, mining, energy, and financial services.[270] Despite those measures on September 3, 2017, North Korea conducted its sixth nuclear test, claiming hydrogen capabilities.[271] Pyongyang quickly improved its ballistic forces by the July 2017 and November 2017 tests of intercontinental missiles.[272] Surprisingly, the Pyongchang Olympics in South Korea encouraged its provocative Northern neighbor to seek détente, more convenient in light of the severe international sanctions and pressure of the Trump administration. The groundbreaking summit of Kim Jong Un and Moon Jae-in on April 27, 2018 opened a path to denuclearization, strengthened by the Panmunjeom Declaration and Pyongyang's willingness to dismantle parts of its nuclear installations, i.e., the Punggye-ri test site, to be visited by US and South Korean experts.[273]

270   US Department of Treasury, *Determination Pursuant to Subsection 2(a)(i) of the Executive Order of March 16, 2016* (2016), https://www.treasury.gov/resource-center/sanctions/Programs/Documents/nk_determination_20160316.pdf.

271   Stratfor, *The History of North Korea's Nuclear Arsenal* (2017), 1–2, https://www.stratfor.com/api/v3/pdf/283911.

272   Stratfor, *The History of North Korea's Nuclear Arsenal*, 1–2.

273   Yoon Young-chan, *Senior Secretary to the President for Public Communication Yoon Young-Chan Briefs Media on North Korea's Shutdown of Nuclear Test Site And Adoption of Seoul Standard Time, April 29, 2018* (2018), http://english1.president.go.kr/activity/briefing.php; Stratfor, *The Inter-Korean Summit, in Summary* (2018), https://worldview.stratfor.com/article/inter-korean-summit-north-korea-south-us; The Korean Culture and Information Service (KOCIS), *Panmunjeom Declaration on Peace, Prosperity and Reunification of the Korean Peninsula, April 27, 2018* (2018), http://www.korea.net/Government/Current-Affairs/National-Affairs/view?subId=641&affairId=656&pageIndex=1&articleId=3412.

Regional Extended Deterrence and Missile Defense in the Twenty-First Century: Theory and Probability Analysis

1. Extended Deterrence. Theory and Practice

This chapter relates to post-Cold War changes in the scope of nuclear and conventional war threats from the perspective of extended deterrence provided by the United States. Extended deterrence may be understood as an effort to use one's deterrent capacity to protect one's allies. BMD in such a case could help to prevent the use of tactical nuclear weapons (TNW) or other WMD.

Historically, extended deterrence in the nuclear age referred to both Cold War superpowers' attempts to broaden their (mostly nuclear-based) deterrence options to safeguard their allies (mainly in Europe and Asia). US' extended deterrence during the Cold War, as Lawrence Freedman noted, relied on the state of strategic balance between superpowers, more effectively encompassing more valuable allies, which led to then-successful extended deterrence of NATO members in Europe and the failed efforts in the Southeast Asia Treaty Organization (SEATO) and Central Treaty Organization (CENTO) areas.[274] The stability-instability paradox undermined the foundations of extended deterrence, by ensuring that nuclear strategic rough equivalence prevented the escalation of conflict to the highest level, and therefore the sides were encouraged to pick a fight at a lower level, on the outskirts of influence of greater powers by offering deterrence-based protection to its weaker allies.[275] Notably, Patrick Mor-

---

274 Freedman, *Deterrence*, 35–36; Conf. US Department of State Archive, *Baghdad Pact (1955) and Central Treaty Organization (CENTO)* (2009), https://2001-2009.state.gov/r/pa/ho/time/lw/98683.htm; US Department of State Office of the Historian, *Milestones: 1953-1960. Southeast Asia Treaty Organization (SEATO), 1954* (2018), https://history.state.gov/milestones/1953-1960/seato.

275 Robert Jervis, "Deterrence, Rogue States, and the US Policy," in *Complex Deterrence. Strategy in the Global Age*, ed. by T.V. Paul, Patrick Morgan, and James Wirtz, Kindle (Chicago: Chicago University Press, 2009), 1882; Freedman, *Deterrence*, 35–36; Glenn Snyder, "The Balance of Power and the Balance of Terror," in *Balance of Power*, ed. by Paul Seabury (San Francisco: Chandler Publishing Company, 1965), 198.

gan distinguished between general deterrence (acting to discourage a potential enemy from military assault with all necessary preparations) and immediate deterrence (attempting to convince an opponent to withhold from attack under crisis conditions).[276]

A critique of the Eisenhower-era massive retaliation doctrine led to Taylor's flexible response based on increased conventional capabilities (and tactical nuclear weapons) implemented by the J. F. Kennedy administration.[277]

Limited war concepts relied on tactical use of nuclear weapons seen as a tool of regular warfare, increasing the chances of extended deterrence and encompassing the allied territory.[278]

Robert Osgood noted that the demands for enlarged conventional NATO forces in the 1960s had little support in Europe apart from Germany, which led to a continued dependency on nuclear deterrence (provided by the US), while Western European allies (especially France, which had withdrawn from NATO in 1966) were dissatisfied with a disparity between their own and US defense capacities, to the extent that made the nuclear naval Multi-Lateral Force (MLF) insufficient in light of concerns related to an overreliance on American assistance and leadership.[279] In this context, Osgood examined the impact of the introduction of the first ABM systems (USSR's around Moscow, installed since 1966, and US' 1967 decision on limited missile defense deployment) in terms of:

- an addendum to strategic forces rather than an independent defensive weapon (due to its technological limitations, far from leak-proof performance),

---

276 Patrick Morgan, *Deterrence Now* (Cambridge: Cambridge University Press, 2003), 80.

277 Taylor, *The Uncertain Trumpet*.

278 On limited war in nuclear era, see Robert E. Osgood, *Limited War Revisited* (Boulder: Westview Press, 1979); William Van Cleave and S.T. Cohen, *Tactical Nuclear Weapons. An Examination of Issues* (London: Macdonald and Jane's, 1978); Bruce Bennett, "On US Preparedness for Limited Nuclear War," in *On Limited Nuclear War in the 21ˢᵗ Century*, ed. by Jeffrey Larsen and Kerry M. Kartchner (Stanford: Stanford Security Studies, 2014).

279 Robert E. Osgood, *Alliances and American Foreign Policy*, ed. by The Johns Hopkins University Press (Baltimore, 1968), 52, 58.

- a possible enhancement of superpowers' advantage over other actors (strengthening bipolarity),

- a defensive tool that, when deployed in Europe, could likely become a source of further dissatisfaction of allies aspiring to defense independence in relation to the US (Germany and France), but would most likely be expected as an additional (equal) protection of allied territory if the US decided to deploy ABM on its soil (while indigenous investments in the production of such systems might be too expensive for European states),

- a potentially attractive alternative to a nuclear weapon program of allies, such as Japan, or (at the same time) a useful enhancement of a nuclear umbrella (also in the case of Britain).[280]

Kahn stipulated that by 1968, the nuclear threshold's breaches should be discussed in the context of defending allied territory and increasing NATO's reliability under the conditions of the still disputable prospects of enlargement of Western European conventional forces.[281] By the late 1960s, US pressure to increase conventional military capacities still seemed to act against the preferences of its European allies, afraid that their conventional units in the bipolar nuclear age would become "cannon fodder," which led to a crisis in NATO.[282] Kahn saw the late 1960s (despite the détente) investments in missile defense (kept to a low level of $1-2 billion annually, with an option to increase such spending in an emergency to $20-30 billion) as a useful confidence-building measure serving the needs of defense in case of:

- small-scale Soviet attacks,

- accidental launches,

- the aggression of minor powers.[283]

---

280 Osgood, *Alliances and American Foreign Policy*, 150–155.

281 Herman Kahn, *On Escalation. Metaphors and Scenarios* (Baltimore: Penguin Books, 1968), 122.

282 Kahn, *On Escalation*, 122.

283 According to Kahn, the benefits of ABM program could be most persuasive in the context of future development of such technology, discovered in learning-by-doing mode. Kahn, *On Escalation*, 157–158.

Missile defense, from Kahn's perspective, could also serve as a:

- psychological warfare instrument,

- technological incentive for the opponent to equip missiles with countermeasures and therefore reduce the yield of warheads,

- force improvement against warning attacks,

- cost-effective adjustment in active-passive defenses ratio.[284]

Nuclear Sharing was a form of extended deterrence based on allocations of nuclear warhead (tactical) to allies, as US nuclear weapons leases to NATO and South Korea during the Cold War.[285]

Osgood assessed that by 1979, NATO's view of its optimal position led to a vision of forward conventional defense in light of strategic parity and the tactical nuclear advantage of the Soviet Union (seeing conventional war as more preferable to Western Europe), while such a posture demanded high expenses at least.[286]

Notably, the 1979 dual track decision on Pershing II deployments and further negotiations with the USSR kept the NATO on equal grounds in confronting the Soviet SS-20 IRBMs threat.[287]

Barry Posen noted that by the end of 1980s, both security dilemma and the cohesion of nuclear and conventional capacities were among the underestimated potential weaknesses of the NATO-Soviet balance, while NATO's conventional means of defense (including a massive air presence) could be seen by the Soviet side as offensively endangering its command and control and even its strategic force survivability.[288] John Mearsheimer stressed that due to the strategic balance of the 1970s and that there were no prospects for an advantage provided by TNW,

---

284 Kahn, *On Escalation*, 157–158.

285 Julian Schofield, *Strategic Nuclear Sharing* (Houndmills: Palgrave Macmillan, 2014), 16–17, 111–112.

286 Osgood, *Limited War Revisited*, 60–61.

287 Stephen Pifer and others, *US Nuclear and Extended Deterrence: Considerations and Challenges* (2010), 6, https://www.brooings.edu/wp-content/uploads/2016/06/06_nuclear_deterrence.pdf%0A; Conf. Federation of American Scientists (FAS), *RT-21M / SS-20 Saber* (2000), https://fas.org/nuke/guide/russia/theater/rt-21m.htm.

288 Barry Posen, *Inadvertent Escalation. Conventional Wars and Nuclear Risks*, Kindle (Ithaca: Cornell University Press, 2013), 297, 348, 4951.

NATO's expectations concerning conventional deterrence grew significantly by 1983, while the Warsaw Pact retained an overall manpower advantage and quantitative superiority in tanks and artillery, partly softened by NATO's qualitative edges.[289] While examining the blitzkrieg probability for the Soviet side, Mearsheimer emphasized the threat of an assault through the Fulda Gap from the Thuringian Bulge leading to Frankfurt, where the plain terrain allowed armored units to move swiftly, with Fulda River as the only obstacle.[290]

US efforts to link BMD, enlarged by Reagan's SDI, with extended deterrence brought tactical/theatre-range results (Patriot, Aegis, and THAAD), while the ICBM-capable SBI (providing plans for boost-phase intercept) failed to materialize (though BP seemed to be close to deliver, but as the 1989 attempts proved, it remained an unsuccessful attempt of an orbital BMD).[291]

NMD and TMD of the 1990s, as Shinichi Oshigawa noted, could contribute to allies' needs for greater credibility of deterrence through damage limitation, yet those missile defense systems could still fail against Russia or China.[292]

Notably, the post-September 9, 2001 US investments increased its Aegis capacities, introduced operational THAAD, raised PAC-3 effectiveness and brought a perspective of partly reliable long-range missile defense in the form of GMD and GBI.

2. Analyses of Extended Deterrence Based on Empirical Evidence

Paul Huth distinguished the following sets of (extended) deterrence factors, contributing to the success or failure of attempts to defend an ally from an aggression, including:

- structural features, i.e., a military balance between the sides of

---

289   John J. Mearsheimer, *Conventional Deterrence*, Kindle (Ithaca: Cornell University Press, 2016), 3146, 3187-3202, 3322.

290   Mearsheimer, *Conventional Deterrence*, 3146, 3187-3202, 3322.

291   Baucom, "The Rise and Fall of Brilliant Pebbles," 143–146; Lockheed Martin, *Missile Defense*; SMDC/ARSTRAT Historical Office, 10; Reagan, *Address to the Nation*; Baucom, *US Missile Defense Program*; Cooper and others, *Missile Defense*, 2–3.

292   Shinichi Oshigawa, *Missile Defense and Deterrence* (Tokyo, 2002), 33, http://www.nids.mod.go.jp/english/publication/kiyo/pdf/bulletin_e2001_2.pdf%0A.

the conflict (attacker-protégé-defender) and the protégé's value to the defending power,

- behavioral features, encompassing the previous actions of the defender in military confrontations (firm or weak), diplomatic strategies chosen by the defending power (flexibility allowing the attacker to make peace bargain without damaging one's image), and the current positions of the defender's military forces deployed to prevent an aggression against its ally (signaling a defense commitment that could also be seen as a provocative move by a potential aggressor).[293]

Huth formalized the examination of those features in four-variable model (for probit analyses, an equivalent of multiple regression), based on an equation:

$$y = c + b_1x_1 + b_2x_2 + b_3x_3 + b_4x_4 + u_t$$

where x (indexed from 1 to 4) corresponds to the particular deterrence factors, i.e., military balance of strength between the defender, protégé, and attacker (x_1), the protégé's value to both sides of the potential conflict (x_2), bargaining choices of the defender (x_3), and his previous record in conflict mitigation (x_4). c stands for a constant and u_t presented an error term.[294] The final equation, as Huth explained, included indicators of independent variables of low multicollinearity distinguished by low r^2 values, below 0.3, while for the non-significant indicators, an estimated coefficient (b) and t-ratio was counted.[295]

In Huth's analysis of empirical data of armed conflicts (by 1980s), the attacker followed one of three predominant military strategies, i.e., setting limited aims of the invasion, attempting to seize advantage by quick offensive movements and the war of attrition, while the best deterrence strategy of the defender was:

- diplomacy based on mixed measures of firm defense of the protégé and willingness to seek compromise through bilateral gestures,

---

293 Paul Huth, *Extended Deterrence and the Prevention of War* (New Haven: Yale University Press, 1988), 34–35.

294 Huth, *Extended Deterrence*, 71–73.

295 Huth, 71–73.

- ability to counter the opponent's escalatory military moves by adequate steps ("tit for tat"), i.e., repositioning changing the local ratio of deployments and signaling determination, while defending forces' initial (immediate and short-term) strength (balancing or overarching the opponents' strength) played a critical role in preventing the aggression.[296]

Similarly, in Huth's equation, a previous bargaining record (firm) of the defender in relations of the possible attacker could strongly influence deterrence outcome.[297] Due to Huth's probit analysis, the defender's nuclear threats had no significance in the success of extended deterrence.[298] As Huth's analysis explained in "Extended Deterrence and the Prevention of War," it did not confirm the hypothesis of the importance of military alliance and economic ties between the defender and protégé in the deterrence result.[299]

In the 1980s, Huth and Bruce Russett evaluated on the basis of historical data analysis that immediate extended deterrence could fail without short-term military advantage of the defender, while nuclear forces did not play a significant role in such cases and massive retaliation was overrated, as the Cuban crisis proved.[300]

Curtis Signorino and Ahmer Tarar relied upon a different, revised statistical model of empirical analysis and reached different conclusions on the

---

296 Huth, 51–52, 57, 75–76.

297 Huth, 81–83.

298 Huth, 81–83.

299 Although the previous Huth-Russett 1988 analysis gave a different account of the matter, confirming the value of alliance for successful deterrence, while the 1984 probit analysis of those scholars verified the value of an alliance for the positive outcome of extended deterrence negatively. The analyzed falsified hypothesis claimed that successful extended deterrence decreased when the protégé is considered to be a supplier of important economic resources for the military-related needs of the defender, while the value of potential gains from aggression (in terms of military balance) grows in such a scenario. Huth, 47, 83; Paul Huth and Bruce Russett, "Deterrence Failure and Crisis Escalation," *International Studies Quarterly* 32, no. 1 (1988): 40–42, http://www.jstor.org/stable/2600411%0A; Paul Huth and Bruce Russett, "What Makes Deterrence Work? Cases from 1900 to 1980," *World Politics* 36, no. 4 (1984): 515–516, http://www.jstor.org/stable/2010184; Conf. Bruce Russett, "The Calculus of Deterrence," *The Journal of Conflict Resolution* 7, no. 2 (1963): 97–109, http://www.jstor.org/stable/172796.

300 Huth and Russett, "Deterrence Failure and Crisis Escalation," 29–30, 38.

matter of immediate deterrence, leading to the high significance of military alliances, the long-term balance of strength and nuclear weapons, a.o., under conditions of the defense of a protected country by an ally, who extended deterrence to stop an external invasion.[301]

Zagare and Kilgour found that extended deterrence (in the context of allied territory) was necessarily less reliable than general deterrence, apart from vitally important areas, as one might assume, noting that if it had been otherwise, the strategic balance would depend on the viability (effectiveness) of threats on tactical level.[302] Those scholars estimated that the higher the value of the defended state-protégé, the more likely the defender would risk conflict to protect it, while for the challenger, the value of the "pawn" (contested country) in defending the powers' schemes may condition the willingness to attack (the attack is more likely when the pawn is seen as highly valuable to the defending power and seems attractive for the challenger in the defender's perception).[303] Those benefits from controlling the pawn (for the challenger and defendant) in Kilgour and Zagare's model must be relatively extensive so that extended deterrence could play a significant part in the scenario of defending such a state.[304]

The Kilgour-Zagare game-theoretic model of extended deterrence related to Bruce Bueno de Mesquita's model (calculations connected with "Correlates of War"); de Mesquita explained that the nation's security level could be defined as a sum of the utilities gained by possible adversaries of this state by challenging it, i.e.,

$$\Sigma_{j \neq i} \; E(U_{ji})$$

for state i and challengers j, so the smaller the sum is the safer a given state is, while when the sum becomes negative, i can obtain concessions by challenging j.[305]

---

301   Curtis S. Signorino and Ahmer Tarar, "A Unified Theory and Test of Extended Immediate Deterrence," *American Journal of Political Science* 50, no. 3 (2006): 587, 592.

302   Zagare and Kilgour, *Perfect Deterrence*, 305.

303   Marc Kilgour and Frank Zagare, "Uncertainty and the Role of the Pawn in Extended Deterrence," *Synthese* 100 (1994): 381.

304   Kilgour and Zagare, "Uncertainty and the Role of the Pawn in Extended Deterrence," 381.

305   Bruce Bueno de Mesquita, "The War Trap Revisited: A Revised Expected Utility

Quackenbush examined the extended deterrence scenario (using a binomial and multinomial logit model) reaching the conclusion that although a highly reliable alliance serves the successful outcome of the deterrent posture in the case of a threat to a protégé, both allies will attempt to avoid being seen as more dedicated than the other ally (in a defender-defended relationship) in order not to be attacked first by the challenger.[306] The latter power was expected to choose the more engaged side in the defense pact as the prime target of the planned assault, hoping that by doing so, it could neutralize the more active state of the relationship and allow it to win the war without being countered by the partner of the opponent (less motivated to pay its due to fulfill its obligations).[307]

The Kilgour-Zagare model stated that the expected outcome in challenger-defender extended deterrence game could by measured by the following utilities (first for the challenger, second for the defender):

status quo $(0,0)$,
challenger's victory $(R_{ch} + n_{ch}, -g_{def} - R_{def})$
defender's victory $(-g_{ch}, n_{def})$
conflict (war) $(-c_{ch} + p_{ch}(R_{ch} - d_{ch}), -c_{def} - p_{def}d_{def} - (1 - p_{def})R_{def})$,

where R_{ch} and R_{def} represent the initial value of the contested country (a "pawn") for the challenging and defending power, respectively, n_{ch} and n_{def} state represent the benefits gained in the case of the other power's reiteration ("concession"), $-g_{ch}$ and $-g_{def}$ represent the costs of concessions, $-c_{ch}$ and $-c_{def}$ represent the costs of being engaged in an armed conflict, $-d_{ch}$ and $-d_{def}$ represent the reduced estimated value of the disputed area ("pawn") after the war, p_{ch} and p_{def} represent the probabilities for each side that it could exercise the control over the country of concern (the "pawn") as a result of war.[308]

Lisa Carlson referred to the problem analyzed by Kilgour and Zagare by adding a model in which the dilemma of a challenger (attacker) and a

---

Model," *The American Political Science Review* 79, no. 1 (1985): 157, 167, http://www.jstor.org/stable/1956125; Kilgour and Zagare, 380, 384, 410; Zeev Maoz, *Correlates of War* (2019), http://www.correlatesofwar.org/people.

306 Quackenbush, *Understanding General Deterrence*, 137–138.

307 Quackenbush, 137–138.

308 Kilgour and Zagare, 382–383; Frank Zagare and Marc Kilgour, "Alignment Patterns, Crisis Bargaining, and Extended Deterrence: A Game-Theoretic Analysis," *International Studies Quarterly* 47 (2003): 587–615.

defender in the case of a disputed status of a protégé was to be solved on the basis of the cost (of war) resistance prediction for each side, i.e., the attacking power was more willing to engage in combat if it estimated that it could tolerate a higher cost of armed conflict than the defender in such a case.[309]

Alastair Smith estimated that an alliance in the case of extended deterrence makes an attack against a defended protégé less likely, but at the same time, in bargaining schemes war would be more probable than concessions, while the contested country would have more incentives (assured by the deterrer) to resist than to give up its position under a pressure of a threatening power.[310]

Matthew Fuhrmann and Todd Sechser (using a binomial probability model) evaluated that over a 50-year period, it was more than three times more likely that a state not having a nuclear umbrella (provided by an ally) would be attacked than in the case of a side defended by a nuclear-capable supporter (the exact probabilities reached the level of 0.156 in the first scenario and 0.047 in the second).[311] Nevertheless, a deployment of nuclear weapons on allied territory in the sense of protection from the conflict could not be confirmed by statistical significance, as the Fuhrmann and Sechser's study proved.[312] Such a conclusion leads to a conviction that nuclear deployments play little role in increasing the effectiveness of extended deterrence in the context of possible attacks against allies of nuclear powers offering protection to their endangered partners. (Among the examined problems that could disorient statistical analytics were US bombs and allies in the case of Greek-Turkish Cyprus conflict of 1974 and the British-Argentinian Falkland conflict of 1982, where nuclear and

---

309   Lisa Carlson, "Crisis Escalation: An Empirical Test in the Context of Extended Deterrence," *International Interactions* 24, no. 3 (1998), 237.

310   Alastair Smith, "Extended Deterrence and Alliance Formation," *International Interactions* 24, no. 4 (1998): 317.

311   Matthew Fuhrmann and Todd S. Sechser, "Signaling Alliance Commitments: Hand-Tying and Sunk Costs in Extended Nuclear Deterrence," *American Journal of Political Science* 58, no. 4 (2014): 928–929, 931–932; Matthew Fuhrmann and Todd S. Sechser, "Appendices for "Signaling Alliance Commitments: Hand-Tying and Sunk Costs in Extended Nuclear Deterrence," *American Journal of Political Science* (2014): 19–20, https://onlinelibrary.wiley.com/action/downloadSupplement?-doi=10.1111%2Fajps.12082&attachmentId=86330477.

312   Fuhrmann and Sechser, "Signaling Alliance Commitments," 928–929, 931–932; Fuhrmann and Sechser, "Appendices for 'Signaling Alliance Commitments'" 19–20.

nonnuclear US allies were counterparts; those were examined as non-interfering with the overall result.)[313] What seems disturbing, however, in relation to the conclusion of the non-significance of nuclear deployments in terms of being a target of violent conflict (external invasion) in the quoted Fuhrmann-Sechser study is the unclear empirical evidence of any case, when a country hosting its protectors' nuclear weapons was attacked (notwithstanding the mentioned Cyprus case of conflict between two US allies, both hosting US nuclear bombs).[314] Notably, NATO members were covered by the Nuclear Sharing of the US tactical arsenal.[315]

Another case would be to prove that nuclear states are less likely to be attacked by nonnuclear powers, which could be questioned empirically by the Korean war, the Vietnam war, or the Falklands war, not to mention (post)colonial conflicts. Historical evidence shows rather that the allies of nuclear powers that do not possess any nuclear deterrents (allies' or their own) on their territory could be attacked and destroyed, as in the cases of South Korea (1950) and South Vietnam (1975),[316] both US allies, Kuwait in 1989, or those enjoying US support, such as Georgia (2008) and Ukraine (2014).

Notably, Daehee Bak confirmed statistically that the defending allies' power and their contiguous position (alliance proximity) could discourage a potential challenger from taking hostile steps, but the effect of geographical distance of a defender to protégé was decreasing over time.[317]

3. Deterrence Theory and Extended Deterrence after the Cold War

The first wave of deterrence theory, developed by Brodie, was focused on game changing, the role of the atomic bomb as a possible weapon

---

313 Fuhrmann and Sechser, "Signaling Alliance Commitments" 928–29, 931–32; Fuhrmann and Sechser, "Appendices for "Signaling Alliance Commitments,'" 19–20.

314 Fuhrmann and Sechser, "Signaling Alliance Commitments," 928–929, 931–932; Fuhrmann and Sechser, "Appendices for "Signaling Alliance Commitments,'" 19–20.

315 Schofield, *Strategic Nuclear Sharing*, 16–17, 111–112; Michael Rühle, "NATO and Extended Deterrence in a Multinuclear World," *Comparative Strategy* 28, no. 1 (2009), 16, https://doi.org/10.1080/01495930802679686.

316 US Department of State Office of the Historian, *Milestones in the History of US Foreign Relations, Ending the Vietnam War, 1969-1973* (2018), https://history.state.gov/milestones/1969-1976/ending-vietnam.

317 Bak Daehee, "Alliance Proximity and Effectiveness of Extended Deterrence," *International Interactions* 44, no. 1 (2018), 121.

of offense and defense in the time of US nuclear advantage. The second wave of deterrence theory, formed in the thermonuclear era, clarified the principles of mutual strategic deterrence, nuclear retaliation, and massive targeted strikes, making first steps towards strategic balance, extended deterrence, and limited war.

As Steff noted, the third wave of deterrence theory, following the first (in the late 1940s) and second (in the 1950s), has been filled with disappointment in ineffective extended deterrence, visible in the Vietnam War context.[318] The third wave relied on psychological decision analysis and undermined previous claims on rational decision-makers.

The fourth wave of deterrence theory in the post-Cold War second nuclear age focused on rogue states, regional conflicts, and the proliferation of WMD among lesser powers, including terrorists.[319]

Thomas Christensen stressed the significance in the post-Cold War environment of revisionist powers, China, and Russia in strategic planning.[320]

Thomas Mahnken (and similarly, Bruce Bennett) described five main scenarios of limited nuclear conflicts in the post-Cold War era (concluding that extended deterrence became more questionable than in a bipolar world):

- an attack to demonstrate the potential of a nuclear arsenal (in Mahnken's hypothetical scenario, such an assault could be performed by Iran against Israel's Negev desert reactor),

- a nuclear attack against carefully chosen targets (e.g., a North Korean strike against the US Okinawa base Kadena),

- selectively disarming and weakening ("incapacitating attack"),

---

318   Steff, 20; Jervis, "Deterrence Theory Revisited"; George and Smoke, *Deterrence in American Foreign Policy.*

319   Jeffrey Knopf, "The Fourth Wave in Deterrence Theory Research," *Contemporary Security Policy* 31, no. 1 (2010): 1–33, https://calhoun.nps.edu/bitstream/ handle/10945/38341/inc_knopf_CSP-31-1_2010.pdf;sequence=4; Lupovici, "The Emerging Fourth Wave of Deterrence Theory"; Jervis, "Deterrence Theory Revisited."

320   Thomas J. Christensen, "The Contemporary Security Dilemma: Deterring a Taiwan Conflict," *The Washington Quarterly* 25, no. 4 (2002): 9, 13–15, 17–18, https://doi. org/10.1162/016366002760252509.

such as a Russian nuclear-propelled electromagnetic impulse attack during a hypothetical conflict at NATO's eastern flank against the Alliance's command and control communication infrastructure,

- a nuclear blow supporting conventional forces on the battlefield, as in a hypothetical escalation of the China-Taiwan conflict by Chinese nuclear strike against US bases in the region,

- actions aimed at the nuclear arsenal of a collapsing state (hypothetically Pakistan, in a disturbing scenario of a loss of control over its nuclear forces and a threat of terrorist takeover, countered by US and Indian efforts to destroy the arsenal under such conditions).[321]

4. US Extended Deterrence in the Far East

In the Far East in the twenty-first century, US' extended deterrence was strengthened by conventional forces redeployments, favoring the Asia-Pacific theater due to growing Chinese military prowess, a.o.[322]

The US' strategic shift (rebalancing to Asia) corresponded to tailored extended deterrence since 2012 in the Obama administration, which was focused on DPRK.[323]

In light of the present day North Korean crisis, the matter of the redeployment of US tactical nuclear weapons was raised by South Korean political powers. Notably, all such weapons were removed after the Cold War by Bush Sr.'s administration.[324] Se Young Jang noted that US warheads in South Korea (as a form extended deterrence) were reduced from below

---

321 Thomas Mahnken, "Future Scenarios of Limited Nuclear Conflict," in *On Limited Nuclear War in the 21ˢᵗ Century*, ed. by Jeffrey Larsen and Kerry M. Kartchner (Stanford: Stanford Security Studies, 2014), 131–143; Bennett, "On US Preparedness for Limited Nuclear War," 216–217.

322 Robert A. Manning, *The Future of US Extended Deterrence in Asia to 2025* (2014), 7, https://www.files.ethz.ch/isn/184441/Future_US_Ext_Det_in_Asia.pdf.

323 Justin Anderson, Jeffrey Larsen and Polly Holdorf, *Extended Deterrence and Allied Assurance: Key Concepts Adn Current Challenges for US Policy* (2013), 121, https://www.usafa.edu/app/uploads/OCP69.pdf.

324 Joseph F. Pilat, "A Reversal of Fortunes? Extended Deterrence and Assurance in Europe and East Asia 1," *Journal of Strategic Studies* 39, no. 4 (2016): 581, https://doi.org/10.1080/01402390.2016.1168016.

1000 in the 1960s to 540 in 1976 to 150 in the mid-1980s.[325] The North Korean nuclear program reached highest priority level for the US deterrence policy after Pyongyang decided to withdraw from the Six-Party Talks on denuclearization in 2009, with Kim Jong Un's quickly moving toward nuclear development after 2011, and as Scott Snyder analyzed, becoming a tool in the process of consolidating power.[326]

Since the early 2000s, among the top issues in the US-South Korean defense partnership arose the transfer of operational command and control (OPCON) from the US to South Korea. OPCON remained under UN (US in this case) control until 1978, when South Korean-US Combined Forces Command (CFC) was formed. Since 1994, Seoul has regained peacetime OPCON control and the wartime command over its forces rested in CFC.[327] After the 2006-2007 US-South Korean consultations, Republic of Korea (ROK) was to reassert wartime OPCON in 2012, but in the context of DPRK nuclear-ballistic progress, it decided to postpone the process.[328] In 2014, the Obama administration saw an opportunity for an OPCON transfer in 2015, but prospects were eventually delayed.[329] The Trump administration's focus on North Korea's nuclear threats led to increased attention on Seoul's capacities in terms of missile defense, i.e., preemptive skills, Kill Chain, and Korean Air and Missile Defense (KAMD) conditioning planned OPCON transfer, while US' extended deterrence was to cover all capacities (including nuclear) to protect its South Korean ally.[330] Conditions for OPCON transfer were to be set

---

325 Se Young Jang, "The Evolution of US Extended Deterrence and South Korea's Nuclear Ambitions," *Journal of Strategic Studies* 39, no. 4 (2016): 506, https://doi.org/10.1080/01402390.2016.1168012.

326 Scott Snyder, *Confronting the North Korean Threat: Reassessing Policy Options, Statement before the United States Senate Committee on Foreign Relations, US Senate, 1st Session, 115th Congress, January 31, 2017* (2017), 4, https://www.foreign.senate.gov/imo/media/doc/013117_Snyder_Testimony.pdf.

327 James Minnich, "The Year 2012. South Korea's Resumption of Wartime Operational Control," *Military Review* (2011), 2–3, https://www.armyupress.army.mil/Portals/7/military-review/Archives/English/MilitaryReview_20110630_art004.pdf.

328 Minnich, "The Year 2012," 2–3.

329 The White House, *Joint Fact Sheet: The United States-Republic of Korea Alliance: A Global Partnership* (2014), https://obamawhitehouse.archives.gov/the-press-office/2014/04/25/joint-fact-sheet-united-states-republic-korea-alliance-global-partnership.

330 The White House, *Joint Statement between the United States and the Republic of Korea,*

precisely in bilateral Annual Security Consultative Meetings (defense ministries consultations) by 2018, while South Korean defenses in terms of WMD crisis prevention were strengthened by US THAAD deployments.[331]

Notably, South Korea deployed its own Aegis-capable ships (KDX-III destroyers), apart from PAC and THAAD engagement.[332]

Clint Work stressed that under President Moon (declaring the will to take operational wartime control in the time of increased ballistic and nuclear provocations by DPRK in Autumn 2017), the success of negotiated OPCON transfer was to depend on South Korean command and control improvements in war-fighting dimensions by Kill Chain preemptive defense system, the KAMD system and Korea Massive Punishment and Retaliation.[333] The actual OPCON wartime transfer to South Korea was expected in January 2018 by the early 2020s.[334]

Based on NPR 2010 Extended Deterrence Dialogue (EDD) between the US and Japan, US and South Korea established the Extended Deterrence Policy Committee (EDPC).[335] EDPC talks since 2011 were to lead to a bilateral deterrence strategy.[336] In the US Department of State in mid-2018,

---

June 30, 2017 (2017), https://www.whitehouse.gov/briefings-statements/joint-state ment-united-states-republic-korea/.

331 US Department of Defense, *Joint News Conference with Secretary Mattis and South Korean Defense Minister Song Young-Moo in Seoul, October 27, 2017* (2017), https://www.defense.gov/News/Transcripts/Transcript-View/Article/1356752/joint-news-conference-with-secretary-mattis-and-south-korean-defense-minister-s/.

332 House Armed Services Committee (V. Brooks testimony), *Statement of General Vincent K. Brooks, Commander, United Nations Command; Republic of Korea and United States Combined Forces Command; and United States Forces Korea, February 14, 2018* (2018), 7, https://docs.house.gov/meetings/AS/AS00/20180214/106847/HHRG-115-AS00-20180214-SD002.pdf.

333 Clint Work, "The Long History of South Korea's OPCON Debate," *The Diplomat* (November 2017), https://thediplomat.com/2017/11/the-long-history-of-south-koreas-opcon-debate/.

334 Lee Chi-dong, "S Korea to Streamline OPCON Transition Procedures," *Yonhap News Agency* (January 19, 2018), http://english.yonhapnews.co.kr/news/2018/01/19/0200000000AEN20180119000951315.html.

335 Brad Roberts, *The Case for US Nuclear Weapons in the 21st Century*, Kindle (Stanford: Stanford University Press, 2016), 202.

336 Samman Chung, "North Korea's Nuclear Threats and Counter-Strategies," *The Journal of East Asian Affairs* 30, no. 2 (2016): 110–13, 114, 117, 124–126, http://www.

those frameworks, i.e., the US-Japan EDD and the Deterrence Strategy Committee (DSC) between the US and South Korea (combining former EDPC and Counter-Missile Capabilities Committee), were coordinated by the Office of Strategic Stability and Deterrence Affairs (SSD) in the Bureau of Arms Control, Verification and Compliance (AVC).[337] In early 2018, the framework of EDPC was labeled the Extended Deterrence Strategy and Consultation Group (EDSCG), operated next to Joint Chiefs of Staff (JCS)'s annual Military Committee Meetings and Security Consultative Meeting (SCM).[338]

Ralph Cossa and Brad Gloserman noted that (in the context of the Obama administration's US NPR 2010) Japanese security circles were concerned that the US could adopt a no-first-use policy in the matter of nuclear weapons that would make Japan less protected (in the area of nuclear deterrence) from a North Korean biological or chemical WMD arsenal, leaving nuclear retaliation possibly off the table in such a case.[339]

As Don Oberdorfer noted, the Jimmy Carter administration reduced nuclear weapons in South Korea to 250 warheads, and by 1989 those were further reduced to 100 warheads.[340]

---

jstor.org/stable/44160975.

337 US Department of State, *Office of Strategic Stability and Deterrence Affairs (AVC/ SSD)* (2018), https://www.state.gov/t/avc/c23758.htm; US Department of Defense, *Press Statement 8th Korea-US Integrated Defense Dialogue (KIDD) September 24, 2015* (2015), https://www.defense.gov/Portals/1/Documents/pubs/Press_ Statement_8th_KIDD_Sep24_OSD_FINAL.pdf.

338 House Armed Services Committee (V. Brooks testimony), 4.

339 Ralph A. Cossa and Brad Glosserman, "Extended Deterrence and Disarmament," *The Nonproliferation Review* 18, no. 1 (2011): 131–132, https://doi.org/10.1080/10 736700.2011.549177.

340 Reduced from the high level of 763 warheads (by 1972), as Don Oberdorfer stressed, recalling William Arkin's data (based on an interview with this US nuclear researcher and supported by US government planning, including Kissinger's National Security Decision Memorandum - NSDM 178 of July 1972, partially classified as of June 2019). Don Oberdorfer and Robert Carlin, *The Two Koreas. A Contemporary History*, Kindle (New York: Basic Books, 2014), 4730-4743, 11414; Conf. Henry A. Kissinger, *National Security Decision Memorandum 178, July 18, 1972, Subject: FY 1973 Nuclear Weapons Deployment Authorization* (1972), https://www.nixonlibrary.gov/sites/default/files/virtuallibrary/docu ments/nsdm/nsdm_178.pdf.
According to NSDM 230 of August 1973, US (tactical) nuclear forces (TNF) in Asia should provide for emergence defense options in case of conventional de-

The Panmunjeom Declaration created a perspective of denuclearization of North Korea, which had claimed in earlier months that it possesed thermonuclear and ICBM capability.[341] The US-North Korea (Trump-Kim Jong-Un) summit in Singapore held on June 12, 2018 brought a stronger commitment of denuclearization of the Korean Peninsula by DPRK.[342]

In the context of North Korea's nuclearization, Andrew O'Neill stated that the reliability of US' extended deterrence in the region and credible nuclear threats posed by the US to counter attempted aggression could prevent new potential nuclear powers (with high technological potential) from developing their own arsenals (including Japan, South Korea, Taiwan, and Australia).[343] O'Neill argued that North Korea's provocative military stance was a result of its nuclear developments, as new nuclear powers tend to engage in conventional hostilities more self-assured that their newly designed possessive weapons would prevent strategically threatening escalation scenarios (as the stability-instability paradox explains), which does not mean in the 2010 perspective that Pyongyang saw US' extended nuclear deterrence on Korean Peninsula as unreliable.[344]

O'Neil found that (US') extended nuclear deterrence helped to support non-proliferation efforts in the defended countries, such as Japan, South Korea, and Australia.[345]

New democracies prove to be more bellicose than older ones, as seen in

---

fense failure against China's (and its communist ally) attack (TNF could be engaged in an early stage of conflict against major Chinese aggression) or an attack of another opponent in Asia, including Korea, Japan, or the Philippines. Henry A. Kissinger, *National Security Decision Memorandum 230, August 9, 1973, Subject: US Strategy and Forces for Asia* (1973), 1, https://www.nixonlibrary.gov/sites/default/files/virtuallibrary/documents/nsdm/nsdm_230.pdf.

341 Jae-in and Jong-un, *Panmunjeom Declaration for Peace.*

342 The White House, *Joint Statement of President Donald J. Trump of the United States of America and Chairman Kim Jong Un of the Democratic People's Republic of Korea at the Singapore Summit, June 12, 2018.*

343 Andrew O'Neil, "Extended Nuclear Deterrence in East Asia: Redundant or Resurgent?" *International Affairs* 87, no. 6 (2011): 1447–1448, 1457.

344 O'Neil, "Extended Nuclear Deterrence in East Asia," 1447–1448, 1457.

345 Andrew O'Neil, *Asia, the US and Extended Nuclear Deterrence. Atomic Umbrellas in the Twenty-First Century,* Kindle (London: Routledge, 2013), 122–123.

the context of territorial disputes by Huth and Todd Allee (confirmed statistically).[346]

5. Eastern Europe: US Forward Deployments

The deficiencies of nuclear deterrence in Cold War Europe were discussed, a.o., in the context of the abandoned MLF and, as Kahn stressed, in reference to Charles de Gaulle's concerns of European defense in the case of nuclear attack (not fully assured by US guarantees only), which were the basis for Kahn's vision of a European Strategic Defense Community, which could enforce a retaliation mechanism in response to nuclear assault, implemented by a commanding general, whose orders might be overridden by a voting committee (to deescalate, when needed, or keep the orders intact to allow the retail blow, as a tactical response of joined armed forces).[347]

A multi-lateral force was promoted and abandoned by the Kennedy administration, which was supposed to encompass a naval nuclear-armed force ready to defend Europe.

Jane Sharp noted that the conservative parties in Europe (in UK, Germany, and France) were not pleased with the Reagan-Gorbachev 1987 INF treaty with full reductions of intermediate-range nuclear missiles as lowering the threshold of US deterrence in Europe, while centrist and left-leaning circles generally favored the agreement.[348]

The B-61 European reduction of US tactical nuclear weapons found no adequate reductions on the Russian side, and no treaty, as Iskander tactical nuclear-tipped missiles in Kaliningrad posed a hazard to the Eastern flank of NATO, increasing the role of Polish BMD perspectives (such a

---

346   Paul Huth and Todd Allee, *The Democratic Peace and Territorial Conflict in the Twentieth Century* (Cambridge: Cambridge University Press, 2002), 287, https://www.questia.com/read/107600727/the-democratic-peace-and-territorial-conflict-in-the.

347   Kahn's proposal referred to the growing Soviet nuclear potential in the 1960s. Kahn, *On Escalation*, 264–266.

348   At the time, Europe's conservative governments were afraid that the INF could lead to more reliance on conventional forces and the need to increase those in Europe. Jane M. O. Sharp, "The Problem of Extended Deterrence in NATO," in *Arms Control and Disarmament*, ed. by Paolo Foradori, Giampiero Giacomello, and Alessandro Pascolini (Cham: Springer International Publishing, 2018), 176, https://doi.org/10.1007/978-3-319-62259-0_13.

challenge lead to non-support for the withdrawal of the remaining 200 US B-61 nuclear tactical bombs from Europe, because of inadequate Russian reductions).[349]

Among the perils to the New START follow-up was the matter of the INF decline in 2019. New perils with the Iran nuclear deal abandoned by the US included a growing tension between Washington and Tehran, while before Trump and Obama, the Iranian ballistic and nuclear threat justified US-backed BMD investments in Eastern Europe.

The scenarios of the New Cold War era also included European nuclear forces based in French and British arsenals.[350]

Notably, Obama's European Reassurance Initiative was transformed into Trump's European Deterrence Initiative (EDI), with increased multi-billion funding.

By 2018, US-led BMD efforts in Eastern Europe included the construction of two Aegis Ashore bases in Poland and Romania and PAC-3 exports to those countries.

Gen. Ben Hodges, former commander of US Army Europe (2014-2017), claimed in June 2018 that permanent deployments of US forces in Poland are not necessary to deter Russia; instead, a rotational forward presence of NATO forces in East European allies could have this effect, while a long-time base could endanger relations with Russia and the alliance's cohesion.[351] Alexander Lanoszka stressed that Poland and Taiwan shared similar concerns in relation to Russia and China, respectively, while the military advantage of those powers raised the need to invest in indigenous anti-access/area denial (A2/AD) capacities.[352]

Eerik Marmei and Gabriel White stressed that European Reassurance

---

349 James M. Acton, "Chapter Two: Extended Deterrence," *Adelphi Series* 50, no. 417 (2010):. 40, https://doi.org/10.1080/19445571.2010.567044.

350 Jeffrey Larsen, "US Extended Deterrence and Europe: Time to Consider Alternative Structures?" in *The Future of Extended Deterrence. The United States, NATO, and Beyond*, ed. by Stéfanie Von Hlatky and Andreas Wenger, Kindle (Washington DC: Georgetown University Press, 2015), 59.

351 Ben Hodges, "Don't Put US Bases in Poland," *Politico* (June 4, 2018), https://www.politico.eu/article/dont-put-us-bases-in-poland/.

352 Alexander Lanoszka, *Atomic Assurance: The Alliance Politics of Nuclear Proliferation*, eBook (Ithaca: Cornell University Press, 2018), 183.

Initiative, launched in 2014 by Obama due to the Russian threat (later the Trump administration's EDI, supported in the FY 2017 by $3.4 billion, increased to $4.7 billion in FY 2018 NDAA) enabled the funding of an additional (the third or fourth in crisis time) Army Armored Brigade Combat Team, including 4000-5000 soldiers, 90 tanks, 90 fighting vehicles, a purchase of Javelin anti-tank missiles for Estonia, and radio equipment for Lithuania and Sentinel Air Defense radars for Latvia (each for $33 million), whereas the 2018 EDI spending assisted the additional rotational presence of the Combat Aviation Brigade, located in Latvia, Poland, and Romania (using 2200 personnel, 10 Chinooks, 50 Blackhawks, and 24 Apache helicopters).[353]

The EDI funding for FY2019 was increased in the Trump administration's budget request to $6.53 billon.[354] The Increased Presence line of effort of EDI ($1.87 billion) supported 9900 personnel in US European Command (USEUCOM), Army Rotational Forces (formerly Armored Brigade Combat Team) for $920 million, the Combat Aviation Brigade (CAB) for $100 million, and $22 million to supply NATO Enhanced Forward Presence (eFP) by a US battalion strengthening Mechanized Task Forces, a.o., in the land component.[355] EDI's naval component consisted of Theater Anti-Submarine Warfare ($85.2 million) and US Marine Corps rotational presence ($29 million), while the air component included Air Superiority Presence ($110 million) by US F-15C/D from the RAF Base Lakenheath and Combat Air Forces training and exercise ($126 million).[356] Exercise and training FY2019 EDI's pillar received a $290 million funding request. The Enhanced Prepositioning line of effort was to receive $3.2 billion to support equipment deliveries to the theater for the army (equipment for two ABCT and two Fires Brigades, a.o.), air force (bases), and missile defense (PAC) to include JASSM-ER deliveries as well. An improved infrastructure pillar was supported by $830 million,

353 Eerik Marmei and Gabriel White, *European Deterrence Initiative. Bolstering the Defence of the Baltic States* (Tallin, 2017), 1–4, https://www.icds.ee/fileadmin/media/IMG/2017/Publications/ICDS_Policy_Paper_European_Deterrence_Initiative_Eerik_Marmei-Gabriel_White_December_2017.pdf.

354 Office of the Under Secretary of Defense (Comptroller) EDI FY2019, *European Deterrence Initiative Budget Fiscal Year (FY) 2019, Justification Book*, 2018, 1, http://comptroller.defense.gov/Portals/45/Documents/defbudget/fy2019/fy2019_EDI_JBook.pdf.

355 Office of the Under Secretary of Defense (Comptroller) EDI FY2019, 1–2, 4.

356 Office of the Under Secretary of Defense (Comptroller) EDI FY2019, 2, 4–6, 21.

introduced to finance new army military constructions (storage, transport) in Romania, Bulgaria, and Poland, as well as navy and air bases.[357]

US air defense artillery (SHORAD) was redeployed to Europe in 2018 (in the New Cold War context).[358]

The overall funding for European Reassurance Initiative (later EDI) through National Defense Authorization Acts from FY 2015 to FY 2018 passed by Congress reached $9.8 billion.[359] The NDAA FY 2019 included a restriction by the US Secretary of Defense on using funds for EDI military construction projects before submitting those to the congressional defense committees for approval.[360]

EDI counters increased the Russian threat since Russia's aggression against Ukraine in 2014 by supporting US troops deployments (after reductions that led to a decrease from 200,000 in the 1980s to 33,000 in 2015).[361]

In 2009, it still might have seemed appropriate to imagine a successful NATO-Russia missile defense cooperation in light of Obama's pro-Russian gesture, a withdrawal from previously planned missile defense GMD sites in Poland and Czechia to provide for narrower, Aegis-based, Iranian-oriented deployments.[362]

---

357 Office of the Under Secretary of Defense (Comptroller) EDI FY2019, 8, 11, 14.

358 Kyle Rempfer, "European Mission for First Time since Cold War," *Military Times* (April 2, 2018), https://www.militarytimes.com/flashpoints/2018/04/02/us-air-defense-artillery-brigade-begins-new-european-mission-for-first-time-since-cold-war/; Conf. Meghann Myers, "Back to Europe," *Army Times* (March 19, 2017), https://www.armytimes.com/news/your-army/2017/03/19/back-to-europe-the-army-is-sending-more-troops-tanks-and-helicopters-to-deter-russia/; Jane's, *Ramping Up* (2017), http://www.janes.com/images/assets/344/74344/Ramping_up_US_Army_Europe_building_forces_and_capability.pdf.

359 US House of Representatives, *National Defense Authorization Act FY 2019, H.R. 5515, June 5, 2018* (US House of Representatives, 2018), 920, https://www.congress.gov/115/bills/hr5515/BILLS-115hr5515pcs.pdf.

360 US House of Representatives, *National Defense Authorization Act FY 2019, H.R. 5515, June 5, 2018,* 1349; US House of Representatives, *Report of the Committee on Armed Services House of Representatives on National Defense Authorization Act FY 2019, May 15, 2018* (2018), 292, https://www.congress.gov/115/crpt/hrpt676/CRPT-115hrpt676.pdf.

361 Jen Judson, "Funding to Deter Russia Reaches $6.5B in FY19 Budget," *DefenseNews* (February 12, 2018), https://www.defensenews.com/land/2018/02/12/funding-to-deter-russia-reaches-65b-in-fy19-defense-budget-request/.

362 Oliver Thränert, "NATO, Missile Defence and Extended Deterrence," *Survival* 51,

The lack of forward deployed US (or NATO) forces in Eastern Europe could lead to the further threat of Russian-led hybrid warfare against such allies as the Baltic states, after the annexation of Crimea and the attack against Ukraine, as Lanoszka explained, by hybrid warfare strategy, including regular and irregular coordinated military actions to provide for a control of an escalation of the conflict, while violating the attacked countries' territorial and domestic safety, as well as their economy, by actions presented as local insurgencies.[363] In the case of Ukraine attacked by Russia in 2014 on the Crimean Peninsula Lanoszka stressed the lack of regular warfare and no deployment of Russian regular forces until the region was under control[364]. In fact as BBC informed in February "thousands" of Russian soldiers were clandestinely sent to Crimean bases[365]. Russian regular forces (aside from Berkut special forces of Yanukovych regime) attacked regular Ukrainian units on the Crimean, using the advantage of the Black Sea fleet over Ukrainian forces and treason in the high ranks of Ukraine's army and navy to win without major combat (on March 18, as BBC reported, pro-Russian unit killed an Ukrainian army officer in Simferopol while storming military base)[366].

Those regular Russian units were not using their official uniforms but were dressed without distinctions; they still were regular, acting in a manner that was a breach of international law. As *The Guardian* noted, the removal of Russian soldier IDs attacking Ukraine (Crimea) was a clear violation of international law (as Jonathan Eyal of Royal United Services Institute confirmed), but the International Committee of the Red Cross did not offer support to legal charges against Russia for such actions.[367]

Apart from the two discussed cases, US' extended deterrence plays a significant role in protection of its Middle Eastern allies, particularly the

---

no. 6 (2009): 63, 73–74, https://doi.org/10.1080/00396330903461674.

363 Alexander Lanoszka, "Russian Hybrid Warfare and Extended Deterrence in Eastern Europe," *International Affairs* 92, no. 1 (2016): 178.

364 Lanoszka, "Russian Hybrid Warfare and Extended Deterrence in Eastern Europe," 178.

365 John Simpson, "Russia's Crimea Plan Detailed, Secret and Successful," *BBC News* (March 19, 2014), http://www.bbc.com/news/world-europe-26644082.

366 Simpson. "Russia's Crimea Plan Detailed."

367 Ewen MacAskill, "Russian Troops Removing ID Markings 'Gross Violation,'" *The Guardian* (March 6, 2014), https://www.theguardian.com/news/defence-and-security-blog/2014/mar/06/ukraine-gross-violation-russian-troops.

Gulf Cooperation Countries (GCC) countries and Israel, which are challenged by Iran, terrorist threats, and the local domestic conflicts in Syria and Yemen. Yair Evron assessed that by 2012, the US retained all means to provide for a successful extended protection of its Arab (GCC) allies from Iranian threats by both deterrence by denial (undermining any Iran's military attempts to threaten those countries) and by punishment, i.e., striking to deprive Iran of its critically important means of armed expansion.[368] In Evron's perspective, the relative regional quantitative inferiority of US land-based armed forces (and GCC's) in comparison to Iran could be effectively balanced by air and naval superiority, technological edges, and crisis deployments of additional ground units.[369]

Trump's Iran deal withdrawal in 2018 could be used by Tehran's regime to quickly built nuclear weapons.[370] Michael Rühle stressed that Nuclear Sharing increased transparency in NATO, while views on a world free of nuclear weapons were premature at best in a multinuclear world (the second nuclear age).[371]

PAC BMD performance in the Yemeni war could reach 66% by July 2018 (from 2014).[372]

To conclude, BMD has become an increasingly useful tool for twenty-first-century extended deterrence, but its performance must be improved to provide for a close to leak-proof performance important in the defense of densely inhabited areas or WMD crises.

6. BMD Probability Analysis in the Extended Deterrence Context

BMD could successfully enhance the reliability of extended deterrence by a firmer first strike (preventive options against WMD threats) posture

---

368 Yair Evron, "Extended Deterrence in the Middle East," *The Nonproliferation Review* 19, no. 3 (2012): 386–387, https://doi.org/10.1080/10736700.2012.734186.

369 Evron, "Extended Deterrence in the Middle East," 386–387.

370 Jonathan Marcus, "A Clear Signal from Tehran, in: Iran to Boost Uranium Enrichment If Nuclear Deal Fails," *BBC News* (June 5, 2018), http://www.bbc.com/news/world-middle-east-44365078.

371 Rühle, "NATO and Extended Deterrence in a Multinuclear World," 16.

372 CSIS Missile Threat, *Interactive: The Missile War in Yemen* (2018), https://missilethreat.csis.org/missile-war-yemen/; Panel of Experts on Yemen, *Final Report of the Panel of Experts on Yemen, UN Security Council Document S/2018/193, January 2017* (2017), 14–16, https://www.un.org/en/ga/search/view_doc.asp?symbol=S/2018/193.

or active defense opportunity. Its effectiveness may be hampered though by still being too far to reach leak-proof defense capacities, important in the case of WMD danger. The probability analysis proves an extensive need for SSKP improvement beyond 90% to provide for leak-proof opportunity, as merely adding more interceptors would not suffice.

Such observations could be confirmed empirically by a re-examination of PAC combat use since the 1991 Kuwait war.

James Lebovic assessed that BMD below SSKP = 95% would not be reliable.[373]

In the Union of Concerned Scientists' analysis (following Wilkening's model), BMD non-leak-proof probability is based on the equation

$$1 - P(0) = 1 - p^n$$

where $P(0)$ stands for a leak-proof intercept (0 warheads defeating the BMD system), p represents a SSKP (the likelihood that the incoming warhead would be intercepted by a single defending intercepting missile), and n is the number of incoming warheads.[374]

In G. Lewis's model, the layered defense intercept probability was measured as:

$$P(x) = 1 - (1 - p)^n$$

where p stands for the interceptors (layers) SSKP and n represents the number of layers (interceptors),[375]

Wilkening measured the layered BMD probability (in the case of flawless cooperation between the layers/interceptors) using the equation (bullet operator represents multiplication symbol)

$$K_W = 1 - L_1 \cdot L_2 \dots L_m$$

where L stood for the probability that a warhead would defeat the particular layer (interceptor).[376] Such a performance occurs when the layers

---

373 James Lebovic, "The Law of Small Numbers: Deterrence and National Missile Defense," *The Journal of Conflict Resolution* 46, no. 4 (2002): 470–472.

374 Grego, Lewis and Wright, *Shielded from Oversight. The Disastrous US Approach to Strategic Missile Defense. Appendix* 8, 1, 5; Wilkening, 187–188.

375 George N. Lewis, "Technical Controversy," 1418-1438.

376 Wilkening, 195, 213–214; Michael V. Finn and Glenn A. Kent, *Simple Analytic Solu-*

do not interfere in any negative way with each other, the condition some scholars (as Peter Zimmermann in the SDI context) found unlikely due to possible flaws in the cooperation between particular elements in BMD systems.[377]

Notably, in the case of interceptors (layers) of the same SSKP, the layers' overall reliability is the same in those two equations presented above (G. Lewis's and Wilkening's), but obviously the latter simple equation allows us to point out cases where the layers have a different SSKP level.

In Fred Hoffman's report referring to the Soviet threat, each of the 4 layers possessed a 50% reliability, so the defeat probability stood at 0.0625 for L_1 x L_2 x L_3 x L_4, i.e., the overall effectiveness of the system reached 1 0.0625 = 0.9375%, which meant destruction of 4687 out of 5000 Soviet warheads in a hypothetical all-out strike; such an outcome left the MAD paradigm intact, but for a higher probability of BMD layers, like 80%, then the defeat probability of 0.2 for each layer led to 1 0.0016 = 99.84% reliability of 4 layers, making the defense strong enough to challenge MAD (Zimmermann questioned such a perspective due to problematic cooperation between the layers).[378]

Wilkening's mode of BMD effectiveness was based on a binomial distribution (Bernoulli trial, with binomial coefficient "W over x" written as $_WC_x$):

$$P(x) = {_WC_x} \cdot q^x \cdot (1-q)^{W-x} = {_WC_x} \cdot (1-K_W)^x \cdot (K_W)^{W-x} =$$
$$\{W!/[x! \cdot (W-x)!]\} \cdot (1-K_W)^x \cdot K_W^{W-x}$$

tions to Complex Military Problems (Santa Monica, 1985), 33–38, https://www.rand. org/content/dam/rand/pubs/notes/2007/N2211.pdf.

377   Peter Zimmerman, "Pork Bellies and the SDI," *Foreign Policy* 63 (1986): 78–79, http://www.jstor.org/stable/1148757; Wilkening, 187-188, 191.

378   Fred Hoffman, *Ballistic Missile Defenses and US National Security, Summary Report Prepared for the Future Security Strategy Study* (1983), 9, A-16, http://www. dod.mil/pubs/foi/Reading_Room/Homeland_Defense/469.pdf; Zimmerman, "Pork Bellies and the SDI," 78–79; Wilkening, 187–188, 191. For more on the statistical analysis of BMD effects, see Michael Armstrong's works: Michael J. Armstrong, "A Verification Study of the Stochastic Salvo Combat Model," *Annals of Operations Research* 186, no. 1 (2011): 23–28, https://doi.org/10.1007/s10479-011-0889-0; Michael J. Armstrong, "The Effectiveness of Rocket Attacks and Defenses in Israel," *Journal of Global Security Studies* 3, no. 2 (2018): 113–132, https://doi.org/10.1093/ jogss/ogx028.

where $K_w(q)$ is the probability of a successful interception of an incoming warhead, W is the number of attacking warheads, and x is the number of warheads defeating the BMD system.[379]

In the examined set of probabilities of a leak-proof interception (binomial distribution), the growth of BMD reliability due to SSKP improvement was particularly high in the cases of a multiple-warhead salvo attack (41-50 warheads) in the scenario of using 5 interceptors against each of the incoming missiles (Table 1). Similarly, a significant growth of benefits from an increase in SSKP was visible in the case of using 4 interceptors against each of 30-40 incoming warheads (Table 6).

Table 1. 5 warheads attacking in a salvo, probabilities of 0-5 warheads defeating the missile defense at SSKP levels 84%-96%.

warheads defeating the defense (out of 5)	SSKP =96%	SSKP =94%	SSKP =92%	SSKP =90%	SSKP =88%	SSKP =86%	SSKP =84%
0	0.815	0.734	0.659	0.590	0.528	0.470	0.418
1	0.170	0.234	0.287	0.328	0.360	0.383	0.398
2	0.014	0.030	0.050	0.073	0.098	0.125	0.152
3	0.001	0.002	0.004	0.008	0.013	0.020	0.029
4	0.000	0.000	0.000	0.000	0.001	0.002	0.003
5	0.000	0.000	0.000	0.000	0.000	0.000	0.000

Source: own counting (using Microsoft Excel) according to the equation (bullet operator represents multiplication symbol)

$$P(x) = \{W!/[x! \cdot (W - x)!]\} \cdot (1 - K_w)^x \cdot K_w^{W-x}$$

based on Wilkening's model (Bernoulli distribution), where $P(x)$ stood for a probability of defeating the BMD by x incoming warheads, K_w meant the probability of interception of an attacking warhead by an interceptor, and W stood for the amount of attacking warheads, and

$$P(0) = 1 - (1 - p)^n$$

based on G. Lewis's model, for p counted for a leak-proof defense in the cases of attacks of 5, 6, 7, ... 30 incoming warheads (in Bernoulli distribution) using n additional interceptors.

Wilkening, 187-188, 191. G. Lewis, 1299-1689. See also MDA, *Ballistic Missile Defense Intercept Flight Test Record.*

---

379   Wilkening, 187–188, 191, 195, 213–214.

Chart 1. 5 warheads attacking in a salvo, probabilities of 0-5 warheads defeating the missile defense at SSKP levels 84%-96%.

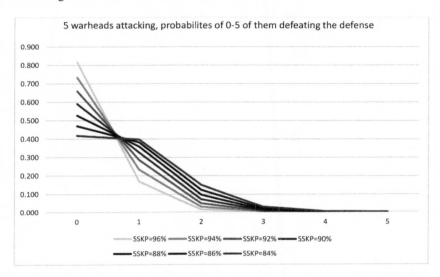

Source: own counting based on Wilkening, 187-188, 191 and G. Lewis, 1418-1438.

Table 2. 10 warheads attacking in a salvo, probabilities of 0-7 warheads defeating the missile defense at SSKP levels 84%-96%.

warheads defeating the defense (out of 10)	SSKP =96%	SSKP =94%	SSKP =92%	SSKP =90%	SSKP =88%	SSKP =86%	SSKP =84%
0	0.665	0.539	0.434	0.349	0.279	0.221	0.175
1	0.277	0.344	0.378	0.387	0.380	0.360	0.333
2	0.052	0.099	0.148	0.194	0.233	0.264	0.286
3	0.006	0.017	0.034	0.057	0.085	0.115	0.145
4	0.000	0.002	0.005	0.011	0.020	0.033	0.048
5	0.000	0.000	0.001	0.001	0.003	0.006	0.011
6	0.000	0.000	0.000	0.000	0.000	0.001	0.002
7	0.000	0.000	0.000	0.000	0.000	0.000	0.000

Source: own counting based on Wilkening, 187-188, 191 and G. Lewis, 1418-1438.

Chart 2. 10 warheads attacking in a salvo, probabilities of 0-7 warheads defeating the missile defense at SSKP levels 84%-96%.

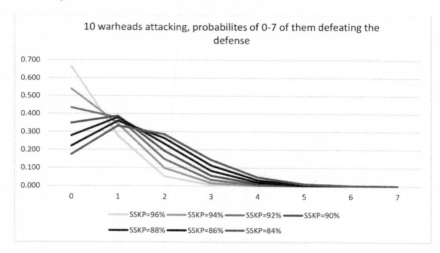

Source: own counting based on Wilkening, 187-188, 191 and G. Lewis, 1418-1438.

Table 3. 20 warheads attacking in a salvo, probabilities of 0-10 warheads defeating the missile defense at SSKP levels 84%-96%.

warheads defeating the defense (out of 20)	SSKP =96%	SSKP =94%	SSKP =92%	SSKP =90%	SSKP =88%	SSKP =86%	SSKP =84%
0	0.442	0.290	0.189	0.122	0.078	0.049	0.031
1	0.368	0.370	0.328	0.270	0.212	0.159	0.117
2	0.146	0.225	0.271	0.285	0.274	0.247	0.211
3	0.036	0.086	0.141	0.190	0.224	0.241	0.241
4	0.006	0.023	0.052	0.090	0.130	0.167	0.195
5	0.001	0.005	0.015	0.032	0.057	0.087	0.119
6	0.000	0.001	0.003	0.009	0.019	0.035	0.057
7	0.000	0.000	0.001	0.002	0.005	0.012	0.022
8	0.000	0.000	0.000	0.000	0.001	0.003	0.007
9	0.000	0.000	0.000	0.000	0.000	0.001	0.002
10	0.000	0.000	0.000	0.000	0.000	0.000	0.000

Source: own counting based on Wilkening, 187-188, 191 and G. Lewis, 1418-1438.

Chart 3. 20 warheads attacking in a salvo, probabilities of 0-10 warheads defeating the missile defense at SSKP levels 84%-96%.

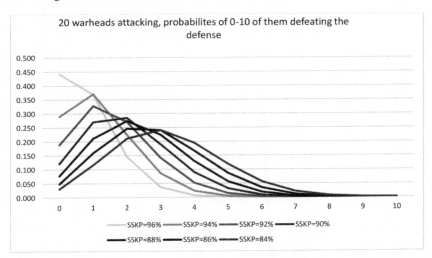

Source: own counting based on Wilkening, 187-188, 191 and G. Lewis, 1418-1438.

Table 4. 35 warheads attacking in a salvo, probabilities of 0-10 warheads defeating the missile defense at SSKP levels 84%-96%.

warheads defeating the defense (out of 35)	SSKP =96%	SSKP =94%	SSKP =92%	SSKP =90%	SSKP =88%	SSKP =86%	SSKP =84%
0	0.240	0.115	0.054	0.025	0.011	0.005	0.002
1	0.349	0.256	0.164	0.097	0.054	0.029	0.015
2	0.248	0.278	0.243	0.184	0.126	0.080	0.048
3	0.113	0.195	0.232	0.225	0.189	0.144	0.101
4	0.038	0.100	0.162	0.200	0.206	0.187	0.154
5	0.010	0.039	0.087	0.138	0.174	0.189	0.182
6	0.002	0.013	0.038	0.076	0.119	0.154	0.173
7	0.000	0.003	0.014	0.035	0.067	0.104	0.137
8	0.000	0.001	0.004	0.014	0.032	0.059	0.091
9	0.000	0.000	0.001	0.005	0.013	0.029	0.052
10	0.000	0.000	0.000	0.001	0.005	0.012	0.026

Source: own counting based on Wilkening, 187-188, 191 and G. Lewis, 1418-1438.

Chart 4. 35 warheads attacking in a salvo, probabilities of 0-7 warheads defeating the missile defense at SSKP level 96%.

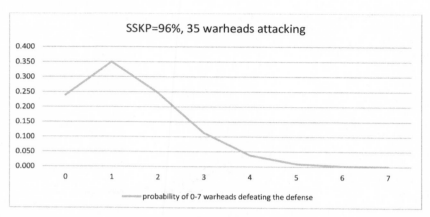

Source: own counting based on Wilkening, 187-188, 191 and G. Lewis, 1418-1438.

Chart 5. 35 warheads attacking in a salvo, probabilities of 0-10 warheads defeating the missile defense at SSKP levels 84%-96%.

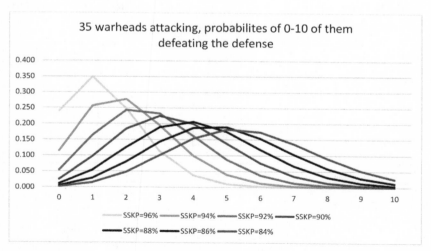

Source: own counting based on Wilkening, 187-188, 191 and G. Lewis, 1418-1438.

Table 5. SSKP 89%, up to 29 warheads attacking in a salvo, leak-proof interception probability for 1-5 interceptors.

Warhead/ Interceptors	1	2	3	4	5
1	0.89	0.99	1.00	1.00	1.00
2	0.79	0.96	0.99	1.00	1.00
3	0.70	0.91	0.97	0.99	1.00
4	0.63	0.86	0.95	0.98	0.99
5	0.56	0.80	0.91	0.96	0.98
6	0.50	0.75	0.87	0.94	0.97
7	0.44	0.69	0.83	0.90	0.95
8	0.39	0.63	0.78	0.86	0.92
9	0.35	0.58	0.73	0.82	0.88
10	0.31	0.53	0.67	0.78	0.85
11	0.28	0.48	0.62	0.73	0.80
12	0.25	0.43	0.57	0.68	0.76
13	0.22	0.39	0.53	0.63	0.71
14	0.20	0.35	0.48	0.58	0.66
15	0.17	0.32	0.44	0.53	0.62
16	0.15	0.29	0.40	0.49	0.57
17	0.14	0.26	0.36	0.45	0.52
18	0.12	0.23	0.32	0.41	0.48
19	0.11	0.21	0.29	0.37	0.44
20	0.10	0.19	0.26	0.34	0.40
21	0.09	0.17	0.24	0.30	0.36
22	0.08	0.15	0.21	0.27	0.33
23	0.07	0.13	0.19	0.25	0.30
24	0.06	0.12	0.17	0.22	0.27
25	0.05	0.11	0.15	0.20	0.24
26	0.05	0.09	0.14	0.18	0.22
27	0.04	0.08	0.12	0.16	0.20
28	0.04	0.08	0.11	0.14	0.18
29	0.03	0.07	0.10	0.13	0.16

Source: own counting based on Wilkening, 187-188, 191 and G. Lewis, 1418-1438.

Chart 6. SSKP 89%, up to 29 warheads in a salvo, leak-proof interception probability for 1-5 interceptors.

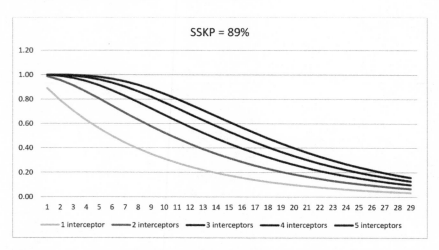

Source: own counting based on Wilkening, 187-188, 191 and G. Lewis, 1418-1438.

Table 6. Probability of a leak-proof interception in a scenario of using 4 interceptors against each of the incoming warheads out of 30-40 attacking in a salvo at SSKP levels between 84% and 96%.

x	84%	85%	86%	87%	88%	89%	90%	91%	92%	93%	94%	95%	96%
30	0.02	0.03	0.04	0.06	0.08	0.12	0.16	0.22	0.29	0.38	0.49	0.62	0.75
31	0.02	0.03	0.04	0.05	0.07	0.10	0.14	0.20	0.27	0.36	0.47	0.60	0.73
32	0.02	0.02	0.03	0.05	0.07	0.09	0.13	0.18	0.25	0.34	0.45	0.58	0.72
33	0.01	0.02	0.03	0.04	0.06	0.08	0.12	0.17	0.23	0.32	0.43	0.56	0.70
34	0.01	0.02	0.02	0.03	0.05	0.07	0.11	0.15	0.21	0.30	0.41	0.54	0.68
35	0.01	0.01	0.02	0.03	0.04	0.07	0.10	0.14	0.20	0.28	0.39	0.52	0.67
36	0.01	0.01	0.02	0.03	0.04	0.06	0.09	0.13	0.18	0.26	0.37	0.50	0.65
37	0.01	0.01	0.01	0.02	0.03	0.05	0.08	0.12	0.17	0.25	0.35	0.48	0.63
38	0.01	0.01	0.01	0.02	0.03	0.05	0.07	0.11	0.16	0.23	0.33	0.46	0.61
39	0.00	0.01	0.01	0.02	0.03	0.04	0.06	0.10	0.15	0.22	0.31	0.44	0.60
40	0.00	0.01	0.01	0.02	0.02	0.04	0.06	0.09	0.13	0.20	0.30	0.42	0.58

Source: own counting based on Wilkening, 187-188, 191 and G. Lewis, 1418-1438.

Chart 7. Probability of a leak-proof interception in a scenario of using 4 interceptors against each of the incoming warheads out of 30-40 attacking in a salvo at SSKP levels between 84% and 96%.

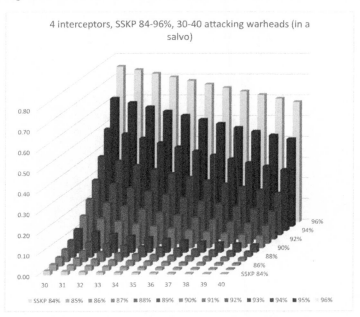

Source: own counting based on Wilkening, 187-188, 191 and G. Lewis, 1418-1438.

Table 7. Probability of a leak-proof interception in a scenario of using 5 interceptors against each of the warheads incoming out of 41-50 attacking in a salvo at SSKP levels between 86% and 96%.

x	86%	87%	88%	89%	90%	91%	92%	93%	94%	95%	96%
41	0.01	0.02	0.03	0.04	0.06	0.10	0.15	0.23	0.34	0.48	0.65
42	0.01	0.01	0.02	0.04	0.06	0.09	0.14	0.22	0.32	0.46	0.63
43	0.01	0.01	0.02	0.03	0.05	0.08	0.13	0.20	0.30	0.44	0.61
44	0.01	0.01	0.02	0.03	0.05	0.08	0.12	0.19	0.29	0.42	0.60
45	0.01	0.01	0.02	0.03	0.04	0.07	0.11	0.18	0.27	0.41	0.58
46	0.00	0.01	0.01	0.02	0.04	0.06	0.10	0.17	0.26	0.39	0.56
47	0.00	0.01	0.01	0.02	0.03	0.06	0.10	0.15	0.24	0.38	0.55
48	0.00	0.01	0.01	0.02	0.03	0.05	0.09	0.14	0.23	0.36	0.53
49	0.00	0.01	0.01	0.02	0.03	0.05	0.08	0.13	0.22	0.34	0.52
50	0.00	0.00	0.01	0.01	0.03	0.04	0.07	0.13	0.21	0.33	0.50

Source: own counting based on Wilkening, 187-188, 191 and G. Lewis, 1418-1438.

Chart 8. Probability of a leak-proof interception in a scenario of using 5 interceptors against each of the incoming warheads out of 41-50 attacking in a salvo at SSKP levels between 86% and 96%.

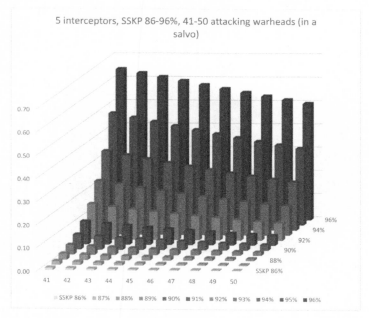

5 interceptors, SSKP 86-96%, 41-50 attacking warheads (in a salvo)

Source: own counting based on Wilkening, 187-188, 191 and G. Lewis, 1418-1438.

7. Finite Deterrence, Minimum Deterrence, Basic Deterrence

In 1990, Harold Feiveson and Frank von Hippel used the term *finite deterrence* to label more than a minimum size of superpower START nuclear forces, seeing the level of below 2000 warheads as too difficult to achieve by two superpowers' negotiations without agreement concerning other nuclear powers.[380]

Frank Marzari explained that finite deterrence was a posture formed by McNamara, based on survivability of the larger portion of nuclear forces through hardened underground silos, airborne avoidance of a first strike surprise, and SLBM deployments, which (cementing MAD policy) was also recommended by the US Secretary of Defense to his Soviet coun-

---

380   Harold Feiveson and Frank von Hippel, "Beyond START: How to Make Much Deeper Cuts," *International Security* 15, no. 1 (1990): 155–156, https://www.jstor.org/stable/2538985.

terparts (as preventing both sides from losing its nuclear force through a surface first strike).[381]

Richard Ned Lebow stated that in the 1960s' MAD scheme, "finite deterrence" was an alternative to the nuclear war-fighting doctrine (MAD); due to the cautiousness of USSR and Western leaders regarding nuclear war, a sufficient nuclear force included only a couple hundred warheads. However, this view had very low support in the US government.[382] According to J. David Singer, in the 1960s' MAD discussion between overkill and finite deterrence, in the latter, the finite or minimum MT requirements related to the ability to destroy enemy cities by a finite number of warheads would mean that the countervalue (counter-city) posture would be more savvy than a counter-force, as much more expansive, and with up to a 50% chance of destroying an enemy's missile by one's own missile (in an attempt to destroy the enemy's nuclear forces).[383]

Leverett Saltonstall explained that in the 1960s' discussion between counterforce and finite deterrence, the latter led to a threat to enemy society.[384] That posture, finite counter-city, is also labeled countervalue.[385]

Michael Miller noted that Cooperative Threat Reduction relied on the premise that nuclear materials are finite and may be secured.[386]

As Jeremy Stocker explained, after the Cold War, Britain kept a minimum deterrence force as an absolute necessity, while France and China maintained a similar policy with a larger stockpile.[387]

Zagare and Kilgour found that the point of a threat becoming potent was

---

381   Frank Marzari, "The Prospects for Strategic Stability in the 1970s," *Canadian Journal of Political Science* 4, no. 4 (1971): 542.

382   Richard Ned Lebow, *Avoiding War, Making Peace* (Cham: Springer, 2017), 129–160.

383   J. David Singer, *Deterrence, Arms Control, and Disarmament: Toward a Synthesis in National Security Policy* (Columbus: Ohio State University, 1962), 70.

384   Leverett Saltonstall, "Western Military Strength and Security," *The Annals of the American Academy of Political and Social Science*, 336 (1961): 63, https://www.jstor.org/stable/1032804.

385   Sloan, 57.

386   Michael Miller, "Nuclear Attribution as Deterrence," *The Nonproliferation Review*, 14, no. 1 (2007): 46, https://doi.org/10.1080/10736700601178465.

387   Jeremy Stocker, "Nuclear Deterrence," *The Adelphi Papers* 46, no. 386 (2007): 56, https://doi.org/10.1080/05679320701266356.

linked to the point of minimum cost of successful deterrence in a continuum of costs model.[388]

Damon Coletta stressed that the opponents of MAD underestimated a scenario of challenging a more powerful defender (not being able to use its full military potential in all local fields of operations) by an aggressor caring less of finite (due to its conventional dimension) war costs than the defender.[389] Colin Gray, explaining the process of escalating a regional conflict, found that a superpower protector needs strong reasons to risk through expanding its finite assets (including moral) in a regional-scale row (which became visible under a Bush Sr. new world order).[390]

As Robert Harkavy summarized, among doctrines related to nuclear deterrence, it is important to mention first and second strike doctrine, minimum and maximum deterrence, symmetrical and asymmetrical posture, finite/proportional dilemma, the problem of extended deterrence, limited, conventional, general and immediate, among others.[391]

Morgan clarified that post Cold War decline of Russia's conventional forces led to its increased reliance on nuclear forces, which at the same time were framed into a minimum deterrence posture, due to the low likelihood of nuclear attack and no permanent necessity of deterrence in great power relations, from the 2003 perspective.[392] As Thérèse Delpech stressed, China in the early twenty-first century has maintained a minimum deterrence policy in its nuclear posture doctrine.[393] Austin Long evaluated that by 2008, Russia's and China's nuclear forces were only providing basic deterrence, were unable to disarm US land-based triad component, and were far from first strike ability, while even a 5% chance of retaliation causing

---

388 Zagare and Kilgour, *Perfect Deterrence*, 292.

389 Damon Coletta, "Space and Deterrence," *Astropolitics* 7, no. 3 (2009): 178, https://doi.org/10.1080/14777620903372982.

390 Colin S. Gray, "Deterrence and Regional Conflict: Hopes, Fallacies, and 'Fixes,'" *Comparative Strategy* 17, no. 1 (1998): 57, https://doi.org/10.1080/01495939808403131.

391 Robert E. Harkavy, "Triangular or Indirect Deterrence/Compellence: Something New in Deterrence Theory?" *Comparative Strategy* 17, no. 1 (1998): 63, https://doi.org/10.1080/01495939808403132.

392 Morgan, *Deterrence Now*, 247.

393 Thérèse Delpech, *Nuclear Deterrence in the 21ˢᵗ Century: Lessons from the Cold War for a New Era of Strategic Piracy* (Santa Monica: RAND, 2012), 36, https://www.questia.com/read/122637778/nuclear-deterrence-in-the-21st-century-lessons-from.

destruction of even only two major US cities could seem a viable hedge against a possible US nuclear operation against Russia or China.[394] Michael Chase and Arthur Chan noted that PLA rocket force control over both nuclear and conventional deterrence caused ambiguity in terms of signaling, whether deterrence action is nuclear or conventional.[395]

John Baylis explained that mid-1950s thermonuclear and ballistic progress led to the British vision of cost-saving minimum deterrence posture for the West (according to the Director of Scientific Research at the Ministry of Supply, Robert Cockburn, corresponding with the Air Defence subcommittee), leading to the abandonment of a fully fledged race of arms between both superpowers, while the West would only need to deploy a minimum nuclear force able to destroy the USSR.[396]

Louis Rene Beres stressed from the 1987 nonproliferation progress perspective, both superpowers should restructure their nuclear postures towards minimum deterrence (and to return to such a strategy).[397]

Cimbala confirmed in early 2000s that START III models other than SLBM-based deterrence performs better than other triad force structures as a minimum (surviving) retaliation force in both more difficult (day-to-day alert and riding out an attack) and more convenient (generated alert, launch on warning) scenario of enemy assault under 2500 or 1500 warhead limit regimes.[398]

---

394 Austin Long, *Deterrence: From Cold War to Long War: Lessons from Six Decades of Rand Deterrence Research* (Santa Monica: RAND, 2008), 64, https://www.questia.com/read/122660182/deterrence-from-cold-war-to-long-war-lessons-from.

395 Michael Chase and Arthur Chan, *China's Evolving Approach to "Integrated Strategic Deterrence"* (Santa Monica: RAND, 2016), 52, https://www.questia.com/read/125655759/china-s-evolving-approach-to-integrated-strategic.

396 John Baylis, *Ambiguity and Deterrence: British Nuclear Strategy, 1945-1964* (New York: Oxford University Press, 1995), 188–189; Cambridge University, *The Papers of Sir Robert Cockburn* (2019), https://janus.lib.cam.ac.uk/db/node.xsp?id=EAD%2FGBR%2F0014%2FROCO; Churchill College Cambridge, *Guide to Holdings* (2019), https://www.chu.cam.ac.uk/archives/collections/guide-holdings/.

397 Louis Rene Beres, "Approaching Armageddon: Nuclear Proliferation and Nuclear War in the Middle East," in *Challenges to Deterrence: Resources, Technology, and Policy,* ed. by Stephen Cimbala (New York: Praeger, 1987), 135.

398 Stephen Cimbala, "Triage of Triads: Does the United States Really Need Three Strategic-Retaliatory Forces?" in *Deterrence and Nuclear Proliferation in the Twenty-First Century,* ed. by Stephen Cimbala (Westport: Praeger, 2001), 126–127.

Following Elizabeth Dauber (1993), the minimum ability of deterrence under Command, Control, and Communications (C3) US capacities was to provide a certain retaliation under Soviet attack, i.e., the retaliation force must have had been survivable ("close to intact") enough to secure an operationalized and coordinated attack (if the Soviet Union attacked first) ordered by National Command Authority.[399]

Timothy Crawford explained that pivots (being equal militarily to adversaries) by joining any side (among two rival adversaries) could change the outcome of the war, but not be able to overwhelm both combined adversaries.[400]

According to Feiveson, Richard Ullman, and von Hippel, the early stages of finite or minimum deterrence was rooted late in the Eisenhower administration's US Navy advocacy, leading to a vision of 232 survivable Polaris missiles that were able to cause MAD effects (but not all 645 airfields hosting Soviet strategic bombers targeted by Strategic Air Command, SAC, and tactical nuclear weapons), while Kennedy's science adviser, Jerome Wiesner, supported a vision of only few hundred survivable warheads as sufficient.[401]

Alan Wolfe explained that during the Carter administration, the two discussed reforms to the triad policy (Congressional Budget Office, CBO, *US Strategic Nuclear Forces, and Deterrence Policies and Procurement Issues* of April 1977, showing alternatives to the Rumsfeld-Schlesinger doctrine and high costs, seen by Wolfe as criticism) included finite deterrence as a minimal option leading to retaliation sufficiency in the con-

---

399 Cori Elizabeth Dauber, *Cold War Analytical Structures and the Post Post-War World: A Critique of Deterrence Theory* (Westport: Praeger, 1993), 42, https://www.questia. com/read/106747502/cold-war-analytical-structures-and-the-post-post-war.

400 Timothy W. Crawford, *Pivotal Deterrence: Third-Party Statecraft and the Pursuit of Peace* (Ithaca: Cornell University Press, 2003), 30, https://www.questia.com/ read/106760350/pivotal-deterrence-third-party-statecraft-and-the; Conf. Frank P. Harvey, *The Future's Back: Nuclear Rivalry, Deterrence Theory, and Crisis Stability after the Cold War* (Montreal: McGill-Queens University Press, 1997), https://www. questia.com/read/96176256/the-future-s-back-nuclear-rivalry-deterrence-theory; Bruce Russett, *The Prisoners of Insecurity: Nuclear Deterrence, the Arms Race, and Arms Control* (San Francisco: W.H. Freeman, 1983), https://www.questia.com/read/ 98393071/the-prisoners-of-insecurity-nuclear-deterrence-the.

401 Harold Feiveson, Richard Ullman and Frank von Hippel, "Reducing US and Soviet Nuclear Arsenals," *Bulletin of the Atomic Scientists* (1985), 145.

text of soft non-military target destruction and possible cancellation of B-1 and M-X programs in the overall triad reduction scheme, to provide for a cheaper strategic force, with CBO estimates of ca. \$3 billion annual savings and up to \$6.9 billion by 1982.[402] Still, as Wolfe explained, the conventional costs would be higher, while a second reform plan of "limited nuclear options" increased flexibility by enhancing finite deterrence to adapt it to limited war scenarios involving nuclear weapons (B-1 and M-X were to be cancelled in this scheme as well), but the funding for sea-launched cruise missiles, new interceptors, or warning systems would be provided, and the cost saving plan would include, according to CBO, \$2.3 billion immediately and \$4.5 billion by 1982 (since 1977).[403] Another discussed option in the CBO report (showing alternatives to counterforce, i.e., a second strike and options to destroy the enemy nuclear force, was essential equivalence, most demanding in terms of funding, but keeping pace with the Soviet Union in strategic weaponry (and its possible potential in reaching megatonnage advantage).[404]

---

402   Alan Wolfe, "Carter Plays with Fire. Obsession with Nuclear Strategy," *The Nation* (September 24, 1977), 267.

403   Wolfe, "Carter Plays with Fire," 267.

404   G. Philip Hughes and C. R. Neu, *US Strategic Nuclear Forces, Deterrence Policies and Procurement Issues* CBO, (1977), 27–32, https://www.cbo.gov/sites/default/files/95th-congress-1977-1978/reports/77doc600_0.pdf.

CHAPTER V

Since the Gulf War to Layered BMD:
an Overview of US PAC Intercept Performance

The aim of this chapter is to point out the significance of improvements in BMD effectiveness from the time of the US-led coalition formed to liberate Kuwait (occupied by Hussein's Iraq from August 1990 until Operation Desert Storm) until the ongoing twenty-first-century attempts to provide for a leak-proof interception of warheads in the case of military aggression. Notably, the mixed record of the PAC-2 units' interception attempts during the 1990-1991 Gulf War (in the context of Iraq's ballistic attacks against Saudi Arabia and Israel) gave rise to assumptions of low performance of the US-designed new BMD systems employed at tactical level.[405] Further analysis proved many of those concerns valid and led to a more detailed study of US tactical missile defense reliability, evolutionarily increased since 1991, through the Iraq War of 2003,[406] to the time of layered regional BMD systems in Eastern Europe and East Asia.

1. The Controversy of PAC Performance in 1991

According to Jeremiah Sullivan, Dan Fenstermacher, Daniel Fisher, Ruth Howes, O'Dean Judd, and Roger Speed (reporting on the basis of an earlier overview by Steven Hildreth), ca. 80 out of all Iraqi Scud missiles used against Saudi Arabia and Israel managed to land in (or near) the attacked countries, while PAC interceptors were able to engage 44 of them (probably 16 in the Israeli theater of operations and 28 in Saudi Arabia),

---

405 Sullivan and others, "Technical Debate over Patriot Performance in the Gulf War," 42, 55; Conf. Samson, *American Missile Defense*, 101; Hildreth, *Evaluation of US Army Assessment*; Shuey, *Theater Missile Defense*; Postol and Lewis, "Video Evidence on the Effectiveness of Patriot during the 1991 Gulf War," 34; Postol, *Optical Evidence Indicating Patriot High Miss Rates*; Schubert and Kraus, *The Whirlwind War*, 236–250.

406 Conf. Joel D. Rayburn and others, *The US Army in the Iraq War, Vol. 1 Invasion – Insurgency – Civil War, 2003-2006, and Vol. 2 Surge and Withdrawal, 2007-2011*, ed. by Joel D. Rayburn and Frank K. Sobchak (Carlisle Barracks: US Army War College Press, 2019), https://ssi.armywarcollege.edu/pubs/download.cfm?q=1373; Conf. Jon Finer, 'The Last War- and the Next? Learning the Wrong Lessons from Iraq," *Foreign Affairs* 98, no. 4 (2019): 183–191.

which did not mean a clear interception. The US Army evaluation of Patriot performance was corrected (as lower than previously assessed) from 96% effective (in March 1991) to 69% (in May 1991) and 59% (in April 1992).[407] On February 26, 1991, the US Central Command (CENT-COM) confirmed that an Iraqi Scud missile launched from South Iraq hit barracks occupied by American troops, killing 28 soldiers and leaving 100 wounded.[408] On February 28, 1991, the overall number of Scud missiles fired at Israel and Saudi Arabia reached 81.[409] In March 1991, Gen. Richard Beltson (US Army, responsible for missile procurement) reported to Congress that the Patriot deficiencies included:

- old gas engines, which tend to cause malfunctions,

- the misidentification of attacking missiles' debris, leading to tracking failures.

Beltson explained that the PAC firing doctrine during the Kuwait war led to using 2 interceptors against each incoming Scud right after detecting the attacking missile (in some cases even 4 interceptors were used).[410]

Beltson estimated that PAC effectiveness during the Kuwait war was 95% (mostly in the Saudi defense context, stressing that the PAC system was used in an automatic launch in Saudi Arabia and manually in Israel) on the basis of 45 interceptions out of 47 engagements. The December 1991 reassessments of the US Army (Brigadier General Robert Drolet) reported by Hildreth set PAC-2 reliability at 80% of engagements of attacking tactical ballistic missiles in Saudi Arabia and 50% in Israel.[411]

According to the US Army experts' report during the Kuwait war, 158 PAC-2 missiles were used, whereas by the end of the war, there were as many as ca. 3000 Patriot interceptors deployed, including earlier PAC-1 (full-scale PAC-2 production started after the war broke out).[412] In January 1991, the coalition command could use 480 PAC-2 missiles deployed

---

407   Sullivan and others, 42.

408   Hildreth, *Evaluation of US Army Assessment*, 51–54.

409   Hildreth, *Evaluation of US Army Assessment*, 51–54.

410   Hildreth, *Evaluation of US Army Assessment*, 51–54.

411   Hildreth, *Evaluation of US Army Assessment*, 51–54.

412   Schubert and Kraus, 243.

in the area of conflict.[413] The PAC-2 MIM 104C missile operational range reached 160 km.[414]

William Rosenau stressed that the Iraqi Scud missiles (since January 18, 1991 used to attack Israel, Saudi Arabia, and Bahrain) despite their low technological performance posed a strategic threat of a break-up of the coalition built to liberate Kuwait, occupied by Hussein's Iraq.[415] The Iraqi regime could use at the time 2 Scud (Soviet R-17)-based missiles: al-Hussein, with a 600-650 km range, and al-Abbas, with a range of 750-900 km, deployed (as Rosenau pointed out referring to the US Department of Defense report on intelligence estimates) on 28 fixed launchers at five missile sites (in Western Iraq) and some amount of mobile launchers (probably 36, but the number was not confirmed).[416]

The overall Iraqi Scud force probably included 600 missiles, according to US intelligence estimates.[417] Rosenau noted that the pursuit of Iraqi Scuds in Western Iraq was conducted by (apart from air observation and attacks) helicopter-deployed US and British (SAS) special operation forces, aimed to find Scud launcher locations and deliver them to the air force to bomb them.[418] As Rosenau concluded, the "Scud hunt" should not be seen as decisive in reducing the daily rate of Scud launches (from 4.7 launches per day in the first week of Operation Desert Storm to 1.5 per day in the later weeks of the war), as Iraq regained capability to use Scuds more intensively in the last days of the campaign.[419]

---

413   Hildreth, *Evaluation of US Army Assessment*, 1.

414   Wisher, 9.

415   William Rosenau, *Special Operations Forces and Elusive Ground Targets. Lessons from Vietnam and the Persian Gulf War* (Santa Monica, 2001), 29–32, https://www.rand.org/pubs/monograph_reports/MR1408.html.

416   Rosenau, 29–32.

417   Richard Cheney, *Conduct of the Persian Gulf War. Final Report to the Congress* (Washington, DC, 1992), 129, http://www.dtic.mil/dtic/tr/fulltext/u2/a249270.pdf.

418   SAS teams also engaged Iraqi launchers directly with close combat missiles. Rosenau, 37, 39–40.

419   Which could be understood as proof of Iraqi skill to adapt to the Scud hunt pressure and to overcome it after a couple of weeks of operations. Rosenau, 42. On the "Scud hunt," see also the establishments of Gordon and Trainor. Michael Gordon and Bernard Trainor, *The General's War. The Inside Story of the Conflict in the Gulf* (Boston: Back Bay Books, 1995), 227–248.

The US Department of Defense estimated that Scud attacks against Israel offered Hussein a strategic advantage, while Patriot units used against those missiles were not fully ready to counter warheads equipped with WMD, which led to a conclusion that further BMD improvements were necessary to counter such WMD threats posed by Third World countries in the future.[420] Tony DelGenis reported that the losses caused by Iraqi Scuds attacks (39 missiles) against Israel included 13 killed, 1020 wounded, and 12,000 private houses or offices damaged.[421]

Theodore Postol, the most radical critic of the Gulf War US missile defense performance, claimed (relying on media videotapes of PAC-2 attempts to intercept Scud missiles) that Patriot was a "near total failure in terms of its ability to destroy, damage, or divert Scud warheads."[422] Similarly, the Chair of US House Government Operations Subcommittee on Legislation and National Security, John Conyers, wrote that there was no strong evidence to claim that PAC-2 shot more than "a few" Iraqi Scud missiles during the Gulf War.[423] Joseph Cirincione judged that in the 1990s, right-wing politicians in the US lost the missile defense debate, a.o., due to the low performance of PAC-2 during the Gulf War, as MIT's Postol's arguments suggested.[424]

The September 1992 report of the GAO stressed that after the US Army revised its estimate of Gulf War PAC-2 performance in April 1992 (to 70% effectiveness in Saudi Arabia and 40% effectiveness in Israel), it could not prove with the "strongest evidence" more than 9% of Patriot interceptions out of 25% claimed as strongly reliable.[425] According to the revised assessment of the Army, PAC-2 engagements were 52% effective

---

420   Cheney, *Conduct of the Persian Gulf War*, xiii.

421   Tony DelGenis, "Israel's Gulf War Experience: A Brief Synopsis," *Middle East Policy* 2 (1997): 80, http://dx.doi.org/10.1111/j.1475-4967.1997.tb00266.x.

422   Theodore Postol and Robert Stein, "Patriot Experience in the Gulf War. Correspondence," *International Security* 17, no. 1 (1992): 226; Theodore Postol, "Lessons of the Gulf War Experience with Patriot," *International Security* 16, no. 3 (1991): 119–171.

423   John Conyers, "The Patriot Myth: Caveat Emptor," *Arms Control Today* 22, no. 9 (1992): 3, http://www.jstor.org/stable/23625004.

424   Joseph Cirincione, "Why the Right Lost the Missile Defense Debate," *Foreign Policy* 106 (1997): 45–46, http://www.jstor.org/stable/1149173.

425   Henry Hinton and others, *Operation Desert Storm. Data Does Not Exist to Conclusively Say How Well Patriot Performed* (Washington, DC, 1992), 3, https://www.gao.gov/assets/220/216867.pdf; Conf. Conyers, 3; Sullivan and others, 42.

in terms of destroying enemy warheads, including 25% engagements that were hit-to-kill effective with high certainty.[426] The GAO's February 1992 report stated that the failure of PAC interception of a Scud on February 25, 1991, which led to the tragic losses in the barracks and death of 28 US soldiers, occurred due to the extensive length of work of the Dhahran PAC battery (over 100 hours), which deepened the inaccuracy in calculations used to track the attacking missile (the necessary additional software, needed to limit the inaccuracy, arrived too late, on February 26, 1991).[427]

Anthony Cordesman and Abraham Wagner assessed that during the Kuwait war, Patriot provided perfect air defense protection and limited BMD, which had a more psychological than hit-to-kill effect, but (importantly) increased the morale of soldiers and helped to prevent Israeli engagement in the conflict.[428] Israeli engagement could have caused the dissolution of the Arab part of the coalition formed to drive Hussein's Iraq out of Kuwait.[429] Roger Handberg estimated that Patriot deployment in Israel, though militarily ineffective in attempts to intercept the incoming Scud missiles, played a politically crucial role by providing the Israeli government with an excuse (in the eyes of the public opinion) to not respond militarily to the Iraqi attacks, and therefore, the US BMD helped to secure the political conditions necessary to win the war against Iraq.[430]

David Denoon stressed that the PAC-2 missiles (originally anti-aircraft weapons) were adapted for BMD purposes to provide for the defense of small areas, not as a hedge against missile attacks aimed at cities, and (importantly) they were not prepared to deal with Iraqi Scuds (which, due to

---

426   Henry Hinton and others, *Operation Desert Storm*, 3.

427   Ralph Carlone and others, *Patriot Missile Defense. Software Problem Led to System Failure at Dhahran, Saudi Arabia* (Washington, DC, 1992), 1, https://www.gao.gov/assets/220/215614.pdf.

428   Anthony Cordesman and Abraham Wagner, *The Lessons of Modern War, Vol. 4 The Gulf War* (Westview Press, 1996), 20, https://www.questia.com/read/101412956/the-gulf-war.

429   Barry Schneider, *Future War and Counterproliferation: US Military Responses to NBC Proliferation Threats* (Westport: Praeger, 1999), 128–129, https://www.questia.com/read/15397470/future-war-and-counterproliferation-u-s-military.

430   Roger Handberg, *Ballistic Missile Defense and the Future of American Security: Agendas, Perceptions, Technology, and Policy* (Westport: Praeger, 2002), 65, https://www.questia.com/read/106742722/ballistic-missile-defense-and-the-future-of-american.

metallurgic deficiencies, often break into pieces while descending towards the targets).[431] Albert Mauroni explained that the disintegration of Scud missiles in the air were falsely interpreted by the Pentagon as successful PAC-2 interceptions, leading to (later corrected) claim referring to the hit-to-kill rate reaching more than 90% (reduced after further inquiries to as low as 9% confirmed interceptions).[432] Alberto Bin, Richard Hill, and Archer Jones observed that the over-optimistic first reports of PAC-2 interceptions could be partly attributed to the software configuration, informing of an intercept success when Patriot missiles were detonated near Scuds (even in cases when they could not destroy the Scud).[433] At the same time, PAC engagement critics saw pieces of disintegrated Scud missiles falling on the ground as a sufficient proof that the interception failed (even when the Iraqi missile was destroyed), because such debris could cause casualties or damage (especially in Israel).[434] Barry Schneider pointed out that in the dispute on the PAC-2 reliability during the Gulf War, Postol's critique was correct in terms of the US Army's overreliance on Patriot's intercept capabilities (confirmed by the corrected hit-to-kill ratio).[435] However, as Schneider stressed, the final identification of interception effects was not possible without the data on Iraqi missile targets (unavailable to the US), which could decisively prove whether the interceptors managed to change the course of flight of Scud warheads or collided only with the less important pieces of self-disintegrated missiles.[436] Williamson Murray and Robert Scales explained that the imperfect PAC-2 interception attempts during the Gulf War were connected to conventional warhead design, used against targets by an explosion spreading out metal elements, not effective enough to prevent some Scuds from break-

431   David Denoon, *Ballistic Missile Defense in the Post-Cold War Era* (Boulder: Westview Press, 1995), 2, https://www.questia.com/read/89750824/ballistic-missile-defense-in-the-post-cold-war-era.

432   Albert Mauroni, *Chemical-Biological Defense: US Military Policies and Decisions in the Gulf War* (Westport: Praeger, 1998), 97, https://www.questia.com/read/10674 3486/chemical-biological-defense-u-s-military-policies.

433   Alberto Bin, Richard Hill and Archer Jones, *Desert Storm: A Forgotten War* (Westport: Praeger, 1998), 101, https://www.questia.com/read/120739370/desert-storm-a-forgotten-war.

434   Bin, Hill and Jones, *Desert Storm*, 101.

435   Schneider, *Future War and Counterproliferation*, 128–129.

436   Schneider, 128–129.

ing through such explosions, whereas the improved PAC-3, deployed to support the 2003 US intervention in Iraq, were aimed at destroying very fast targets (as planned, missiles reaching even a speed close to Mach 10, including Iraqi missiles of Mach 4-7 velocity) by a direct collision (which proved to be the most reliable of all methods used before).[437]

As Mauroni reported, according to US intelligence estimates, the pre-Kuwait War Iraqi WMD arsenal included chemical agents (mustard gas), nerve gases (tabun, sarin, and cyclosarin), and (in development) soman, nerve gas VX, and hallucinogen BZ, whereas the Iraqi-possessed Soviet-produced delivery tools of those weapons consisted of multiple rocket launchers, Iraq-designed rockets launched by helicopters, aerial bombs, artillery guns, mortars and (according to Israeli sources) chemical warheads carried by Scud missiles.[438] As Mauroni noted, during the Kuwait war, the overall Iraqi chemical arsenal could encompass 1000-4000 tons of nerve agents and mustard gases, while Iraq was able to produce 150 tons of mustard gas, 5-10 tons of tabun, 20 tons of sarin, monthly.[439]

Michael Gordon noted that just before Iraqi attack on Kuwait, the Iraqi servicemen were interrupted while attempting to move US equipment designed to trigger nuclear warheads across the border, whereas in her conversation, US ambassador April Glaspie raised the Iraqi WMD threat with Hussein.[440] After the Iraqi attack against Kuwait, in October 1990, according to US declassified records, the Iraqi Military Industry Commission was examining an offer from Pakistani nuclear scientist, Abdul Qadeer Khan, to provide Iraq with nuclear weapons.[441] In 1992, the

---

437   Including highly advanced Russian BMD developments, which were still not battle-field-checked. Williamson Murray and Robert Scales, *The Iraq War: A Military History* (Cambridge, Massachusetts: Belknap Press, 2003), 265, https://www.questia.com/library/119021308/the-iraq-war-a-military-history.

438   Mauroni, *Chemical-Biological Defense*, 26–27.

439   Mauroni, 26–27.

440   Michael Gordon, "The Last War Syndrome. How the United States and Iraq Learned the Wrong Lessons from Desert Storm," in *Into the Desert: Reflections on the Gulf War*, ed. by Jeffrey Engel (New York: Oxford University Press, 2013), 121, https://www.questia.com/read/121322606/into-the-desert-reflections-on-the-gulf-war.

441   Conflict Records Research Center, *Correspondence between the MIC and the Petro Chemical Group Regarding a Letter from A.Q. Khan Offering Assistance in Developing Iraq's Nuclear Weapons Program*, CRRC Record Number: SH-MICN-D-000-741, Document Date: 6 Oct 1990 (1990), http://crrc.dodlive.mil/files/2013/06/SH-MICN-

White House was concerned about foreign support (visible before the 1990-1991 war) in Iraqi attempts to reestablish its nuclear program, shattered by an Israeli air strike against Osiraq in 1981 (a year after Desert Storm, Washington examined possible nuclear cooperation between Algeria and Iraq after the electoral success of Algerian Islamic fundamentalist party).[442]

It is worth stressing that due to the establishment of the US Iraq Survey Group (ISG) and the British John Chilcot reports, Iraq most likely destroyed its WMD arsenal after the 1991 war, despite the pre-2003 George W. Bush administration statements on the threat posed by the Hussein regime's chemical weapons (and hypothetical nuclear attempts, including Niger's uranium ore), which were not confirmed by US investigations after the invasion in March 2003 (Operation Iraqi Freedom).[443] According to the Iraq Survey Group report, there was no evidence of WMD in Hussein's possession in 2003 and weapons of that sort existing in Iraq most likely had no military importance (if those materials really stayed in Iraq).[444]

2. PAC Improved Performance During the 2003 Iraq War

Gordon and Bernard Trainor stressed that during Operation Iraqi Freedom, PAC-3 missiles proved to be effective enough to counter the Iraqi short-range Al-Samoud and Ababil missiles, while the use of naval cruise missiles (Seersuckers) against land targets surprised the invading coalition and its reconnaissance systems.[445] Samson noted that despite the official claims of 100% reliability in Operation Iraqi Freedom, the PAC-2 and PAC-3 (54 of the latter generation out of 1069 PAC interceptors were

D-000-741.pdf; Omar Al-Jaffal, "Iraq's Defunct Military Industry," *Al Monitor*, July 1, 2015, https://www.al-monitor.com/pulse/originals/2015/07/iraq-military-industry-war-islamic-state.html.

442 Edmund J. Hull, *Memorandum for Jonathan T. Howe through Richard N. Haass, Subject: Algeria: New Islamic Electoral Success and Old Stories on Nuclear Cooperation with Iraq*, Bush Presidential Records, White House Office of Records Management, WHORM, Date 01/06/92 (1992), https://bush41library.tamu.edu/files/persian-gulf/41-CO004-322949/41-co004-322949.pdf.

443 Duelfer, *Comprehensive Report*, 64; Chilcot, *The Report of the Iraq Inquiry*, 77–78.

444 Duelfer, 64.

445 Michael Gordon and Bernard Trainor, *Cobra II. The Inside Story of the Invasion and Occupation of Iraq*, Kindle (New York: Pantheon Books, 2006), 3544.

used in the Spring 2003 invasion) record was mixed, while it was possible to confirm their engagement against 9 out of 23 Iraqi missiles launched (no Scud missiles were reported), among which modified the Chinese anti-ship cruise missiles CSSC-3 Seersuckers were most difficult to track on radars and intercept.[446] Patriot missiles' performance in the Iraq war was also disappointing, as Samson stressed, in terms of the recognition of air units, which led to friendly fire against one British and two US aircrafts (destroying one and tracking another), confirmed by government assessments and explained by radar malfunction, "*ghost tracks*", i.e., false images leading to bad targeting.[447] Richard Dean Burns stressed that Gen. Kadish's views on PAC-3 use during the 2003 invasion were optimistic, despite not having a fully clear test performance, and the official record of 100% effective interception based on 9 successful attempts out of 9 engagements (including 7 PAC-2 and 2 PAC-3 interceptions) did not refer to all 23 missiles fired by Iraq and fratricide accidents.[448] The Defense Science Board Task Force report on Patriot performance in the 2003 war estimated that among the reasons for friendly fire (in air defense mode) were incorrect combat identification, flawed situational awareness (in terms of communication and data processing), and operation system deficiencies (a.o., protocols and software not being well suited to the combat scenario in Iraq, where the ratio of friendly to foe aircraft reached 4000 to 1, while PAC systems design headed towards serious missile attack scenarios).[449]

The Congressional Research Service (CRS) report stated that the mistaken fatal use of PAC-2 against a British Tornado on March 23, 2003 (which killed two crew members while shooting down the aircraft), an incident on March 25 (the misidentification of a US F-16, treated by PAC as a target, leading to the destruction of Patriot radar by the aircraft), and

446 Samson, 104–105.

447 Samson, 104–105, 119–120; Conf. Office of the Under Secretary of Defense for Acquisition, *Report of the Defense Science Board Task Force on Patriot System Performance* (2002), https://www.acq.osd.mil/dsb/reports/2000s/ADA435837.pdf; Christopher Bolkcom, "Friendly Fire," in *Iraq War: Defense Program Implications for Congress,* ed. by Ronald O'Rourke (Washington, DC: Congressional Research Service, 2003), 54–58, https://www.globalsecurity.org/military/library/report/crs/iraq_defense.pdf.

448 Richard Dean Burns, *The Missile Defense Systems of George W. Bush. A Critical Assessment* (Santa Barbara: Praeger, 2010), 74–75.

449 Office of the Under Secretary of Defense for Acquisition, *Report of the Defense Science Board Task Force on Patriot System Performance,* 2.

a tragic identification failure of PAC-3 on April 2, causing the death of a F/A-18C pilot (the fighter was shot down) could be attributed to:

- electromagnetic interference (from too many PAC systems close to each other),

- human mistakes, or

- digital identification and communication technology malfunctions.[450]

As Christopher Bolkcom noted, the British Tornado's accidental destruction by a PAC-2 could be connected to the unexpected air route of the British airplane (beyond the secured Kuwait-Iraq air corridor), while its identification-friend-or-foe (IFF) technologies, damaged during the mission, were not able to communicate effectively with the US units.[451] In the case of the F-16 incident, according to CRS expertise, the PAC team was operating in automatic mode, hiding from Iraqi artillery, whereas in the case of the F/A-18C, the accident was probably due to human error of the PAC crew, which took the US fighter for an enemy missile (the possible remedy fro such mistakes could come from improved battle-management communication technologies, such as Link-16).[452]

The RAND report stressed that PAC-2 GEM and PAC-3 were successful against Ababil 100 missiles (on March 20, March 21, March 24, March 25, and March 27), and Al-Samoud missiles (on March 23, March 27, and April 1) intercepted by (altogether) 21 GEM missiles, accompanied by 2 PAC-2 (destroying 6 targets, apart from 1 false target tracked by 1 missile) and 4 PAC-3 interceptors (including 2 used against 1 destroyed Ababil missile and 2 against a target destroyed on April 1).[453] Apart from Seersuckers, the unengaged missiles (Ababil) were labeled by the RAND report as having no danger of causing any damage ("harmless trajectory").[454]

---

450 Bolkcom, "Friendly Fire," 55–56.

451 Bolkcom, 55–56.

452 Bolkcom, 55–56.

453 Bruce Pirnie and others, "Air Operations," in *Operation Iraqi Freedom. Decisive War, Elusive Peace*, ed. by Walter Perry and others (Santa Monica: RAND, 2015), 177–178, https://www.rand.org/content/dam/rand/pubs/research_reports/RR1200/RR1214/RAND_RR1214.pdf.

454 Pirnie and others, "Air Operations," 177–178.

3. The Stages of PAC Improvements

The Gulf War BMD deployments, as well as the later PAC-3 introduction to arms sales contracts, could be seen as steps towards regional layered missile defense systems, created with the participation of US allies threatened by missiles in their neighborhood. The twenty-first century's layers or additional interceptors in a layered BMDS are rooted in the Cold War US BMD efforts, including Reagan's SDI. The 1980s' SDI-era visions of BMD systems reaching intercontinental capacities involved, next to space-based systems, a layered system that included 4 layers, each possessing a 50% kill probability, which left the MAD paradigm unharmed due to a likely leakage of 50% of attacking warheads through each of the four layers, letting more than 300 strategic warheads (ca. 312 out of 5000 Soviet warheads in hypothetical all-out attack) reach their targets.[455] The main US post-Cold War effort to improve BMD systems was justified in terms of rogue countries' capabilities (dictatorships armed with WMD and threatening their neighbors with armed invasion) in the area of WMD-oriented missile technologies.[456]

A mobile air defense (future Patriot[457]) concept appeared in 1961 (in US Army Missile Command). In 1965, the Surface-Air-Missile (SAM-D) development program began, leading to tests in 1970 and full-scale development in 1976, commenced under the name Patriot (to honor the 200th anniversary of the Declaration of Independence), bringing the new operational equipment to the Army by 1985.[458] PAC was modified in the mid-1980s, including the introduction of 8 launchers in a battery (PAC-2 used 4 missiles per launcher), with MIM-104 missile reaching a speed of Mach 3.[459]

---

455 Hoffman, *Ballistic Missile Defenses.*

456 Donald H. Rumsfeld and others, *Executive Summary of the Report of the Commission to Assess the Ballistic Missile Threat to the United States (Pursuant to Public Law 201 104ᵗʰ Congress, July 15, 1998)* (1998), https://fas.org/irp/threat/bm-threat.htm; Conf. Robert Kagan and William Kristol, *Present Dangers. Crisis and Opportunity in American Foreign and Defense Policy* (San Francisco: Encounter Books, 2000).

457 Phased Array Tracking Radar to Intercept on Target. NATO, *PATRIOT Deployment* (2015), https://www.nato.int/nato_static_fl2014/assets/pdf/pdf_2015_05/2015 0508_1505-Factsheet-PATRIOT_en.pdf.

458 CSIS Missile Threat, *Patriot* (2018), https://missilethreat.csis.org/system/patriot/.

459 PBS, "Weapons: MIM-104 Patriot," *PBS* (2018), https://www.pbs.org/wgbh/pages/

Notably, in 1991 PAC-2, which was designed to attack Soviet cruise and air targets at Mach 2, attempted to intercept an Iraqi Scud reaching Mach 5 (3750 mph).[460] The controversial outcomes led to further significant PAC improvements. As Wisher explained, Patriot developments after the Gulf war included PAC-3 Configuration 1 (1994-1995) with Guidance Enhanced Missile (GEM), PAC-3 Configuration 2 (1996-1997), and PAC-3 Configuration 3 (1998-2000) with GEM+ Missile and PAC-3 Missile.[461]

According to the 2000 GAO report, due to the Army's expectations, PAC-3 costs increased from $3.9 billion in 1994 to $6.9 billion in 2000 (for 1200 and 1012 missiles, respectively).[462] PAC-3 used 16 missiles per launcher.[463] The US Army expected to receive (in 2000) 2200 PAC-3 missiles for 2 consecutive wars, as strategically planned.[464]

The 2013 Patriot battery (a battalion consisted of up to 6 such batteries) included 4 GEM-T launchers (with 4 fragmentation warhead interceptors each) and 2 PAC-3 launchers (with 16 guided missiles each, using direct collision, hit-to-kill kinetic interception).[465] If each battalion consisted of 4 fire units (batteries), and each of them employed 6 launchers, the PAC intercept force by 2025 could consist of up to 5760 missiles (if PAC-3 interceptors were to be used, i.e., 16 missiles per launcher).[466]

---

frontline/gulf/weapons/patriot.html. Scud-D reached a speed of Mach 5 in flight. Military Factory, "SS-1 (Scud)/9P117," *Military Factory* (2017), https://www.militaryfactory.com/armor/detail.asp?armor_id=24.

460   Carlone and others, *Patriot Missile Defense*, 6.

461   Wisher, 8–9, 18.

462   Allen Li, Bob Levin and others, *Missile Defense* (Washington, DC, 2000), 4, https://www.gao.gov/assets/240/230417.pdf.

463   Kyle Mizokami, "Why America's Enemies Fear the Patriot Missile Defense System (Even After Almost 40 Years)," *The National Interest* (March 20, 2017), http://nationalinterest.org/print/blog/the-buzz/why-americas-enemies-fear-the-patriot-missile-defense-system-19833.

464   Li, Levin, and others, *Missile Defense*, 4.

465   US Army Acquisition Corps, *Patriot Overview* (2013), 5, https://www.msl.army.mil/Documents/Briefings/LTPO/LTPO.pdf; J. Michael Gilmore, *Annual Report, Fiscal Year 2014* (Washington, DC, 2015), 133–134, http://www.dote.osd.mil/pub/reports/FY2014/pdf/other/2014DOTEAnnualReport.pdf.

466   US Army Acquisition Corps, 5; Gilmore, *Annual Report*, 133–134.

The US Army's modernization plans included a goal of upgrading all Patriot battalions (15, consisting of typically 4 fire units, up to 6 in each battalion) by 2025 to the Integrated Battle and Command System (IBCS) in the Integrated Air and Missile Defense (IAMD) program (providing for Patriot units radars and launchers connection into a central network with command/control stations).[467] By 2013, eleven US allies used Patriot systems (Germany, Greece, Israel, Japan, Kuwait, Netherlands, Saudi Arabia, South Korea, Spain, Taiwan, and the United Arab Emirates [UAE]).[468] In 2015, Qatar became a Patriot partner country.[469] In January 2013, NATO contributions connected with the Syrian civil war led to the deployment of the first operational Patriot battery in Turkey (under allied command).[470] The first 5 Patriot batteries (operated by 750 soldiers) contributed by NATO countries support the Turkish air defense under Syrian missile threat.[471] In 2015, the US, German, and Dutch PAC batteries were withdrawn from Turkey, while 1 Spanish-operated PAC-2 unit stayed as a replacement, supported by an Italian SAMP/T battery. Turkey decided in 2017 to conclude an agreement with Russia on the purchase of S-400 air defense systems.[472]

The 2015-ready NATO PAC batteries were providing a point defense in the range of 15-20 km (using 4 PAC-2 and 16 PAC-3 missiles per launcher, intercepting at a speed of 5000 km/h) with radars of more than 150 km

---

467   Cristina Chaplain, LaTonya Miller, Kevin O'Neill and others, *Patriot Modernization. Oversight Mechanism Needed to Track Progress and Provide Accountability* (Washington, DC, 2016), 3, 7, 33, https://www.gao.gov/assets/680/679257.pdf.

468   US Army Acquisition Corps, 4.

469   Brian McKeon, "Statement before the Senate Armed Services Subcommittee on Strategic Forces, April 13, 2016 (Principal Deputy under Secretary of Defense for Policy)" (2016), 7, https://www.armed-services.senate.gov/imo/media/doc/McKeon_04-13-16.pdf.

470   NATO, *PATRIOT Deployment*.

471   NATO, *PATRIOT Deployment*.

472   Missile Defense Advocacy Alliance, *Turkey* (2018), http://missiledefenseadvocacy.org/intl-cooperation/turkey/; Ben Hodges, *Department of Defense Press Briefing by General Hodges on Operation Atlantic Resolve, December 9, 2015, US Department of Defense* (Washington, DC, 2015) https://www.defense.gov/News/Transcripts/Transcript-View/Article/633667/department-of-defense-press-briefing-by-general-hodges-on-operation-atlantic-re/; Burak Bekdil, "Turkey Makes Deal to Buy Russian-Made S-400 Air Defense System," *DefenseNews* (2017), https://www.defensenews.com/land/2017/12/29/turkey-russia-reportedly-sign-loan-deal-for-s-400-air-defense-system/.

range.[473] The increased Russian threat in Eastern Europe since the 2014 Russia's aggression against Ukraine led (a.o.) to the Enhanced Forward Presence of NATO battle groups (since the 2016 Warsaw summit conclusions) in Poland, Estonia, Latvia, and Lithuania.[474] Patriot batteries were sent by the US NATO contingents for air defense exercises to Poland (in 2015) and to Lithuania (in 2017).[475]

The MSE unit's initial operational capabilities were dependent upon the first PAC unit being equipped with 12 missiles per fire unit (a Patriot launcher could carry 12 MSE or 6 of the latter and 8 PAC-3s in two canisters, i.e., four packs, instead of 16 PAC-3 missiles in 4 canisters) and the deployment of a battalion consisting of four such fire units.[476]

The August 2016 GAO report for Congress stressed that from 2013 to mid-2016, the Patriot (as "a cornerstone" of the US Army BMD efforts) received $1.1 billion to upgrade its capabilities, while the Army requested an additional $1.8 billion to modernize PAC by 2023.[477]

Michael Elleman and Wafa Alsayed noted that after the Kuwait and Saudi Arabian purchase of PAC-2 (soon after Desert Storm), the US BMD producers had to wait until the next decade for an another contract of such

---

473 NATO, *PATRIOT Deployment*.

474 NATO, *Boosting NATO's Presence in the East and Southeast, March 2, 2018* (2018), https://www.nato.int/cps/en/natohq/topics_136388.htm?selectedLocale=en; Justin Geiger, "Battle Group Poland Is Hailed in Orzysz, Poland," *US Army* (2017), https://www.army.mil/article/186072/battle_group_poland_is_hailed_in_ orzysz_poland; Conf. Anthony Juarez, *Remixing the "Appropriate Mix" Reassessing NATO's Deterrence and Defense Posture in the Face of New Threats* (2016), https://e-reports-ext.llnl.gov/pdf/825301.pdf.

475 Randall Jackson, "Army Europe Air Defense Unit Deploys to Poland for Exercise," *US Army* (2016), https://www.army.mil/article/144818/army_europe_air_defense _unit_deploys_to_poland_for_exercise; John Vandiver, "US Deployed Patriot Missiles to Lithuania for Multinational War Games," *Stars & Stripes* (2017), https://www.stripes.com/news/europe/us-deployed-patriot-missiles-to-lithuania-for-multinational-war-games-1.477426.

476 Defense Acquisition Management, *Patriot Advanced Capability-3 Missile Segment Enhancement (PAC-3 MSE) (Selected Acquisition Report as of FY 2017 President's Budget, March 21, 2016* (2016), 9, http://www.dtic.mil/dtic/tr/fulltext/u2/1019515.pdf; Lockheed Martin, *PAC-3 Missile Segment Enhancement (MSE). Delivering Increased Range and Altitude* (2015), https://www.lockheedmartin.com/content/dam/lock heed/data/mfc/pc/pac-3-missile-segment-enhancement/mfc-pac-3-mse-pc.pdf.

477 Chaplain, Miller, O'Neill and others, *Patriot Modernization*, 1.

importance. In early 2000s (in light of the Iranian threat), Gulf states' interest in BMD grew significantly, opening a path to the US-UAE PAC-3 procurement agreement of 2008 (followed by the 2011 THAAD delivery deal), Qatar's official plan of PAC acquisition, Kuwait and Saudi PAC-2/PAC-3 upgrades, and further THAAD negotiations of the latter buyers.[478]

As Hildreth noted, THAAD was proposed in 1987 and first tested in 1995.[479] MDA's THAAD plans for 2025 included a deployment of 7 batteries, 428 interceptors, and 7 radars.[480] According to "The Military Balance," in 2018, the US armed forces operated 480 Patriot missiles and 42 THAAD.[481] According to MDA's FY 2019 budget, each of the 7 THAAD batteries (armed with 6 launchers and 48 missiles) was operated by 95 soldiers (MDA's responsibilities included "unique or developmental items" and the Army's obligations were related to operation and common items).[482]

Among the MDA, the most recent major accomplishment was the first successful test intercept of ICBM in May 2017.[483] The costs of 20 addi-

---

478 Michael Elleman and Wafa Alsayed, "Ballistic Missile Defense Cooperation in the Arabian Gulf," in *Regional Missile Defense from a Global Perspective*, ed. by Catherine McArdle Kelleher and Peter Dombrowski, Kindle (Stanford: Stanford University Press, 2015), 3273-3282; Gawdat Bahgat, "Missile Proliferation in the Middle East," *The Journal of Social, Political, and Economic Studies* 31, no. 4 (2006): 399+, https://www.questia.com/read/1P3-1229863001/missile-proliferation-in-the-middle-east.

479 Steven Hildreth, *Defense Primer: Ballistic Missile Defense* (Washington, DC, 2016), https://fas.org/sgp/crs/natsec/IF10541.pdf.

480 Cristina Chaplain, LaTonya Miller, Matthew Ambrose, and others, *Missile Defense. Some Progress Delivering Capabilities, but Challenges with Testing Transparency and Requirements Development Need to Be Addressed* (Washington, DC, 2017), 105, https://www.globalsecurity.org/space/library/report/gao/684963.pdf.

481 John Chipman, "Chapter Three: North America," *The Military Balance* 118, no. 1 (2018): 49, https://doi.org/10.1080/04597222.2018.1416979.

482 Office of the Under Secretary of Defense—Comptroller, *Missile Defense Agency, Procurement, Defense-Wide (Includes O&M and MILCON). Defense-Wide Justification Book Volume 2b of 2, Department of Defense Fiscal Year 2019 Budget Estimates, Washington, DC, February 2018* (2018), LVII, http://comptroller.defense.gov/Portals/45/Documents/defbudget/fy2019/budget_justification/pdfs/02_Procurement/U_PROCUREMENT_MasterJustificationBook_Missile_Defense_Agency_PB_2019_1.pdf; MDA, *Terminal High Altitude Area Defense Fact Sheet*; Office of the Under Secretary of Defense - Comptroller, *Program Acquisition Costs by Weapon System FY 2018* (2017), 4–3, http://comptroller.defense.gov/Portals/45/Documents/defbudget/fy2018/fy2018_Weapons.pdf.

483 MDA, *Fiscal Year (FY) 2019 Budget Estimates Overview*, 2018, https://www.mda.mil/

tional long-range GBI in the Midcourse BMD layer and 20 silos (to increase the GBI number to 64 by 2023) were set at the level of ca. $1.8 billion, according to the FY 2019 budget plan.[484] MDA appropriations from 1985 to 2017 reached $190 billion, including its predecessor organizations, i.e., SDIO and Ballistic Missile Defense Organization (BMDO).[485]

4. Israeli BMD Improvements Supported by the US Since the 1991 PAC-2 Introduction

Among the most important regional BMD improvements after the Gulf War are the US-Israeli Arrow (middle range) and Iron Dome (short range) intercept missiles cooperation, leading to the deployment of a combat-capable Israel's missile defense, used to defend settlements attacked by Hamas rockets (since 2012).[486] According to the 2016 ten-year memorandum of understanding between the United States and Israel, the US has committed to supporting Israeli missile defense in the amount of $500 million annually since 2019.[487] In the framework of $38 billion US security support, this replaced the previous $30 billion package implemented by 2018 (overall, mostly military United States assistance to Israel reached ca. $134.8 billion 1946-2016, including $91.6 billion in

---

global/documents/pdf/budgetfy19.pdf.

484   Office of the Under Secretary of Defense - Comptroller, *Missile Defense Agency, Procurement, Defense-Wide (Includes O&M and MILCON). Defense-Wide Justification Book Volume 2b of 2, Department of Defense Fiscal Year 2019 Budget Estimates*, Washington, DC, February 2018, 2b–13.

485   MDA and predecessor organizations funding. MDA, *Historical Funding for MDA FY85-17 Fiscal Year (FY in Billions)* (2017), https://www.mda.mil/global/documents/pdf/FY17_histfunds.pdf.

486   IDF, *Operation Pillar of Defense (2012)* (2018), https://www.idf.il/en/minisites/wars-and-operations/operation-pillar-of-defense-2012/; Duncan Clarke, "The Arrow Missile: The United States, Israel and Strategic Cooperation," *Middle East Journal* 48, no. 3 (1994): 475–491, http://www.jstor.org/stable/4328717; Eyal Pecht, Asher Tishler and Nir Weingold, "On the Choice of Multi-Task R&D Defense Projects: A Case Study of the Israeli Missile Defense System," *Defence and Peace Economics* 24, no. 5 (2013): 429–448, https://doi.org/10.1080/10242694.2012.717205.

487   Jeremy Sharp, *US Foreign Aid to Israel* (Washington, DC, 2018), 1; Thomas Harvey, "Statement before the House Armed Services Subcommittee on Strategic Forces, June 7, 2017" (2017), 9–10, http://docs.house.gov/meetings/AS/AS29/20170607/106064/HHRG-115-AS29-Wstate-HarveyT-20170607.pdf; The White House, *Fact Sheet: Memorandum of Understanding Reached with Israel* (2016), https://obamawhitehouse.archives.gov/the-press-office/2016/09/14/fact-sheet-memorandum-understanding-reached-israel.

military assistance, $34.3 billion in economic funding, and $5.1 billion in missile defense support).[488]

Choices made by Israel since its participation in Reagan's SDI, through the shocking experience of Iraqi Scud attacks during the Gulf War (and low PAC-2 performance), led to the creation of partly indigenous missile defense systems, based on US technologies introduced with Washington's financial support. Israel managed to build layered missile defense system of high effectiveness and a broad set of possible targets, including short range artillery and missile threats (countered by Iron Dome), short-to-middle range ballistic threats (intercepted by David's Sling), and a medium-range BMD component: the Arrow system. The experience of the Gulf War and Islamist radical groups short-range rocket attacks forced Israel to invest heavily in own BMD responses. Next to the United States, aside from its Arab Gulf allies, Israel remains one of the few countries forced to test its BMD capabilities in combat. For those reasons, it seems useful to focus on the Israeli BMD results, which could contribute to further analysis of layered missile defense systems, developed in the first and second decades of the twenty-first century for the needs of the Far East (South Korea and Japan) and East European (Poland and Romania) allies of the US that are threatened by regional missile hazards.

Before the development of the Israeli BMD, its capabilities to counter WMD threats in the neighborhood were largely based on first strike (preventive) assault options, using the outreach of Israel's air forces. Israeli attack against Osiraq in 1981 stopped Hussein's nuclear weapon program.[489] Similarly, in 2007, the Israeli air force prevented Bashar Assad's Syria from further development of its WMD capacities through air strikes against Syrian nuclear installations.[490]

---

488 Jeremy Sharp, *US Foreign Aid to Israel*, 1; T. Harvey, 9–10; The White House, *Fact Sheet: Memorandum of Understanding Reached with Israel*.

489 Israel's government (a nuclear weapon state since the 1960s, most likely) was afraid that Hussein would use nuclear weapons to wage war against Israel. Kinga Szabó, *Anticipatory Action in Self Defense. Essence and Limits under International Law* (Berlin: Springer, 2011), 179–181.

490 David Sanger and Mark Mazzetti, "Israel Struck Syrian Nuclear Project, Analysts Say," *The New York Times* (2017), http://www.nytimes.com/2007/10/14/washington/14weapons.html; David Makovsky, "The Silent Strike. How Israel Bombed a Syrian Nuclear Installation and Kept It Secret," *The New Yorker* (September 17, 2012), https://www.newyorker.com/magazine/2012/09/17/the-silent-strike; Aaron

Israel attempted to improve BMD by engagement in foreign cooperation within the framework of SDI since the late 1980s. Since the beginning of the US-Israeli BMD cooperation in 1986, a key component of the future layered Israeli missile defense system was designed: an Arrow missile.[491] Duncan Clarke explained that the beginning of the US engagement in Israeli Arrow missile development was connected to an abandonment of Israeli fighter Lavi investments, which had been supported by the US ($1.5 billion) and could compete with the F-16. To make it up to the Israelis, Washington started investing in Arrow through SDIO, accepted by the Israeli Defense Forces (IDF) and Israeli Air Force with hesitation (based on the earlier first strike doctrine as a hedge against possible WMD attacks).[492] Ephraim Sneh presented Arrow as one of the components of Israeli four circles of defense (state-of-the art in year 2005), consisting of passive defenses (shelters), active defenses (Arrow), responsive defenses (boost phase BMD aimed at WMD threat), and preemptive defense (long-range strikes).[493]

A disappointing period concerning the newly developed US BMD capacities came with the international coalition's efforts to drive Hussein's Iraq out of Kuwait, when the deployment of PAC-2 used against attacking Scud missiles (in January and February 1991) could not help avoid losses on Israeli soil. Martin Van Creveld wrote that during Desert Storm, the first PAC-2 fire units deployed in Israel were US-operated, while those delivered later were controlled also by Israeli troops, proving "almost useless" (as an air-defense, not BMD weapon) against Iraqi Scuds.[494] The benefits from engaging PAC-2 in Israel were mostly political, allowing the US to persuade the Israeli government not to engage in the war against

---

Kalman, "Israel Used 17 Tons of Explosives to Destroy Syrian Reactor in 2007, Magazine Says," *The Times of Israel*, 2012, https://www.timesofisrael.com/israel-uses-17-tons-of-explosives-to-destroy-syrian-reactor/.

491 Jewish Virtual Library (JVL), *Arrow Missile Program, Jewish Virtual Library (JVL)* (2018), http://www.jewishvirtuallibrary.org/arrow-missile-program (accessed August 24, 2018).

492 Clarke, "The Arrow Missile," 477–479.

493 Ephraim Sneh, *Navigating Perilous Waters: An Israeli Strategy for Peace and Security* (London: Routledge, 2005), 88–89.

494 The remaining parts of used PAC missiles could also cause damage while falling. Martin Van Creveld, *The Sword and the Olive: A Critical History of the Israeli Defense Forces* (New York: PublicAffairs, 1998), 331–332.

Iraq.[495] Further Israeli efforts to increase its BMD potential in cooperation with the US were largely inspired by threats within a close neighborhood, i.e., the growing rocket and missile abilities of radical Islamist anti-Israeli groups (such as Hezbollah and Hamas) and the support of the authoritarian Middle Eastern regimes of Syria, Iraq, and Iran for armed strikes aimed against Israel (with potential ballistic and WMD options).

A further increase of Israeli efforts connected with BMD was stimulated by the Lebanon conflict (and Hezbollah attacks), along with the Hamas rocket threats from Gaza and the West Bank. Iron Dome and David's Sling BMD became the world's first operational and combat-proven intercept systems, reaching 80-90% reliability in the 2012 and 2014 Israeli Gaza operations, countering the rocket threat posed by radical Islamist groups to the inhabitants of Israel.[496]

Another important stimuli to invest in Israeli BMD came from authoritarian Iran under the leadership of the radical populist, Mahmud Ahmadinejad, who publicly denied the Holocaust and (as reported in 2005) called to wipe Israel from the map of the Middle East (apart from Iranian support for terrorist groups and its missile and nuclear programs).[497]

Israeli engagement in BMD grew after the 2006 Lebanon war, when Israel was attacked by thousands of Hezbollah missiles.[498] In the context of the Lebanon war's missile threat, the Israeli defense establishment took steps to reconsider chemical laser projects as BMD solutions, including Nauti-

---

495   Michael O'Hanlon, "Alternative Architectures and US Politics," in *Rockets' Red Glare: Missile Defenses and the Future of World Politics*, ed. by James Wirtz and Jeffrey Larsen (Boulder: Westview Press, 2001), 116.

496   Although the critics of Israeli BMD quoted in the following parts of the text undermined the official claims of Iron Dome effectiveness.

497   Nadav Morag, "The Strategic Impact of an Iranian Nuclear Weapons Capability on Israel," in *Nuclear Threats and Security Challenges*, ed. by Samuel Apikyan and David Diamond (Dordrecht: Springer, 2015), 139; Nazila Fathi, "Wipe Israel 'off the Map' Iranian Says," *The New York Times* (2005), http://www.nytimes.com/2005/10/27/world/africa/wipe-israel-off-the-map-iranian-says.html; Louis Charbonneau, "In New York, Defiant Ahmadinejad Says Israel Will Be 'Eliminated,'" *Reuters* (2012), https://www.reuters.com/article/us-un-assembly-ahmadinejad/in-new-york-defi ant-ahmadinejad-says-israel-will-be-eliminated-idUSBRE88N0HF20120924.

498   Inna Lazareva, "The Iron Dome: What Is It and How Does It Work?" *The Telegraph* (July 10, 2014), http://www.telegraph.co.uk/news/worldnews/middleeast/israel/10960091/The-Iron-Dome-what-is-it-and-how-does-it-work.html.

lus-Skyguard (co-developed with US contractor Northrop Grumman).[499]
The 1990s program implemented as Tactical High Energy Laser (THEL)
with US-Israeli cooperation was cancelled in 2005 due to technical problems (though they proved to be effective against rocket targets in late
1990s tests), and was reorganized in 2006 by Northrop Grumman.[500]

Iron Dome was introduced in 2011.[501] David's Sling's has been in service since July 2016, protecting Israel from Hamas and Iranian threats.[502]
Raytheon presented David's Sling (co-developed with Israeli Rafael Advanced Defense Systems), which as been operational since 2017 as medium-range air defense system (and mid-tier Israeli layered BMD); its two-
stage Stunner (destroying targets kinetically, while Tamir used a blast
warhead) missile's version named SkyCeptor offered to Poland in 2016 as
a part of a planned Wisła BMD in the framework of the Patriot contract
was also examined as a possible US choice.[503] Rafael was built in 1948 as a
R&D company of the Israeli Defense Ministry, but its engagement in Iron
Dome, despite its close links to IDF, was labeled as a private company.[504]

IDF's first combat operations using Iron Dome were conducted within
the framework of the operation Pillar of Defense, implemented in 2012
against terrorist groups in Gaza (Hamas and Islamic Jihad) and the missile

499   David Eshel, "Missile/Rocket Defense Emerges as Top Israeli Priority," *Military Technology*, 12 (2006), 34–37.

500   Ian Siperco, "Shield of David: The Promise of Israeli National Missile Defense," *Middle East Policy* XVII, no. 2 (2010): 134–135, http://www.mepc.org/shield-david-promise-israeli-national-missile-defense.

501   IDF, *Clear Skies Ahead Meet the Soldiers of the Iron Dome* (2013), https://www.idf.il/en/minisites/israeli-air-force/clear-skies-ahead-meet-the-soldiers-of-the-iron-dome/.

502   David's Sling was introduced as a stationary platform, while Iron Dome remained mobile. IDF, *New David's Sling Anti-Missile System Protects Israel from Long Range Threats* (2017), https://www.idf.il/en/minisites/israeli-air-force/new-david-s-sling-anti-missile-system-protects-israel-from-long-range-threats/.

503   Raytheon, *David's Sling Weapon System* (2018), https://www.raytheon.com/capabilities/products/davidssling/; Barbara Opall-Rome, "US-Israel Team Ramp-up Interceptor Builds," *DefenseNews* (2017), https://www.defensenews.com/smr/2017/08/03/us-israel-teams-ramp-up-interceptor-builds.

504   Peter Dombrowski, Catherine Kelleher and Eric Auner, "Demistyfing Iron Dome," *The National Interest* (July 2013), http://nationalinterest.org/print/article/demystifying-iron-dome-8649; Rafael, *Welcome to Rafael* (2018), http://www.rafael.co.il/4324-en/Marketing.aspx.

threat posed by those organizations to the Israeli population.[505] During the next similar Israeli operation (Protective Edge) in July-August 2014, aimed against terrorist actions (rocket attacks targeted at South Israel), the IDF used Iron Dome to intercept part of the rockets fired against the Israeli population (according to the IDF, Iron Dome intercepted 692 rockets, while ca. 4500 rockets were used by the enemy).[506] According to media reports, during the 2014 operation, Iron Dome attempted to intercept 799 targets, successfully hitting 735 and failing to hit 64.[507]

Naval Iron Dome became formally operational in 2017 (with Tamir interceptors).[508] Israel adapted the Sa'ar 6 corvette (built in Germany) to equip the Navy with Iron Dome launchers.[509] Naval Iron Dome was designed to protect cargo vessels, Navy ships, and the energy infrastructure.[510]

Raytheon claimed that Iron Dome was more than 90% effective (2011-2017 against more than 1500 targets), with Tamir missiles (its subcomponents provided by Raytheon since 2014) having a range of 4-70 km, in 10 batteries (3-4 launchers, equipped with 20 Tamir missiles each), confirming that Iron Dome was seen by the US as a model for its similar system aimed to deliver forward protection of deployed troops ("Sky-Hunter").[511] Until November 2017, Iron Dome intercepted around 1700

---

505 IDF, *Operation Pillar of Defense (2012)*; Conf. Judah Ari Gross, Toi Staff and Dov Lieber, "Iron Dome Deployed in Greater Tel Aviv Area as IDF Girds for Possible Attack," *The Times of Israel* (November 14, 2017), https://www.timesofisrael.com/iron-dome-deployed-in-tel-aviv-area-as-idf-girds-for-possible-gaza-attack/.

506 IDF, *Operation Protective Edge (July/August 2014)* (2018), https://www.idf.il/en/minisites/wars-and-operations/operation-protective-edge-julyaugust-2014/.

507 That would mean Iron Dome's Tamir missiles were 92% effective at the time; the numbers came from Mitch Ginsburg's reporting (quoting Channel 2). Mitch Ginsburg, "Iron Dome Gets Mysterious Upgrade," *The Times of Israel* (2015), https://www.timesofisrael.com/iron-dome-to-get-mysterious-upgrade/.

508 IDF, *The Naval "Iron Dome" Is Ready for Action* (2017), https://www.idf.il/en/minisites/israeli-navy/the-naval-iron-dome-is-ready-for-action/.

509 Anna Ahronheim, "IDF Declares Naval Iron Dome System Operational," *Jerusalem Post* (November 27, 2017), http://www.jpost.com/Israel-News/IDF-declares-Naval-Iron-Dome-system-operational-515337.

510 Globes, "IDF Conducts Successful Naval Iron Dome Trial" (November 27, 2017), http://www.globes.co.il/en/article-idf-conducts-successful-naval-iron-dome-trial-1001213462.

511 One battery could protect 60,000 square miles. Raytheon, *Iron Dome Weapon System. Short-Range Air Defense* (2018), https://www.raytheon.com/capabilities/products/irondome/.

targets.[512] Baker Spring and Michaela Bendikova noted that the price of Tamir interceptors was more than $100,000 in 2011.[513] In 2017, Britain decided to buy Iron Dome for the Falklands to protect them from a possible Argentinian threat based on French-bought Super Entendard jets.[514]

Notably, critics (MIT's Postol) claimed that the 2012 Iron Dome effectiveness was 5%, not 90%.[515] Postol wrote in the context of 2012 Israeli operations on the basis of video recordings that in order to destroy Grad rockets, Iron Dome interceptors would have to engage them from their front, while in most cases, they approached from the sides or back, being unable to destroy the approaching rocket's warhead (and explained low Israeli losses to civil defense efforts, not BMD).[516]

Yiftah Shapir responded to Postol's claim of Iron Dome's 5% rate of intercepts by stressing that video clips recorded by civilian witnesses and placed online were not clear enough to distinguish between one or two explosions or to conclude that evidence was presented of a failed attempt to destroy Grad's warhead by a Tamir missile.[517]

The US Army tested Tamir missiles in 2016 against unmanned air vehicles. Boyd Collins, "US Army Successfully Demonstrates Iron Dome Missile from New Interceptor Launch Platform," *US Army* (April 20, 2016), https://www.army.mil/article/166397/U_S__Army_successfully_demonstrates_Iron_Dome_missile_from_new_interceptor_launch_platform.

512 IsraelDefense, "Israel's Sea-Based Iron Dome Declared Operational" (November 28, 2017), http://www.israeldefense.co.il/en/node/31961.

513 Baker Spring and Michaela Bendikova, *Israel and the Iron Dome System: A Lesson for the United States* (Washington, DC), https://www.heritage.org/defense/report/israel-and-the-iron-dome-system-lesson-the-united-states.

514 Jerusalem Post and Globes, "UK to Purchase Israeli Iron Dome Defense System to Defend Falklands" (November 25, 2017), http://www.jpost.com/Israel-News/UK-to-purchase-Israeli-Iron-Dome-defense-system-to-defend-Falklands-515160.

515 Michael Peck, "Russia Mocks America for Buying Israel's Iron Dome," *The National Interest* (November 4, 2017), http://nationalinterest.org/blog/the-buzz/russia-mocks-america-buying-israels-iron-dome-23023.

516 Theodore Postol, "The Evidence That Shows Iron Dome Is Not Working," *Bulletin of the Atomic Scientists*, 2014, https://thebulletin.org/evidence-shows-iron-dome-not-working7318.

517 Yiftah Shapir, *How Many Rockets Did Iron Dome Shoot Down?* (The Institute for National Security Studies [INSS], 2013), http://www.inss.org.il/publication/how-many-rockets-did-iron-dome-shoot-down/.

IDF sources claimed that the performance of Iron Dome was improved from the interception rate of 84% in 2012 to 90% in 2014.[518] Luiz Bandeira stressed that the use of Iron Dome against Qassam rockets on November 14-15, 2014 (when Israeli interceptors destroyed 105 of 274 Hamas rockets) cost $5.2 million ($50,000 per missile), whereas the cost of Qassam rockets was estimated to be a few hundred dollars.[519] Iron Dome was supposed to eliminate the rocket threat to Israel posed by Gaza Strip groups and those operating from the West Bank of Jordan.[520] David Hafemeister stressed that the 2012 Iron Dome use against rocket attacks (with an estimated 80-90% success rate) was the first example of combat use of theater BMD.[521]

As Eyal Pecht, Asher Tishler, and Nir Weingold noted, David's Sling intercept range was 250 km, Arrow 2's intercept capabilities covered a 90 km range (at a 10-50 km altitude), and Arrow 3 was supposed to reach targets at the exo-atmospheric level (above 100 km) within a range of 90 km.[522] According to those scholars, the defense of a medium-sized Israeli city (with a success probability of 80%, i.e., performance/probability at 0.8) against short range rockets (Kassam, Katyusha, or Grad) required two Iron Dome fire units (each consisting of 3 launchers with 60 interceptors altogether), while a procurement of one Iron Dome unit cost $66 million.[523]

The large part of Israeli BMD accomplishments could be attributed to the long-lasting US military engagement in Israel's defense and co-development of technologies critically important for its layered intercept sys-

---

518 Emily Landau and Azriel Bermant, "Iron Dome Protection: Missile Defense in Israel's Security Concept," in *The Lessons of Operation Protective Edge*, ed. by Anat Kurz and Shlomo Brom (Tel Aviv: The Institute for National Security Studies, 2014), 37–42, http://www.inss.org.il/he/wp-content/uploads/sites/2/systemfiles/SystemFiles/Iron Dome Protection_ Missile Defense in Israel's Security Concept.pdf.

519 Luiz Bandeira, *The Second Cold War. Geopolitics and the Strategic Dimensions of the USA* (Cham: Springer, 2017), 317.

520 Daniel Byman, *A High Price: The Triumphs and Failures of Israeli Counterterrorism* (New York: Oxford University Press, 2011), 358.

521 David Hafemeister, *Nuclear Terrorism and Proliferation in the Post-9/11 World* (Cham: Springer, 2016), 99.

522 Pecht, Tishler and Weingold, 439–441.

523 Pecht, Tishler and Weingold, 439–441.

tem.[524] Jeremy Sharp noted that since its emergence after World War II, Israel is the largest recipient of US assistance, reaching $127.4 billion by 2016, whereas the US assistance for Israel in 2019-2028 includes $500 million annually to support the Israeli BMD.[525]

MDA's 2016 budget report signified that the ongoing US-Israeli missile defense cooperation (from 1986 to 2016), the US supported Arrow, Upper Tier, and David's Sling through overall funding for those systems (until 2014), reaching $1.123 billion, while the 2015 aid was as high as $269 million (and $268 million in 2016).[526] The Obama administration-era budget estimates decreased those funds to $100-110 million annually from 2017 to 2021.[527] The Trump era 2017 MDA budget for FY 2018 included $1.56 billion in support for the Israeli missile defense from 2018 to 2022 (ca. 380 million annually from 2019 to 2022), apart from the support for three previously mentioned projects.[528] The National Defense Authorization (NDA) for 2018 included up to $92 million for Israel to buy Tamir interceptors for Iron Dome, up to $120 million for David's Sling and up to $120 million for Arrow 3.[529] Karako stressed that between

---

524   Jack Detsch, "Congress Deepens US-Israel Missile Alliance," *Al Monitor* (November 9, 2017), https://www.al-monitor.com/pulse/originals/2017/11/congress-us-israel-missile-alliance-threat-iran-hezbollah.html.

525   Jeremy Sharp, *US Foreign Aid to Israel*, Summary.

526   Office of the Under Secretary of Defense - Comptroller, *Missile Defense Agency Defense-Wide Justification Book Research, Development, Test and Evaluation (RDTE) Volume 2a of 2 FY 2017* (2016), 627, http://comptroller.defense.gov/Portals/45/Documents/defbudget/FY2017/budget_justification/pdfs/03_RDT_and_E/MDA_RDTE_MasterJustificationBook_Missile_Defense_Agency_PB_2017_1.pdf.

527   Office of the Under Secretary of Defense - Comptroller, *Missile Defense Agency Defense-Wide Justification Book Research, Development, Test and Evaluation (RDTE) Volume 2a of 2 FY 2017*, 627.

528   Office of the Under Secretary of Defense (Comptroller), *Missile Defense Agency Defense-Wide Justification Book Research, Development, Test and Evaluation (RDTE) Volume 2a of 2 FY 2018* (2017), 535, http://comptroller.defense.gov/Portals/45/Documents/defbudget/FY2018/budget_justification/pdfs/03_RDT_and_E/U_RDTE_MasterJustificationBook_Missile_Defense_Agency_PB_2018_Vol2a_Vol2b.pdf.

529   US Congress, *National Defense Authorization (NDA) Act for Fiscal Year 2018*, Public Law 115-91, December 12, 2017 (2017), 131 Stat. 1778-1779, https://www.govinfo.gov/content/pkg/PLAW-115publ91/pdf/PLAW-115publ91.pdf; US Congress (sponsor Mac Thornberry), *National Defense Authorization Act for Fiscal Year 2018*,

1998 and 2012, MDA spent 1-3% of its budget on Israeli-related funding.[530] Notably, US assistance for Iron Dome reached $1.4 billion from 2011 to 2016.[531]

Israeli policies in the area of BMD development, conducted since the 1980s, led to major progress in terms of deployments of combat-ready layered intercept systems, operational since the beginning of the second decade of the twenty-first century. Among the leading accomplishments of Israeli defense establishment was a successful (and partly US-funded) cooperation with the BMD technology leader, the US, which secured for the Israel the prime-ranked place among missile defense developers and producers in international comparisons. The experience of largely failed PAC efforts in Israel during the Gulf War, as well as radical Islamists and Iranian ballistic (or WMD) threats in the neighborhood, were seen as the factors in the 1990s and early 2000s for increased Israeli investments in BMD technologies. The layered system designed to protect Israel from rocket and short range ballistic threats, based on Iron Dome, David's Sling, and Arrow components, could be a model for US-based twenty-first-century missile defense solutions. The controversial dimensions of Israeli BMD achievements included (apart from the Desert Storm Scud intercept re-evaluations) the validity of the official rate of Iron Dome interceptions during IDF's 2012 and 2014 Gaza operations. The broad range of

---

House of Representatives (H.R.) 2810 (US House of Representatives, 2017) https://www.congress.gov/115/bills/hr2810/BILLS-115hr2810enr.pdf, https://www.congress.gov/bill/115th-congress/house-bill/2810; Conf. US Congress (sponsor John McCain).

530   Thomas Karako, Wes Rumbaugh and Ian Williams, *The Missile Defense Agency and the Color of Money. Fewer Resources, More Responsibility* (Washington, DC, 2016), 25, https://missilethreat.csis.org/wp-content/uploads/2016/12/MDA-and-the-Color-of-Money.pdf; Conf. Jen Judson, "Report: US Aid for Israel Missile Defense Competes With MDA Priorities," *DefenseNews* (July 29, 2016), https://www.defensenews.com/home/2016/07/29/report-us-aid-for-israel-missile-defense-competes-with-mda-priorities/.

531   In 2016, the cost of Iron Battery was estimated at $50 million (and $50,000 per missile). Jacob Lokshin, *Iron Dome (Israel)* (2016), http://missiledefenseadvocacy.org/missile-defense-systems-2/allied-air-and-missile-defense-systems/allied-intercept-systems-coming-soon/iron-dome-israel/; Gili Cohen, "Why Does Israel Need Three Different Missile Defense Systems?" *Haaretz* (2015), https://www.haaretz.com/.premium-why-does-israel-need-3-anti-missile-systems-1.5346632; Rebecca Shimoni Stoil, "US House Okays Funding Boost for Israel's Missile Defense," *The Times of Israel* (June 17, 2016), http://www.timesofisrael.com/us-house-okays-huge-funding-for-israels-missile-defense/.

disparity between the defender's and critics' views of Iron Dome's effectiveness (creating a gap between the official 80-90% and critically-viewed less than 10% intercept rate) could encourage further studies in the area of BMD reliability analysis.

5. Layered US-Led BMD Systems in the Twenty-First Century: The Cases of Eastern Europe and East Asia

The twenty-first century's US-led BMD investments included East European deployments, i.e., a modified concept of the George W. Bush administration's GMD system's GBI site in Poland and radar in Czech, replaced after 2009 by the Obama administration's EPAA, leading to Aegis Ashore sites at the Romanian Deveselu and Polish Redzikowo bases.[532] The limited scope (due to Russian pressure) of East European investments led to the abandonment of the deployment of ICBM-capable interceptors and the introduction of medium-range Aegis Ashore missile defense bases.

East Asian US-led BMD developments (countering the North Korean nuclear threat) included the introduction of the THAAD system to South Korea in 2017 and planned Aegis Ashore bases in Japan, next to previous Patriot batteries deployments in Japan and South Korea and US-Japanese Aegis cooperation (the co-development of SM-3 Block IIA missile and Japan's construction of four Japanese Aegis Congo-class destroyers).[533]

A huge increase in the MDA budget after September 11th (increased more than twice), could be connected to the US ABM treaty withdrawal[534] and the higher threats from the war on terror, leading to a further re-

---

532 Ministry of Foreign Affairs Republic of Poland, *Polish-US Missile Defence Negotiations* (2012), http://www.msz.gov.pl/en/foreign_policy/security_policy/missile_defence/md_negotiations/; US Embassy & Consulate in Poland, *United States and Poland Start Construction of Redzikowo Missile Defense Facility, May 18, 2016* (2016), https://pl.usembassy.gov/facility.

533 Cheryl Pellerin, "US, South Korean Military Leaders Reinforce Alliance," *US Department of Defense* (August 24, 2017), https://www.defense.gov/News/Article/Article/1288096/us-south-korean-military-leaders-reinforce-alliance; MDA, *Aegis Ballistic Missile Defense*; Mari Yamaguchi, "Japan to Buy Aegis Ashore Missile Defense Systems," *DefenseNews* (December 19, 2017), https://www.defensenews.com/land/2017/12/19/japan-to-buy-aegis-ashore-missile-defense-systems.

534 US Department of State, *Treaty Between The United States of America and The Union of Soviet Socialist Republics on The Limitation of Anti-Ballistic Missile Systems (ABM Treaty)* (2017), https://2009-2017.state.gov/t/avc/trty/101888.htm.

gional focus on BMD. The Polish GMD base agreement was concluded in August 2008 to be amended in July 2010 to introduce Aegis interceptors in place of previously planned GBIs (agreement had been enforced since September 2011).[535] As Hildreth and Carl Ek, noted, the George W. Bush administration' GMD plan in Poland and Czechia (cancelled by Obama in 2009) was estimated to cost $4 billion (for the base of 10 interceptors and additional infrastructure, scheduled for completion in 2013).[536]

Obama's EPAA missile defense plan was divided into four stages:

1. deploy Aegis naval units in the Mediterranean and early warning radar in Turkey, connected with NATO BMD preparations (implemented from 2009 to 2011),

2. build an Aegis Ashore base in Romania and develop an Aegis missile SM-3 Block IB (until 2015),

3. implement a fielding plan of a second Aegis Ashore base (in Poland) and provide for a SM-3 Block IIA missile (set in 2018 perspective),

4. develop an ICBM-interception capable SM-3 Block IIB missile (cancelled).[537]

EPAA's stage four was cancelled in 2013, most likely due to Russian expectations of limiting (NATO and US-led) BMD deployments near Russia's borders and its overall negative approach to Western BMD investments in Europe.[538]

---

535 US Department of State, *Agreement between the Government of the United States of America and the Government of the Republic of Poland Concerning the Deployment of Ground-Based Ballistic Missile Defense Interceptors in the Territory of the Republic of Poland, Done at Warsaw, 20ᵗʰ* (2011), https://www.state.gov/documents/organization /180542.pdf; US Department of State, *Protocol Amending the Agreement between the Government of the United States of America and the Government of the Republic of Poland Concerning the Deployment of Ground-Based Ballistic Missile Defense Interceptors in the Territory of the Republic of Poland* (2010), https://www.state.gov/documents/ organization/180543.pdf; Ministry of Foreign Affairs Republic of Poland, *Polish-US Missile Defence Negotiations*.

536 Steven Hildreth and Carl Ek, *Long-Range Ballistic Missile Defense in Europe, September 23, 2009* (2009), 1, https://fas.org/sgp/crs/weapons/RL34051.pdf.

537 The White House, *Fact Sheet: Implementing Missile Defense in Europe, September 15, 2011.*

538 Syring, *Department of Defense Briefing by Vice Adm. Syring*; Durkalec, "The Role of Missile Defence in NATO Deterrence," 20; Conf. Jaganath Sankaran, *The United States'*

As Jaganath Sankaran explained, SM-3 IIA velocity of 4.5 km per second was enough to intercept Iranian missiles (in the latter case, the velocity required to perform an interception could vary from between 2.0-2.5 km/s, when BMD was launched from Turkey, to 3.5-4.0 km/s, when interceptors were launched from London), but interception of Russian ICBMs by SM-3 IIA from Aegis units on the North Sea or Barents Sea would be impossible (requiring speeds from 4.6-4.7 km/s to 5.1-5.2 km/s, depending on the location of ICBM sites).[539] Notably, ICBM missiles could reach a boost phase powered velocity of Mach 20 (15,000 mph, 4.17 mps, ca. 6.67 km/s) and reentry velocity at this level.[540]

Similarly, as in the case of East European BMD developments, the US and Japan signed an agreement on Aegis Ashore in December 2017 (driven by the North Korean missile and nuclear threat, which had been growing since the successful ICBM and thermonuclear tests of Pyongyang in the summer/autumn), which led to the deployment of two such bases by 2023.[541] Japanese missile defense efforts by 2017 included the deployment of 4 Kongo-class Aegis destroyers (and 2 additional Aegis-adapted) armed with SM-3 Block IB interceptors with a range of 380 miles (and co-development of Block IIA, intercepting at a range of 1300 miles), as well as a purchase of PAC-3 (with a 12-mile range), deployed in thirteen sites by 2013.[542]

European Phased Adaptive Approach Missile Defense System. Defending Against Iranian Threats Without Diluting the Russian Deterrent, 2015, https://www.rand.org/pubs/research_reports/RR957.html.

539   Jaganath Sankaran, "Missile Defense Against Iran Without Threatening Russia," *Arms Control Today* 43, no. 9 (2013): 19, http://www.jstor.org/stable/23629550.

540   Jane Gibson and Kenneth Kemmerly, "Intercontinental Ballistic Missiles," in *AU-18 Space Primer. Air Command and Staff College, Space Research Electives Seminars*, ed. by Brian C. Tichenor (Maxwell Air Force Base: Air University Press, 2009), 235–48 (236–37) http://space.au.af.mil/au-18-2009/au-18_chap18.pdf.

541   The Mainichi, "Japan Decides to Introduce New Missile Defense amid N. Korea Threat" (December 19, 2017), https://mainichi.jp/english/articles/20171219/p2g/00m/0dm/045000c; Missile Threat Center for Strategic and International Studies Missile Defense Project, *Missiles of North Korea* (2018), https://missilethreat.csis.org/country/dprk; Stratfor, *North Korea: Pyongyang Launches Its Longest-Range Missile Yet, November 28, 2017* (2017), https://worldview.stratfor.com/article/north-korea-pyongyang-launches-its-longest-range-missile-yet; Stratfor, *Why North Korea Won't Stop, September 3, 2017* (2017), https://worldview.stratfor.com/article/why-north-korea-wont-stop.

542   Kyle Mizokami, "Everything You Need to Know: Japan's Missile Defenses," *The Nation-*

Apart from the previous Aegis SM-3 Block IIA US-Japan cooperation (and PAC deployments), Aegis destroyers were independently developed by South Korea.[543] The 2017 THAAD deployment in South Korea was criticized by China (as threatening Beijing's deterrence capabilities), though its range (124 miles or 200 km), when positioned in the chosen Seongju location, could not even protect Seoul.[544] New perspectives on ending the North Korean crisis appeared in 2018, when Pyongyang showed willingness to negotiate denuclearization and stopping ballistic tests (if those were not tactical moves, as in the previous attempts to negotiate a lasting consensus).[545]

The layered capabilities of BMD systems involved possible interoperability between its layers and (in the future) probably also within the broader alliance defense networks, including US longer-range capabilities. In 2017, the US Defense Security Cooperation Agency (DSCA) labeled $10.5 billion prepared sales of IBCS for PAC-3 Missile Segment Enhancement (MSE) interceptors (totaling 208 plus 11 test missiles) for Poland, one of its major contracts.[546] The contract included, a.o., four radar sets (AN/MPQ-65), sixteen launching stations M903, two future and six current IBCS Engagement Operations Centers (EOC), as well as six engagement operations from the IBCS EOCs DSCA.[547]

---

al Interest (September 2, 2017), http://nationalinterest.org/blog/the-buzz/every thing-you-need-know-japans-missile-defenses-22155.

543   Tae-Hyung Kim, "South Korea's Missile Defense Policy: Dilemma and Opportunity for a Medium State," *Asian Politics & Policy* 1, no. 3 (2009): 380, https://doi.org/10.1111/j.1943-0787.2009.01131.x.

544   Chery Kang, "'THAAD' Anti-Missile System Can't Protect South Korea from Missile Attacks by Itself," *CNBC* (September 11, 2017), https://www.cnbc.com/2017/09/11/south-korea-missile-defense-thaad-system-cant-do-the-job-alone.html.

545   Rodger Baker, *Cheeseburgers in the Workers' Paradise* (2018), https://worldview.stratfor.com/article/united-states-north-korea-trump-kim-jong-un-summit-nuclear-talks; Stratfor, *North Korea: Pyongyang Invites US Dialogue and Washington Considers Its Next Steps, March 9, 2018* (2018), https://worldview.stratfor.com/article/north-korea-united-states-dialogue-denuclearization-talks-trump-kim-meeting; Sarah Sanders, *Press Briefing by Press Secretary Sarah Sanders, The White House, March 9, 2018* (2018), https://www.whitehouse.gov/briefings-statements/press-briefing-press-secretary-sarah-sanders-030918.

546   DSCA, *Poland - Integrated Air and Missile Defense (IAMD) Battle Command System (IBCS)-Enabled Patriot Configuration-3+ with Modernized Sensors and Components, November 17, 2017* (Washington, DC, 2017), http://www.dsca.mil/sites/default/files/mas/poland_17-67.pdf.

547   Defense Security Cooperation Agency (DSCA).

Marek Świerczyński wrote that the price for Polish Patriot contract (justified by a newly developed IBCS system and new PAC-3 MSE missiles, as well as a broad offset, including the production of cheaper SkyCeptor missiles in Poland, based on the Israeli Stunner missile) seemed tremendously high to the Polish government and the media.[548] Offset probably increased the price of PAC-3 MSE (Poland planned to buy 208 such missiles, serving in 12 fire units and equipped with 48 launchers) much above the price of $5.7 million per missile for the US military.[549]

The US-Polish PAC-3 contract worth $10.5 billion was seen as too expensive at 7 billion zlotys (ca. $2 billion), while the offset for Poland's Wisła air and missile defense raised the MSE price.[550] Notably, Romania bought PAC-3 in a cheaper and more easily accessible configuration than the latest Polish-chosen configuration, which was developed for $3.9 billion (including 56 GEM-T missiles and 168 MSE interceptors).[551]

According to the US Department of Defense budget reports, from 1997 to 2017, Patriot costs exceeded $20 billion, including its development (surpassing $6.4 billion) and procurement expenditures (reaching ca. $14 billion).[552] Other US BMDS segments (THAAD, Aegis, and GMD) without Aegis destroyers cost more than $92 billion (in procurement and R&D) in FYs 1997-2017 (the overall MDA appropriations from 1997 to

---

548   Marek Świerczyński, "Gdzie Te Patrioty?" *Polityka* 3143, no. 2 (2018): 22–23.

549   Świerczyński, "Gdzie Te Patrioty?"; Conf. Marek Świerczyński, "Offset Na Miarę (Małych) Możliwości," *Polityka Insight* (March 24, 2018), https://www.polityka. pl/tygodnikpolityka/kraj/1742944,1,polska-na-ostatniej-prostej-do-podpisania-kontraktu-na-patrioty.read.

550   Jen Judson, "Poland Has Sticker Shock over 'Unacceptable' Price Tag for Patriot Buy," *DefenseNews* (December 6, 2017), https://www.defensenews.com/land/2017/12/06/poland-surprised-by-high-price-tag-for-its-long-awaited-patriot-purchase/; Ministry of National Defense of Poland, *Modernizacja i Rozwój Sił Zbrojnych RP* (2017), http://www.mon.gov.pl/aktualnosci/artykul/najnowsze/modernizacja-i-rozwoj-sil-zbrojnych-82017-12-22/ htm.

551   DSCA, *Romania—Patriot Air Defense System and Related Support and Equipment* (Washington, DC, 2017), http://www.dsca.mil/sites/default/files/mas/romania_17-35.pdf; US Army Program Executive Office Missiles& Space, *Lower Tier Project Office* (2018), https://www.msl.army.mil/Pages/ltpo/patriot.html.

552   Costs derived from the US Department of Defense (Comptroller) fiscal years 1998-2019 budget reports (http://comptroller.defense.gov/Portals/45/Documents/defbudget) and US Department of Navy fiscal years 1998-2019 Justification Books, http://www.secnav.navy.mil/fmc/fmb/Pages/Fiscal-Year-2017.aspx.

2017 reached $151.2 billion),[553] while those naval units were above $58 billion. THAAD improvements from 1997 to 2017 cost ca. $13 billion in R&D, while the procurement of those systems cost about $4.2 billion. Aegis investments (1997-2017) were supported by ca. $35 billion (excluding destroyers, which were built by the Navy for the cost of $54 billion in procurement and ca. $4 billion in R&D expenses).[554] Ronald O'Rourke reported that by 2022, the Aegis naval units size will grow to 51 ships (from 33 in 2017), equipped with 602 SM-3 missiles (420 in 2017), while by 2018, the Aegis force consisted of CG-47(-73) Ticonderoga class cruisers (27 ships procured between 1978 and 1988) and Arleigh Burke class destroyers (62 procured in 1985-2005 period and 15 procured in FYs 2010-2017).[555,]

GMD development (previously, under the Clinton administration, National Missile Defense) were most costly of all BMD elements (apart from Aegis naval units, excluded from budget assessments of missile defense), with the expenditures reaching $40 billion R&D costs through 20-year investments, from 1997 to 2017.

6. Probability Analysis in the Context of PAC Improvements

As Hildreth noted, the discussion of layered BMD systems (developed conceptually since the 1960s) was invigorated by SDI, which drew attention to the perspective of stopping large-scale Soviet ICBM attacks using a four-layer defense system, with a probability of interception measured as a multiplied warhead survival likelihood for each of the layers, which led to a (disputed) conclusion on a perspective of a near-decisive intercept.[556] As Zimmerman explained, at a high enough effectiveness for each

---

553   MDA, *Historical Funding for MDA FY85-17 Fiscal Year (FY in Billions)*.

554   Costs derived from US Department of Defense fiscal years 1998-2019 budget reports.

555   Ronald O'Rourke, *Navy Aegis Ballistic Missile Defense (BMD) Program: Background and Issues for Congress*, 2019, 1–2, 6, https://crsreports.congress.gov/product/pdf/RL/RL33745.

556   Steven Hildreth, "Layered Defense," in *Missile Defense: The Current Debate*, ed. by Steven Hildreth (Washington, DC: Congressional Research Service, 2005), 11–13, https://fas.org/sgp/crs/weapons/RL31111.pdf.

Hildreth referred to Zimmerman's critique of SDI's layered defense effectiveness (discussed in the following lines).

layer (reaching 80%), leaving a leakage of 20% in an optimistic scenario, it would be possible (calculating the outcome by multiplying each layer's leakage in a four-layered system) to imagine a successful defense against even 6000 warheads (if, what the quoted scholar saw as unlikely, the layers performance in terms of hardware/software communication and cooperation with each other would be flawless).[557] In the 1980s, a measurement based on the multiplication of each layer's effectiveness, a ratio of $0.2 \times 0.2 \times 0.2 \times 0.2 = 0.0016$ (%) passing out of 6000, i.e., 9.6 (warheads), left ca. 10 warheads unmatched by missile defense, and in the case of 90%-effective layers multiplied ($0.1 \times 0.1 \times 0.1 \times 0.1 = 0.0001$), there would remain only 1 (exactly 0.6) warhead hitting the target (notably, Zimmerman saw such an outcome as unlikely because the layers in his analysis were not seen as independent from each other).[558] As mentioned in the previous chapters, according to Wilkening's model, in the case of separate layers with non-significant deficiencies in cooperating, the layered defense effectiveness (K_W) equaled (bullet operator represents multiplication)

$$K_W = 1 - L_1 \cdot L_2 \ldots L_m$$

where L_i stands for the probability of defeating the i-th layer of defense by the attacking warhead.[559]

G. Lewis measured the layered defense in terms of using additional interceptors against one attacking warhead using the equation

$$P(0) = 1 - (1 - p)^n$$

where p is a single intercept probability and n stands for the number of interceptors used.[560]

Grego, Lewis, and Wright (on the basis of the previous Wilkening model) described the probability of penetration of the defense by one or more warheads as the equation

$$1 - P(0) = 1 - p^n$$

where p stands for the probability of a single interception, and n stands

---

557   Zimmerman, 78–79.

558   Zimmerman, 78–79.

559   Wilkening, 187–88, 191.

560   Lewis, "Technical Controversy," 1418-1429.

for a quantity of attacking warheads (e.g., the probability of penetration of one or more warheads through the defenses when the single intercept probability reached 94% and 6 warheads attacked simultaneously could be measured as $1 - 0.95^5 = 1 - 0.69 = 0.31$).[561]

The probabilistic modeling used in the following tables to investigate the outcome of interception attempts is based on the equation (as mentioned previously)

$$P(x) = \{W!/[x! \cdot (W - x)!]\} \cdot (1 - K_w)^x \cdot K_w^{W-x}$$

(bullet operator in the equation represents multiplication) following Wilkening's model (a Bernoulli binomial distribution), where $P(x)$ stands for a probability of defeating the BMD by x incoming warheads, K_w represents the probability of interception of an attacking warhead by an interceptor, and W stands for the number of attacking warheads.[562]

The following Tables 1, 2, and 3 and Charts 1, 2, and 3 show the probabilities of leak-proof interception in scenarios of additional interceptors (from 1 to a fully hypothetical 15) against each of the incoming warheads in attacks of up to 35 warheads. The decreasing probability of a leak-proof interception related to SSKP, examined at effectiveness levels of 85%, 90%, and 95% could be partly balanced by an introduction of additional interceptors (Tables 1-3 and, Charts 1-3). The probable gains from using those additional missiles at the analyzed SSKP levels were compared to point out the most likely benefits from further R&D efforts in the area of BMD (Tables 4-5). Table 4 presents the valid effects of R&D efforts in the area of interceptors' SKKP, while in a scenario of using 5 interceptors against each of the incoming warheads, the probability of a leak-proof interception due to the improvement of SSKP grew by 20-30 percentage points (when 10-25 warheads attacked) and by 15-10 percentage points (when 30-35 warheads attacked). Table 5 shows the highest gains from increasing SSKP from 90 to 95% in a scenario of using additional interceptors (5 against each of the incoming warheads) during a defense against a salvo attack of up to 35 warheads. The net gains were most visible in a hypothetical defense against 20-35 attacking warheads using 5 interceptors at 95% reliability, where the gain from further technological improve-

---

561 Grego, Lewis and Wright, *Shielded from Oversight. The Disastrous US Approach to Strategic Missile Defense. Appendix 8*, 1, 5; Wilkening, 187–188, 191.

562 Wilkening, 187–88, 191.

ments (to raise SSKP by 5 percentage points, from 90 to 95%) reached 40-50 percentage points in probable effectiveness (hit-to-kill ratio). In the cases of SSKP levels at 85% and 90%, the leak-proof probability of interception against a 35-warhead salvo using 5 interceptors against each of the attacking missiles was as low as 2% and 12%, respectively (Tables 1 and 2 and Charts 1 and 2). If the SSKP level reached 95% in a 35-warhead salvo attack scenario, an engagement of 5 interceptors against each of 35 incoming warheads provided for a relatively high 60% probability of a leak-proof defense (Table 3 and Chart 3).

Chapter Summary

To summarize, the 1990-1991 Gulf War and the US invasion of Iraq in 2003 provided incentive to further active investments in increasing the reliability of PAC missiles. The long post-Desert Storm investigation led to a reassessed estimation of their likely effectiveness, much lower than it was claimed by the US Army in the first weeks after January-February 1991 Iraq's Scud missiles attacks against Saudi Arabia and Israel. After the early statements of PAC-2 kill performance (reaching beyond 90% and presented as outstanding), the US Army had to revise its previous claims and locate the accomplishments of Patriot interceptors at the level of 70% at best, including up to a 25% hard-proven intercept record. The imperfect reliability of military records and the necessary corrections of the Patriot performance reports strengthened the criticism of those missile defense systems, seen also as a possible main arms trade contract offer of the United States for its allies (a.o., Israel and the Gulf monarchies, later the Far East and East European partners) threatened by missile and WMD proliferation. The 1990s debate on PAC-2 reliability and the extremely broad range of its possible performance seen from the perspective of its critics and defendants (between 9% and 70%) encouraged further improvements of BMD systems (leading to PAC-3, THAAD, Aegis, and GMD deployments) and missile defense effectiveness probability analysis studies. After the Spring 2003 US invasion of Iraq, the PAC reliability assessment (a claim of 100% effectiveness) had to be re-evaluated to include friendly fire accidents and cruise intercept deficiencies. The twenty-first-century layered BMD systems constructed by the United States in Eastern Europe and in the Far East (due to Iranian and North Korean threats), using PAC-3, Aegis, and THAAD interceptors, confirmed the scale of US missile defense investments, leading to theater-range operational capability and

drew attention to the implication of deployments for the possible regional balance of power, countered by the authoritarian Russian and Chinese
regimes as a threat to their deterrent capabilities. Notably, improved PAC
missile defense systems were sold by the mid-second decade of the twenty-first-century to twelve US-allied countries, while two additional purchase contracts were in implementation by 2018 (in the case of Poland
and Romania). Among the highly ranked present-day accomplishments
in the area of layered missile defense systems were Israeli US-supported
Iron Dome and David's Sling and Arrow, which were successful against
short range rocket attacks against civilian targets. The BMD effectiveness
probability calculations presented in the tables and charts are based on a
binomial distribution and earlier academic records employing probabilistic theory to examine the benefits of SSKP improvements in the scenarios of multiple warheads salvo attacks (reducing the summed intercept
capabilities of BMD missiles) and engagement of additional interceptors
(increasing the intercept probability). The probabilistic analysis proved
that increased SSKP improves a multiple-warhead intercept significantly
stronger than proportionally, reaching as high level as additional 40-50
percentage points in leak-proof intercept probability for a 5 percentage
points increase in SSKP (beyond 90%).

Table 1. SSKP reaching 85%, leak-proof intercept probabilities for 1-15 interceptors (columns) and 1-35 warheads attacking in a salvo (verses).

q-tity	1	2	3	4	5	6	7	8	9	10	11	12	13	14	15
1	0.85	0.98	1.00	1.00	1.00	1.00	1.00	1.00	1.00	1.00	1.00	1.00	1.00	1.00	1.00
2	0.72	0.92	0.98	0.99	1.00	1.00	1.00	1.00	1.00	1.00	1.00	1.00	1.00	1.00	1.00
3	0.61	0.85	0.94	0.98	0.99	1.00	1.00	1.00	1.00	1.00	1.00	1.00	1.00	1.00	1.00
4	0.52	0.77	0.89	0.95	0.98	0.99	0.99	1.00	1.00	1.00	1.00	1.00	1.00	1.00	1.00
5	0.44	0.69	0.83	0.90	**0.95**	0.97	0.98	0.99	0.99	1.00	1.00	1.00	1.00	1.00	1.00
6	0.38	0.61	0.76	0.85	0.91	0.94	0.96	0.98	0.99	0.99	0.99	1.00	1.00	1.00	1.00
7	0.32	0.54	0.69	0.79	0.86	0.90	0.93	0.95	0.97	0.98	0.99	0.99	0.99	1.00	1.00
8	0.27	0.47	0.61	0.72	0.80	0.85	0.89	0.92	0.94	0.96	0.97	0.98	0.98	0.99	0.99
9	0.23	0.41	0.55	0.65	0.73	0.79	0.84	0.88	0.91	0.93	0.94	0.96	0.97	0.97	0.98
10	0.20	0.35	0.48	0.58	**0.67**	0.73	0.78	0.83	0.86	0.89	0.91	0.93	0.94	0.95	0.96
11	0.17	0.31	0.42	0.52	0.60	0.67	0.72	0.77	0.81	0.84	0.87	0.89	0.91	0.92	0.94
12	0.14	0.26	0.37	0.46	0.54	0.60	0.66	0.71	0.75	0.78	0.82	0.84	0.86	0.88	0.90
13	0.12	0.23	0.32	0.40	0.47	0.54	0.59	0.64	0.69	0.72	0.76	0.79	0.81	0.84	0.86
14	0.10	0.19	0.28	0.35	0.42	0.48	0.53	0.58	0.62	0.66	0.70	0.73	0.76	0.78	0.80
15	0.09	0.17	0.24	0.31	**0.37**	0.42	0.47	0.52	0.56	0.60	0.63	0.67	0.70	0.72	0.75
16	0.07	0.14	0.21	0.27	0.32	0.37	0.42	0.46	0.50	0.54	0.57	0.60	0.63	0.66	0.69
17	0.06	0.12	0.18	0.23	0.28	0.32	0.37	0.41	0.44	0.48	0.51	0.54	0.57	0.60	0.62
18	0.05	0.10	0.15	0.20	0.24	0.28	0.32	0.36	0.39	0.42	0.45	0.48	0.51	0.54	0.56
19	0.05	0.09	0.13	0.17	0.21	0.24	0.28	0.31	0.34	0.37	0.40	0.43	0.45	0.48	0.50
20	0.04	0.08	0.11	0.15	**0.18**	0.21	0.24	0.27	0.30	0.33	0.35	0.38	0.40	0.43	0.45

	0.03	0.06	0.10	0.13	0.15	0.18	0.21	0.24	0.26	0.28	0.31	0.33	0.35	0.37	0.39
21	0.03	0.06	0.10	0.13	0.15	0.18	0.21	0.24	0.26	0.28	0.31	0.33	0.35	0.37	0.39
22	0.03	0.06	0.08	0.11	0.13	0.16	0.18	0.20	0.23	0.25	0.27	0.29	0.31	0.33	0.35
23	0.02	0.05	0.07	0.09	0.11	0.13	0.16	0.18	0.19	0.21	0.23	0.25	0.27	0.29	0.30
24	0.02	0.04	0.06	0.08	0.10	0.12	0.13	0.15	0.17	0.18	0.20	0.22	0.23	0.25	0.26
25	0.02	0.03	0.05	0.07	**0.08**	0.10	0.11	0.13	0.14	0.16	0.17	0.19	0.20	0.22	0.23
26	0.01	0.03	0.04	0.06	0.07	0.08	0.10	0.11	0.12	0.14	0.15	0.16	0.17	0.19	0.20
27	0.01	0.02	0.04	0.05	0.06	0.07	0.08	0.10	0.11	0.12	0.13	0.14	0.15	0.16	0.17
28	0.01	0.02	0.03	0.04	0.05	0.06	0.07	0.08	0.09	0.10	0.11	0.12	0.13	0.14	0.15
29	0.01	0.02	0.03	0.04	**0.04**	0.05	0.06	0.07	0.08	0.09	0.09	0.10	0.11	0.12	0.13
30	0.01	0.02	0.02	0.03	0.04	0.04	0.05	0.06	0.07	0.07	0.08	0.09	0.09	0.10	0.11
31	0.01	0.01	0.02	0.03	0.03	0.04	0.04	0.05	0.06	0.06	0.07	0.08	0.08	0.09	0.09
32	0.01	0.01	0.02	0.02	0.03	0.03	0.04	0.04	0.05	0.05	0.06	0.06	0.07	0.07	0.08
33	0.00	0.01	0.01	0.02	**0.02**	0.03	0.03	0.04	0.04	0.05	0.05	0.05	0.06	0.06	0.07
34	0.00	0.01	0.01	0.02	0.02	0.02	0.03	0.03	0.04	0.04	0.04	0.05	0.05	0.05	0.06
35	0.00	0.01	0.01	0.01	0.02	0.02	0.02	0.03	0.03	0.03	0.04	0.04	0.04	0.05	0.05

Source: own counting (using Microsoft Excel) according to the equation (bullet operator represents multiplication)

$$P(x) = \{W! / [x! \cdot (W-x)!]\} \cdot (1 - K_w)^x \cdot K_w^{W-x}$$

based on Wilkening's model (Bernoulli distribution), where P(x) stands for a probability of defeating the BMD by x incoming warheads, K_w represents the probability of interception of an attacking warhead by an interceptor, and W stands for the amount of attacking warheads, and

$$P(0) = 1 - (1-p)^n$$

based on G. Lewis's model, for p counted for a leak-proof defense in the cases of attacks of 5, 6, 7, … 30 incoming warheads (in Bernoulli distribution) using n additional interceptors.

Wilkening, 187-188, 191. G. Lewis, 1299-1689. Conf. MDA, *Ballistic Missile Defense Intercept Flight Test Record.*

Table 2. At SSKP reaching 90%, leak-proof intercept probabilities for 1-15 interceptors and 1-35 attacking warheads.

q-tity	1	2	3	4	5	6	7	8	9	10	11	12	13	14	15
1	0.90	0.99	1.00	1.00	1.00	1.00	1.00	1.00	1.00	1.00	1.00	1.00	1.00	1.00	1.00
2	0.81	0.96	0.99	1.00	1.00	1.00	1.00	1.00	1.00	1.00	1.00	1.00	1.00	1.00	1.00
3	0.73	0.93	0.98	0.99	1.00	1.00	1.00	1.00	1.00	1.00	1.00	1.00	1.00	1.00	1.00
4	0.66	0.88	0.96	0.99	1.00	1.00	1.00	1.00	1.00	1.00	1.00	1.00	1.00	1.00	1.00
5	0.59	0.83	0.93	0.97	**0.99**	1.00	1.00	1.00	1.00	1.00	1.00	1.00	1.00	1.00	1.00
6	0.53	0.78	0.90	0.95	0.98	0.99	1.00	1.00	1.00	1.00	1.00	1.00	1.00	1.00	1.00
7	0.48	0.73	0.86	0.93	0.96	0.98	0.99	0.99	1.00	1.00	1.00	1.00	1.00	1.00	1.00
8	0.43	0.68	0.82	0.89	0.94	0.97	0.98	0.99	0.99	1.00	1.00	1.00	1.00	1.00	1.00
9	0.39	0.62	0.77	0.86	0.91	0.95	0.97	0.98	0.99	0.99	1.00	1.00	1.00	1.00	1.00
10	0.35	0.58	0.72	0.82	**0.88**	0.92	0.95	0.97	0.98	0.99	0.99	0.99	1.00	1.00	1.00
11	0.31	0.53	0.68	0.78	0.85	0.90	0.93	0.95	0.97	0.98	0.98	0.99	0.99	0.99	1.00
12	0.28	0.49	0.63	0.73	0.81	0.86	0.90	0.93	0.95	0.96	0.97	0.98	0.99	0.99	0.99
13	0.25	0.44	0.59	0.69	0.77	0.83	0.87	0.90	0.93	0.95	0.96	0.97	0.98	0.98	0.99
14	0.23	0.41	0.54	0.65	0.73	0.79	0.84	0.87	0.90	0.93	0.94	0.96	0.97	0.97	0.98
15	0.21	0.37	0.50	0.60	**0.68**	0.75	0.80	0.84	0.87	0.90	0.92	0.94	0.95	0.96	0.97
16	0.19	0.34	0.46	0.56	0.64	0.71	0.76	0.81	0.84	0.87	0.90	0.91	0.93	0.94	0.95
17	0.17	0.31	0.42	0.52	0.60	0.67	0.72	0.77	0.81	0.84	0.87	0.89	0.91	0.92	0.94
18	0.15	0.28	0.39	0.48	0.56	0.62	0.68	0.73	0.77	0.80	0.83	0.86	0.88	0.90	0.91
19	0.14	0.25	0.35	0.44	0.52	0.58	0.64	0.69	0.73	0.77	0.80	0.82	0.85	0.87	0.89
20	0.12	0.23	0.32	0.40	**0.48**	0.54	0.60	0.65	0.69	0.73	0.76	0.79	0.81	0.84	0.86

21	0.11	0.21	0.29	0.37	0.44	0.50	0.56	0.60	0.65	0.69	0.72	0.75	0.78	0.80	0.82
22	0.10	0.19	0.27	0.34	0.40	0.46	0.52	0.56	0.61	0.65	0.68	0.71	0.74	0.77	0.79
23	0.09	0.17	0.24	0.31	0.37	0.43	0.48	0.52	0.57	0.60	0.64	0.67	0.70	0.73	0.75
24	0.08	0.15	0.22	0.28	0.34	0.39	0.44	0.49	0.53	0.56	0.60	0.63	0.66	0.69	0.71
25	0.07	0.14	0.20	0.26	**0.31**	0.36	0.41	0.45	0.49	0.53	0.56	0.59	0.62	0.65	0.67
26	0.06	0.13	0.18	0.23	0.28	0.33	0.37	0.41	0.45	0.49	0.52	0.55	0.58	0.61	0.63
27	0.06	0.11	0.16	0.21	0.26	0.30	0.34	0.38	0.42	0.45	0.48	0.51	0.54	0.57	0.59
28	0.05	0.10	0.15	0.19	0.24	0.28	0.31	0.35	0.38	0.42	0.45	0.48	0.50	0.53	0.55
29	0.05	0.09	0.13	0.18	0.21	0.25	0.29	0.32	0.35	0.38	0.41	0.44	0.47	0.49	0.52
30	0.04	0.08	0.12	0.16	**0.19**	0.23	0.26	0.29	0.32	0.35	0.38	0.41	0.43	0.45	0.48
31	0.04	0.07	0.11	0.14	0.18	0.21	0.24	0.27	0.30	0.32	0.35	0.37	0.40	0.42	0.44
32	0.03	0.07	0.10	0.13	0.16	0.19	0.22	0.24	0.27	0.29	0.32	0.34	0.37	0.39	0.41
33	0.03	0.06	0.09	0.12	0.15	0.17	0.20	0.22	0.25	0.27	0.29	0.31	0.34	0.36	0.38
34	0.03	0.05	0.08	0.11	0.13	0.16	0.18	0.20	0.22	0.25	0.27	0.29	0.31	0.33	0.34
35	0.03	0.05	0.07	0.10	**0.12**	0.14	0.16	0.18	0.20	0.22	0.24	0.26	0.28	0.30	0.32

Source: own counting based on the models in Wilkening, 187-188, 191 and G. Lewis, 1299-1689.

Table 3. At SSKP reaching 95%, leak-proof intercept probabilities for 1-15 interceptors and 1-35 attacking warheads.

q-tity	1	2	3	4	5	6	7	8	9	10	11	12	13	14	15
1	0.95	1.00	1.00	1.00	1.00	1.00	1.00	1.00	1.00	1.00	1.00	1.00	1.00	1.00	1.00
2	0.90	0.99	1.00	1.00	1.00	1.00	1.00	1.00	1.00	1.00	1.00	1.00	1.00	1.00	1.00
3	0.86	0.98	1.00	1.00	1.00	1.00	1.00	1.00	1.00	1.00	1.00	1.00	1.00	1.00	1.00
4	0.81	0.97	0.99	1.00	1.00	1.00	1.00	1.00	1.00	1.00	1.00	1.00	1.00	1.00	1.00
5	0.77	0.95	0.99	1.00	**1.00**	1.00	1.00	1.00	1.00	1.00	1.00	1.00	1.00	1.00	1.00
6	0.74	0.93	0.98	1.00	1.00	1.00	1.00	1.00	1.00	1.00	1.00	1.00	1.00	1.00	1.00
7	0.70	0.91	0.97	0.99	1.00	1.00	1.00	1.00	1.00	1.00	1.00	1.00	1.00	1.00	1.00
8	0.66	0.89	0.96	0.99	1.00	1.00	1.00	1.00	1.00	1.00	1.00	1.00	1.00	1.00	1.00
9	0.63	0.86	0.95	0.98	0.99	1.00	1.00	1.00	1.00	1.00	1.00	1.00	1.00	1.00	1.00
10	0.60	0.84	0.94	0.97	**0.99**	1.00	1.00	1.00	1.00	1.00	1.00	1.00	1.00	1.00	1.00
11	0.57	0.81	0.92	0.97	0.99	0.99	1.00	1.00	1.00	1.00	1.00	1.00	1.00	1.00	1.00
12	0.54	0.79	0.90	0.96	0.98	0.99	1.00	1.00	1.00	1.00	1.00	1.00	1.00	1.00	1.00
13	0.51	0.76	0.88	0.94	0.97	0.99	0.99	1.00	1.00	1.00	1.00	1.00	1.00	1.00	1.00
14	0.49	0.74	0.87	0.93	0.96	0.98	0.99	1.00	1.00	1.00	1.00	1.00	1.00	1.00	1.00
15	0.46	0.71	0.85	0.92	**0.96**	0.98	0.99	0.99	1.00	1.00	1.00	1.00	1.00	1.00	1.00
16	0.44	0.69	0.82	0.90	0.94	0.97	0.98	0.99	0.99	1.00	1.00	1.00	1.00	1.00	1.00
17	0.42	0.66	0.80	0.89	0.93	0.96	0.98	0.99	0.99	1.00	1.00	1.00	1.00	1.00	1.00
18	0.40	0.64	0.78	0.87	0.92	0.95	0.97	0.98	0.99	0.99	1.00	1.00	1.00	1.00	1.00
19	0.38	0.61	0.76	0.85	0.91	0.94	0.96	0.98	0.99	0.99	0.99	1.00	1.00	1.00	1.00
20	0.36	0.59	0.74	0.83	**0.89**	0.93	0.96	0.97	0.98	0.99	0.99	1.00	1.00	1.00	1.00

21	0.34	0.57	0.71	0.81	0.88	0.92	0.95	0.96	0.98	0.98	0.99	0.99	1.00	1.00	1.00
22	0.32	0.54	0.69	0.79	0.86	0.90	0.94	0.96	0.97	0.98	0.99	0.99	0.99	1.00	1.00
23	0.31	0.52	0.67	0.77	0.84	0.89	0.92	0.95	0.96	0.97	0.98	0.99	0.99	0.99	1.00
24	0.29	0.50	0.65	0.75	0.82	0.87	0.91	0.94	0.96	0.97	0.98	0.98	0.99	0.99	0.99
25	0.28	0.48	0.62	0.73	**0.80**	0.86	0.90	0.93	0.95	0.96	0.97	0.98	0.99	0.99	0.99
26	0.26	0.46	0.60	0.71	0.78	0.84	0.88	0.91	0.94	0.95	0.97	0.97	0.98	0.99	0.99
27	0.25	0.44	0.58	0.68	0.76	0.82	0.87	0.90	0.93	0.94	0.96	0.97	0.98	0.98	0.99
28	0.24	0.42	0.56	0.66	0.74	0.80	0.85	0.89	0.91	0.93	0.95	0.96	0.97	0.98	0.98
29	0.23	0.40	0.54	0.64	0.72	0.78	0.83	0.87	0.90	0.92	0.94	0.95	0.96	0.97	0.98
30	0.21	0.38	0.52	0.62	**0.70**	0.77	0.82	0.86	0.89	0.91	0.93	0.94	0.96	0.97	0.97
31	0.20	0.37	0.50	0.60	0.68	0.75	0.80	0.84	0.87	0.90	0.92	0.94	0.95	0.96	0.97
32	0.19	0.35	0.48	0.58	0.66	0.73	0.78	0.82	0.86	0.88	0.91	0.92	0.94	0.95	0.96
33	0.18	0.33	0.46	0.56	0.64	0.70	0.76	0.80	0.84	0.87	0.89	0.91	0.93	0.94	0.95
34	0.17	0.32	0.44	0.54	0.62	0.68	0.74	0.79	0.82	0.85	0.88	0.90	0.92	0.93	0.94
35	0.17	0.30	0.42	0.52	**0.60**	0.66	0.72	0.77	0.80	0.84	0.86	0.89	0.91	0.92	0.93

Source: own counting based on the models of Wilkening, 187-188, 191 and G. Lewis, 1299-1689.

Case Study. Yemen Missile War and Patriot Interceptors: A New Perspective on Tactical BMD?

1. Introduction. PAC and the Middle Eastern Challenge: The Case of Yemen

The chapter is focused on the Patriot missile defense engagements during the Saudi intervention in Yemen against the Houthi rebels (since 2015), compared with the Israeli Iron Dome operations against Hamas (2012, 2014) and the PAC performance during both US-Iraq wars. PAC became an asset of US allies endangered by missile or rocket attacks in 1991, but the technological deficiencies did not provide for a fully successful defense in the case of multiple warheads attacks or very fast targets. Further investments raised the test and combat effectiveness of Patriot, though by 2018, critics still undermined its real time performance, it reached close to 70% reliability in the Yemeni case. The included probabilistic analysis of BMD reliability against salvo warhead attacks, which examined the attempts of increasing defense chances by engaging additional interceptors or improving its single shot reliability.

The main hypotheses standing behind the presented argumentation claim that the gap between official and critically-assessed records of Patriot combat engagements remained much too broad; the public records may set the disparity range at the level of 20 percentage points (as in the Yemeni case), i.e.. between close to 50% and just below 70% intercept accuracy. Importantly, probabilistic analyses could signal an advantage of SSKP improvements (to levels of 90% and beyond) over the mere engagement of additional interceptors (although that is also necessary) in the context of possible WMD crisis. Only more than 90%-reliable interceptors (strengthened by using couple of them in each engagement attempt) could bring closer leak-proof intercept chances against warheads engaged in a salvo, as the analyzed scenarios of up to 35 missile attacks show.[563]

---

563   Lebovic, "The Law of Small Numbers," 470–72; Wilkening, 187–88, 191; Lewis, "Technical Controversy," 1418–1438; Grego, Lewis and Wright, *Shielded from Oversight. The Disastrous US Approach to Strategic Missile Defense. Appendix 8*, 1, 5.

2. The Background of PAC Engagement
Against Yemen Missile Threat

As soon as Yemeni Houthi rebels used missiles to attack Riyadh (after earlier civilian targets), which was defended by PAC, controversy arose around its performance. PAC was praised by Washington but criticized as leaking.[564] A critical view of PAC reliability in that context claimed that they were a total failure, and were not able to intercept any missiles at all, as Jeffrey Lewis argued.[565] Similar controversies arose after Iron Dome combat use by the IDF in 2012 and 2014, echoing earlier criticism of PAC during both Iraq wars.

The case of the Yemen civil war became a significant reality check for missile defense units worldwide, as the records of intervening Saudi Arabia and its allies proved.

Notably, among the monographs on the ongoing Yemeni conflicts (apart from other references), the analyses relied on Ginny Hill's, Marieke Brandt's, Asher Orkaby's, Shelagh Weir's, Helen Lackner's, Victoria Clark's, and Gregory Johnsen's.[566]

---

564 Jeff Daniels, "Raytheon's Patriot Defense System Likely Failed to Stop Saudi Missile Attack," CNBC, 2017, https://www.cnbc.com/2017/12/04/patriot-defense-system-likely-failed-in-saudi-ballistic-missile-attack.html; Max Fisher, Eric Schmitt, Audrey Carlsen, Malachy Browne, "Did American Missile Defense Fail in Saudi Arabia," *The New York Times* (2017), https://www.nytimes.com/interactive/2017/12/04/world/middleeast/saudi-missile-defense.html (accessed August 23, 2018).

565 Jeffrey Lewis, "Patriot Missiles Are Made in America and Fail Everywhere," *Foreign Policy*, 2018, https://foreignpolicy.com/2018/03/28/patriot-missiles-are-made-in-america-and-fail-everywhere/ (accessed August 23, 2018).

566 Ginny Hill, *Yemen Endures. Civil War, Saudi Adventurism and the Future of Arabia*, Kindle (Oxford: Oxford University Press, 2017); Marieke Brandt, *Tribes and Politics in Yemen. A History of the Houthi Conflict*, Kindle (Oxford: Oxford University Press, 2017); Asher Orkaby, *Beyond the Arab Cold War. The International History of the Yemen Civil War, 1962-68*, Kindle (New York: Oxford University Press, 2017); Shelagh Weir, *A Tribal Order: Politics and Law in the Mountains of Yemen* (Austin: University of Texas Press, 2007); Helen Lackner, *Yemen in Crisis. Autocracy, Neo-Liberalism and the Disintegration of a State* (London: Saqi Books, 2017); Victoria Clark, *Yemen. Dancing on the Heads of Snakes* (New Haven: Yale University Press, 2010); Gregory D. Johnsen, *The Last Refuge. Yemen, Al-Qaeda and America's War in Yemen*, Kindle (New York: W. W. Norton & Company, 2014); Conf. Isa Blumi, *Destroying Yemen. What Chaos in Arabia Tells Us about the World* (Oakland: University of California Press, 2018).

As Orkaby explained, the Houthi insurgency (*Ansar Allah* 'God supporters') was rooted in protests against discrimination in North Yemen (and the Wahhabi influence) after it unified with the South in 1990; the killing of Hussein Badreddin al-Houthi (co-leader of the movement) by the Yemeni military in 2004 triggered an insurgency under the Houthi family name.[567] US military engagement in Yemen under Ali Abdullah Saleh's presidency was seen as support for his regime, who was accused of exaggerating the threat of al-Qaeda in the Arabian Peninsula (AQAP) to keep power in the divided country. By 2010, Houthi rebels waged an open armed revolt.[568]

Shelagh Weir explained that in the 1980s, the influence of Sunni Wahhabism was growing in the North Yemeni provinces, finding fertile ground in local Zaydi-Shiism (and attracting fighters to the mujahedeen campaign in Afghanistan) after past Saudi efforts to gain the upper hand in Yemen (through support for Yemeni loyalists against republicans backed by Egypt in the 1962-1970 civil war).[569] Nevertheless, in 1990, Saudis were hugely disappointed by the lack of Yemen's condemnation of the Iraqi aggression against Kuwait, which led to expulsions of Yemeni workers from the Kingdom.[570] Notably, Osama bin Laden (son of a prominent Yemen-born Saudi entrepreneur) became by 1990 a prominent figure among the Jeddah Yemeni community leading to the Afghan campaign.[571]

---

567   Asher Orkaby, "Yemen's Humanitarian Nightmare. The Real Roots of the Conflict," *Foreign Affairs* 96, no. 6 (2017): 94; Orkaby, *Beyond the Arab Cold War,* 207; Conf. Clark, 269; Noel Brehony, "Yemen and the Huthis: Genesis of the 2015 Crisis," *Asian Affairs* 46, no. 2 (2015): 237, https://doi.org/10.1080/03068374.2015.1037162.

568   Hill, *Yemen Endures,* 149–152.

569   Weir, *A Tribal Order,* 280, 296; Conf. Clive Jones, "A Tribal Order: Politics and Law in the Mountains of Yemen," *Middle Eastern Studies* 47, no. 2 (2011): 435–436, https://doi.org/10.1080/00263206.2011.544104.

   In the 1960s civil war, Riyadh was supporting dynastic Imamate (Zaydi-Shiite) in North, while revolutionaries received Nasserite and Iraqi Ba'athist support. Jesse Ferris, *Nasser's Gamble: How Intervention in Yemen Caused the Six-Day War and the Decline of Egyptian Power* (Princeton: Princeton University Press, 2013), 2; Barak Salmoni, Bryce Loidolt and Madeleine Wells, *Regime and Periphery in Northern Yemen: The Huthi Phenomenon* (Santa Monica: RAND, 2010), 85.

570   Weir, 296.

571   Hill, 120, 134, 149–152. Osama bin Laden's father, Muhammad, emigrated from Hadhramat (Yemen) to Saudi Arabia in the 1930s. Rohan Gunaratna, *Inside Al Qaeda. Global Network of Terror* (New York: Columbia University Press, 2002), 16.

In 2009, al-Qaeda networks in Saudi Arabia and Yemen were merged in AQAP and the US responded with special operations conducted in cooperation with Yemen and Saudi Arabia within the Obama administration's strategy.[572]

The influence of 2011 Arab Spring increased social resistance against Saleh's continued rule, as G. Hill explained, opening a path to a negotiated transition in November.[573] Unfortunately, under the temporary President (former Vice President) Abd Rabbu Mansur Hadi, security conditions worsened, and by September 2014, Houthis had consolidated their administration in the Northern province of Saada and were able take control of Sana'a (Saleh's supporters offered no resistance on Houthi's march and joined their ranks in the capital).[574] The US decided to move the embassy out of Sana'a under a Houthi-Saleh alliance, despite the joint interest in defeating AQAP.[575] AQAP forces in Yemen by 2015 were estimated to be from a couple hundred to a couple thousand militants.[576]

3. The Role of PAC Missile Defense in Saudi-Led Intervention in Yemen

In 2014, Yemen became again fully divided by a civil war, when Houthi rebels formed an alliance with Saleh (with some troops supporting the former head of state), which led to Saudi Arabia's intervention and

---

572 Hill, 149–152; Conf. Jiadong Zhang, "Terrorist Activities in Yemen and the US Countermeasures," *Journal of Middle Eastern and Islamic Studies (in Asia)* 4, no. 1 (2010): 113–114, https://doi.org/10.1080/19370679.2010.12023150.

573 Hill, 200, 249, 265–272; Conf. Johnsen, *The Last Refugee*, 269; Michael Knights, "The Military Role in Yemen's Protests: Civil-Military Relations in the Tribal Republic," *Journal of Strategic Studies* 36, no. 2 (2013): 277, https://doi.org/10.1080/0140 2390.2012.740660.

574 Hill, 200, 249, 265–272; Conf. Johnsen, 269; Knights, "The Military Role in Yemen's Protests," 277.

575 Hill, 200, 249, 265–272; Conf. Brandt, *Tribes and Politics in Yemen*, 9111, 10177-10198, 10656-10678.

Brian Perkins noted, though, that after 9/11, Houthis adopted anti-American and anti-Israeli slogans. Brian M. Perkins, "Yemen: Between Revolution and Regression," *Studies in Conflict & Terrorism* 40, no. 4 (2017): 307, https://doi.org/10.1080/105 7610X.2016.1205368.

576 Maria-Louise Clausen, "Understanding the Crisis in Yemen: Evaluating Competing Narratives," *The International Spectator* 50, no. 3 (2015): 25, https://doi.org/10.108 0/03932729.2015.1053707.

Houthi missile attacks countered by Saudi PAC units deployed first near the Yemeni border.[577]

The Saudi-led intervention in Yemen started with major operations in March 2015 (Operation Decisive Storm) after the plea from an over-thrown president Hadi to intervene.[578] The Saudi operation began to prevent Houthis from seizing Aden, which was abandoned by Hadi, who fled to Saudi Arabia.[579] Apart from air strikes, the ground operations of the Saudi-led coalition included a successful amphibious operation in the port of Aden in July 2015 (where Hadi had formed a new government after he fled from Sana'a) and further (limited) advances northwards.[580]

The UN panel of experts reported in 2018 that the number of Houthi missiles attacking Saudi Arabia between June 2015 and November 2016 reached 60.[581] By the end of 2016, Saudi authorities confirmed detection of 37 missiles (Scud and Tochka; some of the latter were intercepted), which entered Saudi Arabia between June and November 2016, attacking civilian targets.[582]

4. The Controversy of Iranian Arms Deliveries for Houthis

Shia Houthi rebels enjoyed Iranian military support (including missiles and rocket launchers) in their campaign against the Saudi-led Sunni coalition, though it remained difficult to prove a broad scale of such deliveries in the UN.[583] Earlier records of Iran's arm supplies to Houthis were con-

---

577 Frank Gardner, "Yemen Conflict: The View from the Saudi Side," *BBC* (2016), https://www.bbc.com/news/world-middle-east-38239782.

578 Ralph Shield, "The Saudi Air War in Yemen: A Case for Coercive Success through Battlefield Denial," *Journal of Strategic Studies* 41, no. 3 (2018): 463, https://doi.org /10.1080/01402390.2017.1308863; Jane's, "Yemeni Rebels Enhance Ballistic Missile Campaign," *Jane's* (2017), http://www.janes.com/images/assets/330/72330/ Yemeni_rebels_enhance_ballistic_missile_campaign.pdf.

579 Marcel Serr, "Understanding the War in Yemen," *Israel Journal of Foreign Affairs* 11, no. 3 (2017): 359, https://doi.org/10.1080/23739770.2017.1419405.

580 Shield, "The Saudi Air War in Yemen," 466. By 2017, Houthis remained under Abdul Malik al-Huthi's leadership. Lackner, *Yemen in Crisis*, 150.

581 Panel of Experts on Yemen, *Final Report of the Panel of Experts on Yemen*, 35, 148–235.

582 Gardner, "Yemen Conflict."

583 Panel of Experts on Yemen, 25–27; Amir Magdy Kamel, "The JCPOA: How Iran's Grand Strategy Stifled the US," *Middle Eastern Studies* 54, no. 4 (2018): 718, https://

firmed when Iranian vessels with arms for rebels were seized in January 2013 by US and Yemen units (and most likely such assistance increased after 2014, as Thomas Juneau assessed).[584]

The Trump administration (together with the UK, France, and Germany) strongly backed Houthi missile delivery-related sanctions against Iran, seeing clear evidence of such supplies (enabling attacks against Saudi cities and vessels delivering humanitarian assistance to Yemen).[585]

Examples of Iranian military backing of the Houthis appeared to be insufficient to introduce UN restrictive measures, however. The UN Yemen panel reported no large-scale Iranian arms sales to Houthis, aside from 2064 Iranian-made weapons (discovered during 2015 and 2016 maritime seizures of four vessels arriving to deliver arms to Houthis, including 2 Iranian-manufactured modifications of RPG-7 rocket launchers, 1998 pieces of modified AK-47 and 64 Hoshdar-M sniper rifles, produced only in Iran).[586] In those seized vessels, altogether 300 RPG-7 rocket launchers were found.[587] Iranian missiles, such as Shahab 1-3 and Zelzal were among those used by Houthis, apart from Soviet and modified (North Korean) Scuds.[588]

---

doi.org/10.1080/00263206.2018.1427583; Marko Valenta and Jo Jakobsen, "Nexus of Armed Conflicts and Migrations to the Gulf: Migrations to the GCC from War-Torn Source Countries in Asia, Africa and the Arab Neighbourhood," *Middle Eastern Studies* 54, no. 1 (2018): 35–36, https://doi.org/10.1080/00263206.2017.1365058.

584 Thomas Juneau, "Iran's Policy towards the Houthis in Yemen: A Limited Return on a Modest Investment," *International Affairs* 92, no. 3 (2016): 655–658; Carole Landry, "Iran Arming Yemen's Houthi Rebels since 2009: UN Report," *Middle East Eye* (May 1, 2015), https://www.middleeasteye.net/news/iran-arming-yemens-huthi-rebels-2009-un-report-1170499355.

585 US Embassy in Yemen, *Joint Statement by France, Germany, the United Kingdom, and the United States* (February 27, 2018), https://ye.usembassy.gov/pr-02282018/; The White House, *Statement by the Press Secretary on Saudi Arabia and Yemen* (December 21, 2017), https://www.whitehouse.gov/briefings-statements/statement-press-secretary-saudi-arabia-yemen; The White House, *Statement by the Press Secretary on the Houthi Missile Strike on a Turkish Wheat Ship* (May 25, 2018), https://www.whitehouse.gov/briefings-statements/statement-press-secretary-houthi-missile-strike-turkish-wheat-ship/.

586 Panel of Experts on Yemen, 25–27; United Nations, *Security Council Renews Sanctions against Yemen, Rejects Alternate Draft after Veto by Russian Federation* (February 26, 2018), https://www.un.org/press/en/2018/sc13225.doc.htm.

587 Panel of Experts on Yemen, 25–27, 143–45.

588 Panel of Experts on Yemen, 25–27, 143–45; Shaul Shay, "Iranian Rocketry in the

The February 2018 draft UN Security Council resolution introducing sanctions on Iran for supporting Houthi rebels was vetoed by Russia.[589] According to the UAE June 2018 report to the UN, Iranian weapons (including missiles and drones) were smuggled into Yemen by Houthis through Hudaydah port,[590] which the Emirates attempted to seize through a military operation launched on June 13[591] (the operation of the coalition to reclaim the city was stopped on July 1, but on July 26, air strikes were renewed).[592]

5. Houthi Missile Attacks and PAC Defense

The UN Yemen panel reported that from June 16, 2015 to November 26, 2016, the Saudi-led coalition shot down 28 missiles and rockets out of 60 (including Qaher-1 and Scud), stressing that economically the Houthi-Saleh alliance benefited from the lower costs of attacking missiles comparing to PAC-3.[593] The Kingdom of Saudi Arabia confirmed 10 interceptions in the June 2015 to November 2016 incidents (Table 2).[594] Emile

Service of the Houthis in Yemen," *IsraelDefense* (2016), http://www.israeldefense. co.il/en/content/iranian-rocketry-service-houthis-yemen.

589   Bruce Riedel, "What You Need to Know about the Latest Houthi Attack on Riyadh," *Brookings Institution* (2018), https://www.brookings.edu/blog/order-from-chaos/2018/03/27/what-you-need-to-know-about-the-latest-houthi-attack-on-riyadh/; Jeremy Sharp, *Yemen: Civil War and Regional Intervention* (Washington, DC, 2018), 4, https://fas.org/sgp/crs/mideast/R43960.pdf; BBC, "Yemen War: Saudis Shoot down Missiles Fired by Houthi Rebels," *BBC* (March 26, 2018), https://www.bbc. co.uk/news/world-middle-east-43536751; UN Security Council, *United Kingdom of Great Britain and Northern Ireland: Draft Resolution, S/2018/156* (UN Security Council, 2018), http://digitallibrary.un.org/record/1473784/files/S_2018_156-EN.pdf; Security Council Report, *UN Documents for Yemen* (2018), https://www. securitycouncilreport.org/un-documents/yemen.

590   Lana Nusseibeh, *Letter Dated 13 June 2018 from the Permanent Representative of the UAE to the UN, S/2018/607* (2018), 3, https://undocs.org/S/2018/607.

591   Peter Salisbury, "The New Front in Yemen. What's at Stake in Hodeidah," *Foreign Affairs*(June 27, 2018), https://www.foreignaffairs.com/articles/middle-east/2018-06-27/new-front-yemen.

592   Solène Metais, *Yemen: The Battle for Al-Hudaydah as a Turning Point in the Civil War*, *European Strategic Intelligence and Security Center* (July 17, 2018), http://www.esisc. org/publications/briefings/yemen-the-battle-for-al-hudaydah-as-a-turning-point-in-the-civil-war; Middle East Monitor, "Coalition Renews Strikes on Yemen's Main Port City" (July 27, 2018), https://www.middleeastmonitor.com/20180727-coalition-renews-strikes-on-yemens-main-port-city.

593   Panel of Experts on Yemen, 35, 148–150.

594   Panel of Experts on Yemen, 35, 148–150.

Hokayem and David Roberts reported that there were 375 Saudi civilian casualties caused by Houthi rockets in Najran by February 2016.[595] Houthi missile attacks also caused large losses in the Emirates (participating actively in the Saudi-led intervention); in September 2015, 83 men were killed at a military base (most likely a missile-hit ammunition depot exploded).[596]

In July 2015, the US agreed to send 600 PAC-3 missiles to Saudi Arabia for $5.4 billion, while in October 2017, it confirmed the sale of 360 THAAD missiles and 44 launchers for $15 billion.[597] The US has supported Saudi policy aimed against the Houthi rebellion in Yemen since 2014, giving aid to the intervention since 2015.[598]

By November 2017, Raytheon claimed more than 100 successful intercepts of Yemen-launched tactical missiles, including over 90 of PAC-2 Guided Enhanced Missile-T with a blast fragmentation warhead (aside from Lockheed's kinetic-kill PAC-3 also used by the Saudis) with a huge majority in Saudi Arabia or Yemen and only a few over UAE.[599]

The first attacks of Scud-similar missiles against Riyadh occurred in November 2017, while the overall number of missiles fired by Houthis against Saudi Arabia reached 100 by March 2018.[600] In late March 2018, the Saudis claimed the intercept of 7 Houthi missiles attacking four Saudi cities using PAC-3 interceptors, but debris from one of them fell close to Riyadh airport, causing one fatality.[601] The coalition claimed intercep-

---

595   Emile Hokayem and David Roberts, "The War in Yemen," *Survival* 58, no. 6 (2016): 168.

596   Hokayem and Roberts, "The War in Yemen," 168.

597   Barbara Opall-Rome, "Raytheon: Arab-Operated Patriots Intercepted over 100 Tactical Ballistic Missiles since 2015," *DefenseNews* (2017), https://www.defensenews. com/digital-show-dailies/dubai-air-show/2017/11/14/raytheon-saudi-based-patriots-intercepted-over-100-tbms-since-2015/.

598   Jeremy Sharp and Christopher Blanchard, *The War in Yemen: A Compilation of Legislation in the 115th Congress* (Washington, DC, 2018), 1, https://fas.org/sgp/crs/ mideast/R45046.pdf.

599   Opall-Rome, "Raytheon"; Raytheon, *Patriot by the Numbers*, 2018, https://www. raytheon.com/sites/default/files/capabilities/rtnwcm/groups/public/docu ments/content/patriot-by-the-numbers-pdf.pdf.

600   Riedel, "What You Need to Know about the Latest Houthi Attack on Riyadh"; Gardner.

601   Saeed Al-Batati and Rick Gladstone, "Saudis Claim to Intercept 7 Missiles Fired at

tions of 3 missiles over Riyadh and 4 others fired against Najran, Jizan, Khamis, and Mushait.[602]

By July 2018, the recognized number of ballistic missiles fired by Houthis at Saudi Arabia since 2015 had reached 161.[603] By July 10, 2018, the publicly known intercept result was 106 Yemeni missiles.[604] That would mean that the effectiveness of the PAC BMD in combat grew to 66% since 2016, when it remained relatively low, at 47%.

Notably, by late 2016, anti-ship Houthi missile attacks were assessed as a threat to sea movement through Bab al-Mandeb and even world maritime trade.[605] In July 2018, Houthis managed to attack two Saudi oil tankers in the Red Sea and damage one of them, which led to a suspension of Saudi oil shipments through the Bab el-Mandeb strait route on July 25, and resumed on August 2.[606]

Cities From Yemen," *The New York Times* (March 25, 2018), https://www.nytimes.com/2018/03/25/world/middleeast/saudi-arabia-yemen-missile-houthi.html; Marwa Rashad, Sarah Dadouch and Abdulrahman Al-Ansi, "Barrage of Missiles on Saudi Arabia Ramps up Yemen War," *Reuters* (March 26, 2018), https://www.reuters.com/article/us-yemen-security-missiles/barrage-of-missiles-on-saudi-arabia-ramps-up-yemen-war-idUSKBN1H21HQ; Riedel.

602   Haaretz, "Saudi Arabia's US-Made Patriot Missile Defense System 'Malfunctions,'" *Reuters* (March 27, 2018), https://www.haaretz.com/middle-east-news/saudi-patriot-missile-malfunctions-crashes-in-rdential-area-1.5940630; Al-Batati and Gladstone, "Saudis Claim to Intercept 7 Missiles Fired at Cities From Yemen"; Stratfor, "Saudi Arabia: Missile Strikes on Riyadh Mark Third Anniversary of War on Houthis" (March 26, 2018), https://worldview.stratfor.com/article/saudi-arabia-missile-strikes-riyadh-mark-third-anniversary-war-houthis.

603   Middle East Monitor, "Houthi Missile Kills One in Saudi Arabia" (August 9, 2018), https://www.middleeastmonitor.com/20180809-houthi-missile-kills-one-in-saudi-arabia; Middle East Monitor, "161 Ballistic Missiles Fired at Saudi Arabia since 2015" (July 17, 2018), https://www.middleeastmonitor.com/20180717-161-ballistic-missiles-fired-at-saudi-arabia-since-2015.

604   CSIS Missile Threat, *Interactive: The Missile War in Yemen*.

605   Panel of Experts on Yemen, 14–16.

606   Stratfor, "Saudi Arabia, Yemen: What's Next for Red Sea Oil Shipments After Houthi Attack" (July), https://worldview.stratfor.com/article/saudi-arabia-yemen-whats-next-red-sea-oil-shipments-houthi-attack-strait-ship; Stratfor, "Saudi Arabia: Oil Shipments Through Bab El-Mandeb Strait Resumed" (August 2, 2018), https://worldview.stratfor.com/situation-report/saudi-arabia-oil-shipments-through-bab-el-mandeb-strait-resumed; Middle East Monitor, "Saudi Arabia Resumes Oil Shipments through Bab El-Mandab" (August 2, 2018), https://www.middleeastmonitor.com/20180802-saudi-arabia-resumes-oil-shipments-through-bab-el-mandab.

Notably, the assassination of independent Saudi journalist (for the Washington Post) Jamal Khashoggi by Saudi intelligence (most likely with crown prince Mohammed bin Salman's [MBS's] backing) in the Saudi consulate in Istanbul on October 2, 2018 shook the reliability of the Saudi monarchist regime despite the King's ordered investigation. The US' most powerful Arab ally seemed to resemble a tyrannous and dangerous rogue state (but as Stratfor assessed, the assassination did not lead to an open conflict between Turkey and Saudi Arabia, competing for Sunni leadership, although Turkish president Recep Erdogan accused the Saudis of the planned murder of the journalist).[607]

In November 2018, the US Treasury introduced sanctions against 17 Saudi official servicemen involved in Khashoggi's assassination.[608] Stratfor mentioned that the Washington Post confirmed a CIA report on MBS's responsibility for giving orders to kill Jamal Khashoggi.[609] The June 2019 UN report stated that the role of the Saudi crown prince in Khashoggi assassination demands further investigation.[610]

---

607 Stratfor, *Why Turkey Isn't Burning Bridges With Saudi Arabia Over Khashoggi, October 29, 2018* (2018), https://worldview.stratfor.com/article/why-turkey-isnt-burning-bridges-saudi-arabia-over-khashoggi; Stratfor, *Saudi Arabia: King Salman Orders Restructuring of Saudi Intelligence Personnel, October 22, 2018* (2018), https://worldview.stratfor.com/situation-report/saudi-arabia-king-salman-orders-restructuring-saudi-intelligence-personnel; Conf. Charles Glass, *Seeing Khashoggi's Fate as a Death Foretold, October 24, 2018* (2018), https://worldview.stratfor.com/article/seeing-khashoggis-fate-death-foretold.

608 US Department of Treasury, *Treasury Sanctions 17 Individuals for Their Roles in the Killing of Jamal Khashoggi, November 15, 2018,* https://home.treasury.gov/news/press-releases/sm547.

609 Stratfor, *US, Saudi Arabia: CIA Concludes Saudi Crown Prince Ordered Khashoggi's Killing, Report Says, November 17, 2018,* 2018, https://worldview.stratfor.com/situation-report/us-saudi-arabia-cia-concludes-saudi-crown-prince-ordered-khashoggis-killing-report; Shane Harris, Greg Miller and Josh Dawsey, "CIA Concludes Saudi Crown Prince Ordered Jamal Khashoggi's Assassination," *The Washington Post* (November 16, 2018), https://www.washingtonpost.com/world/national-security/cia-concludes-saudi-crown-prince-ordered-jamal-khashoggis-assassination/2018/11/16/98c89fe6-e9b2-11e8-a939-9469f1166f9d_story.html?utm_term=.32b7e192bc38.

610 United Nations, *Saudi Arabia in Spotlight as UN-Appointed Independent Investigator Publishes Full Khashoggi Findings, June 19, 2019* (2019), https://news.un.org/en/story/2019/06/1040821; Stratfor, *Saudi Arabia: U.N. Report Turns Up the Heat on Crown Prince Over Khashoggi Murder, June 19, 2019* (2019), https://www.stratfor.com/situation-report/saudi-arabia-un-report-turns-heat-crown-prince-over-khashoggi-murder-mbs.

6. Summary and Analysis: The Improvement of Patriot Engagements Since 1990-1991 (US-Iraq Wars and After)

a) Summary: PAC Performance During Desert Storm

Historically, the debate on PAC's combat performance began with its mixed record of interception attempts of Iraqi Scuds attacking Saudi Arabia and Israel in early 1991.[611] During the Kuwait war, 158 PAC-2 missiles were used, whereas up to the end of the war, there were as many as ca. 3000 Patriot interceptors deployed, including the earlier PAC-1; PAC-2 production on a full scale started after the war broke out.[612] As Rosenau noted, the Iraqi regime could use during the Kuwait War two types of Scud (Soviet R-17-based) missiles (of relatively low technological performance): al-Hussein, with a 600-650 km range, and al-Abbas, with a range of 750-900 km, deployed on 28 fixed launchers at five missile sites (in Western Iraq) and on some amount (probably 36) of mobile launchers.[613] The "Scud hunt" in Western Iraq of US and British Special Forces was not a decisive factor in the reduction of the daily rate of Scud attacks.[614] The overall Iraqi Scud force included probably 600 missiles, and 81 of them directly threatened targets in Saudi Arabia and Israel after launch.[615]

The losses caused by Iraqi Scuds (39 missiles) in Israel included 13 killed, 1020 wounded, and 12,000 private houses or offices damaged.[616] Relying on video recordings of PAC-2 attempts to intercept Scud missiles, Postol sustained that Patriot was almost completely ineffective during the Kuwait war.[617]

PAC interceptors were able to attack 44 out of 80 Iraqi Scuds during the Kuwait war (probably 16 in the Israeli theater of operations and 28 in Saudi Arabia), which did not mean a clear interception.[618] Notably, the US

---

611 Sullivan and others, 42, 45; Samson, 101; Hildreth, *Evaluation of US Army Assessment*; Shuey; Postol and Lewis, 4; Postol, *Optical Evidence Indicating Patriot High Miss Rates*; Schubert and Kraus.

612 Schubert and Kraus, 243.

613 Rosenau, 29–32.

614 Rosenau, 39–42; Gordon and Trainor, *The General's War*, 230–248.

615 Cheney, 129; Hildreth, *Evaluation of US Army Assessment*, 2, 51–54.

616 DelGenis, "Israel's Gulf War Experience," 80.

617 Postol and Stein, 226; Postol, "Lessons of the Gulf War Experience with Patriot."

618 Sullivan and others, 42.

Army's evaluation of Patriot performance was lowered from 96% effective (in March 1991) to 69% (in May 1991) and below 60% in April 1992.[619] The April 1992 US Army revision of Gulf War PAC-2 performance estimation setting its effectiveness at 70% of in Saudi Arabia and 40% in Israel could not provide absolute certainty of interceptions of more than 9% of the targets.[620] Due to the revised assessment of the Army, PAC-2 engagements were 52% effective in terms of destroying enemy warheads, including 25% highly certain warhead interceptions.[621] The most visible failure of PAC interception of a Scud on February 25, 1991 (Dhahran) led to the loss of 28 US soldiers.[622]

b) Summary: PAC Performance During the 2003 Iraq War

The improved PAC-3, deployed to support the 2003 US intervention in Iraq, were aimed at destroying very fast targets (close to Mach 10) by colliding with them directly.[623] During the operation, no Scud attacks were reported, and the Iraqi missiles appeared to be less challenging.

PAC 2003 performance was also disappointing in terms of air unit recognition, which led to friendly fire against one British and two US aircrafts (destroying one and tracking another), confirmed by government assessments and explained by radar malfunction (false images leading to wrong targeting).[624]

The US Department of Defense report on Patriot performance in the 2003 war estimated that among the reasons for friendly fire were ill combat identification, flawed situational awareness (in terms of communication and data processing), and operation system deficiencies (protocols and software were not well suited to the combat scenario in Iraq, where the ratio of friendly to foe aircraft reached 4000 to 1, and the PAC systems design headed towards serious missile attack scenarios).[625]

---

619   Sullivan and others, 42.

620   Henry Hinton and others, *Operation Desert Storm*, 3.

621   Henry Hinton and others, *Operation Desert Storm*, 3.

622   Carlone and others, 1.

623   Murray and Scales, *The Iraq War*, 265.

624   Samson, 104–105, 119–120.

625   Office of the Under Secretary of Defense for Acquisition, *Report of the Defense Science Board Task Force on Patriot System Performance*, 2; Bolkcom, 55–56.

In the context of the 2003 US intervention in Iraq, it is worth stressing that due to the establishment of the US ISG, Iraq most likely destroyed its WMD arsenal just after the 1991 Kuwait war, despite the pre-2003 George W. Bush administration statements regarding the threat posed by the Hussein regime's chemical weapons and hypothetical nuclear attempts, which were not confirmed by investigations after the invasion in March 2003.[626]

c) Summary: Israeli Patriot-Related BMD Improvements

The Israeli engagement in BMD grew after 2006 Lebanon war, when Israel was attacked by thousands of Hezbollah's missiles, including Iranian-supplied ones.[627] As Stratfor assessed, Hezbollah possessed a 10,000 strong arsenal of rockets during the 2006 war, managing to launch 120 per day on average (causing $3.5 billion losses in Israel's economy), despite Israeli early strikes against longer-range rockets.[628] By 2018, Hezbollah's Iranian backed rocket arsenal grew to 130,000.[629] IDF's first combat operations using Iron Dome were conducted within a framework of the Pillar of Defense operation, implemented in 2012 against radical Islamist (Hamas and Islamic Jihad) groups attacking from Gaza and during operation Protective Edge from July to August 2014, aimed against Hamas rocket attacks targeted at South Israel.[630]

During the 2012 IDF operations, 1506 rockets were fired against Israel from Gaza.[631] A total of 421 of those were intercepted by Iron Dome and 58 hit populated areas: the BMD shot down 28% of all rockets used, while the leakage of the system related to the protection of populated areas could be analyzed at a minimum 12.1% level to consider also the attacking rockets that didn't hit the targets (152) and those used against

---

626   Duelfer, 64; Chilcot, 77–78; Robert Jervis, *Why Intelligence Fails. Lessons from the Iranian Revolution and the Iraq War*, Kindle (Ithaca: Cornell University Press, 2010), 74; Ali A. Allawi, *The Occupation of Iraq. Winning the War, Losing the Peace* (New Haven: Yale University Press, 2007), 80–81.

627   Lazareva, "The Iron Dome"; Siperco, "Shield of David," 128.

628   Stratfor, *The Missile Arsenal at the Heart of the Israeli-Iranian Rivalry* (August 8, 2018), https://worldview.stratfor.com/article/missile-arsenal-heart-israeli-iranian-rivalry.

629   Stratfor, *The Missile Arsenal at the Heart of the Israeli-Iranian Rivalry*.

630   IDF, *Operation Pillar of Defense (2012)*; IDF, *Operation Protective Edge (July/August 2014)*; Conf. Byman, *A High Price*, 358.

631   IDF, *Operation Pillar of Defense (2012)*.

unpopulated locations (875).[632] IDF reported six Israeli fatalities and 240 injured in the time of Pillar of Defense operation.[633] During the 2014 operation Protective Edge, ca. 4500 rockets were used against Israel and 692 were shot down by Iron Dome (15% of all attacking, including those not heading towards populated areas).[634]

Michael Armstrong assessed that the real Iron Dome's interception result related to the fact that the "hazardous" (targeted at population areas) rockets were below 32% in 2012 and 59-75% in 2014.[635] In 2014, Israeli defense officials quoted by Emily Landau and Azriel Bermant claimed that the performance of Iron Dome improved from the interception rate of 84% in 2012 to 90% in 2014,[636] referring to rockets aimed at populated areas.

The Iron Dome performance seemed much lower in the assessments of BMD critics.[637] The comparison of the costs of missiles used by the attacker and the defender in the Israeli BMD case appeared to favor the offense.

Notably, Saudi Arabia expressed interest in buying the Israeli Iron Dome system after extensive Houthi missile attacks in early 2018 (reportedly in 2015, Saudis rejected such on offer).[638] By 2018, the Iron Dome purchase

---

632 IDF, *Operation Pillar of Defense (2012)*; Conf. Michael J. Armstrong, "Modeling Short-Range Ballistic Missile Defense and Israel's Iron Dome System," *Operations Research* 62, no. 5 (2014): 1028–1039.

633 IDF, *Operation Pillar of Defense (2012)*.

634 IDF, *Operation Protective Edge (July/August 2014)*.

635 Michael J. Armstrong, "The Effectiveness of Rocket Attacks and Defenses in Israel," 113–116; Conf. Michael J. Armstrong, "Modeling Short-Range Ballistic Missile Defense and Israel's Iron Dome System"; Michael J. Armstrong, "Iron Dome: Neither a 'Bluff' nor the 'End of Rockets,'" *The National Interest* (April 7, 2018), https://nationalinterest.org/feature/iron-dome-neither-bluff-nor-the-end-rockets-25269.

636 Landau and Bermant, "Iron Dome Protection," 37–38; Ginsburg, "Iron Dome Gets Mysterious Upgrade."

637 Peck, "Russia Mocks America for Buying Israel's Iron Dome"; Alex Gatopoulos, "How Successful Was Israel's Iron Dome?" *Al Jazeera* (September 8, 2014), http://www.aljazeera.com/news/middleeast/2014/08/israel-iron-dome-gaza-rockets-201481712494436388.html.

638 Defense Industry Daily (after Basler Zeitung), "Iron Dome Sees Israel Ramp up, Raytheon Partnership for US Market" (January 11, 2018), https://www.defenseindustrydaily.com/iron-dome-deployment-exports-07039; Benjamin Weinthal, "Report: Saudi Arabia Sought to Buy Israel's Iron Dome System," *Jerusalem Post* (January 9, 2018), https://www.jpost.com/Middle-East/Report-Saudi-Arabia-sought-to-buy-Israels-Iron-Dome-system-533185; The New Arab, "Saudi Arabia

was also negotiated between Israel and Azerbaijan.[639]

7. Probability Analysis in Scenarios of Hypothetical PAC-Level Effective BMD Engagements

The most recent case of Patriot used by Saudi Arabia against Yemeni Houthi missile attacks (compared to intercept records in US operations against Hussein's Iraq and during the Israeli Iron Dome combat engagements) could delineate PAC's effectiveness at ca. 70% reliability (Table 1).

By May 2017, MDA's test results proved PAC-3 to be 86% reliable.[640] Within the next few months, by mid-2018, PAC-3's test performance was lifted to 88%, including 30 successful intercepts in 34 tests.[641]

In the context of missile defense analyzed in a binomial distribution, Lebovic noted that its 95% reliability seemed to be the minimum statistical requirement, as systems of lower effectiveness could be swiftly defeated by attacking warheads.[642]

The introduced probability analysis could help to predict the possible necessary SSKP improvements, allowing a distant leak-proof intercept perspective against salvo missile/rocket attacks.

Table 3 and Figure 1 show the probabilities (in Bernoulli's binomial distribution following Wilkening's model) of defeating the BMD system by a given number of warheads, from 0 to 12, in a scenario of a salvo attack of 35 warheads and SSKP's reaching 85%, 90% (close to test performance

---

'Looking to Buy' Israel's Iron Dome System" (January 9, 2018), https://www.alaraby.co.uk/english/news/2018/1/9/saudi-arabia-looking-to-buy-israels-iron-dome-system; Times of Israel, "Saudi Arabia 'Rejects Israeli Offer to Supply Iron Dome'" (May 23, 2015), http://www.timesofisrael.com/saudi-arabia-rejected-israeli-offer-of-iron-dome/?fb_comment_id=720779021366241_72092 4811351662#f268bdd6541325.

639   Michael J. Armstrong, "Iron Dome: Neither a 'Bluff' nor the 'End of Rockets'"; Stratfor, "Azerbaijan: Deal Reached With Israel for Iron Dome" (December 19, 2016), https://worldview.stratfor.com/article/azerbaijan-deal-reached-israel-iron-dome; Ilgar Gurbanov, "Azerbaijan's Defense Minister Visits Israel, as Bilateral Ties Grow Stronger," *Eurasia Daily Monitor* 14, no. 117 (2017), https://jamestown.org/pro gram/azerbaijans-defense-minister-visits-israel-as-bilateral-ties-grow-stronger.

640   MDA, *Ballistic Missile Defense Intercept Flight Test Record (as of May 30, 2017)*.

641   MDA, *Ballistic Missile Defense Intercept Flight Test Record (as of March 2018)* (2018), https://www.mda.mil/global/documents/pdf/testrecord.pdf.

642   Lebovic, 470–472.

of PAC-3), and 95% (the hypothetical future performance of short-range BMD).

In the first scenario of SSKP equaling 85%, 5 warheads would defeat the BMD with a (relatively highest) probability of ca. 18,8%, while other most probable scenarios include:

- 4 warheads defeating the defense, in such a case $p(x) = 17.2\%$,
- 6 warheads passing through the defense with a probability of 16.6% (see Table 3, Figure 1).

The next example regarding a salvo attack of 35 warheads and interceptors of SSKP equaling 90% presents the highest probability (22.5%) of 3 warheads defeating the BMD, while at the SSKP level of 95%, it would be more likely that only 1 warhead would defeat the defense, with a probability of 30.6% (underlined in Table 3).

The following tables and figures show the probabilities of leak-proof interception in scenarios of engaging additional interceptors against each of the incoming warheads in attacks of up to 35 warheads. The decreasing probability of a leak-proof interception related to growing number of warheads attacking in a salvo, examined at SSKP levels of 85%, 90%, and 95% could be partly balanced by an introduction of additional interceptors (Tables 4, 5, and 6 and Figures 2, 3, and 4). In a scenario of using 5 interceptors against each of the incoming warheads, the highest gains from SSKP improvements (85-90-95%) were most visible in a hypothetical defense against 20-35 simultaneously attacking warheads, where the gain from 90-95% SSKP growth reached 40-50 percentage points of increased leak-proof intercept probability (Tables 5 and 6).

Summarizing, a mere increase in the number of interceptors would not bring closer a leak-proof interception without a rise of SSKP above 90%, while SSKP improvements could also be more budget friendly (lowering demand for additional missiles), noting the high unit costs of interceptors like PAC-3 MSE (ca. $5 million).[643]

---

643   US Army Financial Management & Comptroller, *US Army Justification Book of Missile Procurement. FY 2018 Budget Amendment* (2017), 21–22, https://www.asafm.army. mil/documents/BudgetMaterial/FY2018/MSLS_Army_FY18BA_20171108.pdf; Office of the Under Secretary of Defense - Comptroller, *Program Acquisition Costs by Weapon System FY 2018*, 4–6.

Conclusion

To summarize, the presented cases of combat use of PAC from 1991 to 2018 could not rule out by themselves the most significant doubts concerning Patriot's real-time performance. It is hardly imaginable to provide for a combat-proven tactical BMD for such regions as Middle East without the efforts to deliver PAC units for the sake of civilians endangered by rocket/missile attacks, with the local contributions of Middle Eastern US allies. The latest examples of PAC combat use during the Yemeni conflict could prove that its reliability stands slightly below 70%. The Gulf War of 1990-1991 and the US invasion of Iraq in 2003 gave incentive to further active investments in increasing the reliability of PAC missiles. Among the present-day accomplishments in missile defense, the Israeli US-supported BMD appeared to be partly successful in the cases of short range rocket attacks against civilian targets. The probabilistic analysis proved that the increased SSKP improved multiple-warhead interception significantly stronger than proportionally. Such evidence could support investments in further SSKP improvements as giving clearer benefits over the plain addition of multiple interceptors.

Table 1. PAC results of intercept 1991-2018.

Case	Test Performance		Yemen War		Israeli Iron Dome Operations		Iraq	Kuwait War (1991)	
year/location	by 2017	2001-2018	2015-2016	2015-2018	2012	2014	2003	Saudi Arabia	Israel
SSKP% approx.	86	88	44	66	32 (28)**	59-75 (15)**	39 (100*)	70? 9~, 25^, 52^^	40?
number of attacking missiles/ rockets	29	34	60	161	1506	ca. 4500	23	42	39
missiles/ rockets intercepted	25	30	28	106	421	692	9*	28/29?	16?

* interception attempts, ** in relation to rockets threatening populated areas, in brackets the intercepted rockets as a percent of all used including those not targeted at populated areas and not chosen as intercept targets (after M. Armstrong), ~ strongest evidence, ^ highly certain intercept, ^^ warhead destruction, ? disputed

Sources: UN Security Council, *Final Report of the Panel of Experts on Yemen*, 35, 148-150; Missile Threat, *Interactive: The Missile War in Yemen*; Middle East Monitor, "161 ballistic missiles fired at Saudi Arabia since 2015"; Samson, 104-105; Burns, 74-75; Pirnie, Miller, O'Neil, Haynes; 177-178; Hinton, Schmitt, Carlsen, Browne, 3; DelGenis, 80; Sullivan, Fenstermacher, Fisher, Howes, Judd, Speed, 42; Hildreth, 2; MDA, *Ballistic Missile Defense Intercept Flight Test Record (as of March 2018)*; MDA, *Ballistic Missile Defense Intercept Flight Test Record (as of May 30, 2017)*; Armstrong, "The Effectiveness of Rocket Attacks and Defenses in Israel," 113-132. Raytheon, Iron Dome Weapon System, 2018. IDF, *Operation Pillar of Defense (2012)*, 2018. IDF, Operation Protective Edge (July/August 2014), 2018.

Table 2. Houthi missiles intercepts by PAC units (June 16, 2015-November 26, 2016).

date	intercept record (success = 1, fail = 0)	Saudi confirmation of interception (yes = 1, no = 0)
16.6.2015	1	0
26.08.2015	1	0
26.08.2015	0	1
15.10.2015	0	0
4.12.2015	0	0
9.12.2015	0	0
9.12.2015	0	0
11.12.2015	0	0

13.12.2015	0	0
18.12.2015	0	0
19.12.2015	0	0
19.12.2015	0	0
20.12.2015	0	0
21.12.2015	0	1
21.12.2015	0	1
22.12.2015	0	0
23.12.2015	0	0
26.12.2015	0	1
27.12.2015	1	0
27.12.2015	0	0
28.12.2015	1	0
30.12.2015	1	0
31.12.2015	1	0
1.1.2016	0	0
7.1.2016	0	1
8.2.2016	0	0
8.2.2016	0	1
9.2.2016	0	1
13.2.2016	0	1
9.5.2016	0	1
9.5.2016	0	1
13.5.2016	0	0
20.5.2016	0	0
31.5.2016	1	0
6.6.2016	1	0
3.7.2016	1	0
23.7.2016	1	0
23.7.2016	0	0
10.8.2016	1	0
10.8.2016	1	0
16.8.2016	0	0
19.8.2016	1	0
26.8.2016	0	0
31.8.2016	0	0
2.9.2016	0	0
10.9.2016	0	0
10.9.2016	0	0
12.9.2016	1	0
3.10.2016	0	0
4.10.2016	0	0
8.10.2016	0	0
9.10.2016	1	0
20.10.2016	0	0

20.10.2016	0	0
28.10.2016	1	0
1.11.2016	0	0
1.11.2016	0	0
1.11.2016	0	0
15.11.2016	1	0
26.11.2016	1	0
overall = 28/60	**18**	**10**

Source: UN Security Council, *Final Report of the Panel of Experts on Yemen*, 35, 148-150.

Chart 1. Probabilities of defeating the BMD by a given number of warheads at SSKP levels of 85%, 90% and 95% in the case of a salvo attack of 35 warheads.

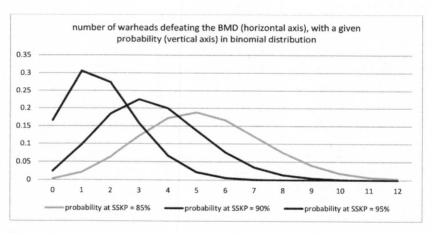

Source: own counting based on Wilkening's model of Bernoulli distribution. Wilkening, 187-191.

Chart 2. SSKP 85%, leak-proof intercept probabilities for 1-15 interceptors and 1-35 attacking warheads.

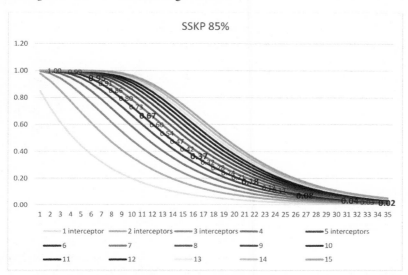

Source: own counting based on the models of Wilkening and G. Lewis. Wilkening, 187-191; G. Lewis, 1418-1438; Grego, Lewis, Wright, 1, 5.

Chart 3. SSKP 90%, leak-proof intercept probabilities for 1-15 interceptors and 1-35 attacking warheads.

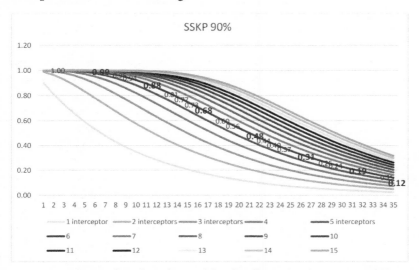

Source: own counting based on the models of Wilkening and G. Lewis. Wilkening, 187-191; G. Lewis, 1418-1438; Grego, Lewis, Wright, 1, 5.

Chart 4. SSKP 95%, leak-proof intercept probabilities for 1-15 interceptors and 1-35 attacking warheads.

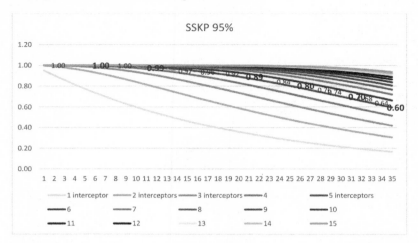

Source: own counting based on the models of Wilkening and G. Lewis. Wilkening, 187-191; G. Lewis, 1418-1438; Grego, Lewis, and Wright, 1, 5.

Table 3. Probabilities of defeating the BMD by a given number of warheads at SSKP levels of 85%, 90% and 95% in the case of a salvo attack of 35 warheads.

Number of Warheads Defeating the BMD	Probability at SSKP = 85%	Probability at SSKP = 90%	Probability at SSKP = 95%
0	0.003	0.025	0.166
1	0.021	0.097	**0.306**
2	0.063	0.184	0.274
3	0.122	**0.225**	0.158
4	0.172	0.200	0.067
5	**0.188**	0.138	0.022
6	0.166	0.076	0.006
7	0.121	0.035	0.001
8	0.075	0.014	0.000
9	0.040	0.005	0.000
10	0.018	0.001	0.000
11	0.007	0.000	0.000
12	0.003	0.000	0.000

Source: own counting (using Microsoft Excel) according to the equation (bullet operator represents multiplication)

$$P(x) = \{W!/[x! \cdot (W-x)!]\} \cdot (1 - K_W)^x \cdot K_W^{W-x}$$

based on Wilkening's model of Bernoulli distribution, where $P(x)$ stands for a probability of defeating the BMD by x incoming warheads, K_W represents the probability of interception of an attacking warhead by an interceptor, and W stands for the amount of attacking warheads. Wilkening, 187-191.

Table 4. Leak-proof intercept probabilities (SSKP = 85%) for 1-5 interceptors (columns) and 1-35 warheads attacking in a salvo (verses).

Interceptors Warheads	1	2	3	4	5
1	0.85	0.98	1.00	1.00	1.00
2	0.72	0.92	0.98	0.99	1.00
3	0.61	0.85	0.94	0.98	0.99
4	0.52	0.77	0.89	0.95	0.98
5	0.44	0.69	0.83	0.90	**0.95**
6	0.38	0.61	0.76	0.85	0.91
7	0.32	0.54	0.69	0.79	0.86
8	0.27	0.47	0.61	0.72	0.80
9	0.23	0.41	0.55	0.65	0.73
10	0.20	0.35	0.48	0.58	**0.67**
11	0.17	0.31	0.42	0.52	0.60
12	0.14	0.26	0.37	0.46	0.54
13	0.12	0.23	0.32	0.40	0.47
14	0.10	0.19	0.28	0.35	0.42
15	0.09	0.17	0.24	0.31	**0.37**
16	0.07	0.14	0.21	0.27	0.32
17	0.06	0.12	0.18	0.23	0.28
18	0.05	0.10	0.15	0.20	0.24
19	0.05	0.09	0.13	0.17	0.21
20	0.04	0.08	0.11	0.15	**0.18**
21	0.03	0.06	0.10	0.13	0.15
22	0.03	0.06	0.08	0.11	0.13
23	0.02	0.05	0.07	0.09	0.11
24	0.02	0.04	0.06	0.08	0.10

26	0.01	0.03	0.04	0.06	0.07
27	0.01	0.02	0.04	0.05	0.06
28	0.01	0.02	0.03	0.04	0.05
29	0.01	0.02	0.03	0.04	0.04
30	0.01	0.02	0.02	0.03	**0.04**
31	0.01	0.01	0.02	0.03	0.03
32	0.01	0.01	0.02	0.02	0.03
33	0.00	0.01	0.01	0.02	0.02
34	0.00	0.01	0.01	0.02	0.02
35	0.00	0.01	0.01	0.01	**0.02**

Source: own counting (using Microsoft Excel) according to the equation (bullet operator represents multiplication)

$$P(x) = \{W! / [x! \cdot (W - x)!]\} \cdot (1 - K_w)^x \cdot K_w^{W-x}$$

based on Wilkening's model of Bernoulli distribution, where $P(x)$ stood for a probability of defeating the BMD by x incoming warheads, K_w meant the probability of interception of an attacking warhead by an interceptor, and W stood for the amount of attacking warheads,

and

$$P(0) = 1 - (1 - p)^n$$

based on Lewis's model, where p was a single intercept probability and n stood for the number of interceptors used. In this analyses p was counted for a leak-proof defense in the cases of attacks of 5, 6, 7, ... 30 incoming warheads (in Bernoulli distribution) using n additional interceptors.

The probability of a penetration of the defense by one or more warheads as an equation:

$$1 - P(0) = 1 - p^n$$

where p stood for the probability of a single interception, and n for a quantity of attacking warheads after Grego, Lewis and Wright (on the basis of the previous Wilkening's modeling). Wilkening, 187-191; G. Lewis, 1418-1438; Grego, Lewis, Wright, 1, 5.

Table 5. Leak-proof intercept probability growth due to SSKP improvement from 85% to 90% in multiple warheads attack scenarios (from 5 to 35) and the use of 5 interceptors against each of the attacking warhead.

amount of attacking warheads	5	10	15	20	25	30	35
SSKP 85%	95	67	37	18	8	4	2
SSKP 90%	99	88	68	48	31	19	12
net benefit	*4*	*21*	*31*	*30*	*23*	*15*	*10*

Source: own counting based on the models of Wilkening and G. Lewis. Wilkening, 187-191; G. Lewis, 1418-1438; Grego, Lewis, Wright, 1, 5.

Table 6. Leak-proof intercept probability growth due to SSKP improvement from 90% to 95% in multiple warheads attack scenarios (from 5 to 35) and the use of 5 interceptors against each of the attacking warhead.

amount of attacking warheads	5	10	15	20	25	30	35
SSKP 90%	99	88	68	48	31	19	12
SSKP 95%	100	99	96	89	80	70	60
net benefit	*1*	*11*	*28*	*41*	*49*	*51*	*48*

Source: own counting based on the models of Wilkening and G. Lewis. Wilkening, 187-191; G. Lewis, 1418-1438; Grego, Lewis, Wright, 1, 5.

Final Conclusions

Among the top twenty-first challenges of fourth wave of deterrence theories include finding a balance between the traditional challenges of the rivalry between great/minor powers on a global/regional scale and the new growing threat of international terrorism (in particular jihadist terrorism) able to engage greater military force in the entire regional theater of operations, as in the case of the Taliban and Al-Qaeda Middle East branches (ISIS, AQAP, a.o.). The US deterrence doctrines developed in the time of the US-Soviet rivalry are not suited to the twenty-first-century regional scope of deployments, against regional enemies equipped with ballistic or rocket forces. The experience of the Kuwait war allowed the US to adapt to the regional scale of operations, shifting its strategic views from a Soviet, global challenge to the threat coming from regional hegemonic authoritarian powers armed with WMD. Since the 1990s, the US BMD efforts have been reoriented from the focus on the Soviet threat (as in the time of Reagan's SDI) to smaller scale missile challenges, as the one posed by Hussein's Iraq, and later North Korea or Iran.

While the long-range missile defense based on space interceptors (SDI) proved to be too difficult to deploy before the demise of the USSR, the US BMD efforts were centered on supporting forward deployed units by tactical (terminal stage) missile defenses, including PAC (and later THAAD). Middle-tier missile defense was still based on modernized naval Aegis capacities. Among the new challenges of post-Cold War deterrence (supported by missile defense) were those concerning new US allies from the former Soviet bloc in Eastern Europe. The growing Iranian threat, as well as new conditions of US global engagements after September 11th, 2001 (and the end of the ABM treaty), led to the concept of the third site of US long-range missile defense (after Alaska and California) in Poland: according to a 2008 agreement, a GMD base would protect the US from Iranian missiles.

Under Obama, the latter concept (criticized by Russia) was reshaped toward Aegis Ashore bases in Poland and Romania. New US BMD deployments supporting extended deterrence efforts to defend Far East allies in the case of North Korean missile and nuclear provocations included Aegis ships introduced by Japan and THAAD deployments in Korea. In the 2010s, after the Russian aggression against Ukraine in 2014, the great power rivalry between Putin's Russia and the West was labeled the New Cold War. New US deterrence and BMD challenges included the end of the INF treaty, as well as China's growing military might. Still, by the end of 2010s, the US' combat proven BMD skills (tested in the Iraq wars, Israeli counter-Hamas operations, and the Yemen civil war) were below the levels of leak-proof defense probability. Among the advantages of such new systems were growing numbers of layers and the broader area of forward deployments (engaging the Cold War and new US allies).

ADDENDUM

BMD costs after the Cold War: Tables

Table 1. Patriot development costs since 1996 to 2006 ($ millions).

year	'97	'98	'99	'00	'01	'02	'03	'04	'05	'06
R&D:										
PAC-3	383	243	237	221	80	131	176	-	-	-
PAC Improvement	-	-	-	-	12	9	42	46	32	-
Patriot MEADS	59	50	12	49	53	64	102	388	312	290
Procurement:										
PAC-3	219	317	187	377	362	730	607	617	470	
Patriot Mods	-	-	-	50	23	25	149	225	66	302
Patriot MEADS	-	-	-	-	-	-	-	-	-	550

Source: data derived from US Department of Defense (Comptroller) budget reports FY1998-FY2019, http://comptroller.defense.gov/Portals/45/Documents/defbudget (accessed March 13, 2018).

Table 2. Patriot development costs since 2007 to 2017 ($ millions).

year	07	08	09	10	11	12	13	14	15	16	17	Total 1997-2017
R&D:												
PAC-3	-	11	-	11	11	-	45	34	58	88	82	**2162**
Spares	-	-	-	11	7	5	7	10	37	33	34	**142**
PAC Improvement	-	-	-	-	-	-	-	-	-	-	-	**141**
Patriot MEADS	323	402	455	571	451	-	-	-	-	-	-	**3579**
MSE	-	-	-	-	122	86	63	86	34	2	-	**393**
Total R&D												**6417**
Procurement:												
PAC-3	495	995	511	396	628	731	1009	326	184	242	197	**9886**
Patriot Mods	-	-	-	-	-	-	-	-	-	-	-	**839**
Patriot MEADS	-	-	-	-	-	-	-	-	-	-	-	**550**
MSE	-	-	-	-	-	75	8	690	533	515	809	**2630**
Total procurement												**13905**

Source: data derived from US Department of Defense (Comptroller) budget reports FY1998-FY2019, http://comptroller.defense.gov/Portals/45/Documents/defbudget (accessed March 13, 2018).

Table 3. BMD components and Aegis destroyers' costs since 1997 to 2006 ($ millions).

Year	'97	'98	'99	'00	'01	'02	'03	'04	'05	'06
THAAD:										
R&D	616	387	432	590	541	819	864	861	914	1121
Aegis (Navy Theater Wide, NTW, and Navy Area Theater, NAT, since 2006 Aegis R&D):										
R&D (NTW)	304	438	366	371	456	-	-	-	-	893
R&D (NAT)	300	292	242	303	270	96	-	-	-	
support equipment	31	23	89	80	44	154	152	95	62	99
procurement NAT	9	15	43	18	-	-	-	-	-	-
Standard Missile (SM) and Aegis BMD improvements										
SM Mods procurements	17	50	45	41	49	35	54	50	51	57
SM-6/SM-2:										
procurement	209	176	212	196	172	155	151	146	149	144
R&D	9	1	11	1	1	14	24	74	111	149
Spares	5	1	8	13	-	-	-	-	-	-
Aegis destroyers:										
procurement	3638	3530	2724	2667	3282	3066	2681	3270	3557	147
R&D	85	78	176	241	185	320	331	216	149	220
GMD (NMD):										
R&D GMD	811	936	1678	950	1858	3655	3056	3712	4468	2391
MKV	-	-	-	-	-	-	-	-	-	48

Source: data derived from US Department of Defense (Comptroller) budget reports FY1998-FY2019, and US Department of Navy Justification Books, FY 1998-2019, http://www.secnav.navy.mil/fmc/fmb/Pages/Fiscal-Year-2017.aspx (accessed March 13, 2018).

Table 4. BMD components and Aegis destroyers' costs since 1997 to 2006 ($ millions).

Year	'07	'08	'09	'10	'11	'12	'13	'14	'15	'16	'17	All 1997-2017
THAAD:												
R&D	1082	1034	951	690	421	381	267	252	271	219	255	**12969**
procurement			105	419	584	605	417	572	450	448	567	**4165**
Aegis:												
Aegis R&D	1125	1214	1054	1419	1531	1139	959	886	850	883	1021	**12973**
support equipment	77	89	87	99	82	42	75	60	-	-	-	**1295**
Aegis Ashore procurement	-	-	-	-	-	-	-	131	-	31	57	**219**
Land-based Aegis Missile SM-3 R&D	-	-	-	-	286	299	244	125	121	29	40	**1145**
SM3 Block IIA co-development	-	-	-	248	300	458	417	297	259	165	102	**2246**
SM-3 procurement	-	-	-	226	283	378	463	581	663	712	577	**3884**
SM-6 (pre-2010 SM-2) procurement	137	158	221	189	247	357	333	300	405	417	491	**4964**
SM R&D	177	215	223	150	93	56	47	61	50	111	91	**1666**
Spares	-	-	-	-	-	7	15	19	16	17	5	**106**
Aegis destroyers:												
procurement	354	48	199	2484	2900	2081	4504	2086	2933	4267	3745	**54165**
R&D	175	152	197	172	196	212	163	183	87	274	149	**3960**
GMD (NMD):												
R&D	2985	2199	1473	1022	1246	1143	924	1064	1040	1598	1344	**39551**
MKV	134	223	-	-	-	-	-	-	-	-	-	**405**
Total costs (with funds for FY 1997-2006)	without the Aegis destroyers											**92397**
Total costs (with funds for FY 1997-2006)	with the Aegis destroyers											**150521**

Source: data derived from US Department of Defense (Comptroller) budget reports FY1998-FY2019 and US Department of Navy Justification Books, FY 1998-2019.

Table 5. Missile Segment Enhancement (MSE) planned procurement since 2017 (for PAC) in $ millions.

MSE Procurement	Prior Years	2017	2018	2019	2020	2021	2022	2023	To Complete	Total
quantity	312	169	240	240	93	160	160	196	148	1718
costs (mln)	1819.6	809.2	1106.0	1131.3	512.8	734.2	727.0	813.3	793.4	8446.8
unit cost (mln)	5.8	4.8	4.6	4,7	5.5	4.6	4.5	4.1	5.4	4.9

Source: US Army Justification FY2019, http://comptroller.defense.gov/Portals/45/Documents/defbudget/fy2019/army/procurement/PB19_MSLS.pdf.

Table 6. BMD THAAD FY 2019 budget perspective ($ millions).

BMD Terminal Defense Segment	Prior	2017	2018	2019	2020	2021	2022	2023	To Complete	Total (R&D until 2023)
R&D	1254	183	278	198	179	177	157	139	unknown	1311
quantity	229	36	84	82	37	28	21	28	8	553
procurement	3598	567	961	874	416	414	424	434	133	7822
unit cost	16	16	11	11	11	15	20	16	17	14

Source: Missile Defense Agency. "Research, Development, Test & Evaluation, Defense-Wide. Defense-Wide Justification Book Volume 2a of 5." Washington, DC: Department of Defense Fiscal Year 2019 Budget Estimates, February 2018, 2a-43, http://comptroller.defense.gov/Portals/45/Documents/defbudget/fy2019/budget_justification/pdfs/03_RDT_and_E/U_RDTE_MasterJustificationBook_Missile_Defense_Agency_PB_2019_1.pdf (accessed March 13, 2018).

Missile Defense Agency. "Procurement, Defense-Wide (includes O&M and MILCON). Defense-Wide Justification Book Volume 2b of 2." Washington, DC: Department of Defense Fiscal Year 2019 Budget Estimates, February 2018, 2b-1 http://comptroller.defense.gov/Portals/45/Documents/defbudget/fy2019/budget_justification/pdfs/02_Procurement/U_PROCUREMENT_MasterJustificationBook_Missile_Defense_Agency_PB_2019_1.pdf (accessed March 13, 2018).

Table 7. Costs of 20 additional GBI and 20 silos equipment increase ($ millions)

GBI missile and silo	2017	2018	2019	2020	2021	total
units		10	14	8	8	40
mln	47	268	524	520	411	1770
unit cost		26.8	37.43	65	51.37	44.25

Source: Missile Defense Agency. "Procurement, Defense-Wide (Includes O&M and MILCON). Defense-Wide Justification Book Volume 2b of 2."

Table 8. MDA (SDIO, BMDO) appropriations ($ billions)

year	presidential request	appropriation granted
1985	1.8	1.4
1986	3.7	2.8
1987	4.8	3.2
1988	5.2	3.6
1989	4.5	3.7
1990	4.6	4
1991	4.5	2.9
1992	5.2	4.1
1993	5.4	3.8
1994	3.8	2.8
1995	3.2	2.8
1996	2.9	3.4
1997	2.8	3.7
1998	2.6	3.8
1999	3.6	3.5
2000	3.3	3.6
2001	4.5	4.8
2002	8.3	7.8
2003	6.7	7.4
2004	7.7	7.7
2005	9.2	9
2006	7.8	7.8
2007	9.3	9.4
2008	8.9	8.7

2009	9.3	9
2010	7.8	7.9
2011	8.4	8.5
2012	8.6	8.4
2013	7.8	8.3
2014	7.7	7.6
2015	7.4	7.8
2016	8.1	8.3
2017	7.5	8.2
total	196.9	189.7

Source: Missile Defense Agency, "Historical Funding for MDA FY85-17 Fiscal Year (FY in Billions)," https://www.mda.mil/global/documents/pdf/FY17_histfunds.pdf (accessed March 11, 2018).

Table 9. MDA expenditures in FY 2019 budget plan ($ millions)

category/year	2018	2019	2020	2021	2022	2023	2018-23
operations & maintenance	504.1	499.8	502.7	535.4	525.7	567.8	3135.5
procurement	2417.5	2432	1945.1	1669.8	1294.9	1486.4	11245.7
R&D	6798.2	6777.3	6868.5	6878.6	6815.4	6665	40803
construction	203	206.2	52.2	178	647.5	190.8	1477.7
total	**9922.8**	**9915.3**	**9368.5**	**9261.8**	**9283.5**	**8910**	**56661.9**

Source: Missile Defense Agency. "2018-23 Budget Summary $ Millions," https://www.mda.mil/global/documents/pdf/budgetfy19_summary.pdf (accessed March 13, 2018).

Table 10. MDA 2018-2021 funding.

$ millions/year	2018	2019	2020	2021*
2018 funding	7886	8003	8222	8326
2019 increased funding	9923	9915	9368^	9262
US Department of Defense budget	670.6^^	685.0^^^	718.3^^^^	713.5~

*FY2019 plans.

^ overall missile defense funding reached $13.6 billion in FY2020 budget request (out of $718 billion defense funding).

^^actual, ^^^enacted, ^^^^request, ~FY2020 request plan.

Source: MDA, PB 2019-23 Budget Summary $ Millions, https://www.mda.mil/global/documents/pdf/budgetfy19_summary.pdf.

^Deputy Under Secretary of Defense (Comptroller) Elaine McCusker, *in Department of Defense News Briefing on the President's Fiscal Year 2020 Defense Budget*, US Department of Defense, March 12, 2019, https://dod.defense.gov/News/Transcripts/Tran script-View/Article/1783618/department-of-defense-news-briefing-on-the-presi dents-fiscal-year-2020-defense//.

^^-^^^^ Office of the Under Secretary of Defense (Comptroller)/Chief Financial Officer, Defense Budget Overview. United States Department of Defense Fiscal Year 2020 Budget Request, March 2019, 1-10, https://comptroller.defense.gov/Portals/45/Documents/defbudget/fy2020/fy2020_Budget_Request_Overview_Book.pdf.

˜ National Defense Budget Estimates for FY 2020, Office of the Under Secretary of Defense (Comptroller), May 2019, 7, https://comptroller.defense.gov/Portals/45/Documents/defbudget/fy2020/FY20_Green_Book.pdf. Conf. MDA, https://www.mda.mil/global/documents/pdf/budgetfy20.pdf, https://www.mda.mil/global/documents/pdf/budgetfy19.pdf, https://comptroller.defense.gov/Portals/45/Documents/defbudget/fy2020/budget_justification/pdfs/02_Procurement/PROC_Vol2_MDA_PROC_OM_MILCON_PB20_Justification_Book_Final.pdf,

References

Acton, James M. "Chapter Two: Extended Deterrence." *Adelphi Series* 50 (2010): 39–56, https://doi.org/10.1080/19445571.2010.567044.

Ahronheim, Anna. "IDF Declares Naval Iron Dome System Operational." *Jerusalem Post*, November 27, 2017, http://www.jpost.com/Israel-News/IDF-declares-Naval-Iron-Dome-system-operational-515337.

Al-Batati, Saeed, and Rick Gladstone. "Saudis Claim to Intercept 7 Missiles Fired at Cities From Yemen." *The New York Times*, March 25, 2018, https://www.nytimes.com/2018/03/25/world/middleeast/saudi-arabia-yemen-missile-houthi.html.

Al-Jaffal, Omar. "Iraq's Defunct Military Industry." *Al Monitor*, July 1, 2015, https://www.al-monitor.com/pulse/originals/2015/07/iraq-military-industry-war-islamic-state.html.

Allawi, Ali A. *The Occupation of Iraq. Winning the War, Losing the Peace.* New Haven: Yale University Press, 2007.

Anderson, Justin, Jeffrey Larsen, and Polly Holdorf. *Extended Deterrence and Allied Assurance: Key Concepts Adn Current Challenges for US Policy.* 2013, https://www.usafa.edu/app/uploads/OCP69.pdf.

Armstrong, Clare. *V-2 Rocket Attacks and Defense.* 1945, http://usacac.army.mil/cac2/cgsc/carl/eto/eto-042.pdf.

Armstrong, Michael J. "A Verification Study of the Stochastic Salvo Combat Model." *Annals of Operations Research* 186 (2011): 23–38, https://doi.org/10.1007/s10479-011-0889-0.

———. "Iron Dome: Neither a 'Bluff' nor the 'End of Rockets.'" *The National Interest*, April 7, 2018, https://nationalinterest.org/feature/iron-dome-neither-bluff-nor-the-end-rockets-25269.

———. "Modeling Short-Range Ballistic Missile Defense and Israel's Iron Dome System." *Operations Research* 62 (2014): 1028–1039.

———. "The Effectiveness of Rocket Attacks and Defenses in Israel.", *Journal of Global Security Studies* 3 (2018): 113–132, https://doi.org/10.1093/jogss/ogx028.

Bahgat, Gawdat. "Missile Proliferation in the Middle East." *The Journal of Social, Political, and Economic Studies* 31 (2006): 399+, https://www.questia.com/read/1P3-1229863001/missile-proliferation-in-the-middle-east.

Baker, Rodger. *Cheeseburgers in the Workers' Paradise*. 2018, https://worldview.stratfor.com/article/united-states-north-korea-trump-kim-jong-un-summit-nuclear-talks.

Ballistic Missile Defense Organization (US Department of Defense). *User Operational Evaluation System (UOES) THAAD Missile Configuration*. 2000, http://fas.org/spp/starwars/program/38112.pdf.

Bandeira, Luiz. *The Second Cold War. Geopolitics and the Strategic Dimensions of the USA*. Cham: Springer, 2017.

Baucom, Donald. "The Rise and Fall of Brilliant Pebbles." *The Journal of Social, Political and Economic Studies* 29 (2004): 143–190, http://highfrontier.org/oldarchive/Archive/hf/The Rise and Fall of Brilliant Pebbles -Baucom.pdf.

———. *US Missile Defense Program, 1944-1994: A Protracted Revolution*. 1995, www.dtic.mil/dtic/tr/fulltext/u2/a338560.pdf.

Baylis, John. *Ambiguity and Deterrence: British Nuclear Strategy, 1945–1964*. New York: Oxford University Press, 1995.

BBC. "Yemen War: Saudis Shoot down Missiles Fired by Houthi Rebels." *BBC*, March 26, 2018, https://www.bbc.co.uk/news/world-middle-east-43536751.

BBC News. "America Withdraws from ABM Treaty." December 13, 2001, http://news.bbc.co.uk/2/hi/americas/1707812.stm.

———. "Iran Nuclear Deal: Tehran May Increase Uranium Enrichment." May 8, 2019, https://www.bbc.com/news/world-middle-east-48197628.

———. "What We Know about North Korea's Missile Programme." *BBC*, August 10, 2017, http://www.bbc.com/news/world-asia-17399847.

Begg, David, Stanley Fischer, and Rudiger Dornbusch. *Economics*. London: McGraw-Hill Higher Education, 2008.

Bekdil, Burak. "Turkey Makes Deal to Buy Russian-Made S-400 Air Defense System." *DefenseNews*, 2017, https://www.defensenews.com/land/2017/12/29/turkey-russia-reportedly-sign-loan-deal-for-s-400-air-defense-system/.

Bennett, Bruce. "On US Preparedness for Limited Nuclear War." in *On Limited Nuclear War in the 21st Century*. Edited by Jeffrey Larsen and Kerry M. Kartchner. Stanford: Stanford Security Studies, 2014.

Bentzen, Naja. *Ukraine and the Minsk II Agreement. On a Frozen Path to Peace?*, 2016, http://www.europarl.europa.eu/RegData/etudes/BRIE/2016/573951/EPRS_BRI(2016)573951_EN.pdf.

Bentzen, Naja and Evarts Anosovs. *Minsk Peace Agreement: Still to Be Consolidated on the Ground.* 2015, http://www.europarl.europa.eu/EPRS/EPRS-Briefing-548991-Minsk-peace-summit-FINAL.pdf.

Beres, Louis Rene. "Approaching Armageddon: Nuclear Proliferation and Nuclear War in the Middle East." in *Challenges to Deterrence: Resources, Technology, and Policy*, 128-144. Edited by Stephen Cimbala. New York: Praeger, 1987.

Bin, Alberto, Richard Hill and Archer Jones. *Desert Storm: A Forgotten War*. Westport: Praeger, 1998, https://www.questia.com/read/120739370/desert-storm-a-forgotten-war.

Blumi, Isa. *Destroying Yemen. What Chaos in Arabia Tells Us about the World*. Oakland: University of California Press, 2018.

Boeing. *Ground-Based Midcourse Defense*. 2019, http://www.boeing.com/defense/missile-defense/ground-based-midcourse/index.page#.

Bolkcom, Christopher. "Friendly Fire." In *Iraq War: Defense Program Implications for Congress*, 54-58. Edited by Ronald O'Rourke. Washington DC: Congressional Research Service, 2003, https://www.globalsecurity.org/military/library/report/crs/iraq_defense.pdf.

Bracken, Paul. *The Second Nuclear Age. Strategy, Danger, and the New Power Politics*. New York: St. Martin's Griffin, 2013.

Brandt, Marieke. *Tribes and Politics in Yemen. A History of the Houthi Conflict*. Oxford: Oxford University Press, 2017.

Brehony, Noel, "Yemen and the Huthis: Genesis of the 2015 Crisis." *Asian Affairs* 46 (2015): 232–250, https://doi.org/10.1080/030683 74.2015.1037162.

Brodie, Bernard. "Implications for Military Policy." In *The Absolute Weapon: Atomic Power and World Order*, 70-107. Edited by Bernard Brodie. New York: Harcourt, Brace and Company, 1946.

———. "War in the Atomic Age." In *The Absolute Weapon: Atomic Power and World Order*, 21-69. Edited by Bernard Brodie. New York: Harcourt, Brace and Company, 1946.

Browne, Ryan, Jim Sciutto and Barbara Starr. "Russia Deploys Missile in Apparent Treaty Violation." *CNN*, February 14, 2017, http://edition. cnn.com/2017/02/14/politics/russia-cruise-missile-spy-ship/index. html.

Buncombe, Andrew. "Pentagon Says North Korea's ICBM Was a Missile They've Never Seen before." *The Independent*, July 5, 2017, http:// www.independent.co.uk/news/world/asia/north-korea-missile-icbm-pentagon-trump-not-seen-before-a7825541.html.

Burns, Richard Dean. *The Missile Defense Systems of George W. Bush. A Critical Assessment.* Santa Barbara: Praeger, 2010.

Bush, George W. *Executive Order 13466, June 26, 2008.* 2008, https:// www.treasury.gov/resource-center/sanctions/Documents/nkeo.pdf.

Bush, George W. and Radosław Sikorski. *Agreement between the Government of the United States of America and the Government of the Republic of Poland Concerning the Deployment of Ground-Based Ballistic Missile Defense Interceptors in the Territory of the Republic of Poland, Warsaw, August 20, 2008.* 2008, https://www.state.gov/documents/organization/180542. pdf.

Bush, George W. *The President's State of the Union Address.* 2002, http:// georgewbush-whitehouse.archivep.gov/news/releases/2002/01/ 20020129-11.html.

Byman, Daniel. *A High Price: The Triumphs and Failures of Israeli Counterterrorism.* New York: Oxford University Press, 2011.

Carlone, Ralph, Michael Blair, Sally Obenski and Paula Bridickas. *Patriot Missile Defense. Software Problem Led to System Failure at Dhahran, Saudi Arabia.* Washington DC, 1992, https://www.gao.gov/assets/220/215614.pdf.

Carlson, Lisa. "Crisis Escalation: An Empirical Test in the Context of Extended Deterrence." *International Interactions,* 24 (1998): 225–253

Chanlett-Avery, Emma, Ian Rinehart and Mary Nikitin. *North Korea: US Relations, Nuclear Diplomacy, and Internal Situation.* 2016, https://fas.org/sgp/crs/nuke/R41259.pdf.

Chaplain, Cristina. *Ballistic Missile Defense System Testing Delays Affect Delivery of Capabilities,* 2016 http://www.gao.gov/assets/680/676855.pdf.

———. *Missile Defense: Assessment of DOD's Reports on Status of Efforts and Options for Improving Homeland Missile Defense,* 2016, http://www.gao.gov/assets/680/675263.pdf.

———. *Missile Defense. Mixed Progress in Achieving Acquisition Goals and Improving Accountability,* 2014 http://www.gao.gov/assets/670/662194.pdf.

Chaplain, Cristina, LaTonya Miller, Matthew Ambrose, and Jeff Cherwonik. *Missile Defense. Some Progress Delivering Capabilities, but Challenges with Testing Transparency and Requirements Development Need to Be Addressed,* Washington DC, 2017, https://www.globalsecurity.org/space/library/report/gao/684963.pdf.

Chaplain, Cristina, LaTonya Miller, Kevin O'Neill, James Haynes, Randy Kimmett, Meredith Allen Neice, Jenny Shinn, and others. *Patriot Modernization. Oversight Mechanism Needed to Track Progress and Provide Accountability,* Washington DC, 2016, https://www.gao.gov/assets/680/679257.pdf.

Charbonneau, Louis. "In New York, Defiant Ahmadinejad Says Israel Will Be 'Eliminated.'" *Reuters,* 2012, https://www.reuters.com/article/us-un-assembly-ahmadinejad/in-new-york-defiant-ahmadinejad-says-israel-will-be-eliminated-idUSBRE88N0HF20120924.

Chase, Michael and Arthur Chan. *China's Evolving Approach to "Integrated*

Strategic Deterrence." Santa Monica: RAND, 2016, https://www.questia. com/read/125655759/china-s-evolving-approach-to-integrated-strategic.

Cheney, Richard. *Conduct of the Persian Gulf War. Final Report to the Congress.* Washington DC, 1992, http://www.dtic.mil/dtic/tr/fulltext/ u2/a249270.pdf.

Chi-dong, Lee. "S Korea to Streamline OPCON Transition Procedures." *Yonhap News Agency*, January 19, 2018, http://english.yonhapnews. co.kr/news/2018/01/19/0200000000AEN20180119000951315. html

Chilcot, John. *The Report of the Iraq Inquiry. Executive Summary.* London, 2016, http://www.iraqinquiry.org.uk/media/247921/the-report-of-the-iraq-inquiry_executive-summary.pdf.

Chipman, John. "Chapter One: Defence and Military Analysis." *The Military Balance* 117 (2017): 7–18, https://doi.org/10.1080/04597222. 2017.1271206.

———. "Chapter Six: Asia." *The Military Balance,* 117 (2017): 237–350, https://doi.org/10.1080/04597222.2017.1271212.

———. "Chapter Three: North America." *The Military Balance* 118 (2018): 27–64, https://doi.org/10.1080/04597222.2018.1416979.

———. "Chapter Two: Comparative Defence Statistics." *The Military Balance* 116 (2016): 19–26, https://doi.org/10.1080/04597222.20 16.1127562.

———. "Chapter Two: Comparative Defence Statistics." *The Military Balance* 118 (2018): 19–26, https://doi.org/10.1080/04597222.20 18.1416969.

———. "Chapter Two: Comparative Defence Statistics." *The Military Balance* 119 (2019): 21–27, https://doi.org/10.1080/04597222.20 19.1561026.

Christensen, Thomas J. "The Contemporary Security Dilemma: Deterring a Taiwan Conflict." *The Washington Quarterly,* 25 (2002): 5–21, https://doi.org/10.1162/016366002760252509.

Chul-Jae, Lee. "North May Have Multiple-ICBM Technology." *Korea JoongAng Daily*, July 5, 2017, http://koreajoongangdaily.joins.com/news/article/article.aspx?aid=3035462.

Chung, Samman. "North Korea's Nuclear Threats and Counter-Strategies." *The Journal of East Asian Affairs*, 30 (2016): 83–131, http://www.jstor.org/stable/44160975.

Churchill College Cambridge. *Guide to Holdings*. 2019, https://www.chu.cam.ac.uk/archives/collections/guide-holdings/.

Cimbala, Stephen. *Shield of Dreams. Missile Defenses in US and Russian Nuclear Strategy*. Annapolis: Naval Institute Press, 2008.

———. "Triage of Triads: Does the United States Really Need Three Strategic-Retaliatory Forces?" In *Deterrence and Nuclear Proliferation in the Twenty-First Century*, 119–137. Edited by Stephen Cimbala. Westport: Praeger, 2001.

Cirincione, Joseph. "Why the Right Lost the Missile Defense Debate." *Foreign Policy* 106 (1997): 38–55, http://www.jstor.org/stable/1149173.

Clark University. *Robert H. Goddard Papers*, 2019, https://www2.clarku.edu/research/archives/goddard/articles.cfm.

Clark, Victoria. *Yemen. Dancing on the Heads of Snakes*, New Haven: Yale University Press, 2010.

Clarke, Duncan. "The Arrow Missile: The United States, Israel and Strategic Cooperation." *Middle East Journal* 48 (1994): 475–491, http://www.jstor.org/stable/4328717.

Clausen, Maria-Louise. "Understanding the Crisis in Yemen: Evaluating Competing Narratives." *The International Spectator* 50 (2015): 16–29, https://doi.org/10.1080/03932729.2015.1053707.

Van Cleave, William, and S.T. Cohen. *Tactical Nuclear Weapons. An Examination of Issues*. London: Macdonald and Jane's, 1978.

Cohen, Gili. "Why Does Israel Need Three Different Missile Defense Systems?" *Haaretz*, 2015, https://www.haaretz.com/.premium-why-does-israel-need-3-anti-missile-systems-1.5346632.

Coletta, Damon. "Space and Deterrence." *Astropolitics*, 7 (2009): 171–192, https://doi.org/10.1080/14777620903372982.

Collins, Boyd. "US Army Successfully Demonstrates Iron Dome Missile from New Interceptor Launch Platform." *US Army*, April 20, 2016, https://www.army.mil/article/166397/U_S__Army_successfully _demonstrates_Iron_Dome_missile_from_new_interceptor_ launch_platform.

Commander Navy Installations Command (CNIC). *Naval Support Facility Redzikowo*, 2019, https://www.cnic.navy.mil/regions/cnreurafswa /installations/nsf_redzikowo.html.

Comprehensive Test Ban Treaty Organization (CTBTO) Preparatory Commission. *Status of Signature and Ratification*, 2019, https://www. ctbto.org/the-treaty/status-of-signature-and-ratification/.

Conflict Records Research Center. *Correspondence between the MIC and the Petro Chemical Group Regarding a Letter from A.Q. Khan Offering Assistance in Developing Iraq's Nuclear Weapons Program, CRRC Record Number: SH-MICN-D-000-741, Document Date: 6 Oct 1990*, 1990, http://crrc.dodlive.mil/files/2013/06/SH-MICN-D-000-741.pdf.

Conradi, Peter. *Who Lost Russia? How the World Entered a New Cold War*, Kindle. London: A Oneworld Book, 2017.

Conyers, John. "The Patriot Myth: Caveat Emptor." *Arms Control Today* 22 (1992): 3–10, http://www.jstor.org/stable/23625004.

Cooper, Henry F. *Brilliant Pebbles*, 2016, http://highfrontier.org/ category/brilliant-pebbles/.

Cooper, Henry F., Malcom R. O'Neill, Robert L. Pfaltzgraff and Rowland H. Worrell. *Missile Defense. Challenges and Opportunities for the Trump Administration*, 2016, http://www.ifpa.org/pdf/IWGWhitePaper16. pdf.

Copp, Tara. "'Fort Trump' Would Be the Second US Site in Poland." *Military Times*, September 19, 2018, https://www.militarytimes.com/ news/your-military/2018/09/19/fort-trump-would-be-the-second- us-site-in-poland/.

Cordesman, Anthony and Abraham Wagner. *The Lessons of Modern War, Vol. 4 The Gulf War.*. Westview Press, 1996, https://www.questia.com/read/101412956/the-gulf-war.

Cossa, Ralph A. and Brad Glosserman. "Extended Deterrence and Disarmament." *The Nonproliferation Review* 18 (2011): 125–145, https://doi.org/10.1080/10736700.2011.549177.

Crawford, Timothy W. *Pivotal Deterrence: Third-Party Statecraft and the Pursuit of Peace.* Ithaca: Cornell University Press, 2003, https://www.questia.com/read/106760350/pivotal-deterrence-third-party-statecraft-and-the.

Van Creveld, Martin. *The Sword and the Olive: A Critical History of the Israeli Defense Forces.* New York: PublicAffairs, 1998.

CSIS. *Missile Defense Project, Standard Missile-3 (SM-3), Missile Threat, Center for Strategic and International Studies, June 14, 2016, Last Modified September 28, 2018,* 2016, https://missilethreat.csis.org/defsys/sm-3/.

———. *Missile Threat, KN-18 (MaRV Scud Variant).* https://missilethreat.csip.org/missile/kn-18-marv-scud-variant/.

CSIS Missile Threat. *Interactive: The Missile War in Yemen.* 2018, https://missilethreat.csis.org/missile-war-yemen/.

———. *Patriot,* 2018, https://missilethreat.csis.org/system/patriot/.

———. *SSC-8 (Novator 9M729),* 2019 https://missilethreat.csis.org/missile/ssc-8-novator-9m729/.

Dabrowski, John. *Missile Defense. The First 70 Years,* 2013, https://www.mda.mil/global/documents/pdf/first70.pdf.

Daehee, Bak. "Alliance Proximity and Effectiveness of Extended Deterrence." *International Interactions,* 44 (2018): 107–131.

Daniels, Jeff. "Raytheon's Patriot Defense System Likely Failed to Stop Saudi Missile Attack." *CNBC,* 2017, https://www.cnbc.com/2017/12/04/patriot-defense-system-likely-failed-in-saudi-ballistic-missile-attack.html.

Dauber, Cori Elizabeth. *Cold War Analytical Structures and the Post Post-War World: A Critique of Deterrence Theory.* Westport: Praeger, 1993, https://www.questia.com/read/106747502/cold-war-analytical-structures-and-the-post-post-war.

Davenport, Kelsey. *Missile Technology Control Regime (MTCR).* 2019, https://www.armscontrol.org/factsheets/mtcr.

Day, Matthew. "Russia 'Simulates' Nuclear Attack on Poland." *The Telegraph*, November 1, 2009, http://www.telegraph.co.uk/news/world news/europe/poland/6480227/Russia-simulates-nuclear-attack-on-Poland.html.

Debre, Isabel. "In First, US Deploys THAAD Anti-Missile System in Israel." *DefenseNews*, March 4, 2019, https://www.defensenews.com/land/2019/03/04/in-first-us-deploys-thaad-anti-missile-system-in-israel/.

Defense Acquisition Management. *Patriot Advanced Capability-3 Missile Segment Enhancement (PAC-3 MSE)" (Selected Acquisition Report as of FY 2017 President's Budget, March 21, 2016,* 2016, http://www.dtic.mil/dtic/tr/fulltext/u2/1019515.pdf.

Defense Industry Daily (after Basler Zeitung). "Iron Dome Sees Israel Ramp up, Raytheon Partnership for US Market." January 11, 2018, https://www.defenseindustrydaily.com/iron-dome-deployment-exports-07039.

Defense Security Cooperation Agency (DSCA). *Poland - Integrated Air and Missile Defense (IAMD) Battle Command System (IBCS)-Enabled Patriot Configuration-3+ with Modernized Sensors and Components, November 17, 2017.* Washington DC, 2017, http://www.dsca.mil/sites/default/files/mas/poland_17-67.pdf.

DelGenis, Tony. "Israel's Gulf War Experience: A Brief Synopsis." *Middle East Policy* V (1997): 79–92, http://dx.doi.org/10.1111/j.1475-4967.1997.tb00266.x.

Delpech, Thérèse. *Nuclear Deterrence in the 21st Century: Lessons from the Cold War for a New Era of Strategic Piracy.* Santa Monica: RAND, 2012, https://www.questia.com/read/122637778/nuclear-deterrence-in-the-21st-century-lessons-from.

Denoon, David. *Ballistic Missile Defense in the Post-Cold War Era*. Boulder: Westview Press, 1995, https://www.questia.com/read/89750824/ballistic-missile-defense-in-the-post-cold-war-era.

Detsch, Jack. "Congress Deepens US-Israel Missile Alliance." *Al Monitor*, November 9, 2017, https://www.al-monitor.com/pulse/originals/2017/11/congress-us-israel-missile-alliance-threat-iran-hezbollah.html.

Dodge, Michaela. *President Obama's Missile Defense Policy: A Misguided Legacy*. http://www.heritage.org/defense/report/president-obamas-missile-defense-policy-misguided-legacy.

Dombrowski, Peter, Catherine Kelleher, and Eric Auner. "Demistyfing Iron Dome." *The National Interest*, July 2013, http://nationalinterest.org/print/article/demystifying-iron-dome-8649.

DSCA. *Romania—Patriot Air Defense System and Related Support and Equipment*. Washington DC, 2017, http://www.dsca.mil/sites/default/files/mas/romania_17-35.pdf.

Duelfer, Charles. *Comprehensive Report of the Special Advisor to the DCI on Iraq's WMD. Volume I*. Washington DC, 2004, https://www.cia.gov/library/readingroom/docs/DOC_0001156395.pdf.

Durkalec, Jacek. "The Role of Missile Defence in NATO Deterrence." In *Regional Approached to the Role of Missile Defence in Reducing Nuclear Threats*, 19–28. Edited by Marcin Andrzej Piotrowski. Warsaw: The Polish Institute of International Affairs, 2013, https://www.pism.pl/files/?id_plik=14446.

EEAS. "EU-Democratic People's Republic of Korea (DPRK) Relations." 2016, https://eeas.europa.eu/headquarters/headquarters-homepage/4003/eu-democratic-peoples-republic-korea-dprk-relations_en.

———. *Statement on the Nuclear Test in the DPRK, September 9, 2016*, 2016, https://eeas.europa.eu/headquarters/headquarters-homepage/9582/statement-nuclear-test-dprk_en.

Elleman, Michael and Wafa Alsayed. "Ballistic Missile Defense Cooperation in the Arabian Gulf." In *Regional Missile Defense from a Global Perspective*, 3167-3568. Edited by Catherine McArdle Kelleher and Peter Dombrowski, Kindle. Stanford: Stanford University Press, 2015.

Epperson, Jason. *US Deploys THAAD Anti-Missile System in First Deployment to Romania.* https://www.cnic.navy.mil/regions/cnreurafswa/installations/nsf_deveselu/news/US-deploys-THAAD-anti-missile-system-to-Romania.html.

Esgain, Albert. "The Spectrum of Responses to Treaty Violations." *Ohio State Law Journal* 26 (1965): 1–42, https://kb.osu.edu/dspace/bitstream/handle/1811/68754/OSLJ_V26N1_0001.pdf.

Eshel, David. "Missile/Rocket Defense Emerges as Top Israeli Priority." *Military Technology* 12 (2006): 34–37.

Estonian Presidency of the Council of the EU. *EU Sanctions Map,* 2019, https://www.sanctionsmap.eu/#/main.

EUCOM. *US, Poland Break Ground on Aegis Ashore Site in Poland,* 2016, https://www.eucom.mil/media-library/pressrelease/35358/u-s-poland-break-ground-on-aegis-ashore-site-in-poland.

European Commission Service for Foreign Policy Instruments. *European Union Consolidated Financial Sanctions List,* 2019, https://webgate.ec.europa.eu/europeaid/fsd/fsf/public/files/pdfFullSanctionsList/content?token=dG9rZW4tMjAxNw.

European Council. *Council Common Position 2006/795/CFSP, November 20, 2006.* 2006, http://eur-lex.europa.eu/legal-content/EN/TXT/PDF/?uri=CELEX:32006E0795&from=EN.

———. *Council Common Position 2009/573/CFSP, July 27, 2009,* 2009, http://eur-lex.europa.eu/LexUriServ/LexUriServ.do?uri=OJ:L:2009:197:0111:0116:EN:PDF.

———. *Council Decision 2009/1002/CFSP, December 22, 2009,* 2009, http://eur-lex.europa.eu/LexUriServ/LexUriServ.do?uri=OJ:L:2009:346:0047:0050:EN:PDF.

———. *Council Decision 2010/800/CFSP, December 22, 2010,* 2010, http://eur-lex.europa.eu/LexUriServ/LexUriServ.do?uri=OJ:L:2010:341:0032:0044:EN:PDF.

———. *Council Decision 2011/860/CFSP, December 19, 2011,* 2011, http://eur-lex.europa.eu/legal-content/EN/TXT/PDF/?uri=CELEX:32011D0860&from=EN.

———. *Council Decision 2013/183/CFSP, April 22, 2013*, 2013, http://eur-lex.europa.eu/legal-content/EN/TXT/PDF/?uri=CELEX:32013D0183&from=EN.

———. *Council Decision 2016/849, May 27, 2016, Repealing Decision 2013/183/CFSP*, 2016, http://eur-lex.europa.eu/legal-content/EN/TXT/PDF/?uri=CELEX:32016D0849&from=EN.

———. *Council Decision 2016/849, May 27, 2016*, 2016, http://eur-lex.europa.eu/legal-content/EN/TXT/PDF/?uri=CELEX:32016D0849&from=EN.

———. *Council Regulation 1283/2009, December 22, 2009*, 2009, http://eur-lex.europa.eu/LexUriServ/LexUriServ.do?uri=OJ:L:2009:346:0001:0025:EN:PDF.

———. *Council Regulation 1334/2000, June 22, 2000*, 2000, http://eur-lex.europa.eu/legal-content/EN/TXT/PDF/?uri=CELEX:32000R1334&from=EN.

———. *Council Regulation 296/2013, March 26, 2013*, 2013, http://eur-lex.europa.eu/LexUriServ/LexUriServ.do?uri=OJ:L:2013:090:0004:0009:EN:PDF.

———. *Council Regulation No 329/2007, March 27, 2007*, 2007, http://eur-lex.europa.eu/LexUriServ/LexUriServ.do?uri=OJ:L:2007:088:0001:0011:EN:PDF.

———. *EU Restrictive Measures in Response to the Crisis in Ukraine*, 2019, http://www.consilium.europa.eu/en/policies/sanctions/ukraine-crisis/.

European Union External Action Service. *EU Restrictive Measures in Force*, 2017, https://eeas.europa.eu/sites/eeas/files/restrictive_measures-2017-08-04.pdf.

Everett, Robert. *Report of Defense Science Board on SDIO Brilliant Pebbles Space Based Interceptor Concept.* Washington DC, 1989, http://www.dod.mil/pubs/foi/Reading_Room/Homeland_Defense/06-F-0419_FINAL_RESPONSE-ocrd.pdf.

Evron, Yair. "Extended Deterrence in the Middle East." *The Nonprolifera-*

tion Review 19 (2012): 377–90, https://doi.org/10.1080/10736700. 2012.734186.

Fathi, Nazila. "Wipe Israel 'off the Map' Iranian Says." *The New York Times,* 2005, http://www.nytimes.com/2005/10/27/world/africa/wipe-israel-off-the-map-iranian-says.html.

Federation of American Scientists (FAS). *Patriot TMD,* 2000, http://fas.org/spp/starwars/program/patriot.htm.

———. *RT-21M / SS-20 Saber,* 2000, https://fas.org/nuke/guide/russia/theater/rt-21m.htm.

———. *THAAD TMD,* 2016, http://fas.org/spp/starwars/program/thaad.htm.

Feiveson, Harold, and Frank von Hippel. "Beyond START: How to Make Much Deeper Cuts." *International Security,*15 (1990): 154–180, https://www.jstor.org/stable/2538985.

Feiveson, Harold, Richard Ullman, and Frank von Hippel. "Reducing US and Soviet Nuclear Arsenals." *Bulletin of the Atomic Scientists,* 1985, 144–150.

Ferdinando, Lisa. *Work Joins Groundbreaking for Ballistic Missile Defense Site in Poland,* 2016, https://www.defense.gov/News/Article/Article/759662/work-joins-groundbreaking-for-ballistic-missile-defense-site-in-poland/.

Ferris, Jesse. *Nasser's Gamble: How Intervention in Yemen Caused the Six-Day War and the Decline of Egyptian Power.* Princeton: Princeton University Press, 2013.

Finer, Jon. "The Last War- and the Next? Learning the Wrong Lessons from Iraq." *Foreign Affairs* 98 (2019): 183–191.

Fink, Daniel, Fred Hoffman, and William Delaney. *Final Report of the Defense Science Board/Defense Policy Board Task Force on Ballistic Missile Defense (BMD),* 1991, https://www.dod.mil/pubs/foi/Reading_Room/Homeland_Defense/06-F-0419_FINAL_RESPONSE-ocrd.pdf.

Finn, Michael V. and Glenn A. Kent. *Simple Analytic Solutions to Complex Military Problems.* Santa Monica, 1985, https://www.rand.org/content/dam/rand/pubs/notes/2007/N2211.pdf.

Finn, Peter. "Putin Withdraws Russia From Major Arms Treaty." *The Washington Post*, December 1, 2007, http://www.washingtonpost.com/wp-dyn/content/article/2007/11/30/AR2007113000221.html.

Fisher, Max, Eric Schmitt, Audrey Carlsen, and Malachy Browne. "Did American Missile Defense Fail in Saudi Arabia." *The New York Times*, 2017, https://www.nytimes.com/interactive/2017/12/04/world/middleeast/saudi-missile-defense.html?hp&action=click&pgtype=Homepage&clickSource=story-heading&module=photo-spot-region&region=top-news&WT.nav=top-news.

Frank, Ruediger. "The Political Economy of Sanctions against North Korea." *Asian Affairs* 30 (2006): 5–36, http://www.jstor.org/stable/42704552.

Freedman, Lawrence. *Deterrence*. Cambridge: Polity Press, 2004.

———. *The Evolution of Nuclear Strategy*. London: Palgrave Macmillan UK, 2003, https://doi.org/10.1057/9780230379435.

Fuhrmann, Matthew, and Todd S. Sechser. "Appendices for 'Signaling Alliance Commitments: Hand-Tying and Sunk Costs in Extended Nuclear Deterrence.'" *American Journal of Political Science*, 2014, https://onlinelibrary.wiley.com/action/downloadSupplement?doi=10.1111%2Fajps.12082&attachmentId=86330477.

———. "Signaling Alliance Commitments: Hand-Tying and Sunk Costs in Extended Nuclear Deterrence." *American Journal of Political Science* 58 (2014): 919–932.

Futter, Andrew. *Ballistic Missile Defense and US National Security Policy. Normalisation and Acceptance after the Cold War*. London: Routledge, 2013.

Gallis, Paul. *The NATO Summit at Bucharest, 2008*. 2008, https://fas.org/sgp/crs/row/RS22847.pdf.

Gardner, Frank. "Yemen Conflict: The View from the Saudi Side." *BBC*, 2016, https://www.bbc.com/news/world-middle-east-38239782.

Garner, Rob and Brian Dunbar. "Dr. Robert H. Goddard, American Rocketry Pioneer." *Goddard Space Flight Center National Aeronautics and Space Administration*, 2016, https://www.nasa.gov/centers/god dard/about/history/dr_goddard.html.

Gatehouse, Gabriel. "The Untold Story of the Maidan Massacre." *BBC News Magazine*, February 12, 2015, http://www.bbc.com/news/maga zine-31359021.

Gatopoulos, Alex. "How Successful Was Israel's Iron Dome?" *Al Jazeera*, September 8, 2014, http://www.aljazeera.com/news/middleeast/2014 /08/israel-iron-dome-gaza-rockets-201481712494436388.html.

Geiger, Justin. "Battle Group Poland Is Hailed in Orzysz, Poland." *US Army*, 2017, https://www.army.mil/article/186072/battle_group_ poland_is_hailed_in_orzysz_poland.

George, Alexander L. and Richard Smoke. *Deterrence in American Foreign Policy: Theory and Practice*. New York: Columbia University Press, 1974.

Gibson, Jane and Kenneth Kemmerly. "Intercontinental Ballistic Missiles." In *AU-18 Space Primer. Air Command and Staff College, Space Research Electives Seminars*, 235-248. Edited by Brian C. Tichenor. Maxwell Air Force Base: Air University Press, 2009, http://space.au.af. mil/au-18-2009/au-18_chap18.pdf.

Gilbert, Martin. Attacking Antwerp." *Forbes*, May 6, 2008, https://www. forbes.com/2008/06/05/antwerp-port-wwII-tech-logistics08-cx_ mg_0605antwerp.html.

Gilman, Benjamin A. *Iran Nonproliferation Act of 2000, Public Law 106-178, March 14*. US Congress, 2000, https://www.congress.gov/106/ plaws/publ178/PLAW-106publ178.pdf.

Gilmore, J. Michael. *Annual Report, Fiscal Year 2014*. Washington DC, 2015, http://www.dote.osd.mil/pub/reports/FY2014/pdf/other/2 014DOTEAnnualReport.pdf.

Ginsburg, Mitch. "Iron Dome Gets Mysterious Upgrade." *The Times of Israel*, 2015, https://www.timesofisrael.com/iron-dome-to-get-mysterious-upgrade/.

Glass, Charles. *Seeing Khashoggi's Fate as a Death Foretold, October 24,*

2018. 2018, https://worldview.stratfor.com/article/seeing-khashog gis-fate-death-foretold.

Globes. "IDF Conducts Successful Naval Iron Dome Trial." November 27,2017, http://www.globes.co.il/en/article-idf-conducts-successful-naval-iron-dome-trial-1001213462.

Goddard, Robert H. *A Method of Reaching Extreme Altitudes*, 1919, http://www2.clarku.edu/research/archives/pdf/ext_altitudep.pdf.

———. *US Patents, Rocket Apparatus*, 1914, https://patents.google.com/patent/US1102653.

Golitsina, Natalya and Ron Synovitz. "Photos Link Yanukovych's Troops To Maidan Massacre." *Radio Free Europe, Radio Liberty*, April 2, 2014, https://www.rferl.org/a/ukraine-snipers-sbu-photos-video/2531 8776.html.

Gordon, Michael. "The Last War Syndrome. How the United States and Iraq Learned the Wrong Lessons from Desert Storm." In *Into the Desert: Reflections on the Gulf War*, 112-147. Edited by Jeffrey Engel. New York: Oxford University Press, 2013, https://www.questia.com/read/121322606/into-the-desert-reflections-on-the-gulf-war.

Gordon, Michael and Bernard Trainor. *Cobra II. The Inside Story of the Invasion and Occupation of Iraq*, Kindle. New York: Pantheon Books, 2006.

———. *The General's War. The Inside Story of the Conflict in the Gulf*. Boston: Back Bay Books, 1995.

Gortney, Bill. *Department of Defense Press Briefing by Admiral Gortney in the Pentagon Briefing Room, April 7, 2015*. 2015, https://www.defense.gov/News/Transcripts/Transcript-View/Article/607034/departmentof-defense-press-briefing-by-admiral-gortney-in-the-pentagon-briefin/.

Graham, William. *Antares 230 Successfully Returns with Launch of OA-5 Cygnus*. 2016, https://www.nasaspaceflight.com/2016/10/antares-230-launch-oa-5-cygnus/.

Granath, Bob. *Pegasus XL Mated to L-1011 Stargazer Carrier Aircraft*.

2016, https://www.nasa.gov/image-feature/pegasus-xl-mated-to-l-1011-stargazer-carrier-aircraft.

Gray, Colin. *The Second Nuclear Age*. Boulder: Lynne Rienner, 1999.

Gray, Colin S. "Deterrence and Regional Conflict: Hopes, Fallacies, and 'Fixes.'" *Comparative Strategy* 17 (1998): 45–62, https://doi.org/10.1080/01495939808403131.

Grego, Laura, George N. Lewis and David Wright. *Shielded from Oversight. The Disastrous US Approach to Strategic Missile Defense. Appendix 6. The Ground Based Interceptor and Kill Vehicle*. 2016, http://www.ucsusa.org/sites/default/files/attach/2016/07/Shielded-from-Oversight-appendix-6.pdf.

———. *Shielded from Oversight. The Disastrous US Approach to Strategic Missile Defense. Appendix 8*. Cambridge, Massachusetts, 2016, http://www.ucsusa.org/sites/default/files/attach/2016/07/Shielded-from-Oversight-appendix-8.pdf.

———. *Shielded from Oversight. The Disastrous US Approach to Strategic Missile Defense*. 2016, http://www.ucsusa.org/sites/default/files/attach/2016/07/Shielded-from-Oversight-full-report.pdf.

Gross, Judah Ari, Toi Staff and Dov Lieber. "Iron Dome Deployed in Greater Tel Aviv Area as IDF Girds for Possible Attack." *The Times of Israel*, November 14, 2017, https://www.timesofisrael.com/iron-dome-deployed-in-tel-aviv-area-as-idf-girds-for-possible-gaza-attack/.

Grush, Loren. "Orbital ATK to Launch Antares Rocket This Weekend—Two Years after 2014 Explosion." *The Verge*, 2016, https://www.theverge.com/2016/10/14/13225592/orbital-atk-antares-rocket-launch-2014-explosion.

Gunaratna, Rohan. *Inside Al Qaeda. Global Network of Terror*. New York: Columbia University Press, 2002.

Gurbanov, Ilgar. "Azerbaijan's Defense Minister Visits Israel, as Bilateral Ties Grow Stronger." *Eurasia Daily Monitor* 14 (2017), https://jamestown.org/program/azerbaijans-defense-minister-visits-israel-as-bilateral-ties-grow-stronger.

Gvosdev, Nikolas and Christopher Marsh. *Russian Foreign Policy. Interests, Vectors, and Sectors*, Kindle. Thousand Oaks: CQ Press, 2014.

Haaretz. "Saudi Arabia's US-Made Patriot Missile Defense System 'Malfunctions,'" *Reuters*, March 27, 2018, https://www.haaretz.com/middle-east-news/saudi-patriot-missile-malfunctions-crashes-in-residential-area-1.5940630.

Hafemeister, David. *Nuclear Terrorism and Proliferation in the Post-9/11 World*. Cham: Springer, 2016.

Handberg, Roger. *Ballistic Missile Defense and the Future of American Security: Agendas, Perceptions, Technology, and Policy*. Westport: Praeger, 2002, https://www.questia.com/read/106742722/ballistic-missile-defense-and-the-future-of-american.

Harkavy, Robert E. "Triangular or Indirect Deterrence/Compellence: Something New in Deterrence Theory?" *Comparative Strategy* 17 (1998): 63–81, https://doi.org/10.1080/01495939808403132.

Harris, Shane, Greg Miller and Josh Dawsey. "CIA Concludes Saudi Crown Prince Ordered Jamal Khashoggi's Assassination." *The Washington Post*, November 16, 2018, https://www.washingtonpost.com/world/national-security/cia-concludes-saudi-crown-prince-ordered-jamal-khashoggis-assassination/2018/11/16/98c89fe6-e9b2-11e8-a939-9469f1166f9d_story.html?utm_term=.32b7e192bc38.

Harvey, Frank P. *The Future's Back: Nuclear Rivalry, Deterrence Theory, and Crisis Stability after the Cold War*. Montreal: McGill-Queens University Press, 1997, https://www.questia.com/read/96176256/the-future-s-back-nuclear-rivalry-deterrence-theory.

Harvey, Thomas. "Statement before the House Armed Services Subcommittee on Strategic Forces, June 7, 2017." 2017, http://docs.house.gov/meetings/AS/AS29/20170607/106064/HHRG-115-AS29-Wstate-HarveyT-20170607.pdf.

Hildreth, Steven. *Defense Primer: Ballistic Missile Defense*. Washington DC, 2016, https://fas.org/sgp/crs/natsec/IF10541.pdf.

———. *Evaluation of US Army Assessment of Patriot Antitactical Missile Effectiveness in the War Against Iraq*. Washington DC, 1992, http://www.dtic.mil/get-tr-doc/pdf?AD=ADA344634.

————."Layered Defense." In *Missile Defense: The Current Debate*, 11–13. Edited by Steven Hildreth. Washington DC: Congressional Research Service, 2005, https://fas.org/sgp/crs/weapons/RL31111.pdf.

Hildreth, Steven and Carl Ek, *Long-Range Ballistic Missile Defense in Europe, September 23, 2009*, 2009 https://fas.org/sgp/crs/weapons/RL34051.pdf.

Hill, Fiona and Clifford Gaddy, *New and Expanded Mr Putin. Operative in the Kremlin*, Kindle (Washington DC: Brookings, 2015)

Hill, Ginny. *Yemen Endures. Civil War, Saudi Adventurism and the Future of Arabia*, Kindle (Oxford: Oxford University Press, 2017)

Hinton, Henry L., Lee Edwards, Leon Gill, Stan Lipscomb and J. Klein Spencer. *Ballistic Missile Defense. Issues Concerning Acquisition of THAAD Prototype System*, 1996 http://www.gao.gov/assets/230/222810.pdf.

Hinton, Henry, David Warren, Raymond Dunham, Thomas Gilliam and Barbara Haynes. *Operation Desert Storm. Data Does Not Exist to Conclusively Say How Well Patriot Performed* (Washington DC, 1992) https://www.gao.gov/assets/220/216867.pdf.

Historical Office (Office of the Secretary of Defense). "National Security Strategy." 2019, https://history.defense.gov/Historical-Sources/National-Security-Strategy/.

Hodges, Ben. *Department of Defense Press Briefing by General Hodges on Operation Atlantic Resolve, December 9, 2015, US Department of Defense.* Washington DC, 2015, https://www.defense.gov/News/Transcripts/Transcript-View/Article/633667/department-of-defense-press-briefing-by-general-hodges-on-operation-atlantic-re/.

————. "Don't Put US Bases in Poland." *Politico*, June 4, 2018, https://www.politico.eu/article/dont-put-us-bases-in-poland/.

Hoffman, Fred, *Ballistic Missile Defenses and US National Security, Summary Report Prepared for the Future Security Strategy Study*, 1983, http://www.dod.mil/pubs/foi/Reading_Room/Homeland_Defense/469.pdf.

Hokayem, Emile and David Roberts "The War in Yemen." *Survival* 58 (2016): 157–186.

Hollis, Duncan "Russia Suspends CFE Treaty Participation." *American Society of International Law Insights* 111 (2007), https://www.asil. org/insights/volume/11/issue/19/russia-suspends-cfe-treaty-par ticipation.

House Armed Services Committee (V. Brooks testimony), *Statement of General Vincent K. Brooks, Commander, United Nations Command; Republic of Korea and United States Combined Forces Command; and United States Forces Korea, February 14, 2018,* 2018 https://docs.house. gov/meetings/AS/AS00/20180214/106847/HHRG-115-AS00-20180214-SD002.pdf.

Hughes, G. Philip, and C. R. Neu, *US Strategic Nuclear Forces, Deterrence Policies and Procurement Issues,* 1977 https://www.cbo.gov/sites/de fault/files/95th-congress-1977-1978/reports/77doc600_0.pdf.

Hull, Edmund J., *Memorandum for Jonathan T. Howe through Richard N. Haass, Subject: Algeria: New Islamic Electoral Success and Old Stories on Nuclear Cooperation with Iraq, Bush Presidential Records, White House Office of Records Management, WHORM, Date 01/06/92,* 1992 https://bush41library.tamu.edu/files/persian-gulf/41-CO004-322949/41-co004-322949.pdf.

Huth, Paul. *Extended Deterrence and the Prevention of War.* New Haven: Yale University Press, 1988.

Huth, Paul and Todd Allee. *The Democratic Peace and Territorial Conflict in the Twentieth Century.* Cambridge: Cambridge University Press, 2002, https://www.questia.com/read/107600727/the-democratic-peace-and-territorial-conflict-in-the.

Huth, Paul and Bruce Russett. "Deterrence Failure and Crisis Escalation." *International Studies Quarterly* 32 (1988): 29–45, http://www.jstor. org/stable/2600411%0A.

———. "What Makes Deterrence Work? Cases from 1900 to 1980." *World Politics* 36 (1984): 496–525, http://www.jstor.org/stable/2010184.

IDF. *Clear Skies Ahead Meet the Soldiers of the Iron Dome.* 2013, https://

www.idf.il/en/minisites/israeli-air-force/clear-skies-ahead-meet-the-soldiers-of-the-iron-dome/.

———. *New David's Sling Anti-Missile System Protects Israel from Long Range Threats*, 2017 https://www.idf.il/en/minisites/israeli-air-force/new-david-s-sling-anti-missile-system-protects-israel-from-long-range-threats/.

———. *Operation Protective Edge (July/August 2014)*, 2018 https://www.idf.il/en/minisites/wars-and-operations/operation-protec tive-edge-julyaugust-2014/.

Israel Defense Forces (IDF). *Operation Pillar of Defense (2012)*. 2018, https://www.idf.il/en/minisites/wars-and-operations/operation-pillar-of-defense-2012/.

———. *The Naval "Iron Dome" Is Ready for Action*. 2017, https://www.idf.il/en/minisites/israeli-navy/the-naval-iron-dome-is-ready-for-action/.

IsraelDefense. "Israel's Sea-Based Iron Dome Declared Operational." *IsraelDefense*, November 28, 2017, http://www.israeldefense.co.il/en/node/31961.

Jackson, Randall. "Army Europe Air Defense Unit Deploys to Poland for Exercise." *US Army*, 2016, https://www.army.mil/article/144818/army_europe_air_defense_unit_deploys_to_poland_for_exercise.

Jacobs, Horace and Eunice Engelke Whitney. *Missile and Space Projects Guide 1962*. New York: Springer, 1962.

Jae-in, Moon, and Kim Jong-un. *Panmunjeom Declaration for Peace, Prosperity and Unification of the Korean Peninsula*. 2018, http://www.korea.net/Government/Current-Affairs/National-Affairs/view?affairId=656&subId=641&articleId=3354.

Jane's. *Ramping Up*. 2017, http://www.janes.com/images/assets/344/74344/Ramping_up_US_Army_Europe_building_forces_and_capability.pdf.

———. "Yemeni Rebels Enhance Ballistic Missile Campaign." *Jane's*, 2017, http://www.janes.com/images/assets/330/72330/Yemeni_rebels_enhance_ballistic_missile_campaign.pdf.

Jang, Se Young. "The Evolution of US Extended Deterrence and South Korea's Nuclear Ambitions." *Journal of Strategic Studies*, 39 (2016), 502–520, https://doi.org/10.1080/01402390.2016.1168012.

Jerusalem Post and Globes. 'UK to Purchase Israeli Iron Dome Defense System to Defend Falklands." 25 November 2017 http://www.jpost.com/Israel-News/UK-to-purchase-Israeli-Iron-Dome-defense-system-to-defend-Falklands-515160.

Jervis, Robert. "Deterrence, Rogue States, and the US Policy." In *Complex Deterrence. Strategy in the Global Age*, ed. by T.V. Paul, Patrick Morgan, and James Wirtz, Kindle (Chicago: Chicago University Press, 2009), 1817-2181.

———. "Deterrence Theory Revisited, Review Article, Reviewed Work: Deterrence in American Foreign Policy: Theory and Practice, by Alexander George and Richard Smoke." *World Politics*, 31 (1979), 289–324.

———. *How Statesmen Think. The Psychology of International Politics*, Kindle. Princeton: Princeton University Press, 2017.

———. *Perception and Misperception in International Politics*, Kindle. Princeton: Princeton University Press, 2017.

———. *Why Intelligence Fails. Lessons from the Iranian Revolution and the Iraq War*, Kindle. Ithaca: Cornell University Press, 2010.

Jewish Virtual Library (JVL). *Arrow Missile Program, Jewish Virtual Library (JVL)*. 2018, http://www.jewishvirtuallibrary.org/arrow-missile-program

Johnsen, Gregory D., *The Last Refugee. Yemen, Al-Qaeda and America's War in Yemen*, Kindle. New York: W. W. Norton & Company, 2014.

Johnson, James. *The US-China Military and Defense Relationship during the Obama Presidency*. Cham: Springer International Publishing, 2018, https://doi.org/10.1007/978-3-319-75838-1_5.

Jones, Clive. "A Tribal Order: Politics and Law in the Mountains of Yemen." *Middle Eastern Studies*,47 (2011): 435–436, https://doi.org/10.1080/00263206.2011.544104.

Juarez, Anthony. *Remixing the "Appropriate Mix" Reassessing NATO's Deterrence and Defense Posture in the Face of New Threats.* 2016, https://e-reports-ext.llnl.gov/pdf/825301.pdf.

Judson, Jen. "Funding to Deter Russia Reaches $6.5B in FY19 Budget." *DefenseNews*, February 12, 2018, https://www.defensenews.com/land/2018/02/12/funding-to-deter-russia-reaches-65b-in-fy19-defense-budget-request/.

———. "Poland Has Sticker Shock over 'Unacceptable' Price Tag for Patriot Buy." *DefenseNews*, December 6, 2017, https://www.defensenews.com/land/2017/12/06/poland-surprised-by-high-price-tag-for-its-long-awaited-patriot-purchase/.

———. "Report: US Aid for Israel Missile Defense Competes With MDA Priorities." *DefenseNews*, July 29, 2016, https://www.defensenews.com/home/2016/07/29/report-us-aid-for-israel-missile-defense-competes-with-mda-priorities/.

———. "US Army Terminal Missile Defense System Is Headed to Eastern Europe." *DefenseNews*, April 11, 2019, https://www.defensenews.com/land/2019/04/11/us-army-terminal-missile-defense-system-is-headed-to-eastern-europe/.

Juneau, Thomas. "Iran's Policy towards the Houthis in Yemen: A Limited Return on a Modest Investment." *International Affairs* 92 (2016): 647–663.

Kagan, Robert and William Kristol. *Present Dangers. Crisis and Opportunity in American Foreign and Defense Policy.* San Francisco: Encounter Books, 2000.

Kahn, Herman. *On Escalation. Metaphors and Scenarios.* Baltimore: Penguin Books, 1968.

———. *On Thermonuclear War.* Princeton: Princeton University Press, 1960.

Kalb, Marvin. *Imperial Gamble: Putin, Ukraine, and the New Cold War*, Kindle. Washington DC: Brookings, 2015.

Kalman, Aaron. "Israel Used 17 Tons of Explosives to Destroy Syrian Reactor in 2007, Magazine Says." *The Times of Israel*, 2012, https://www.

timesofisrael.com/israel-uses-17-tons-of-explosives-to-destroy-syri an-reactor/.

Kamel, Amir Magdy. "The JCPOA: How Iran's Grand Strategy Stifled the US." *Middle Eastern Studies* 54 (2018): 706–722, https://doi.org/10. 1080/00263206.2018.1427583.

Kang, Chery. "'THAAD' Anti-Missile System Can't Protect South Korea from Missile Attacks by Itself." *CNBC*, September 11, 2017, https:// www.cnbc.com/2017/09/11/south-korea-missile-defense-thaad- system-cant-do-the-job-alone.html.

Kantrowitz, Arthur. *Laser Propulsion to Earth Orbit.* 1975, http://arc.aiaa. org/doi/abs/10.2514/6.1975-2009.

———. "Laser Propulsion to Earth Orbit – Has Its Time Come?" In *Second Beamed Space-Power Workshop*, 41–56. 1989, http://ntrp.nasa. gov/archive/nasa/casi.ntrp.nasa.gov/19900000827.pdf.

Karako, Thomas, Wes Rumbaugh and Ian Williams. *The Missile Defense Agency and the Color of Money. Fewer Resources, More Responsibility.* Washington DC, 2016, https://missilethreat.csis.org/wp-content/ uploads/2016/12/MDA-and-the-Color-of-Money.pdf.

Karako, Thomas and Ian Williams. *Missile Defense 2020. Next Steps for Defending the Homeland*, 2017, http://espap.eu/orbis/sites/default/ files/generated/document/en/170406_Karako_MissileDefense 2020_Web.pdf.

Kent, Glenn A. and David E. Thaler, *First-Strike Stability and Strategic Defenses. Part II of a Methodology for Evaluating Strategic Forces*, 1990 http://www.dtic.mil/get-tr-doc/pdf?AD=ADA231524.

Kile, Shannon N. and Hans M. Kristensen. *Trends in World Nuclear Forces.* 2017, https://www.sipri.org/sites/default/files/2017-06/fs_1707_ wnf.pdf.

———. "World Nuclear Forces." in *SIPRI Annual Yearbook 2016.* Oxford University Press, 2016, https://www.sipri.org/sites/default/files/SI PRIYB16c16s0.pdf.

———. "World Nuclear Forces." in *SIPRI Annual Yearbook 2017.* Oxford University Press, 2017, https://www.sipri.org/yearbook/2017/11.

————. "World Nuclear Forces." in *SIPRI Yearbook 2018*. Oxford University Press, 2018, https://www.sipri.org/sites/default/files/SIPRI YB18c06.pdf.

————. "World Nuclear Forces." in *SIPRI Yearbook 2015*. Oxford University Press, 2015, https://www.sipri.org/sites/default/files/SIPRI YB15c11s0.pdf.

Kilgour, Marc and Frank Zagare. "Uncertainty and the Role of the Pawn in Extended Deterrence." *Synthese* 100 (1994): 379–412.

Kim, Tae-Hyung. "South Korea's Missile Defense Policy: Dilemma and Opportunity for a Medium State." *Asian Politics & Policy* 1 (2009): 371–389, https://doi.org/10.1111/j.1943-0787.2009.01131.x.

Kissinger, Henry A. *National Security Decision Memorandum 178, July 18, 1972, Subject: FY 1973 Nuclear Weapons Deployment Authorization.* 1972, https://www.nixonlibrary.gov/sites/default/files/virtuallibrary /documents/nsdm/nsdm_178.pdf.

————. *National Security Decision Memorandum 230, August 9, 1973, Subject: US Strategy and Forces for Asia.* 1973, https://www.nixonlibrary. gov/sites/default/files/virtuallibrary/documents/nsdm/nsdm_230. pdf.

Kleppner, Daniel and Frederick K. Lamb. "Report of the American Physical Society Study Group on Boost-Phase Intercept Systems for National Missile Defense: Scientific and Technical Issues." *Review of Modern Physics* 76 (2004), https://journals.aps.org/rmp/pdf/10.1103/Rev ModPhys.76.S1.

Knights, Michael. "The Military Role in Yemen's Protests: Civil-Military Relations in the Tribal Republic." *Journal of Strategic Studies* 36 (2013): 261–288, https://doi.org/10.1080/01402390.2012.740660.

Knopf, Jeffrey. "The Fourth Wave in Deterrence Theory Research." *Contemporary Security Policy* 31 (2010): 1–33, https://calhoun.nps.edu/ bitstream/handle/10945/38341/inc_knopf_CSP-31-1_2010.pdf; sequence=4.

Kramer, Andrew E. and Thom Shanker. "Russia Suspends Arms Agreement Over US Shield." *The New York Times*, July 15, 2007, http:// www.nytimes.com/2007/07/15/world/europe/15russia.html.

Kristensen, Hans M. *Assembled Documents: New START Treaty Aggregate Numbers of Strategic Offensive Arms As of September 1, 2011*, 2011 https://fas.org/programs/ssp/nukes/armscontrol/NewSTART-USnumbers090111.pdf.

———. *New START Data Shows Russian Warhead Increase Before Expected Decrease*, 2016 https://fas.org/blogs/security/2016/10/new-start-data-2016/.

Kuchma, Leonid D., Boris N. Yeltsin, John Major and William J. Clinton. *Letter Dated 7 December 1994 from the Permanent Representatives of the Russian Federation, Ukraine, the United Kingdom of Great Britain and Northern Ireland and the United States of America to the United Nations Addressed to the Secretary General. Annex I.* 1994, https://www.un.org/en/ga/search/view_doc.asp?symbol=S/1994/1399.

Lackner, Helen. *Yemen in Crisis. Autocracy, Neo-Liberalism and the Disintegration of a State.* London: Saqi Books, 2017.

Landau, Emily and Azriel Bermant. "Iron Dome Protection: Missile Defense in Israel's Security Concept." In *The Lessons of Operation Protective Edge*, 37–42. Edited by Anat Kurz and Shlomo Brom. Tel Aviv: The Institute for National Security Studies, 2014, http://www.inss.org.il/he/wp-content/uploads/sites/2/systemfiles/SystemFiles/Iron Dome Protection_ Missile Defense in Israel's Security Concept.pdf.

Landry, Carole. "Iran Arming Yemen's Houthi Rebels since 2009: UN Report." *Middle East Eye*, May 1, 2015, https://www.middleeasteye.net/news/iran-arming-yemens-huthi-rebels-2009-un-report-1170499355.

Lankov, Andrei. *Strategic Stability in the Twenty-First Century: The North Korean Nuclear Threat.* 2018, https://carnegie.ru/commentary/77735.

Lanoszka, Alexander. *Atomic Assurance: The Alliance Politics of Nuclear Proliferation*, eBook. Ithaca: Cornell University Press, 2018.

———. "Russian Hybrid Warfare and Extended Deterrence in Eastern Europe." *International Affairs* 92 (2016): 175–195.

Laqueur, Walter. *Putinism. Russia and Its Future in the West*, Kindle. New York: Thomas Dunne Books, 2015.

Larsen, Jeffrey. "US Extended Deterrence and Europe: Time to Consider Alternative Structures?" In *The Future of Extended Deterrence. The United States, NATO, and Beyond*, 41–70. Edited by Stéfanie Von Hlatky and Andreas Wenger, Kindle. Washington DC: Georgetown University Press, 2015.

Lazareva, Inna. "The Iron Dome: What Is It and How Does It Work?" *The Telegraph*, July 10, 2014 http://www.telegraph.co.uk/news/world-news/middleeast/israel/10960091/The-Iron-Dome-what-is-it-and-how-does-it-work.html.

Lebovic, James. "The Law of Small Numbers: Deterrence and National Missile Defense." *The Journal of Conflict Resolution* 46 (2002): 455–483.

Lebow, Richard Ned. *Avoiding War, Making Peace*. Cham: Springer, 2017.

Legvold, Robert. *Return to Cold War*, Kindle. Cambridge: Polity Press, 2016.

Lele, Ajey. "Missile and Nuclear Conundrums." In *Asian Space Race: Rhetoric or Reality?* 125–141. India: Springer India, 2013. https://doi.org/10.1007/978-81-322-0733-7_10.

Lewis, George N. "Technical Controversy. Can Missile Defense Work?" In *Regional Missile Defense from a Global Perspective*, 1299-1689. Edited by Catherine McArdle Kelleher and Peter Dombrowski, Kindle. Stanford: Stanford University Press, 2015.

Lewis, Jeffrey. "Patriot Missiles Are Made in America and Fail Everywhere." *Foreign Policy*, 2018, https://foreignpolicy.com/2018/03/28/patriot-missiles-are-made-in-america-and-fail-everywhere/.

Li, Allen, Lee Edwards, Stan Lipscomb, and Tom Gordon. *Missile Defense. THAAD Restructure Addresses Problems But Limits Early Capability*. 1999, http://www.gao.gov/assets/230/227724.pdf.

Li, Allen, Bob Levin, Wayne Gilliam and Terry Wyatt. *Missile Defense*. Washington DC, 2000, https://www.gao.gov/assets/240/230417.pdf.

Li, Allen, Tom Schulz, Lee Edwards, Stan Lipscomb, Leon Gill and Tom Gordon. *Ballistic Missile Defense. Improvements Needed in THAAD Acquisition Planning.* 1997, http://www.gao.gov/assets/230/224624.pdf.

Liddell Hart, Basil H. *The Revolution in Warfare.* London: Faber and Faber, 1946.

Lieber, Keir and Daryl Press. "The Rise of US Nuclear Primacy." *Foreign Affairs* 85 (2006): 42–54.

Lindsay, James M., and Michael O'Hanlon. *Defending America. The Case for Limited National Missile Defense.* Washington DC: Brookings, 2001.

Lockheed Martin. *Lockheed Martin Completes 100ᵗʰ THAAD Interceptor,* 2015 http://www.lockheedmatin.com/us/news/press-releases/2015/july/mfc-lockheed-martin-completes-100th-thaad-interceptor.html.

———. *Lockheed Martin Receives $528 Million THAAD Missile Defense Contract,* 2016 http://www.lockheedmartin.com/us/news/press-releases/2016/january/mfc-010416-lockheed-martin-receives-528-million-THAAD-contract.html.

———. *Missile Defense,* 2019 http://www.lockheedmartin.com/us/what-we-do/aerospace-defense/missile-defense.html.

———. *Missile vs. Missile,* 2019 https://www.lockheedmartin.com/en-us/news/features/history/missile-defense.html.

———. *Patriot Advanced Capability-3 (PAC-3®),* 2010 https://www.lockheedmartin.com/content/dam/lockheed-martin/mfc/pc/pac-3/mfc-pac-3-pc.pdf.

———. *Terminal High Altitude Area Defense THAAD,* 2019 https://www.lockheedmartin.com/en-us/products/thaad.html.

Lokshin, Jacob. *Iron Dome (Israel).* 2016, http://missiledefenseadvocacy.org/missile-defense-systems-2/allied-air-and-missile-defense-systems/allied-intercept-systems-coming-soon/iron-dome-israel/.

Long, Austin. *Deterrence: From Cold War to Long War: Lessons from Six Decades of Rand Deterrence Research* (Santa Monica: RAND, 2008) https://www.questia.com/read/122660182/deterrence-from-cold-war-to-long-war-lessons-from.

Lonnquest, John and David Winkler. *To Defend and to Deter: The Legacy of the United States Cold War Missile Program*, 1996 http://www.dtic.mil/cgi-bin/GetTRDoc?Location=U2&doc=GetTRDoc.pdf &AD=ADA337549.

Lucas, Edward. *The New Cold War. Putin's Threat to Russia and the World*, Kindle (London: Bloomsbury, 2014)

Lupovici, Amir. "The Emerging Fourth Wave of Deterrence Theory—Toward a New Research Agenda." *International Studies Quarterly*, 54 (2010), 705–32

MacAskill, Ewen. "Russian Troops Removing ID Markings 'Gross Violation.'" *The Guardian*, March 6, 2014, https://www.theguardian.com/news/defence-and-security-blog/2014/mar/06/ukraine-gross-violation-russian-troops.

MacKinnon, Mark. *He New Cold War. Revolutions, Rigged Elections and Pipeline Politics in the Former Soviet Union*, Kindle. Toronto: Vintage Canada, 2008.

Mahnken, Thomas. "Future Scenarios of Limited Nuclear Conflict." In *On Limited Nuclear War in the 21st Century*. Edited by Jeffrey Larsen and Kerry M. Kartchner. Stanford: Stanford Security Studies, 2014.

Majumdar, Dave. "Does North Korea's New Hwasong-15 ICBM Have Soviet and Chinese "DNA"?." *The National Interest*, November 2017, http://nationalinterest.org/blog/the-buzz/does-north-koreas-new-hwasong-15-icbm-have-soviet-or-chinese-23434.

———. "Here Is Everything We Know (And Don't) About Russia's Mysterious ICBM Tests." *The National Interest*, September 2017, http://nationalinterest.org/blog/the-buzz/here-everything-we-know-dont-about-russias-mysterious-icbm-22502.

———. "Just How Much of a Threat Is Russia's Status-6 Nuclear Torpedo?" *The National Interest*, January 2018, http://nationalinterest.org/blog/the-buzz/just-how-much-threat-russias-status-6-nuclear-torpedo-24094.

———. "Russia's New PAK-DA Stealth Bomber Just Took a Big Step Forward." *The National Interest*, March 2017, http://nationalinterest.org/

blog/the-buzz/russias-new-pak-da-stealth-bomber-just-took-big-step-forward-19656.

———. "The Big Problem Russia's New PAK-FA Stealth Fighter and America's F-22 Share." *The National Interest*, July 2017, http://nationalinterest.org/blog/the-buzz/the-big-problem-russias-new-pak-fa-stealth-fighter-americas-21654.

Makovsky, David. "The Silent Strike. How Israel Bombed a Syrian Nuclear Installation and Kept It Secret." *The New Yorker*, September 17, 2012, https://www.newyorker.com/magazine/2012/09/17/the-silent-strike.

Manning, Robert A. *The Future of US Extended Deterrence in Asia to 2025*, 2014, https://www.files.ethz.ch/isn/184441/Future_US_Ext_Det_in_Asia.pdf.

Mantle, Peter J. *The Missile Defense Equation: Factors for Decision Making*. Reston: American Institute of Aeronautics and Astronautics, 2004.

Maoz, Zeev. *Correlates of War*. 2019, http://www.correlatesofwar.org/people.

Marcus, Jonathan. "A Clear Signal from Tehran. Iran to Boost Uranium Enrichment If Nuclear Deal Fails." *BBC News*, June 5, 2018, http://www.bbc.com/news/world-middle-east-44365078.

Marmei, Eerik and Gabriel White. *European Deterrence Initiative. Bolstering the Defence of the Baltic States*. Tallin, 2017, https://www.icds.ee/fileadmin/media/IMG/2017/Publications/ICDS_Policy_Paper_European_Deterrence_Initiative_Eerik_Marmei-Gabriel_White_December_2017.pdf.

Lockheed Martin. *PAC-3 Missile Segment Enhancement (MSE). Delivering Increased Range and Altitude*, 2015, https://www.lockheedmartin.com/content/dam/lockheed/data/mfc/pc/pac-3-missile-segment-enhancement/mfc-pac-3-mse-pc.pdf.

Marzari, Frank. "The Prospects for Strategic Stability in the 1970s." *Canadian Journal of Political Science* 4 (1971): 541–558.

Mattis, Jim. *Nuclear Posture Review. Preface*, 2018, https://www.defense.gov/News/Special-Reports/0218_npr/, https://media.defense.gov/

2018/Feb/02/2001872886/-1/-1/1/2018-NUCLEAR-POSTURE-REVIEW-FINAL-REPORT.PDF.

Mauroni, Albert. *Chemical-Biological Defense: US Military Policies and Decisions in the Gulf War*. Westport: Praeger, 1998, https://www.questia.com/read/106743486/chemical-biological-defense-u-s-military-policies.

Mayer, Michael. *US Missile Defense Strategy. Engaging the Debate*. Boulder: First Forum Press, 2015.

McKeon, Brian. "Statement before the Senate Armed Services Subcommittee on Strategic Forces, April 13, 2016 (Principal Deputy under Secretary of Defense for Policy)." 2016, https://www.armed-services.senate.gov/imo/media/doc/McKeon_04-13-16.pdf.

McMahon, Scott. *Pursuit of the Shield. The US Quest for Limited Ballistic Missile Defense*. Lanham: University Press of America, 1997.

McNamara, Robert S. *The Essence of Security. Reflections in Office*. New York: Harper & Row, 1968.

MDA, *Ballistic Missile Defense Intercept Flight Test Record (as of March 2018)*. 2018, https://www.mda.miglobal/documents/pdf/testrecord.pdf.

———. *Ballistic Missile Defense Intercept Flight Test Record (as of May 30, 2017)*. 2017, https://www.mda.mil/global/documents/pdf/testrecord.pdf.

Mearsheimer, John J. *Conventional Deterrence*, Kindle. Ithaca: Cornell University Press, 2016.

Meier, Oliver and Steven Pifer. *Russia's Missile Treaty Violations Directly Threaten Europe—so Europe Should Speak Up*. 2017, https://www.brookings.edu/blog/order-from-chaos/2017/05/05/russias-missile-treaty-violations-directly-threaten-europe-so-europe-should-speak-up/.

Melito, Thomas. *North Korea Sanctions*. 2015, http://www.gao.gov/assets/680/670170.pdf.

de Mesquita, Bruce Bueno. "The War Trap Revisited: A Revised Expected

Utility Model." *The American Political Science Review* 79 (1985): 156–177, http://www.jstor.org/stable/1956125.

Metais, Solène, *Yemen: The Battle for Al-Hudaydah as a Turning Point in the Civil War, European Strategic Intelligence and Security Center*. July 17, 2018, http://www.esisc.org/publications/briefings/yemen-the-battle-for-al-hudaydah-as-a-turning-point-in-the-civil-war.

Middle East Monitor. "161 Ballistic Missiles Fired at Saudi Arabia since 2015." July 17, 2018, https://www.middleeastmonitor.com/20180717-161-ballistic-missiles-fired-at-saudi-arabia-since-2015.

———. "Coalition Renews Strikes on Yemen's Main Port City." July 27, 2018, https://www.middleeastmonitor.com/20180727-coalition-renews-strikes-on-yemens-main-port-city.

———. "Houthi Missile Kills One in Saudi Arabia." August 9, 2018, https://www.middleeastmonitor.com/20180809-houthi-missile-kills-one-in-saudi-arabia.

———. "Saudi Arabia Resumes Oil Shipments through Bab El-Mandab." August 2, 2018, https://www.middleeastmonitor.com/20180802-saudi-arabia-resumes-oil-shipments-through-bab-el-mandab.

Military Factory. "SS-1 (Scud)/9P117." *Military Factory* 2017, https://www.militaryfactory.com/armor/detail.asp?armor_id=24.

Miller, Michael. "Nuclear Attribution as Deterrence." *The Nonproliferation Review* 14 (2007): 33–60, https://doi.org/10.1080/10736700601178465.

Minasyan, Sergei. "Moratorium on the CFE Treaty and South Caucasian Security." *Russia in Global Affairs* 3 (2008), http://eng.globalaffairs.ru/number/n_11279.

Ministry of Foreign Affairs Republic of Poland. *Minister Witold Waszczykowski: Redzikowo Base Will Significantly Strengthen Poland's Security.* 2016, http://www.msz.gov.pl/en/news/minister_witold_waszczykowski__redzikowo_base_will_significantly_strengthen_poland_s_security.

———. *Polish-US Missile Defence Negotiations.* 2012, http://www.msz.

gov.pl/en/foreign_policy/security_policy/missile_defence/md_ne gotiations/.

Ministry of National Defense of Poland. *Modernizacja i Rozwój Sił Zbrojnych RP.* 2017, http://www.mon.gov.pl/aktualnosci/artykul/najnow sze/modernizacja-i-rozwoj-sil-zbrojnych-82017-12-22/ htm.

Minnich, James. "The Year 2012. South Korea's Resumption of Wartime Operational Control." *Military Review*, 2011, https://www.armyu press.army.mil/Portals/7/military-review/Archives/English/Mili taryReview_20110630_art004.pdf.

Missile Defense Advocacy Alliance. *Turkey.* 2018, http://missiledefen seadvocacy.org/intl-cooperation/turkey/.

Missile Defense Agency. *A System of Elements.* 2019, https://www.mda. mil/system/elements.html.

———. *Aegis Ashore.* 2019, https://www.mda.mil/system/aegis_ashore. html.

———. *Aegis Ballistic Missile Defense.* 2019, https://www.mda.mil/sys tem/aegis_bmd.html.

———. *Aegis Ballistic Missile Defense Fact Sheet.* 2016, https://www.mda. mil/global/documents/pdf/aegis.pdf.

———. *Aegis Ballistic Missile Defense Testing.* 2017, https://www.mda. mil/global/documents/pdf/aegis_tests.pdf.

———. *Elements. Ground-Based Midcourse Defense (GMD).* 2019, https://www.mda.mil/system/gmd.html.

———. *Elements. Potential New Technologies.* 2019, https://www.mda. mil/system/potential_new_technologies.html.

———. *Fiscal Year (FY) 2019 Budget Estimates Overview.* 2018, https:// www.mda.mil/global/documents/pdf/budgetfy19.pdf.

———. *Fiscal Year (FY) 2020 Budget Estimates, March 7, 2019.* 2019, https://www.mda.mil/global/documents/pdf/budgetfy20.pdf.

———. *Ground-Based Midcourse Defense (GMD) Program Overview, May 24, 2016.* 2016, https://mda.mil/global/documents/pdf/osbp_

16conf_GMD_Next_Follow_On_Barrow.pdf.

———. *Ground-Based Midcourse Defense Fact Sheet*. 2017, https://www.mda.mil/global/documents/pdf/gmdfacts.pdf.

———. *Historical Funding for MDA FY85-17 Fiscal Year (FY in Billions)*. 2017, https://www.mda.mil/global/documents/pdf/FY17_hist-funds.pdf.

———. *Homeland Missile Defense System Successfully Intercepts ICBM Target, May 30, 2017*. 2017, https://www.mda.mil/news/17news0003.html.

———. *Patriot Advanced Capability-3*. 2016, https://www.mda.mil/global/documents/pdf/pac3.pdf.

———. *Terminal High Altitude Area Defense*. 2014, http://www.mda.mil/global/documents/pdf/thaad.pdf.

———. *Terminal High Altitude Area Defense Fact Sheet*. 2016, https://www.mda.mil/global/documents/pdf/thaad.pdf.

Missile Threat Center for Strategic and International Studies Missile Defense Project. *Missiles of North Korea*, 2018, https://missilethreat.csis.org/country/dprk.

Mizokami, Kyle. "Everything You Need to Know: Japan's Missile Defenses." *The National Interest.*, September 2, 2017, http://nationalinterest.org/blog/the-buzz/everything-you-need-know-japans-missile-defenses-22155.

———. "Why America's Enemies Fear the Patriot Missile Defense System (Even After Almost 40 Years)." *The National Interest*, March 20, 2017 http://nationalinterest.org/print/blog/the-buzz/why-americas-enemies-fear-the-patriot-missile-defense-system-19833.

Molas-Gallart, J. "Conversion and Control of Technological Capabilities in the Missile Field: The 'Dual-Use Paradox.'" In *Defense Conversion Strategies*, 193–205. Dordrecht: Springer Netherlands, 1997, https://doi.org/10.1007/978-94-017-1213-2_11.

Montague, L. David and Walter B. Slocombe. *Making Sense of Ballistic Missile Defense: An Assessment of Concepts and Systems for US Boost-Phase*

Missile Defense in Comparison to Other Alternatives, 2012, https://download.nap.edu/cart/download.cgi?record_id=13189.

Morag, Nadav. "The Strategic Impact of an Iranian Nuclear Weapons Capability on Israel." In *Nuclear Threats and Security Challenges*, 135–145, Edited by Samuel Apikyan and David Diamond. Dordrecht: Springer, 2015.

Morgan, Patrick. *Deterrence Now*. Cambridge: Cambridge University Press, 2003.

MTCR. "Missile Technology Control Regime." 2019, http://mtcr.info/partners/.

Murray, Williamson and Robert Scales. *The Iraq War: A Military History*. Cambridge, Massachusetts: Belknap Press, 2003, https://www.questia.com/library/119021308/the-iraq-war-a-military-history.

Myers, Meghann. "Back to Europe." *Army Times*, March 19, 2017, https://www.armytimes.com/news/your-army/2017/03/19/back-to-europe-the-army-is-sending-more-troops-tanks-and-helicopters-to-deter-russia/.

National Institute of Standards and Technology. *Approximate Conversions from US Customary Measures to Metric*. 2010, https://www.nist.gov/pml/weights-and-measures/approximate-conversions-us-customary-measures-metric.

NATO. *Boosting NATO's Presence in the East and Southeast, March 2, 2018*. 2018, https://www.nato.int/cps/en/natohq/topics_136388.htm?selectedLocale=en.

———. *Bucharest Summit Declaration. Issued by the Heads of State and Government Participating in the Meeting of the North Atlantic Council in Bucharest on 3 April 2008*. 2008, http://www.nato.int/cps/in/natohq/official_texts_8443.htm.

———. *NATO, Ballistic Missile Defence Programme*. 2017, https://www.ncia.nato.int/BMD/pages/ballistic-missile-defence.aspx.

———. *NATO, BMD, Where We Are*, 2017 https://www.ncia.nato.int/BMD/Pages/Where-we-are.aspx.

————. *PATRIOT Deployment*, 2015 https://www.nato.int/nato_static_fl2014/assets/pdf/pdf_2015_05/20150508_1505-Factsheet-PATRIOT_en.pdf.

NATO Public Affairs. *Aegis Ashore Missile Defence System in Romania Undergoes Scheduled Update*, 2019 https://www.cnic.navy.mil/regions/cnreurafswa/installations/nsf_deveselu/news/Aegis-Ashore-missile-defence-system-in-Romania-undergoes-scheduled-update.html.

Neufeld, Michael J. *Von Braun. Dreamer of Space, Engineer of War*. New York: Vintage Books, 2007.

Nichols, Michelle. "Russia, US Clash over INF Arms Treaty at United Nations." *Reuters*, October 26, 2018, https://www.reuters.com/article/us-usa-nuclear-russia-un/russia-us-clash-over-inf-arms-treaty-at-united-nations-idUSKCN1N02FI.

Nobel Media AB. "The Nobel Peace Prize for 2009 to President Barack Obama—Press Release." 2017, https://www.nobelprize.org/nobel_prizes/peace/laureates/2009/press.html.

Noonan, John. "Russia "Simulates" Nuclear Attack on Poland." *The Weekly Standard*, November 3, 2009, http://www.weeklystandard.com/russia-simulates-nuclear-attack-on-poland/article/271383.

Northrop Grumman. *Orbital ATK Merged with Northrop Grumman in 2018. Orbital ATK Merger*. 2019, http://investor.northropgrumman.com/orbital-atk-merger.

Northrop Grumman Corporation (Tim Paynter & Steve Movius) & Globe Newswire. *Northrop Grumman Completes Orbital ATK Acquisition, Blake Larson Elected to Lead New Innovation Systems Sector*. 2018, https://northropgrumman.gcs-web.com/news-releases/news-release-details/northrop-grumman-completes-orbital-atk-acquisition-blake-larson; https://www.globenewswire.com/news-release/2018/06/06/1518052/0/en/Northrop-Grumman-Completes-Orbital-ATK-Acquisition-B.

Nuclear Threat Initiative (NTI). *Comprehensive Test Ban Treaty (CTBT)*, 2019, https://www.nti.org/learn/treaties-and-regimes/comprehensive-nuclear-test-ban-treaty-ctbt/.

————. *New START*. 2019, http://www.nti.org/learn/treaties-and-re-gimes/treaty-between-the-united-states-of-america-and-the-russian-federation-on-measures-for-the-further-reduction-and-limitation-of-strategic-offensive-arms/.

Nusseibeh, Lana. *Letter Dated 13 June 2018 from the Permanent Representative of the UAE to the UN, S/2018/607*. 2018, https://undocs.org/S/2018/607.

O'Hanlon, Michael. "Alternative Architectures and US Politics." In *Rockets' Red Glare: Missile Defenses and the Future of World Politics*, 111–136. Edited by James Wirtz and Jeffrey Larsen. Boulder: Westview Press, 2001.

O'Neil, Andrew. *Asia, the US and Extended Nuclear Deterrence. Atomic Umbrellas in the Twenty-First Century*, Kindle. London: Routledge, 2013.

O'Neil, Andrew. "Extended Nuclear Deterrence in East Asia: Redundant or Resurgent?." *International Affairs* 87 (2011): 1439–1457.

O'Neill, Gerard K. "The Colonization of Space." *Physics Today* 27 (1974): 32–40, http://www.nsp.org/settlement/physicstoday.htm.

O'Neill, Malcolm. *Memorandum for Secretary of Defense*. 1993, http://www.dod.mil/pubs/foi/Reading_Room/Selected_Acquisition_Reports/485.pdf.

O'Rourke, Ronald. *Navy Aegis Ballistic Missile Defense (BMD) Program: Background and Issues for Congress*. 2019, https://crsreports.congress.gov/product/pdf/RL/RL33745.

Obama, Barack. *Executive Order 13551, August 30, 2010*. 2010, https://www.treasury.gov/resource-center/sanctions/Programs/Documents/Executive Order 13551.pdf.

————. *Executive Order 13570, April 18, 2011*. 2011, https://www.treasury.gov/resource-center/sanctions/Programs/Documents/04182011_nk_eo.pdf.

————. *Executive Order 13687, January 2, 2015*. 2015, https://www.treasury.gov/resource-center/sanctions/Programs/Documents/13687.pdf.

—————. *Executive Order 13722, March 15, 2016.* 2016, https://www. treasury.gov/resource-center/sanctions/Programs/Documents/nk_ eo_20160316.pdf.

Oberdorfer, Don and Robert Carlin. *The Two Koreas. A Contemporary History*, Kindle. New York: Basic Books, 2014.

Office of the Under Secretary of Defense—Comptroller. *Missile Defense Agency, Procurement, Defense-Wide (Includes O&M and MILCON). De-fense-Wide Justification Book Volume 2b of 2, Department of Defense Fis-cal Year 2019 Budget Estimates, Washington, DC, February 2018.* 2018, http://comptroller.defense.gov/Portals/45/Documents/defbudget/ fy2019/budget_justification/pdfs/02_Procurement/U_PROCURE MENT_MasterJustificationBook_Missile_Defense_Agency_ PB_2019_1.pdf.

—————. *Missile Defense Agency Defense-Wide Justification Book Research, Development, Test and Evaluation (RDTE) Volume 2a of 2 FY 2017.* 2016, http://comptroller.defense.gov/Portals/45/Documents/def budget/FY2017/budget_justification/pdfs/03_RDT_and_E/MD A_RDTE_MasterJustificationBook_Missile_Defense_Agency_ PB_2017_1.pdf.

—————. *Program Acquisition Costs by Weapon System FY 2018.* 2017, http://comptroller.defense.gov/Portals/45/Documents/defbudget/ fy2018/fy2018_Weapons.pdf.

Office of the Under Secretary of Defense (Comptroller). *Missile Defense Agency Defense-Wide Justification Book Research, Development, Test and Evaluation (RDTE) Volume 2a of 2 FY 2018.* 2017, http://comptroller. defense.gov/Portals/45/Documents/defbudget/FY2018/budget_ justification/pdfs/03_RDT_and_E/U_RDTE_MasterJustification Book_Missile_Defense_Agency_PB_2018_Vol2a_Vol2b.pdf.

Office of the Under Secretary of Defense (Comptroller) EDI FY2019. *European Deterrence Initiative Budget Fiscal Year (FY) 2019, Justification Book.* 2018, http://comptroller.defense.gov/Portals/45/Documents /defbudget/fy2019/fy2019_EDI_JBook.pdf.

Office of the Under Secretary of Defense for Acquisition. *Report of the Defense Science Board Task Force on Patriot System Performance.* 2002, https://www.acq.osd.mil/dsb/reports/2000s/ADA435837.pdf.

————. *Treaty between the United States of America and the Union of Soviet Socialist Republics on the Elimination of Their Intermediate-Range and Shorter-Range Missiles*. 1987, https://www.acq.osd.mil/tc/inf/INFte xt.htm.

Opall-Rome, Barbara. "Raytheon: Arab-Operated Patriots Intercepted over 100 Tactical Ballistic Missiles since 2015." *DefenseNews*, 2017, https:// www.defensenews.com/digital-show-dailies/dubai-air-show/2017/ 11/14/raytheon-saudi-based-patriots-intercepted-over-100-tbms-since-2015/.

————. "US-Israel Team Ramp-up Interceptor Builds." *DefenseNews*, 2017, https://www.defensenews.com/smr/2017/08/03/us-israel-teams-ramp-up-interceptor-builds.

Oppenheimer, J. Robert. "Speech to the Association of Los Alamos Scientists, Los Alamos, November 2, 1945." In *Robert Oppenheimer, Letters and Recollections*, 315–325. Edited by Alice Kimball Smith and Charles Weiner. Stanford: Stanford University Press, 1995.

Orbital ATK. *About Leadership*. 2017, http://www.orbitalatk.com/ about/leadership/default.aspx.

————. *David A. Thompson*. 2017, http://www.orbitalatk.com/about/ leadership/files/Thompson_David_OA.pdf.

————. *Flight Systems*. 2016, https://www.orbitalatk.com/flight-systems /overview/.

————. *GMD Boost Vehicle, Fact Sheet*. 2015, https://www.orbitalatk. com/flight-systems/missile-defense-systems/interceptors/docs/ BR06009_3862 GMD_R2.pdf.

————. *Interceptors*. 2016, https://www.orbitalatk.com/flight-systems/ missile-defense-systems/interceptors/default.aspx.

————. *Missile Defense Systems*. 2016, https://www.orbitalatk.com/ flight-systems/missile-defense-systems/overview/default.aspx.

Orkaby, Asher. *Beyond the Arab Cold War. The International History of the Yemen Civil War, 1962-68*, Kindle. New York: Oxford University Press, 2017.

————."Yemen's Humanitarian Nightmare. The Real Roots of the Conflict." *Foreign Affairs* 96 (2017): 93–101.

OSCE. *Russia's Withdrawal from CFE Treaty Work a "Dangerous Move,"* *Says OSCE PA Security Chair.* 2015, http://www.osce.org/pa/144946.

Osgood, Robert E. *Alliances and American Foreign Policy.* Edited by The Johns Hopkins University Press. Baltimore, 1968.

————. *Limited War Revisited.* Boulder: Westview Press, 1979.

Oshigawa, Shinichi. *Missile Defense and Deterrence.* Tokyo, 2002, http://www.nids.mod.go.jp/english/publication/kiyo/pdf/bulletin_e2001_2.pdf%0A.

Panel of Experts on Yemen. *Final Report of the Panel of Experts on Yemen, UN Security Council Document S/2018/193, January 2017.* 2017, https://www.un.org/en/ga/search/view_doc.asp?symbol=S/2018/193.

Payne, Keith. *Deterrence in the Second Nuclear Age*, Kindle. Lexington: The University Press of Kentucky, 1996.

PBS. "Weapons: MIM-104 Patriot." *PBS*, 2018, https://www.pbs.org/wgbh/pages/frontline/gulf/weapons/patriot.html.

Pecht, Eyal, Asher Tishler and Nir Weingold. "On the Choice of Multi-Task R&D Defense Projects: A Case Study of the Israeli Missile Defense System." *Defence and Peace Economics* 24 (2013): 429–448, https://doi.org/10.1080/10242694.2012.717205.

Peck, Michael. "Russia Mocks America for Buying Israel's Iron Dome." *The National Interest*, November 4, 2017, http://nationalinterest.org/blog/the-buzz/russia-mocks-america-buying-israels-iron-dome-23023.

Pellerin, Cheryl. "US, South Korean Military Leaders Reinforce Alliance." *US Department of Defense*, August 24, 2017, https://www.defense.gov/News/Article/Article/1288096/us-south-korean-military-leaders-reinforce-alliance.

Pendleton, John H. *Ballistic Missile Defense. Actions Needed to Address Implementation Issues and Estimate Long-Term Costs for European Capabilities.* 2014, http://www.gao.gov/assets/670/662492.pdf.

Perkins, Brian M. "Yemen: Between Revolution and Regression." *Studies in Conflict & Terrorism* 40 (2017)" 300–317, https://doi.org/10.1080 /1057610X.2016.1205368.

Perrien, Alex *NSF Redzikowo Signs Premiere Training Agreement with Polish Forces.* 2017, https://pl.usembassy.gov/agreement/.

Pew Research Center. *Topline Questionnaire, Pew Research Center Spring 2015 Global Attitudes Survey.* 2015, http://www.pewglobal.org/cate gory/datasets/2015/.

Pifer, Stephen *The Eagle and the Trident. US-Ukraine Relations in Turbulent Times.* Washington DC: Brookings, 2017.

Pifer, Stephen, Richard C. Bush, Martin S. Indyk, Michael O'Hanlon and Kenneth M. Pollack. *US Nuclear and Extended Deterrence: Considerations and Challenges.* 2010, https://www.brookings.edu/wp-content/ uploads/2016/06/06_nuclear_deterrence.pdf%0A.

Pilat, Joseph F. "A Reversal of Fortunes? Extended Deterrence and Assurance in Europe and East Asia 1." *Journal of Strategic Studies* 39 (2016): 580–591, https://doi.org/10.1080/01402390.2016.1168016.

Pirnie, Bruce, John Gordon, Richard Brennan, Forrest Morgan, Alexander Hou and Chad Yost. "Air Operations." In *Operation Iraqi Freedom. Decisive War, Elusive Peace,* 149–182. Edited by Walter Perry, Richard Darilek, Laurinda Rohn and Jerry Sollinger. Santa Monica: RAND, 2015, https://www.rand.org/content/dam/rand/pubs/research_ reports/RR1200/RR1214/RAND_RR1214.pdf.

Pompeo, Michael R. *US Intent To Withdraw from the INF Treaty.* 2019, https://www.state.gov/u-s-intent-to-withdraw-from-the-inf-treaty- february-2-2019/.

Popov, Vladimir. "Western Economic Sanctions and East-West Economic Orientation of Russia." in *The Return of the Cold War. Ukraine, the West and Russia,* ed. by J. L. Black, Michael Johns, and Alanda D. Theriault, Kindle. London: Routledge, 2016.

Posen, Barry. *Inadvertent Escalation. Conventional Wars and Nuclear Risks,* Kindle. Ithaca: Cornell University Press, 2013.

Postol, Theodore. "Lessons of the Gulf War Experience with Patriot." *International Security* 16 (1991): 119–171.

———. *Optical Evidence Indicating Patriot High Miss Rates during the Gulf War.* 2004, http://ee162.caltech.edu/notes/postol.pdf.

———. "The Evidence That Shows Iron Dome Is Not Working." *Bulletin of the Atomic Scientists*, 2014, https://thebulletin.org/evidence-shows-iron-dome-not-working7318.

Postol, Theodore and George N. Lewis. "Video Evidence on the Effectiveness of Patriot during the 1991 Gulf War." *Science & Global Security* 4 (1993): 1–63.

Postol, Theodore and Robert Stein. " Patriot Experience in the Gulf War. Correspondence." *International Security* 17 (1992): 199–240.

Powell, Robert. *Nuclear Deterrence Theory. The Search for Credibility.* Cambridge: Cambridge University Press, 1990.

President of Russia. *Live with President Vladimir Putin—Hot Line (Excerpts), December 24, 2001.* 2001, http://en.kremlin.ru/events/president/transcripts/21457.

PRNews Wire & Northrop Grumman (Tim Paynter & Steve Movius) & Orbital ATK (Barron Beneski). *Northrop Grumman to Acquire Orbital ATK for $9.2 Billion.* 2017, https://www.prnewswire.com/news-releases/northrop-grumman-to-acquire-orbital-atk-for-92-billion-300521034.html.

Quackenbush, Stephen. *Understanding General Deterrence. Theory and Application.* New York: Palgrave Macmillan, 2011.

Quackenbush, Stephen L. "General Deterrence and International Conflict: Testing Perfect Deterrence Theory." *International Interactions* 36 (2010): 60–85, https://doi.org/10.1080/03050620903554069.

Radio Free Europe/Radio Liberty (RFERL). "Russia Fails In Bid To Schedule UN Vote On Nuclear Treaty Spurned By Trump." *RFERL*, October 27, 2018, https://www.rferl.org/a/russia-fails-bid-schedule-un-vote-nuclear-treaty-inf-spurned-by-trump/29566690.html.

Rafael. *Welcome to Rafael.* 2018, http://www.rafael.co.il/4324-en/Marketing.aspx.

Rajan, Menon and Eugene Rumer. *Conflict in Ukraine. The Unwindling of the Post-Cold War Order*, Kindle. Cambridge, MA: The Massachusetts Institute of Technology Press, 2015.

Rashad, Marwa, Sarah Dadouch and Abdulrahman Al-Ansi. "Barrage of Missiles on Saudi Arabia Ramps up Yemen War." *Reuters,* March 26, 2018, https://www.reuters.com/article/us-yemen-security-missiles/barrage-of-missiles-on-saudi-arabia-ramps-up-yemen-war-idUSKBN1H21HQ.

Rayburn, Joel D., Frank K. Sobchak, Jeanne F. Godfroy, Matthew D. Morton, James S. Powell and Matthew M. Zais. *The US Army in the Iraq War, Vol. 1 Invasion – Insurgency – Civil War, 2003-2006, and Vol. 2 Surge and Withdrawal, 2007-2011.* Edited by Joel D. Rayburn and Frank K. Sobchak. Carlisle Barracks: US Army War College Press, 2019, https://ssi.armywarcollege.edu/pubs/download.cfm?q=1373.

Raytheon. *David's Sling Weapon System.* 2018, https://www.raytheon.com/capabilities/products/davidssling/.

————. *Iron Dome Weapon System. Short-Range Air Defense.* 2018, https://www.raytheon.com/capabilities/products/irondome/.

————. *Kill Vehicle.* 2019, http://www.raytheon.com/capabilities/products/ekv/.

————. *Patriot by the Numbers.* 2018, https://www.raytheon.com/sites/default/files/capabilities/rtnwcm/groups/public/documents/content/patriot-by-the-numbers-pdf.pdf.

————. *Raytheon Completes $9.2 Million Space Factory Expansion.* 2018, http://www.raytheon.com/news/feature/factory_expansion.html.

Reagan, Ronald. *A Strategy for Peace in the 80s, October 10, 1980.* 1980, https://www.reaganlibrary.gov/major-speeches-index/10-archives/reference/12-10-19-80.

————. *Address to the Nation on Defense and National Security, 23 March 1983.* 1983, https://www.reaganlibrary.archivep.gov/archives/speeches/1983/32383d.htm.

————. *Inaugural Address, January 20, 1981.* 1981, https://www.reaganlibrary.archives.gov/archives/speeches/1981/12081a.htm.

Rebolledo, Vicente Garrido and Belén Lara Fernández. "Is There a Missile Threat for Europe? Justifications for a European Missile Defence in Europe and in the Mediterranean." 2003, 411–427, https://doi.org/10.1007/978-3-642-55854-2_25.

Rempfer, Kyle. "European Mission for First Time since Cold War." *Military Times*, April 2, 2018, https://www.militarytimes.com/flashpoints/2018/04/02/us-air-defense-artillery-brigade-begins-new-european-mission-for-first-time-since-cold-war/.

Rennack, Diane. *North Korea: Economic Sanctions.* 2006, https://fas.org/sgp/crs/row/RL31696.pdf.

———. *North Korea: Legislative Basis for US Economic Sanctions.* 2019, https://fas.org/sgp/crs/row/R41438.pdf.

Rhyu, Sang-young and Jong-Yun Bae. "The Politics of Economic Sanctions against North Korea: The Bush Administration's Strategy toward a Multilateral Governance." *Pacific Focus* 25 (2010): 112–135, https://doi.org/10.1111/j.1976-5118.2010.01037.x.

Riedel, Bruce. *What You Need to Know about the Latest Houthi Attack on Riyadh, Brookings Institution.* 2018, https://www.brookings.edu/blog/order-from-chaos/2018/03/27/what-you-need-to-know-about-the-latest-houthi-attack-on-riyadh/.

Roberts, Brad. *The Case for US Nuclear Weapons in the 21ˢᵗ Century*, Kindle. Stanford: Stanford University Press, 2016.

Rogers, Keith. "North Korean Missiles Could Reach Las Vegas, Experts Say." *Las Vegas Review-Journal*, April 2017, https://www.reviewjournal.com/news/military/north-korean-missiles-could-reach-las-vegas-experts-say/.

Rogoway, Tyler. "North Korea Sends Missile Flying Over Japan (Updating Live)." *The Drive*, August 28, 2017, http://www.thedrive.com/the-war-zone/13898/north-korea-sends-missile-flying-over-japan-updating-live.

Rosefielde, Steven. *The Kremlin Strikes Back. Russia and the West after Crimea's Annexation*, Kindle. New York: Cambridge University Press, 2017.

Rosenau, William. *Special Operations Forces and Elusive Ground Targets. Lessons from Vietnam and the Persian Gulf War.* Santa Monica, 2001, https://www.rand.org/pubs/monograph_reports/MR1408.html.

Royce, Edward R. *Public Law 114-122, North Korea Sanctions and Policy Enhancement Act of 2016.* US Congress, 2016, https://www.congress.gov/114/plaws/publ122/PLAW-114publ122.pdf.

Rühle, Michael. "NATO and Extended Deterrence in a Multinuclear World." *Comparative Strategy* 28 (2009): 10–16, https://doi.org/10.1080/01495930802679686.

Rumsfeld, Donald H. *Annual Report to the President and the Congress.* 2002, http://history.defense.gov/Portals/70/Documents/annual_reports/2002_DoD_AR.pdf.

Rumsfeld, Donald H., Barry Blechman, Lee Butler, Richard Garwin, William Graham, William Schneider and others. *Executive Summary of the Report of the Commission to Assess the Ballistic Missile Threat to the United States (Pursuant to Public Law 201 104th Congress, July 15, 1998).* 1998, https://fas.org/irp/threat/bm-threat.htm.

Russett, Bruce. "The Calculus of Deterrence." *The Journal of Conflict Resolution* 7 (1963): 97–109, http://www.jstor.org/stable/172796.

———. *The Prisoners of Insecurity: Nuclear Deterrence, the Arms Race, and Arms Control.* San Francisco: W.H. Freeman, 1983, https://www.questia.com/read/98393071/the-prisoners-of-insecurity-nuclear-deterrence-the.

Sablière, Jean-Marc de La. *Letter Dated 13 October 2006 from the Permanent Representative of France to the United Nations Addressed to the President of the Security Council, S/2006/814.* 2006, https://undocs.org/S/2006/814.

Sakwa, Richard. *Frontline Ukraine. Crisis in the Borderlands,* Kindle, London: I. B. Tauris, 2016.

Salisbury, Peter. "The New Front in Yemen. What's at Stake in Hodeidah." *Foreign Affairs,* June 27, 2018, https://www.foreignaffairs.com/articles/middle-east/2018-06-27/new-front-yemen.

Salmoni, Barak, Bryce Loidolt, and Madeleine Wells. *Regime and Periphery in Northern Yemen: The Huthi Phenomenon*. Santa Monica: RAND, 2010.

Saltonstall, Leverett. "Western Military Strength and Security." *The Annals of the American Academy of Political and Social Science* 336 (1961): 62–74, https://www.jstor.org/stable/1032804.

Samson, Victoria. *American Missile Defense. Guide to the Issues*. Santa Barbara: Praeger, 2010.

Sanders, Sarah. *Press Briefing by Press Secretary Sarah Sanders, The White House, March 9, 2018*. 2018, https://www.whitehouse.gov/briefings-state ments/press-briefing-press-secretary-sarah-sanders-030918.

Sandford, Daniel. "Ukraine Crisis: What We Know about the Kiev Snipers." *BBC News*, April 3, 2014, http://www.bbc.com/news/world-eu rope-26866069.

Sanger, David and Mark Mazzetti. "Israel Struck Syrian Nuclear Project, Analysts Say." *The New York Times*, 2017 http://www.nytimes. com/2007/10/14/washington/14weapons.html.

Sankaran, Jaganath. "Missile Defense Against Iran Without Threatening Russia." *Arms Control Today*, 43 (2013), 15–21 http://www.jstor.org/ stable/23629550.

———. *The United States' European Phased Adaptive Approach Missile Defense System. Defending Against Iranian Threats Without Diluting the Russian Deterrent*, 2015 https://www.rand.org/pubs/research_reports/ RR957.html.

Schneider, Barry. *Future War and Counterproliferation: US Military Responses to NBC Proliferation Threats* (Westport: Praeger, 1999) https:// www.questia.com/read/15397470/future-war-and-counterprolifera tion-u-s-military.

Schofield, Julian. *Strategic Nuclear Sharing*. Houndmills: Palgrave Macmillan, 2014.

Schubert, Frank and Theresa Kraus. *The Whirlwind War. The United States Army in Operations Desert Shield and Desert Storm* http://www.history. army.mil/books/www/WWINDX.HTM.

Schulz, Thomas. *Letter to William J. Perry, The Secretary of Defense*, 1997 http://www.gao.gov/assets/90/86108.pdf.

Security Council Report. *UN Documents for Yemen*, 2018 https://www. securitycouncilreport.org/un-documents/yemen.

Seligman, Lara. "Trump's Muscular New Plan to Fend Off Russian and Chinese Missiles." *Foreign Policy*, January 2019 https://foreignpolicy. com/2019/01/17/trumps-muscular-new-plan-to-fend-off-russian-and-chinese-missiles-missile-defense-space/.

Serr, Marcel. "Understanding the War in Yemen." *Israel Journal of Foreign Affairs*, 11 (2017), 357–69 https://doi.org/10.1080/23739770.2017. 1419405.

Shapir, Yiftah. "How Many Rockets Did Iron Dome Shoot Down?" *The Institute for National Security Studies (INSS)*, 2013, http://www.inss. org.il/publication/how-many-rockets-did-iron-dome-shoot-down/.

Sharkov, Damien. "Ukraine Has Found the Weapon Used in the 'Maidan Massacre.'" *Newsweek*, July 14, 2016, http://www.newsweek.com/ ukraine-claims-find-sniper-maidan-massacre-480406.

Sharp, Jane M. O. "The Problem of Extended Deterrence in NATO." On *Arms Control and Disarmament*, 169–181. Edited by Paolo Foradori, Giampiero Giacomello, and Alessandro Pascolini. Cham: Springer International Publishing, 2018, https://doi.org/10.1007/978-3-319-62259-0_13.

Sharp, Jeremy. *US Foreign Aid to Israel*. Washington DC, 2018.

———. *Yemen: Civil War and Regional Intervention*. Washington DC, 2018, https://fas.org/sgp/crs/mideast/R43960.pdf.

Sharp, Jeremy and Christopher Blanchard. *The War in Yemen: A Compilation of Legislation in the 115th Congress*. Washington DC, 2018, https://fas.org/sgp/crs/mideast/R45046.pdf.

Shay, Shaul. "Iranian Rocketry in the Service of the Houthis in Yemen." *IsraelDefense*, 2016, http://www.israeldefense.co.il/en/content/irani an-rocketry-service-houthis-yemen.

Shield, Ralph. "The Saudi Air War in Yemen: A Case for Coercive Success through Battlefield Denial." *Journal of Strategic Studies* 41 (2018): 461–489, https://doi.org/10.1080/01402390.2017.1308863.

Shuey, Robert. *Theater Missile Defense: Issues for Congress* (Washington DC, 2001) http://www.au.af.mil/au/awc/awcgate/crs/ib98028.pdf.

Sieradka, Monika. "Poland Supports US Withdrawal from INF." *Deutsche Welle*, October 25, 2018, https://www.dw.com/en/poland-supports-us-withdrawal-from-inf/a-46049028.

Signorino, Curtis S. and Ahmer Tarar. "A Unified Theory and Test of Extended Immediate Deterrence." *American Journal of Political Science* 50 (2006): 586–605.

Simmons, Katie, Bruce Stokes and Jacob Poushter. *NATO Publics Blame Russia for Ukrainian Crisis but Reluctant to Provide Military Aid. In Russia, Anti-Western Views and Support for Putin Surge.* 2015, http://assets.pewresearch.org/wp-content/uploads/sites/2/2015/06/Pew-Research-Center-Russia-Ukraine-Report-FINAL-June-10-2015.pdf.

Simpson, John. "Russia's Crimea Plan Detailed, Secret and Successful." *BBC News*, March 19, 2014, http://www.bbc.com/news/world-europe-26644082.

Singer, J. David. *Deterrence, Arms Control, and Disarmament: Toward a Synthesis in National Security Policy* (Columbus: Ohio State University, 1962)

Siouris, George. *Missile Guidance and Control Systems* (New York: Springer, 2004)

Siperco, Ian. "Shield of David: The Promise of Israeli National Missile Defense." *Middle East Policy*, XVII (2010): 127–141, http://www.mepc.org/shield-david-promise-israeli-national-missile-defense.

SIPRI. *SIPRI Military Expenditure Database 1949-2018.* 2019, https://www.sipri.org/sites/default/files/SIPRI-Milex-data-1949-2018_0.xlsx.

Sloan, Elinor. *Modern Military Strategy. An Introduction.* New York: Routledge, 2017.

SMDC/ARSTRAT Historical Office. "An Old Concept for a New Era in

Missile Defense." *The Eagle*, 2007, http://www.smdc.army.mil/2008/ Historical/Eagle/HittoKill-AnOldConceptforaNewErainMissileDe fense.pdf.

Smith, Alastair. "Extended Deterrence and Alliance Formation." *International Interactions* 24 (1998): 315–343.

Smith, Rick. *100 Years of Possibility: Celebrating the Centennial Birthday of Dr. Wernher von Braun*. 2012, https://www.nasa.gov/topics/history/ features/vonbraun.html.

Smithsonian National Air and Space Museum. *Missile, Surface-To-Surface, Liquid Propellant, Hermes A-1*. 2019, https://airandspace.si.edu/col lection-objects/missile-surface-surface-liquid-propellant-hermes-1.

―――. *V-2 Missile*. 2019, https://airandspace.si.edu/collection-objects /missile-surface-surface-v-2-4.

Sneh, Ephraim. *Navigating Perilous Waters: An Israeli Strategy for Peace and Security*. London: Routledge, 2005.

Snyder, Glenn. "The Balance of Power and the Balance of Terror." In *Balance of Power*. Edited by Paul Seabury. San Francisco: Chandler Publishing Company, 1965.

Snyder, Scott. *Confronting the North Korean Threat: Reassessing Policy Options, Statement before the United States Senate Committee on Foreign Relations, US Senate, 1ˢᵗ Session, 115th Congress, January 31, 2017*. 2017, https://www.foreign.senate.gov/imo/media/doc/013117_Snyder_ Testimony.pdf.

Spearman, M. Leroy. *Historical Development of Worldwide Guided Missiles*. 1983, https://ntrp.nasa.gov/archive/nasa/casi.ntrp.nasa.gov/19 830027720.pdf.

Spring, Baker and Michaela Bendikova. *Israel and the Iron Dome System: A Lesson for the United States*. Washington DC, https://www.heritage. org/defense/report/israel-and-the-iron-dome-system-lesson-the-united-states.

Spring, Baker and James Gattuso. *"Brilliant Pebbles": The Revolutionary Idea for Strategic Defense*. The Backgrounder, 1990, http://s3.amazon aws.com/thf_media/1990/pdf/bg748.pdf.

Steff, Reuben. *Strategic Thinking, Deterrence and the US Ballistic Missile Defense Project From Truman to Obama.* Farnham: Ashgate, 2013.

Stocker, Jeremy. "Nuclear Deterrence." *The Adelphi Papers* 46 (2007): 43–60, https://doi.org/10.1080/05679320701266356.

Stoil, Rebecca Shimoni. "US House Okays Funding Boost for Israel's Missile Defense." *The Times of Israel,* June 17, 2016, http://www.timesof israel.com/us-house-okays-huge-funding-for-israels-missile-dfense/.

Stratfor. "Azerbaijan: Deal Reached With Israel for Iron Dome." December 19, 2016, https://worldview.stratfor.com/article/azerbaijan-deal-reached-israel-iron-dome.

———. *In Zapad Exercises, Russia Flexes Its Military Strength.* 2009, https://www.stratfor.com/article/zapad-exercises-russia-flexes-its-military-strength.

———. *North Korea: Pyongyang Invites US Dialogue and Washington Considers Its Next Steps, March 9, 2018.* 2018, https://worldview.strat for.com/article/north-korea-unied-states-dialogue-denuclearization-talks-trump-kim-meeting.

———. *North Korea: Pyongyang Launches Its Longest-Range Missile Yet, November 28, 2017.* 2017, https://worldview.stratfor.com/article/north-korea-pyongyang-launches-its-longest-range-missile-yet.

———. *Poland: President Supports US Departure From Nuclear Proliferation Treaty, October 26, 2018.* 2018, https://worldview.stratfor.com/situation-report/poland-president-supports-us-departure-nuclear-proliferation-treaty.

———. *Poland: Warsaw's Push for a US Base Faces and Uphill Climb, September 19, 2018.* 2018, https://worldview.stratfor.com/article/poland-warsaw-tries-win-washington-approval-us-base-polish-soil.

———. *Russia, US: What To Make of an Accusation of a Test Ban Treaty Violation,* 2019, https://worldview.stratfor.com/article/russia-us-what-make-accusation-test-ban-treaty-violation-nuclear-arms-race.

———. *Russia: European Countries Will Be Targeted If They Host US Nuclear Missiles, Putin Says,* 2018 https://worldview.stratfor.com/situa

tion-report/russia-european-countries-will-be-targeted-if-they-host-us-nuclear-missiles-putin.

———. *Russia: UN Draft Resolution to Preserve INF Treaty*, 2018, https://worldview.stratfor.com/situation-report/russia-un-draft-resolution-preserve-inf-treaty.

———. "Saudi Arabia, Yemen: What's Next for Red Sea Oil Shipments After Houthi Attack." July https://worldview.stratfor.com/article/saudi-arabia-yemen-whats-next-red-sea-oil-shipments-houthi-attack-strait-ship.

———. *Saudi Arabia: King Salman Orders Restructuring of Saudi Intelligence Personnel, October 22, 2018*, 2018, https://worldview.stratfor.com/situation-report/saudi-arabia-king-salman-orders-restructuring-saudi-intelligence-personnel.

———. "Saudi Arabia: Missile Strikes on Riyadh Mark Third Anniversary of War on Houthis." March 26, 2018, https://worldview.stratfor.com/article/saudi-arabia-missile-strikes-riyadh-mark-third-anniversary-war-houthis.

———. "Saudi Arabia: Oil Shipments Through Bab El-Mandeb Strait Resumed." August 2, 2018, https://worldview.stratfor.com/situation-report/saudi-arabia-oil-shipments-through-bab-el-mandeb-strait-resumed.

———. *Saudi Arabia: U.N. Report Turns Up the Heat on Crown Prince Over Khashoggi Murder, June 19, 2019*, 2019, https://www.stratfor.com/situation-report/saudi-arabia-un-report-turns-heat-crown-prince-over-khashoggi-murder-mbs.

———. *Stuck Between the US and the EU, Poland Explores Its Options, July 10, 2018*, 2018, https://worldview.stratfor.com/article/stuck-between-us-and-eu-poland-explores-its-options.

———. *The History of North Korea's Nuclear Arsenal*, 2017 https://www.stratfor.com/api/v3/pdf/283911.

———. *The Inter-Korean Summit, in Summary*, 2018 https://worldview.stratfor.com/article/inter-korean-summit-north-korea-south-us.

———. *The Missile Arsenal at the Heart of the Israeli-Iranian Rivalry*, 8 August 2018 https://worldview.stratfor.com/article/missile-arsenal-heart-israeli-iranian-rivalry.

———. *US, Saudi Arabia: CIA Concludes Saudi Crown Prince Ordered Khashoggi's Killing, Report Says, November 17, 2018*, 2018, https://worldview.stratfor.com/situation-report/us-saudi-arabia-cia-concludes-saudi-crown-prince-ordered-khashoggis-killing-report.

———. *US Diplomat Floats the Idea of a Treaty With Iran, September 19, 2018*, 2018, https://worldview.stratfor.com/article/us-diplomat-floats-idea-treaty-iran-nuclear-deal.

———. *Why North Korea Won't Stop, September 3, 2017*, 2017, https://worldview.stratfor.com/article/why-north-korea-wont-stop.

———. *Why Turkey Isn't Burning Bridges With Saudi Arabia Over Khashoggi, October 29, 2018*, 2018, https://worldview.stratfor.com/article/why-turkey-isnt-burning-bridges-saudi-arabia-over-khashoggi.

Sullivan, Jeremiah, Dan Fenstermacher, Daniel Fisher, Ruth Howes, O'Dean Judd and Roger Speed. "Technical Debate over Patriot Performance in the Gulf War." *Science & Global Security* 8 (1999): 41–98.

Świerczyński, Marek. "Gdzie Te Patrioty?" *Polityka* 3143 (2018): 22–23.

———. "Offset Na Miarę (Małych) Możliwości." *Polityka Insight*, March 24, 2018, https://www.polityka.pl/tygodnikpolityka/kraj/1742944,1,polska-na-ostatniej-prostej-do-podpisania-kontraktu-na-patrioty.read.

Syring, James D. *Department of Defense Briefing by Vice Adm. Syring on the Fiscal Year 2016 Missile Defense Agency Budget Request in the Pentagon Briefing Room, February 2, 2015*. 2015, https://www.defense.gov/News/Transcripts/Transcript-View/Article/607005/department-of-defense-briefing-by-vice-adm-syring-on-the-fiscal-year-2016-missi/.

———. *Statement before the House Armed Service Committee Subcommittee on Strategic Forces, June 7, 2017*, 2017, https://www.mda.mil/global/documents/pdf/FY18_WrittenStatement_HASC_SFP.PDF.

———. *Unclassified Statement of Vice Admiral James D. Syring, Director,*

Missile Defense Agency, Before the House Armed Service Committee Subcommittee on Strategic Forces, March 25, 2014, 2014, https://www.mda.mil/global/documents/pdf/ps_syring_032514_HASC.pdf.

Szabó, Kinga. *Anticipatory Action in Self Defense. Essence and Limits under International Law* Berlin: Springer, 2011.

Taylor, Maxwell D. *The Uncertain Trumpet.* New York: Harper & Brothers, 1960.

Teller, Edward. "The Ultimate Defense, 2002." In *Memoirs: A Twentieth-Century Journey in Science and Politics,* ed. by Hoover Institution. Perseus Publishers, http://www.hoover.org/research/ultimate-defense.

Teller, Edward and Judith Schoolery *Memoirs. A Twentieth-Century Journey in Science and Politics.* Cambridge, Massachusetts: Perseus Publishers, 2001.

The Economist. "America Tears up an Arms Treaty and Harms Itself." October 2018, https://www.economist.com/united-states/2018/10/25/america-tears-up-an-arms-treaty-and-harms-itself.

————. "Russia Is Undermining a Symbol of Cold War Diplomacy." December 2017, https://www.economist.com/europe/2017/12/09/russia-is-undermining-a-symbol-of-cold-war-diplomacy.

————. "The Economist Explains. What Are the Minsk Agreements? The Plan to Bring Lasting Peace to Ukraine Is Riddled with Loose Language." September 2016, http://www.economist.com/blogs/economist-explains/2016/09/economist-explains-7.

The Korean Culture and Information Service (KOCIS). *Panmunjeom Declaration on Peace, Prosperity and Reunification of the Korean Peninsula, April 27, 2018,* 2018, http://www.korea.net/Government/Current-Affairs/National-Affairs/view?subId=641&affairId=656&pageIndex=1&articleId=3412.

The Mainichi. " Japan Decides to Introduce New Missile Defense amid N. Korea Threat." December 19, 2017, https://mainichi.jp/english/articles/20171219/p2g/00m/0dm/045000c.

The New Arab. "Saudi Arabia 'Looking to Buy' Israel's Iron Dome System." January 9, 2018, https://www.alaraby.co.uk/english/news/2018/1/9/saudi-arabia-looking-to-buy-israels-iron-dome-system.

The Washington Post. *Putin's Prepared Remarks at 43rd Munich Conference on Security Policy, February 12, 2007 (Transcript)*, 2007, http://www.washingtonpost.com/wp-dyn/content/article/2007/02/12/AR2007021200555.html.

The White House. *ABM Treaty Fact Sheet*, 2001, https://georgewbush-whitehouse.archives.gov/news/releases/2001/12/20011213-2.html.

————. *Dr. Rice Discusses Bilateral Meeting of President Bush and Russian President Putin, July 22, 2001*, 2001, https://georgewbush-whitehouse.archives.gov/news/releases/2001/07/20010722-7.html.

————. *Fact Sheet: Implementing Missile Defense in Europe, September 15, 2011*, 2011, https://obamawhitehouse.archives.gov/the-press-office/2011/09/15/fact-sheet-implementing-missile-defense-europe.

————. *Fact Sheet: Memorandum of Understanding Reached with Israel*, 2016, https://obamawhitehouse.archives.gov/the-press-office/2016/09/14/fact-sheet-memorandum-understanding-reached-israel.

————. *Joint Fact Sheet: The United States-Republic of Korea Alliance: A Global Partnership*, 2014, https://obamawhitehouse.archives.gov/the-press-office/2014/04/25/joint-fact-sheet-united-states-republic-korea-alliance-global-partnershi.

————. *Joint Statement between the United States and the Republic of Korea, June 30, 2017*, 2017, https://www.whitehouse.gov/briefings-statements/joint-statement-united-states-republic-korea/.

————. *Joint Statement of President Donald J. Trump of the United States of America and Chairman Kim Jong Un of the Democratic People's Republic of Korea at the Singapore Summit, June 12, 2018*, 2018, https://www.whitehouse.gov/briefings-statements/joint-statement-president-donald-j-trump-united-states-america-chairman-kim-jong-un-democratic-peoples-republic-korea-singapore-summit/.

————. *National Security Strategy (NSS) of the United States of America. Introduction of Donald J. Trump*, 2017, https://www.whitehouse.gov/wp-content/uploads/2017/12/NSS-Final-12-18-2017-0905.pdf.

———. *President Holds Prime Time News Conference, October 11, 2001,* 2001, https://georgewbush-whitehouse.archives.gov/news/releases/2001/10/20011011-7.html.

———. *President Trump in Poland, July 6, 2017,* 2017, https://www.whitehouse.gov/articles/president-trump-poland/.

———. *President Trump Says the Iran Deal Is Defective at Its Core. A New One Will Require Real Commitments, May 11, 2018,* 2018, https://www.whitehouse.gov/articles/president-trump-says-iran-deal-defective-core-new-one-will-require-real-commitments/.

———. *Press Briefing by National Security Advisor Condoleezza Rice, June 15, 2001,* 2001, https://georgewbush-whitehouse.archives.gov/news/releases/2001/06/20010615-2.html.

———. *Press Briefing by National Security Advisor Condoleezza Rice on President's Travel to Europe, June 6, 2001,* 2001, https://georgewbush-whitehouse.archives.gov/news/releases/2001/06/20010606-6.html.

———. *Press Conference by President Bush and President Putin, (Genoa, Italy), July 22, 2001,* 2001, https://georgewbush-whitehouse.archives.gov/news/releases/2001/07/20010722-3.html.

———. *Press Conference by President Bush and Russian Federation President Putin, (Brdo Pri Kranju, Slovenia), June 16, 2001,* 2001, https://georgewbush-whitehouse.archives.gov/news/releases/2001/06/20010618.html.

———. *Remarks by President Trump and Chairman Kim Jong Un of the Democratic People's Republic of Korea in a 1:1 Conversation, Hanoi, Vietnam, February 27, 2019,* 2019, https://www.whitehouse.gov/briefings-statements/remarks-president-trump-chairman-kim-jong-un-democratic-peoples-republic-korea-11-conversation-hanoi-vietnam/.

———. *Remarks by President Trump and President Duda of the Republic of Poland in Joint Press Conference, September 18, 2018,* 2018, https://www.whitehouse.gov/briefings-statements/remarks-president-trump-president-duda-republic-poland-joint-press-conference/.

———. *Remarks by President Trump Before Air Force One Departure, October 20, 2018,* 2018, https://www.whitehouse.gov/briefings-state

ments/remarks-president-trump-air-force-one-departure-4/.

————. *Response to Russian Statement on US ABM Treaty Withdrawal, December 13, 2001,* 2001, https://georgewbush-whitehouse.archives.gov/news/releases/2001/12/20011213-8.html.

————. *Statement by the Press Secretary on Saudi Arabia and Yemen,* December 21, 2017 ,https://www.whitehouse.gov/briefings-statements/statement-press-secretary-saudi-arabia-yemen.

————. *Statement by the Press Secretary on the Houthi Missile Strike on a Turkish Wheat Ship,* May 25, 2018, https://www.whitehouse.gov/briefings-statements/statement-press-secretary-houthi-missile-strike-turkish-wheat-ship/.

The White House (NSS 2002). *National Security Strategy (NSS) of the United States of America.* Washington DC, 2002, https://www.state.gov/documents/organization/63562.pdf.

The White House (NSS 2010). *National Security Strategy (NSS), May 2010.* 2010, https://obamawhitehouse.archives.gov/sites/default/files/rss_viewer/national_security_strategy.pdf.

The White House (NSS 2015). *National Security Strategy (NSS), February 2015.* 2015, https://obamawhitehouse.archives.gov/sites/default/files/docs/2015_national_security_strategy_2.pdf.

The White House (NSS 2017). *National Security Strategy (NSS) of the United States of America.* 2017, https://www.whitehouse.gov/wp-content/uploads/2017/12/NSS-Final-12-18-2017-0905.pdf.

The White House Office of Managament and Budget. *Historical Tables.* 2019, https://www.whitehouse.gov/wp-content/uploads/2019/03/hist-fy2020.pdf.

Thränert, Oliver. "NATO, Missile Defence and Extended Deterrence." *Survival* 51 (2009): 63–76, https://doi.org/10.1080/00396330903461674.

Times of Israel. "Saudi Arabia 'Rejects Israeli Offer to Supply Iron Dome.'" May 23, 2015, http://www.timesofisrael.com/saudi-arabia-rejected-israeli-offer-of-iron-dome/?fb_comment_id=72077902136

6241_720924811351662#f268bdd6541325.

Traynor, Ian. "Ukraine's Bloodiest Day: Dozens Dead as Kiev Protesters Regain Territory from Police." *The Guardian*, February 21, 2014, https://www.theguardian.com/world/2014/feb/20/ukraine-dead-protesters-police.

Trump, Donald J. "Donald J. Trump." https://www.donaldjtrump.com/.

———. *Remarks by President Trump to the People of Poland, July 6, 2017.* 2017, https://www.whitehouse.gov/briefings-statements/remarks-president-trump-people-poland/.

———. *State of the Union Address.* 2018, https://www.whitehouse.gov/briefings-statements/remarks-president-trump-state-union-address/.

———. *Statement by President Donald J. Trump on the Nuclear Posture Review, February 2, 2018.* 2018, https://www.whitehouse.gov/briefings-statements/statement-president-donald-j-trump-nuclear-posture-review/.

US Army Acquisition Corps. *Patriot Overview*, 2013, https://www.msl.army.mil/Documents/Briefings/LTPO/LTPO.pdf.

US Army Center of Military History. *History of Strategic Air and Ballistic Missile Defense, Vol. I, 1945-1955.* 1975, http://www.history.army.mil/html/books/bmd/BMDV1.pdf.

US Army Financial Management & Comptroller. *US Army Justification Book of Missile Procurement. FY 2018 Budget Amendment.* 2017, https://www.asafm.army.mil/documents/BudgetMaterial/FY2018/MSLS_Army_FY18 BA_20171108.pdf.

US Army Program Executive Office Missiles & Space. *Lower Tier Project Office.* 2018, https://www.msl.army.mil/Pages/ltpo/patriot.html.

US Army Space and Missile Defense Command & MDA. *Ground-Based Midcourse Defense (GMD) Extended Test Range (ETR), Final Environmental Impact Statement, Volume 1 of 3: Chapters 1-4.* 2003, https://www.mda.mil/global/documents/pdf/env_gmd_etr_covch2.pdf.

US Congress. *National Defense Authorization (NDA) Act for Fiscal Year 2018, Public Law 115-91, December 12, 2017.* 2017, https://www.

govinfo.gov/content/pkg/PLAW-115publ91/pdf/PLAW-115publ
91.pdf.

———. *National Missile Defense Act of 1999, Public Law 106-38, 106th Congress, July 22, 1999.* 1999, https://www.congress.gov/106/plaws/publ38/PLAW-106publ38.pdf.

———.*North Korea Nonproliferation Act, October 13, 2006.* 2006, http://uscode.house.gov/statutes/pl/109/353.pdf.

US Congress (sponsor John McCain). *National Defense Authorization Act for Fiscal Year 2017, Public Law 114-328, January 4, 2016.* Washington DC: US Congress, 2016, 2000–2968, https://www.congress.gov/bill/114th-congress/senate-bill/2943/text.

US Congress (sponsor Mac Thornberry). *National Defense Authorization Act for Fiscal Year 2018, House of Representatives (H.R.) 2810.* US House of Representatives, 2017, https://www.congress.gov/115/bills/hr2810/BILLS-115hr2810enr.pdf,https://www.congress.gov/bill/115th-congress/house-bill/2810.

US Department of Defense. *Joint News Conference with Secretary Mattis and South Korean Defense Minister Song Young-Moo in Seoul, October 27, 2017.* 2017, https://www.defense.gov/News/Transcripts/Transcript-View/Article/1356752/joint-news-conference-with-secretary-mattis-and-south-korean-defense-minister-s/.

———. *Press Statement 8th Korea-US Integrated Defense Dialogue (KIDD) September 24, 2015.* 2015, https://www.defense.gov/Portals/1/Documents/pubs/Press_Statement_8th_KIDD_Sep24_OSD_FINAL.pdf.

US Department of Defense. *Missile Defense Review.* 2019, https://media.defense.gov/2019/Jan/17/2002080666/-1/-1/1/2019-MISSILE-DEFENSE-REVIEW.PDF.

US Department of Defense. *Nuclear Posture Review. Executive Summary.* 2018,https://media.defense.gov/2018/Feb/02/2001872886/-1/-1/1/2018-NUCLEAR-POSTURE-REVIEW-FINAL-REPORT.PDF.

———. *Nuclear Posture Review.* 2018, https://media.defense.gov/2018/Feb/02/2001872886/-1/-1/1/2018-NUCLEAR-POSTURE-RE-

VIEW-FINAL-REPORT.PDF.

US Department of Defense (QDR) Donald H. Rumsfeld. *Quadrennial Defense Review Report (QDR), February 6, 2006.* Washington DC, 2006. http://archive.defense.gov/pubs/pdfs/QDR20060203.pdf.

US Department of State. *Adherence to and Compliance with Arms Control, Nonproliferation, and Disarmament Agreements and Commitments.* 2018, https://www.state.gov/documents/organization/280774.pdf.

————. *Agreement between the Government of the United States of America and the Government of the Republic of Poland Concerning the Deployment of Ground-Based Ballistic Missile Defense Interceptors in the Territory of the Republic of Poland, Done at Warsaw, 20th.* 2011, https://www.state.gov/documents/organization/180542.pdf.

————. *Annual Report on Implementation of the New Start Treaty, January 2018.* 2018, https://www.state.gov/wp-content/uploads/2019/05/AVC-New-START-January-2018.pdf.

————. *Annual Report on the Implementation of the New Start Treaty, January 2016.* 2016, https://www.state.gov/t/avc/rls/rpt/2016/255558.htm.

————. *Annual Report on the Implementation of the New Start Treaty, January 2017.* 2017, https://www.state.gov/annual-report-on-implementation-of-the-new-start-treaty-2017/.

————. *Annual Report on the Implementation of the New Start Treaty, January 31, 2012.* 2012, https://www.state.gov/t/avc/rls/rpt/197087.htm.

————. *Diplomacy in Action, Intermediate-Range Nuclear Forces (INF) Treaty.* 2018, https://www.state.gov/t/avc/inf/index.htm.

————. *INF Treaty: At a Glance, Fact Sheet.* 2017, https://www.state.gov/inf-treaty-at-a-glance/.

————. *Iran, Syria and North Korea Nonproliferation Act (INKSNA).* 2019, https://www.state.gov/t/isn/inksna/.

————. *Iran and Syria Nonproliferation Act Sanctions.* 2017, https://www.state.gov/iran-north-korea-and-syria-nonproliferation-act-sanctions/.

————. *Joint Statement of the Fourth Round of the Six-Party Talks, Beijing, September 19, 2005.* 2005, https://www.state.gov/p/eap/regional/c15455.htm.

————. *New START.* 2019, https://www.state.gov/t/avc/newstart/.

————. *New START Treaty Aggregate Number of Strategic Offensive Arms, April 1, 2014.* 2014, http://www.state.gov/documents/organization/224449.pdf.

————. *New START Treaty Aggregate Numbers of Strategic Offensive Arms Fact Sheet, March 1, 2019.* 2019, https://www.state.gov/wp-content/uploads/2019/05/AVC-03012019.pdf.

————. *Office of Strategic Stability and Deterrence Affairs (AVC/SSD).* 2018, https://www.state.gov/t/avc/c23758.htm.

————. *Protocol Amending the Agreement between the Government of the United States of America and the Government of the Republic of Poland Concerning the Deployment of Ground-Based Ballistic Missile Defense Interceptors in the Territory of the Republic of Poland.* 2010, https://www.state.gov/documents/organization/180543.pdf.

————. *Refuting Russian Allegations of US Noncompliance with the INF Treaty, Fact Sheet.* https://www.state.gov/refuting-russian-allegations-of-u-s-noncompliance-with-the-inf-treaty/.

————. *Report on the Reasons That Continued Implementation of the New Start Treaty Is in the National Security Interests of the United States.* 2018, https://www.state.gov/wp-content/uploads/2019/05/AVC-New-START-December-2018.pdf.

————. *Treaty Between The United States of America and The Union of Soviet Socialist Republics on The Limitation of Anti-Ballistic Missile Systems (ABM Treaty).* 2017, https://2009-2017.state.gov/t/avc/trty/101888.htm.

————. *US Response to the Russian Federation's INF Treaty Violation: Integrated Strategy.* 2017, https://www.state.gov/u-s-response-to-the-russian-federations-inf-treaty-violation-integrated-strategy/.

US Department of State Archive. *Baghdad Pact (1955) and Central Treaty Organization (CENTO).* 2009, https://2001-2009.state.gov/r/pa/ho/time/lw/98683.htm.

US Department of State Office of the Historian. *Milestones: 1953-1960. Southeast Asia Treaty Organization (SEATO), 1954*. 2018, https://history.state.gov/milestones/1953-1960/seato.

————. *Milestones in the History of US Foreign Relations, Ending the Vietnam War, 1969-1973*. 2018, https://history.state.gov/milestones/1969-1976/ending-vietnam.

US Department of Treasury. *Determination Pursuant to Subsection 2(a)(i) of the Executive Order of March 16, 2016*. 2016, https://www.treasury.gov/resource-center/sanctions/Programs/Documents/nk_determination_20160316.pdf.

————. *Treasury Sanctions 17 Individuals for Their Roles in the Killing of Jamal Khashoggi, November 15, 2018*. https://home.treasury.gov/news/press-releases/sm547.

US Department of Treasury Office of Foreign Assets Control. *North Korea Sanctions Program*. 2016, https://www.treasury.gov/resource-center/sanctions/Programs/Documents/nkorea.pdf.

————. *Ukraine-/Russia-Related Sanctions*. 2019, https://www.treasury.gov/resource-center/sanctions/Programs/Pages/ukraine.aspx.

————. *Ukraine/Russia-Related Sanctions Program*. 2016, https://www.treasury.gov/resource-center/sanctions/Programs/Documents/ukraine.pdf.

US Embassy & Consulate in Poland. *United States and Poland Start Construction of Redzikowo Missile Defense Facility, May 18, 2016*. 2016, https://pl.usembassy.gov/facility.

US Embassy in Romania. *A "Phased, Adaptive Approach" for Missile Defense in Europe*. 2016, https://ro.usembassy.gov/a-phased-adaptive-approach-for-missile-defense-in-europe/.

US Embassy in Yemen. *Joint Statement by France, Germany, the United Kingdom, and the United States*. February 27, 2018, https://ye.usembassy.gov/pr-02282018/.

US Embassy Warsaw. *US Congressional Delegation Visits Redzikowo, April 19, 2017*. 2017 https://pl.usembassy.gov/u-s-congressional-delegation-visits-redzikowo/.

———. *United States and Poland Start Construction of Redzikowo Missile Defense Facility, May 18, 2016.* 2016 https://pl.usembassy.gov/facility/.

US House of Representatives. *National Defense Authorization Act FY 2019, H.R. 5515, June 5, 2018.* US House of Representatives, 2018, https://www.congress.gov/115/bills/hr5515/BILLS-115hr5515pcs.pdf.

———. *Report of the Committee on Armed Services House of Representatives on National Defense Authorization Act FY 2019, May 15, 2018.* 2018 https://www.congress.gov/115/crpt/hrpt676/CRPT-115hrpt676.pdf.

US Navy. *Fact File. Guided Missile Submarines - SSGN.* 2019, https://www.navy.mil/navydata/fact_display.asp?cid=4100&ct=4&tid=300.

US Strategic Command (DO JOC) James E. Cartwright. *Deterrence Operations Joint Operating Concept (DO JOC).* Washington, DC, 2006, http://www.jcs.mil/Portals/36/Documents/Doctrine/concepts/joc_deterrence.pdf?ver=2017-12-28-162015-337.

UN General Assembly. *Resolution Adopted by the General Assembly on 27 March 2014, 68/262, Territorial Integrity of Ukraine.* 2014, http://www.un.org/en/ga/search/view_doc.asp?symbol=A/RES/68/262.

UN Security Council. *Resolution 1874 (2009), June 12, 2009.* 2009, http://www.un.org/en/ga/search/view_doc.asp?symbol=S/RES/1874(2009).

———. *Resolution 2087 (2013), January 22, 2013.* 2013, http://www.un.org/en/ga/search/view_doc.asp?symbol=S/RES/2087(2013).

———. *Resolution 2094 (2013), March 7, 2013.* 2013, http://www.un.org/en/ga/search/view_doc.asp?symbol=S/RES/2094(2013).

———. *United Kingdom of Great Britain and Northern Ireland: Draft Resolution, S/2018/156,* UN Security Council, 2018, http://digitallibrary.un.org/record/1473784/files/S_2018_156-EN.pdf.

ted Nations. *Package of Measures for the Implementation of the Minsk greements.* 2015, http://peacemaker.un.org/sites/peacemaker.un rg/files/UA_150212_MinskAgreement_en.pdf.

———. *Saudi Arabia in Spotlight as UN-Appointed Independent Investigator Publishes Full Khashoggi Findings, June 19, 2019.* 2019, https://news.un.org/en/story/2019/06/1040821.

———. *Security Council Renews Sanctions against Yemen, Rejects Alternate Draft after Veto by Russian Federation.* February 26, 2018, https://www.un.org/press/en/2018/sc13225.doc.htm.

United Nations Office for Disarmament Affairs. *Comprehensive Nuclear-Test-Ban Treaty (CTBT).* 2019, https://www.un.org/disarmament/wmd/nuclear/ctbt/.

University, Cambridge. *The Papers of Sir Robert Cockburn.* 2019, https://janus.lib.cam.ac.uk/db/node.xsp?id=EAD%2FGBR%2F0014%2FROCO.

UNSC. *UNSC Resolution 1695 (2006), July 15.* United Nations Security Council, 2006, http://www.un.org/en/ga/search/view_doc.asp?symbol=S/RES/1695(2006).

———. *UNSC Resolution 1718 (2006), October 14.* United Nations Security Council, http://www.un.org/en/ga/search/view_doc.asp?symbol=S/RES/1718(2006).

———. *UNSC Resolution 2270 (2016), March 2.* 2016, http://www.un.org/en/ga/search/view_doc.asp?symbol=S/RES/2270(2016).

Valenta, Marko and Jo Jakobsen. "Nexus of Armed Conflicts and Migrations to the Gulf: Migrations to the GCC from War-Torn Source Countries in Asia, Africa and the Arab Neighbourhood." *Middle Eastern Studies* 54 (2018): 22–47, https://doi.org/10.1080/00263206.2017.1365058.

Valento, Anthony J. *Report of Organizational Actions Affecting Basis of Securities, Orbital ATK, Inc.* 2015, http://investor.northropgrumman.com/static-files/4ed20b33-b405-4ac1-95a8-91ec553367bd.

Vandiver, John. "US Deployed Patriot Missiles to Lithuania for Multinational War Games." *Stars & Stripes*, 2017, https://www.stripes.com/news/europe/us-deployed-patriot-missiles-to-lithuania-for-multinational-war-games-1.477426.

Viner, Jacob. "The Implications of the Atomic Bomb for International Relations." *Proceedings of the American Philosophical Society* 90 (1946): 53–58, http://www.jstor.org/stable/3301039.

Voice of America News. "Agreement to Send Armed European Police Force to Eastern Ukraine." October 16, 2016, https://www.voanews.com/a/germany-hosts-meeting-to-review-minsk-agreements-on-ukraine/3557662.html.

Walton, Dale C. "Weapons of Mass Destruction." In *Understanding Modern Warfare*, Kindle, 377–432. Cambridge: Cambridge University Press, 2016.

Weinberger, Sharon. "The Most Outlandish Ideas for Missile Defence Systems." *BBC Future*, 2013, http://www.bbc.com/future/story/20130805-rise-and-fall-of-missile-defences.

Weinthal, Benjamin. "Report: Saudi Arabia Sought to Buy Israel's Iron Dome System." *Jerusalem Post*, January 9, 2018, https://www.jpost.com/Middle-East/Report-Saudi-Arabia-sought-to-buy-Israels-Iron-Dome-system-533185.

Weir, Shelagh. *A Tribal Order: Politics and Law in the Mountains of Yemen.* Austin: University of Texas Press, 2007.

Werrell, Kenneth P. *Archie to SAM. A Short Operational History of Ground-Based Air Defense.* Maxwell Air Force Base, 2005, http://www.dtic.mil/dtic/tr/fulltext/u2/a439255.pdf.

Whitehead, John, Lee Pittenger and Nicholas Colella. "Astrid Rocket Flight Test." *Energy and Technology Review*, 1994, 11–17, https://str.llnl.gov/etr/pdfs/07_94.2.pdf.

Wilkening, Dean. "A Simple Model for Calculating Ballistic Missile Defense Effectiveness." *Science & Global Security* 8 (1999): 183–125, http://scienceandglobalsecurity.org/archive/sgs08wilkening.pdf.

Williams, Terence. *Boeing-Led Missile Defense Team Achieves Intercept in Flight Test, June 22, 2014.* http://boeing.mediaroom.com/Boeing-led-Missile-Defense-Team-Achieves-Intercept-in-Flight-Test.

Winnefeld, James D. *Adm. Winnefeld's Remarks at the Center for Strategic and International Studies.* 2015, http://www.jcs.mil/Media/Speeches/ Article/589289/adm-winnefelds-remarks-at-the-center-for-strategic-and-international-studies/.

Wisher, Robert. "Patriot Air and Missile Defense System." In *Nalysis of System Training Impact for Major Defense Acquisition Programs (MDAPs): Training Systems Acquisition,* 5–20. Edited by Frederick Hartman, 2012, http://www.dtic.mil/cgi-bin/GetTRDoc?AD=ADA570775.

Wolfe, Alan. "Carter Plays with Fire. Obsession with Nuclear Strategy." *The Nation,* September 24, 1977, 265–268.

Wood, Lowell, and Roderick Hyde. *Science and Technology in Space during the Coming Decade.* 1984, https://e-reports-ext.llnl.gov/ pdf/203612. pdf.

Wood, Lowell and Walter Scott. *Brilliant Pebbles,* 1989 https://e-reports-ext.llnl.gov/pdf/212611.pdf.

Work, Clint. "The Long History of South Korea's OPCON Debate." *The Diplomat,* November 2017, https://thediplomat.com/2017/11/the-long-history-of-south-koreas-opcon-debate/.

Wright, Mike. *Notes on Hermann Oberth. Space Pioneer Hermann Oberth Was von Braun Mentor.* 2019, https://history.msfc.nasa.gov/earlyra/ hoberth_notes.html.

Yamaguchi, Mari. "Japan to Buy Aegis Ashore Missile Defense Systems." *DefenseNews,* December 19, 2017 https://www.defensenews.com/ land/2017/12/19/japan-to-buy-aegis-ashore-missile-defense-sy tems.

Yanarella, Ernest. *The Missile Defense Controversy. Technology in Search of Mission.* Lexington: University of Kentucky Press, 2002.

Young-chan, Yoon. *Senior Secretary to the President for Public Communication Yoon Young-Chan Briefs Media on North Korea's Shutdown of Nuclear Test Site And Adoption of Seoul Standard Time, April 29, 2018.* http://english1.president.go.kr/activity/briefing.php.

Zagare, Frank, and Marc Kilgour. "Alignment Patterns, Crisis Bargaining and Extended Deterrence: A Game-Theoretic Analysis." *International Studies Quarterly* 47 (2003): 587–615.

————. *Perfect Deterrence.* Cambridge: Cambridge University Press, 2000.

Zakheim, Dov. "Evaluating the Opportunity and Financial Costs of Ballistic Missile Defense." In *Regional Missile Defense from a Global Perspective,* 5404-5755. Edited by Catherine McArdle Kelleher and Peter Dombrowski, Kindle. Stanford: Stanford University Press, 2015.

Zhang, Jiadong. "Terrorist Activities in Yemen and the US Countermeasures." *Journal of Middle Eastern and Islamic Studies (in Asia)* 4 (2010): 101–115, https://doi.org/10.1080/19370679.2010.12023150.

Zheng, Xu, Suochang Yang, and Dan Fang. "Research on Simulation Identification Technology of Loitering Missile," 2019, 1459–1465, https://doi.org/10.1007/978-981-10-6571-2_176.

Zhu, Shiquan, Zhihua Chen, Hui Zhang, Zhengui Huang, and Huanhao Zhang. "Investigations on the Influence of Control Devices to the Separation Characteristics of a Missile from the Internal Weapons Bay." *Journal of Mechanical Science and Technology* 32 (2018): 2047–2057, https://doi.org/10.1007/s12206-018-0414-3.

Zimmerman, Peter. "Pork Bellies and the SDI." *Foreign Policy* 63 (1986): 76–87, http://www.jstor.org/stable/1148757.

Made in the USA
Las Vegas, NV
13 February 2022

43800274R00173